Discovering and (Re)Covering
the Seventeenth Century Religious Lyric

Medieval & Renaissance Literary Studies

Discovering
and
(Re)Covering
the
Seventeenth Century
Religious Lyric

edited by
Eugene R. Cunnar & Jeffrey Johnson

Duquesne University Press
Pittsburgh, Pennsylvania

Published in the United States of America by

DUQUESNE UNIVERSITY PRESS
600 Forbes Avenue
Pittsburgh, Pennsylvania 15282

Library of Congress Cataloging-in-Publication Data

Discovering and (re)covering the seventeenth century religious lyric/
edited by Eugene R. Cunnar and Jeffrey Johnson.
        p. cm. — (Medieval & renaissance literary studies)
Includes bibliographical references and index.
ISBN 0–8207–0317–6 (alk. paper)
1. Religious poetry, English — History and criticism. 2. English
poetry — Early modern, 1500–1700 — History and criticism. 3. Christianity
and literature — England — History — 17th century. 4. Christian poetry,
English — History and criticism. I. Title: Discovering and recovering
the seventeenth century religious lyric. II. Cunnar, Eugene R. III.
Johnson, Jeffrey, 1957-IV. Title. V. Medieval and Renaissance literary
studies
PR545.R4 D5 2000
821'.0409382—dc21
                                                                00–010420
                                                                CIP

Printed on acid-free paper.

Contents

Preface

In the opening stanza of her dedicatory poem "To the Queenes most Excellent Majestie," Aemilia Lanyer proposes "to view that which is seldome seene." Although what Lanyer specifically has in mind is "A Womans writing of divinist things," the statement is also apropos for a collection of essays discussing devotional lyricists who have historically been overlooked altogether or dismissed as not belonging to the first order of poets. To the extent that the seventeenth century arguably gave rise to the greatest flowering of devotional verse in the English language, it only seems fitting that any critical overviews of the religious lyric in this period account for the wide variety and nuanced complexity of the poems identified within this genre, as well as the theology, politics, and historical circumstances of the individuals who produced them. The essays in this collection, therefore, attempt to redress the neglect these poems and their authors have received, reaffirming the sentiments of An Collins who, in her own "Preface" to her *Divine Songs and Meditacions*, writes that she will not be hindered "From Publishing those Truths I do intend / As strong perfumes will not concealed be."

In addition to celebrating the wider field of the religious lyric in the seventeenth century, the purpose of this volume is to honor the teaching and scholarly career of John R. Roberts. The two editors of this volume are both former students, though at two separate universities, of Professor Roberts, and as such, we represent all those who have had the privilege to benefit in the classroom from his wit and learning. We also represent the scholars of seventeenth century literature whose work has been assisted and enhanced by Jack's scholarship, as well as by his generosity in sharing his time and insights. The essays in this volume are a testimony to the critical reevaluation that Roberts's teaching and research have brought to bear on the seventeenth century religious lyric.

The editors wish to express their gratitude to the individuals and institutions whose assistance has made this volume possible. Our primary debt, of course, is to the authors of the essays, who generously shared with us the fruits of their scholarly labors and who patiently and efficiently responded to our sometimes tedious requests. We are also indebted to our home institutions, College Misericordia and New Mexico State University, for providing financial support for this volume. In particular, we want to acknowledge Michael A. Mac Dowell, President of College Misericordia, whose willing support of this project reflects his belief that scholarly excellence is an expression of the College's mission; and the Arts & Sciences Research Center of New Mexico State University, especially Associate Dean Reed W. Dasenbrock. Likewise Richard Lynch (English Department Chair, College Misericordia) provided material assistance and Cindy Cave offered her secretarial support throughout the duration of this project. Further, we wish to extend our thanks to Professor Al Labriola, who was our liaison to Duquesne University Press, and to Susan Wadsworth-Booth, Editor in Chief, whose professionalism made her a delight to work with. Finally, Jeffrey extends his thanks to his wife, Lee, whose support gives meaning to all of his work; and Gene thanks his partner, Merri, who has a strong hand on what is important in life.

Eugene R. Cunnar
Jeffrey Johnson
July 2000

Introduction

Eugene R. Cunnar &
Jeffrey Johnson

In the first issue of *The John Donne Journal* (1982), John R. Roberts published a revelatory assessment of modern Donne criticism based on his own two volumes of annotated Donne bibliography, which covered the years 1912 to 1978. Roberts points out that while most agree Donne is a major poet "we tend to disagree on exactly what accounts for his greatness or wherein his greatness lies" (59). After illustrating his point, Roberts goes on to argue that "the most disturbing fact about modern Donne criticism is that it concerns itself primarily with less than half of Donne's canon, confining itself narrowly to his secular love poems (a dozen or less of the poems in the *Songs and Sonets* and to a much lesser extent the *Elegies*), to his specifically religious poems (almost exclusively the *Holy Sonnets*, 'Goodfriday, 1613,' and the hymns), and more recently, to the *Anniversaries*" (62). Pointing out that less than one percent of Donne criticism treats the verse epistles, Roberts speculates that one reason for this might be that the verse epistles are "artistic failures" (62). If that were the case, Roberts argues, then such a conclusion would be defended or argued against, which it has not. Roberts concludes that the critical neglect of Donne's verse epistles are the result of

1

"silent neglect" (62). Using less than half Donne's canon has produced the unfortunate result of "what might be called a synecdochical understanding of and appreciation for Donne's total achievement as a poet" (62).

One result of this substituting the part for the whole is that "literary historians, critics, and teachers continue to repeat generalizations about Donne's poetry that although incomplete, partial, misleading, and sometimes incorrect, have about them almost the strength of established fact and the sacredness of a hallowed tradition" (63). Roberts proceeds to suggest that one significant reason for the scholarly and critical neglect of over half the Donne canon may be found in the advent of the New Critics, for whom "Donne's dramatic lyrics not only seemed to support and illustrate their own theories about the nature of good poetry, but perhaps more importantly, the analytical methods and approaches that evolved from their theories were especially effective in interpreting Donne's dramatic lyrics" (63). The New Critics passed on their own implicit and explicit concepts of Donne's poetry to later generations, "who, when confronted with the neglected half of Donne's canon, were predisposed to dismiss as inferior those poems that did not readily conform to the received notion of Donne's poetry" (64). Within twentieth century criticism, Roberts points to the development of two major critical positions. The first is illustrated by Merritt Hughes's warning about modern critics "'kidnapping'" Donne for their own purposes and failing to see Donne in historical contexts. The second is reflected in Kenneth Burke's essay in which he admires Rosemond Tuve's argument on Herbert that "the reader must study and understand the cultural, linguistic, and religious traditions Herbert's poems reflect" (64) but contrasts her attempts at "'re-covery'" with modern critics' attempt "to engage in what he termed "'dis-covery,'" that is, an attempt to find new things about the workings of a poet's mind and art by applying modern terms and techniques that would have been completely alien to the poet's own thinking . . ." (64). According to Burke and Roberts, contemporary Donne criticism can be divided "according to the two major approaches— re-covery and dis-covery" (65).

The purpose of this volume is to extend Roberts's assessment of Donne criticism to the religious lyrics of the seventeenth century. Quite clearly we know that in the seventeenth century the canon was different from the canon we use today. If we are to gain a more accurate and thorough view of the seventeenth century religious lyric, then we must begin to recover and discover those writers that have been silently neglected or overlooked in the present. Consequently, the essays in this volume emphasize and address Anglo-Catholic, High Anglican, and women writers, most of whom have been neglected in recent criticism, with the exception of the ongoing recovery of women writers. Moreover, the majority of criticism over the last couple of decades treats Protestant and Puritan writers, especially since the publication of Barbara Lewalski's influential book on Protestant aesthetics. Her revisionist exclusion of the Catholic tradition from the development of English poetics explored by Louis Martz along with her all-subsuming assertion of a poetics dominated by the Calvinist milieu has stimulated the study of Protestant writers, but has unfortunately also stimulated the neglect of the Anglo-Catholic and High Anglican traditions in poetry. We have deliberately excluded mainstream or canonical Protestant writers from this volume in order to emphasize a wide-ranging group of writers who richly deserve to be recovered and rediscovered if the present scholarly imbalance is to be righted and recontextualized. Unlike many of the collections that focus on Protestant canonical writers, this volume aims to present a different view of the development of the seventeenth century religious lyric. We believe that this is

especially important in light of the recent debate by revision-
ist and antirevisionist historians over the causal role religion
played in the English Revolution.

The current debate (summarized by Cust and Hughes and
by Hughes) over the complex causes of the English revolu-
tion, especially religion, carried on by historians of the seven-
teenth century highlights the importance of the seventeenth
century religious lyric. The recent work of Nicholas Tyacke,
Julian Davies, Kevin Sharpe, Conrad Russell, and Anthony
Milton, among others, has offered alternative views about the
significance of religion and religious differences as a major
cause of the revolution. On the one hand, revisionists have
challenged the old Whig and Marxist views by repositioning
the debate in terms of an aggressive monarch wanting change,
especially the Arminianism in religion activated by Laud,
and the conservative Calvinist reaction to those changes.
Revisionist historians have challenged the older view of an
Anglican establishment confronted by Puritans and have em-
phasized the issues that united Protestants rather than those
dividing them. The rise of Arminianism and its challenge to
Calvinist certainties under Charles I and Laud caused Puri-
tans to become more godly in their crusade to reform church
and society, and to resist what they perceived as the re-intro-
duction of popery. From this perspective, revisionists see the
Puritans as both an aggressive minority and as part of a broad
consensual Anglicanism. In supporting their interpretation of
events, revisionists have privileged manuscript sources over
printed sources, discovering that many individuals could hold
diverse and even contradictory theological positions and doc-
trines. On the other hand, those historians who are loosely
and collectively called "antirevisionists," challenge revision-
ist accounts by developing literary and cultural context-
ualization that emphasizes significant connections between
social changes and conflicting views of religion, politics, and
culture. From this perspective, the Arminian ecclesiastical

policy supported by Charles I and Laud was not something that came out of the blue; instead, it had long-term roots and accorded with Charles I's beliefs in absolute monarchy, a hierarchical society, and an emphasis in ceremony and the sacraments in the Church. To support their views, antirevisionists not only employ manuscript evidence, but also look at print culture that reveals the political/religious/cultural divides as those were experienced and expressed by both sides.

In this context, seventeenth century religious lyrics, especially those written by lesser-known or minor writers, take on added significance as both indicators of the political/religious conflicts, and of gender conflicts, and as influences on those conflicts. We must understand these lyrics both as literary artifacts and as representations of ideological and doctrinal stances that were part of the conflicts that resulted in revolution and the subsequent changing and evolving forms of religious poetry. What becomes clear from the historical debate is that it is misleading to privilege one view to the exclusion of those alternative views that were present in the society. Indeed, the historical debate reveals that many writers were influenced by various traditions and that an individual writer might embrace contradictory positions on theological issues. Within the context of the current historical debate, the focus of this volume is to recover and rediscover those lesser-known (and often now neglected writers) who participated in momentous historical changes, and whose work has enlightened our views of the roles that the seventeenth century religious lyric played in those changes, as well to correct a monolithic approach to those lyrics. Secondly, essays in this volume explore in detail the unique and traditional qualities of women's religious lyrics. Each of the essays in this volume seeks either explicitly or implicitly to make the canon more inclusive rather than exclusive. To paraphrase Kari McBride's essay in this volume, we must rewrite the story of seventeenth century literature in order to tell a more accurate story. McBride concludes that the canon is like "urban light pollution, it erases billions of dimmer stars and leaves us with a manageable set of constellations and bright stars. But it is sometimes interesting to travel to the desert, where darkness reveals the innumerable lights of the night sky and masks the relationships we thought we understood."

Kari B. McBride's essay explores the ways in which selective meditations on the Passion from the late sixteenth and early seventeenth centuries were used for the purposes of literary and religious self-fashioning. Answering Marshall Grossman's question about authority and canonicity, McBride discusses Elizabeth Middleton, Robert Southwell, Aemilia Lanyer, and Giles Fletcher in terms of genre, gender markers, and other markers of identity, which serve as "effects of poetry rather than precursors." Instead of asking "how women as opposed to men deploy particular genres," McBride explores how "a particular genre, a poetic meditation on the Passion, can serve to construct subjectivities." According to McBride, as Christians began the process of separating from Jews, the Passion narrative came to serve "as another type of fiction, one of self-construction through othering." While each of these writers is considered minor, with the exception of Lanyer who is an "exemplar of revisionist literary scholarship," "we mistake the context of these poems if we confine ourselves to a narrow vision of poetry and ignore the large cultural and religious context within which they were written." From such a perspective, these poems on the Passion are not just oddities of a poetic corpus but "reveal a spectrum of attitudes about nationality, religion, gender, and sexuality" while producing individual and corporate identities.

Scott R. Pilarz's essay centers on the necessity of understanding Southwell's writings as tools enabling him to fulfill his Jesuit missionary work in England. In particular, Pilarz believes that the complications of Southwell's being a first-generation Jesuit priest "should be embraced in order to recover his English poetry and prose" precisely because these complications inform Southwell's notion of the self, which, in turn, "subsumed his approach to authorship." Pilarz examines Jesuit foundational documents such as Loyola's *Spiritual Exercises* and other Jesuit documents as informing the poetry. In insisting that Southwell's poetry and prose should be understood as exercises in "pious utilitarianism," Pilarz reads Southwell as a writer whose primary aim was, in accordance with his mandate as a Jesuit priest sent to England, "to confirm Catholics in their faith, to absolve the lapsed, [and] not to battle with heretics." Southwell's return to England was not motivated (as Martz and others have argued) by the intention to reform English poetry on a continental model, but instead to fulfill these goals. Throughout his discussion, Pilarz emphasizes both the conciliatory approach Southwell took with Protestants, as well as Elizabeth I, and the consolation he extended to practicing and lapsed Catholics, specifically in relation to the cultivation of remorse as preparation for the sacrament of confession. In using his religious literature to achieve these goals, Southwell would subsequently refine and redefine the religious lyric.

George Klawitter's essay purposes to redress the neglect of Alabaster's "Ensigns" sonnets, which he shows as being a result of Alabaster's modern editors, G. M. Story and Helen Gardner, who have conflated the three primary manuscripts into appealing form in order to make a minor poet more attractive to readers. Klawitter restores the order in which the poet intended these poems to be read, as well as recovers their Ignatian meditative context. According to Klawitter, the actual manuscripts reflect more accurately the intended meditative sequences while also reflecting on Alabaster's allegiance to two faiths, his imprisonments, and the numerous examinations and cross-examinations he underwent. Restoration of the original sequencing allows us to see the importance of Jesuit influences on the poet and how his poetic craftsmanship "becomes a tool of both aesthetics and religion" as it engages the reader's memory, understanding, and will in the meditative path leading from *via purgativa* to *via illuminativa* to *via unitiva*.

Debra Rienstra argues that Lanyer's work makes "an illuminating" addition to the canon because it turns "conventional practices on their heads" in that she circumvents the gendered rhetorical strategies of male authors by interpreting Scripture as a "blatant critique of patriarchy and class structure." Lanyer's dedication to Mary Sidney, Countess of Pembroke (in *Salve Deus Rex Judaeorum*) reveals how her predecessor enables her own writing project and publication. Pembroke's translation of the Psalms provides Lanyer with the authorization to "interpret Scripture against tradition," especially the tradition of male-dominated exegesis. As a result, Lanyer's volume is more than an exercise of her poetic vocation through a retelling of biblical history; it is instead a public polemic in which Lanyer uses the precedent of Pembroke to establish her own prophetic vocation and voice. For Rienstra, both Pembroke and Lanyer provide "an instructive comparison of how authors of both genders negotiate the dangers and advantages of weaving the Text into their texts."

Although it has become commonplace to read Aemilia Lanyer's "Description of Cooke-ham" in the tradition of the country-house poem, Patrick Cook contends that to place the poem only in that context and not to apply the "explicatory pressures" to it that have been accorded male poets contributes to "a failure to recognize this remarkable text's polyphonic richness." As a result, Cook offers a careful and insightful reading of the poem that reveals how Lanyer grafts onto the country-house poem framework a dramatization of "the affective oscillations of its speaker's spiritual condition," specifically in relation to the theme of exaltation through humility. Thus, Lanyer does not celebrate the traditional "landowner's maintenance of a self-sustaining and harmonious estate," but instead celebrates "Lady Clifford's piety through a meditative engagement with her own salvational history." Cook stresses that it is precisely "the incorporation of this theme into the speaker's mental processes" that transforms Lanyer's poem from a simple country-house narrative into a meditative poem drawing on the "traditional emblematics favored in Protestant meditation" so that she can assign Lady Clifford a priestly role while becoming an humble communicant herself. In discovering this process in the poem, Cook recovers a significant aspect of Lanyer's unique feminist poetics that elevates her into the mainstream of literary tradition.

Robert C. Evans's recognition that Drummond was a writer who received far greater appreciation in his own day than now speaks to the need for clarifying the "aesthetic tastes and intellectual trends" of his era. Aware of the range of current theoretical approaches to literature, Evans argues that no poet "is ever likely to be fully recovered unless we feel that his or her words merit attention *as words*." In his essay, he asks "do these bones live?" Evans suggests that Jonson's denigration of Drummond's love poems may be one reason his poetry is dismissed today. While his love poems may "seem old-fashioned when compared, say, to Donne's," Drummond's religious poetry deserves "more detailed and respectful attention." Through attentive readings of the poems in *Flowres of Sion*, Evans explores a whole range of poetic techniques and figures of speech that discover the riches of Drummond's craftsmanship in his religious poetry and that open the way for further critical exploration.

Kate Narveson argues that recent revisionists' framing of the historical debate in the English Church as one simply defined between Calvinists and anti-Calvinists does not explain the alternative position found in the well-known works of John Donne or the lesser known work of William Austin. Focusing on Austin, but establishing parallels with the life and work of Donne, Narveson argues that Austin's religious prose and poetry show that Donne was "not as anomalous in his piety as is sometimes suggested" and that Austin's religious verse, in particular, "expands our sense of Protestant poetics beyond the lyric form." Narveson's analysis of Austin's writings shows that it was possible for a lay person in Jacobean England to be a firm Protestant "with a comfortable anti-popish bias, a concern for fellowship in edification, and a Scripture-centered devotion," and yet also "to be interested in the church fabric and in patristic and later Roman Catholic writings." Neither a Puritan nor an anti-Calvinist, Austin belongs to "a conformity committed to the faith and worship of the established church that can be called Anglianism." By focusing on three poems on the Passion and two on death, Narveson not only recovers Austin as a serious religious poet, but she also situates his unique brand of Anglicanism within the current historical debate, as promoted by Julian Davies and others, that is moving beyond the traditional polar opposites to a more nuanced understanding of the Church of England and its members.

Acknowledging that Patrick Cary's 13 poems are small in comparison with other writers and that little modern scholarship exists on the poet, Sean McDowell argues nevertheless that the work is important for two reasons. First, McDowell explains, the size and character of the volume questions "some of our habits of critical classification," and second, the volume's focus on the senses as visible signs of Christian truth "suggests a model for how first-person religious lyrics generally present the creation and consecration of the self." Following the lead of Veronica Delany, Cary's modern editor, McDowell shows how these 13 poems were remnants of Cary's earlier life. While these religious poems are generally viewed in the context of Cary's secular poems, McDowell argues they are "the culmination of a spiritual quest that included a conversion to Catholicism and ended in a failed three-and-a-half month attempt at being a Benedictine monk." The writing of these poems echoes biographical circumstances, but more importantly they enact the consecration of the self that Cary's spiritual quest engaged him in. In a detailed reading, McDowell explains how the poet takes charge of his senses, educates them, and redirects them in accordance with God's will. By seeing this pattern in his poems, we are able to see a similar but less visible pattern in such canonical poets as Donne, Herbert, and Vaughan. In a larger sense, rediscovering Cary's religious work opens up possible rediscoveries in more canonical writers.

Using Van Dyck's triptych portrait of Charles I as an extended metaphor through which to understand the unique but connected subjectivities of An Collins, Elizabeth Major, and the anonymous poet known as "Eliza," Patricia Demers explores how each of these women experienced and represented religious melancholy. Demers situates melancholy within the constructs of male writers and artists, then poses a series of questions about that tradition as well as modern scholars' understanding of it. For Demers, the female melancholia expressed by these women goes well beyond the melancholy found in Jacques or Hamlet. Described as "inward, inherently performative, though solitary" it is the product of sensibilities and cultural circumstances that are characterized by sobriety and eschatological insight. Each of these women suffered in "the culture of violence and chaos they inhabited," but each turned their "occlusion, neglect, and retirement" into "poignant, therapeutic cartheses," by transforming loss into religious consolation and assurance. In finding the "kinetic, propulsive conviction (of both fallibility and, proleptically, redemption)" in these three women writers, Demers recovers an important, but neglected aspect of seventeenth century women's subjectivity as well as a tradition of female melancholia.

Michael Rex explores the complex contexts surrounding *Eliza's Babes*, an anonymous work published in 1652. Following Margaret Ezell's contention that early women writers often "do not fit neatly into theological, literary, or canonical spaces," Rex uncovers Eliza's struggle to find Christian comfort and assurance amidst the social, political, and religious turmoil of mid-seventeenth century England. While Eliza seems to embrace a form of moderate Protestantism, as Anthony Milton defines that term, she also incorporates into her work elements of Calvinism, Catholicism, and Laudianism without attempting to reconcile the differences between those theologies. However, from this mix, Rex shows how she "creates a new personal world out of the confusion of the physical world" by achieving a "close, matrimonial relationship with Christ." Thus, Rex's broad analysis of Eliza's writings discovers her engagement with and religious justification for publishing her work; her use of a meditative theology; and her social and political commentary. Her repudiation of the gender, class, and religious differences in her tumultuous world leads her to recover the spiritual world as the only means of her achieving the independence, peace, and reassurance that she seeks.

Ann Hurley argues that we should not consider An Collins a minor poet even though only a single volume of her work in one surviving copy exists. For Hurley, Collins's poetry becomes a way for us to recover and extend our understanding of the range of meditative poems which, in turn, "may lead us to revise our current narrative of the history of seventeenth century poetry, its origins, its forms, and its most skillful practitioners." Hurley identifies this seventeenth century woman as a poet whose philosophical and didactic intent was promoted by her plain style, a style that emphasizes her verse as marked by "the specific mix of exaltation and reflection." In Collins's case, her volume is a record of Protestant doctrine as inspired by her own lived life. Moreover, Collins modifies Calvinism in her search for faith as she shows "the vivifying force of Protestant doctrine on the struggling human soul primarily advocating human comfort." Because her subject matter has excluded her from the standard list of seventeenth century religious writers, we have been prevented from understanding fully the development of the English religious lyric.

In her analysis of Mary Carey's elegy, "Upon ye Sight of my abortive birth," Donna J. Long argues that the poet "engages a wide range of doctrine and negotiates biblical tropes" so that the poem functions as religious lyric. This particular poem, Long explains, allows Carey to focus on the abortive birth while confronting the death of her other children. The poem embodies the "tensions inherent in writing as a mother and as a mourner, and as a 'godly woman' whose sacrifices cause her to question God." Situating Carey's poem within the contexts of early modern women's writing of religious lyrics, Long explores the gendered aspects of the religious lyric as she demonstrates how Carey used the poem to establish elegy as a feminine genre. Because Carey could not contain the loss of her children within the traditional, accepted social and literary norms, she engages in a radical revision of those traditional tropes. These revisions occur within the complex social and religious constructs placed on mother-child-God relationships in which childloss was often understood as God's will or the punishment for one's own sins. Carey revises Calvinist doctrine by juxtaposing her individual sin "against the perfect grace of her body." While her writing about her miscarriage provides us with "insight into the relationships women had with their living and deceased children, and with their own bodies," that writing also allows Carey to recuperate her maternal power and her spiritual assurance. Thus her poem also functions as a religious meditation in which Carey "discovers and recovers 'God's will' in her very sex."

Barry Spurr explores Traherne's reaction to the "'late disordered Times when the Foundations were cast down'" by examining the Anglo-Catholic traditions underlying the poetry and prose. While much is traditional in Traherne, he "breathes new life into these familiar conventions" through the individuality of his expression. The "eccentricities" in Traherne's work derive from its Anglo-Catholic character and his royalism. While he is influenced by Herbert, Traherne's spirituality is focused on his "ecstatic celebration of felicity," including a focus on Creation and Incarnation as opposed to Herbert's focus on Atonement and Redemption. Abhorring "'*Enthusiasme*,'" Traherne practices a Protestant poetics, but not as in Lewalski's "sometimes misleadingly Procrustean phrase" because his is a poetics that is paradoxically situated within Catholic and royalist contexts. One result of the Revolution was a heightened interest in orthodox Anglicanism as well as a new spiritual intensity. Although the Catholic influence on his Anglicanism and poetics is realized in such features as his use of liturgy, his praise of Mary, and his presentation of the sacramental life and holy communion, it is the doctrine of the Incarnation, Spurr explains, that serves as the source for Traherne's poetic inspiration and that embodies the unique nature of his Anglicanism.

The plan of P. G. Stanwood's essay is "to reveal Beaumont as the composer of a 'poetic book,' a work that is no accidental collection, but a thoughtfully organized whole, in a fashion that may recall George Herbert's *The Temple*." In fact, he demonstrates that Beaumont's minor poems, in their familiar rhymes, imagery, verse forms, and themes, have distinct affinities with the verse of Herbert and Crashaw. Beyond these parallels, however, Stanwood explains that Beaumont's religious lyrics have "a systematic and meaningful arrangement that is also chronological," and to that end he provides a general overview of the movement of the collection. The study concludes with an insightful reading of the concluding "cycle" of poems that begins in May 1652 with "The Journé," by which he discovers the daily moods and "the general and personal significance of the special liturgical events that fall during this time" that are "typically descriptive of Beaumont's spiritual conflicts."

Responding to the neglect that Joseph Beaumont's poetry has suffered, Paul Parrish aims in his essay to "identify, and contextualize Beaumont's accomplishments as a lyric poet." Because "the lines between canonical and noncanonical, the literary and the nonliterary, the professional writer and the amateur dilettante, the 'authoritative' print publication and the 'dubious' manuscript version are ever more blurred," we are obligated to reexamine a poet "whom conventional judgment has rendered unimportant or unworthy," especially as "we move beyond a 'great poets' approach to literary history to a more inclusive understanding of what it meant to read and write poetry in the seventeenth century." Parrish provides a brief biographical context for Beaumont, proposes a tentative grouping of the poems, and offers more detailed readings of representative types of poems ranging from the personal and the meditative to poems on biblical figures and contemporary topics. For Parrish, Beaumont is a poet capable of "purposeful and deliberative consideration of topics, of occasions, of Christian values and daily expectations," and it is only by understanding such so-called "minor" poets that we can, Parrish argues, "claim a deeper appreciation of the role poetry truly played in seventeenth century English society and culture."

The essays in this volume cover a wide range of very different poets, particularly women writers and high church and Anglo-Catholic writers, all of whom have been largely excluded from the canon. Our purpose in recovering and rediscovering these writers is to provide an "antirevisionist" correction to the hegemonic emphasis on Protestant/Puritan aesthetics and culture that has long dominated scholarship.

That dominance does not accord with recent findings of historians; nor does it give us an accurate view of seventeenth century religious poetry. Only by understanding the lesser known and neglected writers can we fully understand the changing and diverse variety and historical role of the religious lyrics written in this period. To this purpose, the essayists in this collection have made a significant contribution.

1• Gender and Judaism in Meditations on the Passion

Middleton, Southwell, Lanyer, and Fletcher

Kari Boyd McBride

The four authors whose Passion narratives define this study all attempted to write themselves into some kind of literary identity through poetic meditations on the Passion.[1] Both the way we assess their self-fashioning and the status we accord their works depend significantly on our assumptions about literature, canonicity, and religious and literary subjectivity. The poetry of Robert Southwell has a continuous, if marginal, history, perhaps guaranteed by Ben Jonson's comment that he would have destroyed many of his own poems to have written "The Burning Babe." That poem is dutifully and widely anthologized, but scholarly interest in Southwell's poetry peaked with Louis Martz's 1954 book *The Poetry of Meditation* and more recent studies tend to concentrate on Southwell's recusancy and his prose works and letters.[2]

Aemilia Lanyer's poems have lately been brought into the canon, if one counts anthologization as a sign of canonicity. There has been a small flood of works on Lanyer, which shows no sign of abating, but her relatively recent (re)discovery and the lack of contemporary comment on either her (as poet) or her poetry, as well as the small size of her poetic corpus, circumscribe her influence on the development of genres and on the history of literature. Elizabeth Middleton's unique extant composition, which draws on Southwell's Passion poem, remains unpublished, and her identity unclear. That she is known at all is a testament to the feminist recuperative literary project rather than to either her generic influence or her poetic capacities. Giles Fletcher, whose poems had enthusiastic admirers in earlier centuries, has become a footnote to Milton scholarship because of the latter's admiration for Fletcher's work. His poems seem neither to be read nor studied today.

For all of these authors, Marshall Grossman's comment about Lanyer seems appropriate at some level: "[I]f, as appears to be the case, Lanyer's publication had, in fact, no historical consequence, failed to *cause* anything at all, in what sense (if any) was it a literary historical event? What does it mean — now — for Lanyer so belatedly to enter literary history?" Grossman answers these questions by showing how Lanyer's book and her treatment of the country house genre "present a specific resistance to the recollection of the past as *his*tory."[3] I wish to answer Grossman's question about authority and canonicity from another perspective, attending to genre, certainly, but looking at gender and other markers of identity as effects of poetry rather than simply precursors. I want to ask not how women as opposed to men deploy particular genres (a question that produces one set of illuminating answers), but rather how a particular genre, a poetic meditation on the Passion, can serve to construct a range of subjectivities.

The Passion narrative provides a particularly fruitful context for asking such questions, as its history is one of community and individual definition through the assignation of guilt and the definition of self by contrast to "other" — of apostle by apostate, of true believer by false, of Christian by Jew — in a generic context that has served to authorize the antisemitism and pogroms that mark the history of the West. As Michelle Cliff has noted, the distance between self-definition and self-justification for acts of persecution and violence is frighteningly small, for the process of identity construction can turn the enemy into an object whose distorted image replaces anything resembling the actual being in the oppressor's mind: "The actual being is then denied speech, denied self-definition, self-realization, . . . denied selfhood." It is this dehumanizing process, Cliff says, "that gives the impression of sanity to the process of oppression" and allows persecution to "be defended as logical."[4] I wish to suggest here that, by virtue of the authority and familiarity of the Passion narrative, the dynamics of that process of objectification could serve to construct various identities. The Christian subjectivity interpellated by the Passion narratives and the concomitant othering of the dehumanized Jews became merely subject and object positions available to be filled by alternative categories — "men" as distinguished from (and superior to) "women" or, vice versa, virtuous women in contrast to evil men. The Passion narrative thus functioned as a kind of universal subject/object machine productive of both community and individual identities.

The Passion narrative — the story of Jesus's betrayal, trial, execution, and burial — forms the climax of the four canonical gospels. Though the gospels differ in many details, in their rhetorical purposes, and in their christologies and theologies, they all agree that the Jewish people were primarily responsible for the death of Jesus, a contention that is not historically tenable. Although crucifixion was common throughout the ancient world,[5] and while the Jewish tradition of "crucifying" the already-dead bodies of criminals as public spectacle and deterrent gave way in Jerusalem to live crucifixion in the last centuries B.C.E., often under the authority of the Roman-delegated Jewish leadership, it is ultimately implausible that the Jewish crowds could demand and share in the act of crucifying Jesus over the objections — or even the apathy — of both Pilate and Caiaphas as they are reported to have done in the gospel accounts. That both Roman and Jewish authorities agreed in the judgment is likely;[6] that the Jewish *people* either were consulted or shared in the execution of the judgment is incredible.

Rather than representing historical fact, the gospel condemnation of the Jews represents the response of the early Christian communities to their political circumstances in the second half of the first century. The communities that produced the canonized gospels had particular reasons for blaming the Jews. Mark's point, for instance, is that those closest to Jesus, including his own family and his own people, are the very ones who fail to recognize his true nature, while outsiders, like the Roman centurion, saw that Jesus was "the son of God." Matthew, on the other hand, is written for relatively Jewish (as opposed to relatively Hellenized) Christians; it is concerned with intra-religious politics and blames the Pharisees in particular for their failure to recognize the divinity of Jesus. But the one fact that underlies every gospel portrayal of Jewish guilt is the power and presence of Rome; blaming the Romans for crucifying one's god might very well have been dangerous for gospel writers. So long as Christianity had less political standing than Judaism, the self-defensive fiction of Jewish culpability remained relatively innocuous; as Rome itself became Christian, the fiction of Jewish guilt became unnecessary at the very moment that it became — in the words of John Dominic Crossan — "lethal."[7]

It is at that moment that the gospel accounts of the Passion came to serve predominantly as another type of fiction, one of

self-construction through othering.[8] Just when the Passion
narrative began to function to construct a corporate identity
is hard to say, though I would suppose that identity based on
distinction from the Jews would be dependent on the abso-
lute break of Christianity from Judaism. This break from
Judaism was precipitated both by the changes within Judaism
that followed the destruction of Jerusalem in the year 70 and
by the missionary impulse of Christianity, for by the final
decades of the first century, the majority of Christians were
non-Jews. For post-Constantinian Christians, the identity pro-
duced by the othering of the Jews would have taken on the
kind of mythic quality that most effectively builds autono-
mous selfhood, especially as Christianity was increasingly
coopted by the state and encouraged to articulate a theology
of dominance rather than servanthood, a tendency that was
developing long before the Edict of Milan gave Christianity
official status.[9] Once Christianity is neither Jewish nor mar-
ginalized, Jews can become for Christians fundamentally and
profoundly "not like us" — inhuman and demonized absolute
others. This othering of the Jews also finesses the Jewishness
of Jesus and his followers, who are oddly gentile in the Pas-
sion narratives of the gospels and in the developing Christian
tradition, even in narratives with a relatively low christology.[10]

   Thus, in a sense, the Passion narrative served as a kind of
creation story, generative of identity in ways that even the
Eden narrative could not match, though the Christian tradi-
tion read that story almost from the beginning as defining
male identity by contrast to female.[11] And the centrality of
the Passion narrative to the construction of a dominant
Christian subjectivity was underscored by its repetition in both
the weekly (or, later, daily) celebration of "The Lord's Sup-
per," which contextualizes the eucharist in a recital of the
Passion ("in the same night that he was betrayed, [Jesus]
took bread . . .")[12] and in the yearly cycle of the church year
whose climax is the dramatic (and dramatized) Holy Week

reenactment of the Passion — from the Palm Sunday entrance into Jerusalem, through the Maundy Thursday Last Supper and the Good Friday remembrance of the crucifixion, to the Easter Sunday celebration of the resurrection — a pattern that developed early in the Middle Ages and that was elaborated (for instance, by the addition of the Good Friday Reproaches) over the centuries. The English Protestant reformers, who rejected some elements of the Palm Sunday celebration (like the blessing of the palms), retained the reading of the Passion narratives throughout Holy Week.[13] At the same time, the figure of the crucified Christ, which functioned as synecdochic icon for the entire Passion narrative, was a popular subject in stained glass, paint, and a variety of other media throughout the centuries. (Even Cromwellian iconoclasm in the seventeenth century failed to obliterate entirely that central devotional image from English practice.) Thus an early modern English Christian, Protestant or Catholic, would have been reminded, repeatedly and dramatically, publicly and privately, of the absolute otherness — the inhumanity — of the Jews, whose guilt functioned to construct dominance and identity.

In addition to the presence of these aural and visual representations of the Passion that were defined by liturgical and ecclesiastical forms, one must count the influence of meditative praxis, particularly that of the *Spiritual Exercises* (1548) of Ignatius Loyola, popularized not only by the dissemination of that text but by the many similar treatises spawned by the religious impulses that engendered Loyola's work, including Fray Luis de Granada's *Book of Prayer and Meditation* (1554), "the most popular of all these meditative writers in England at the beginning of the seventeenth century," according to Martz.[14] What all of these devotional exercises had in common was the goal of defining and refining the Christian self through meditation on vividly imagined scenes and events from the life of Christ. Paramount among these was the Passion; contemplation on the details of that narrative, the sense of being there and sharing the pain of Christ's suffering and the sorrow of his followers, produced humility and gratitude, the *sine qua non* of true devotion. Individual Christians, then, would have seen, heard, and rehearsed, publicly and privately, year in and year out, the heinous guilt of the Jews.

This absolute othering was reinforced in early modern England by the seeming absence of the Jews (since their expulsion in the thirteenth century[15]). In Spain, where Jews had lived in thriving communities alongside Christians — and Moslems — for many centuries, identity through othering must have taken a different form, even before Ferdinand and Isabella's Edict of Expulsion of 1492 that drove perhaps 200,000 Jews out of Spain and into the Levant but left behind probably hundreds of thousands of *Marranos*, or *Conversos*, who "chose" to convert rather than leave their homeland. In England, however, there were few Jews *until* the sixteenth century, and their renewed presence there was dramatically preceded, in a sense, (and certainly contextualized) by their demonic characterization in the familiar Passion narratives. James Shapiro has argued that, in England as elsewhere in Europe, the presence of converted Jews resulted in a "destabilization of cultural identity," an identity that was dependent on the essential yet unrecognizable difference between Christians and Jews that *Conversos* undermined.[16] The categories "Jew" and "Christian," thus, never entirely succeed in detaching one from the other; they are always and inevitably relational and only apparently dichotomous. Shapiro argues that the resulting national identity crisis produced various new narratives about difference that transformed the opposition "Christian versus Jew" into "Englishman versus Jew" in a way that was productive of national identity. I would suggest here that the destabilized and destabilizing cultural context portrayed by Shapiro provided opportunities for the production of other individual and corporate identities; that is, the Passion narrative, understood to function as a kind of identity machine along the axes of race and religion, could produce identity along other axes, including nationality (as delineated by Shapiro) as well as gender and sexuality. I wish to suggest here that a variety of social markers in various combinations could be exploited in differing ways to produce authority and identity within the context of this founding narrative of Christianity.

Although Middleton's poem may have been the last of these poems to be written, I begin with it because it represents a kind of base line, the process of oppressive subject formation at its most virulent and explicit. Nothing is known of Middleton outside her one extant work; scholars have been unable to link her with the handful of contemporary women by that name (and nothing is known about any of those women that would provide clues to possible authorship). Middleton's poem, "The Death and Passion of our Lord Jesus Christ; As it was Acted by the Bloodye Jewes, And Registred by The Blessed Evangelists," exists in a unique (unpublished) Bodleian manuscript dated 1637.[17] (Of course, the poem may have been written years or decades earlier, though her quotation from Robert Southwell's "St. Peter's Complaint," provides a *terminus a quo* of 1592.) Her meditation on the Passion is of that masochistic species of religious poetry that aims to prolong the reader's experience of spiritual ecstasy by making the gruesome relation of the Passion narrative last as long as possible, larding scriptural tags with superfluous words. Thus we get gems like this one: "The Spirritt fayne would doe it/But the weake fleshe Is hardly brought unto it" (115).[18] She spends 57 stanzas (of 173) on the agony in the garden, and the poem ends abruptly, with a two-line tag, the moment Jesus dies and there is no more bathos to be wrung from the telling. Middleton's poem, rather than illustrating the way an inventive poet could use the dynamics of the Passion narrative, shows the genre at its most hackneyed.

While the purpose of the poem is apparently meditative, it also functions to assess and assign guilt (and to construct identity through opposition, as the title suggests):

Accompany Thy Saviour O my Soule
In outward Signes of inward grieving woe
Breake forth in sighes and with true teares condole
The Dreadfull Horror that torments him soe
Sith, for thy sake, sorrowe did pierce his Hart
Good Reason, in his Griefe, thowe beare A Part. (95)

Though the poet initially argues here that Jesus died to re-
deem the Christian soul, responsibility is quickly transferred
to the Jews. Indeed, the poem is a textbook case illustrating
the way in which dominant identity is produced through the
othering of the Jews; if the poetry is unoriginal, it is nonethe-
less deadly. Here the inhuman, objectified portrait is produced
by caricaturing the Jews' early modern role as bankers and
merchants. And, as is often the case with such bigotry, there
is in Middleton's poem an inverse relationship between vitriol
and reason: the more heinous the portrait of the Jews, the less
logical the argument. Only Judas has "sold" Christ for profit,
but blind bigotry implicates the Jews, as well, who, by
Middleton's logic, should be commended for "buying" Christ:

Oh yee blood-thyrsty Jewes, that Chapmen weare
Of this choyce Jewell;

*   *   *

Buy Truth and sell it not (sayes Holy writt)
Christ is the Truthe, yet here both bought and sould
Judas the Merchant, Jewes the Chapmen fitt
For suche A merchandize, to be Enrould
In Hells blacke booke. . . .

*   *   *

Unhappy Merchandize, that noe good brought
To him that vented it, Nor any gayne
Unto the chapmen, who this traffique bought.
Only thay Gott theyre labour for theyre payne.
Ill wynde (The Proverbe sayes) blowes no man good
Suche are the fruites of sheading harmles blood. (36, 37, 39)

The mercantile metaphor has, of course, a long history in Christian theology. Christ's precious blood is a commodity exchanged for the souls of sinners; his death purchases human lives. But here the metaphor has been deformed to argue that Christians are saved precisely because Jews are damned.[19]

> Judas Hereby lost his owne Salvation,
> A Heavy losse; never to be Redeem'd.
> The Preistes and Jewes purchast theyre Damnation
> A woefull purchase, not to be esteem'd.
> Only wee Christians Reape the chiefest good
> For wee are Saved by his Precious blood. (40)

Only the deformed portrait of the Jews can make the persecution of them seem logical in this morass of bad poetry and worse argument. But this justified oppression is instantly productive of Christian identity, the "wee" of the poem.

In Middleton's account, furthermore, the "bloodthirsty Jewes" (153) are the agents of the entire drama. They "brought . . . [Christ] before the Judgement Seat" (156), "put on him A purple Roabe," "smote him on the Head / And with theyre fillthy Spittle spauld his face" (157);

> Then to the place of Excecution
> They dragge this spotles Innocent to his End
> Where with A Hellishe Resolution
> Unanimous, They purpose, and intend
> Alive to nayle him to the Cursed Tree
> That not at once, but lingring he should Dye. (159)

Middleton, in a sense, completes the transfer of guilt from Romans to Jews that the gospel accounts began. Further, the account mitigates the Christian guilt that is the *raison d'être* of an atonement theology and of meditative practice. Thus the subjectivity produced by Middleton's poem escapes that spiritual abjection that a meditation on the Passion might otherwise produce. Christian responsibility or guilt is evoked only to be canceled out by the greater guilt of the Jews; the notion that "Christ died for our sins" is superseded by "Christ died at the hands of sinful Jews." Reading Middleton's poem, then, produces not compunction but rather a voyeuristic pleasure in which the subject is not implicated.

While little can be known about Middleton, there is significant and revealing biographical data available about Southwell, Lanyer, and, to a lesser extent, Fletcher. We can thus speculate about the historical and cultural positionings that inflect their elaborations on the Passion narrative. For these poets, the Passion narrative functioned to construct alternative, more complex identities than the simple opposition of Christian and Jew. Robert Southwell, recusant, Jesuit, finally martyr to the Roman cause in England in 1595, brought those histories with him to the project of writing "Saint Peters Complaint," a work that he was probably composing just before his arrest in 1592.[20] The poem is a variation on the Passion narrative tradition, focusing on one scene, the denial of Peter. It is written in the persona of Peter, and borrows heavily from Luigi Tanzillo's *Le Lacrime di San Pietro*.[21] Southwell's poem is constructive of identity in a number of ways, but not most significantly of the identities one would most expect to find in a poem by the Jesuit head of the English Mission, such as Christian versus Jew, or Catholic versus Protestant. The Jews are mentioned only once, when their "Jewish tyrannies" are evoked as crimes *less* heinous than Peter's denial (127).[22] And while the distinction between orthodox Catholic and heretic Protestant is made early on in the poem, it provides merely a springboard to identities based on gender and sexuality that are more important to Southwell and that dominate the poem.

And the poem is manifestly about the construction of identity. The opening stanza of the preface from "The Author to the Reader" invites the reader to "learne by [Peter's] faultes, what in thine owne to mend," that is, to construct a righteous self by contrast to a sinful one. But the concern of the poem quickly shifts from the scriptural contrast between sin and righteousness to a contemporary contrast between the "pagans" who write love lyrics and those who write in the service of Christianity:

> Still finest wits are stilling *Venus* rose.
> In Paynim toyes the sweetest vaines are spent:
> To Christian workes, few have their tallents lent.
>
> (16–18)

Succeeding stanzas again condemn those who "fill volumes with your forged Goddesse praise" and "Devote your fabling wits to lovers layes" (32, 34). This literary self-fashioning, however, soon becomes more complex than the simple dichotomies implied by subject and object, divine and secular, faithful and apostate. For the subjectivity that is being constructed is ultimately a male, homosocial identity constructed "between men," in the words of Eve Kosofsky Sedgwick,[23] across the bodies of women, initially the body of poetry about the bodies of beloved women, but finally a homoerotic subjectivity constructed upon the desirable body of Christ across the corrupt and corrupting bodies of all women. For in Southwell's portrait of Peter's denial, it is the humiliating fact that women prompted his denial of Christ — the servant-girls who assert, "You also were with Jesus the Galilean" — that makes his sin so heinous. (In fact, the number and gender of Peter's accusers vary according by gospel,[24] but the femaleness of the accusers is central to Southwell's argument, and he departs from the biblical text here.) Southwell's Peter reviles himself with the charge that "A puffe of womans wind bred all my fear," "a maidens easie breath/Did blow me down, and blast my soule to death" (150, 168).[25] These are not the ordinary, featureless women of the gospel accounts, but "homely droyles" (drudges or base servants), "ill grac'd" and "despisde" (314, 317), who with fearsome farts and dragon breath can "blast" a man's soul. Here women have assumed the object-position of the cloven-footed, demonic Jews in early modern iconography. Peter's denial becomes a type of Adam's seduction by Eve (who was also portrayed with demonic body parts in contemporary depictions) — the basest of sins by virtue of the baseness of women. So when Southwell summarizes women's nature, it is in the Augustinian tradition of original sin:

> O women, woe to men: traps for their falls,
> Still actors in all tragicall mischances:
> Earthes necessarie evils, captiving thralles,
> Now murdring with your tongs, now with your glances,
> Parents of life, and love: spoylers of both,
> The theefes of Harts: fals do you love or loth.
>
> (319–24)

In contrast to this portrait of women, Southwell paints a picture of Jesus as the true object of desire, elaborating for 20 stanzas on the beauty of Christ (before calling himself back to the "real" purpose of his poem with the remark, "But O, how long demurre I on his eies" [445]), using the language of carnal love that provided the poet with an initial contrast productive of subjectivity. Jesus's eyes are the particular focus of this adoration:

> You flames devine that sparkle out your heats,
> And kindle pleasing fires in mortall hearts:
> You nectared Aumbryes of soule feeding meats,
> You graceful quivers of loves dearest darts:
> You did vouchsafe to warme, to wound, to feast:
> My cold, my stony, my now famishde breast.
>
> *   *   *
>
> These blasing comets, lightning flames of love,
> Made me their warming influence to know:
> My frozen hart their sacred force did prove,
> Which at their lookes did yeeld like melting snow.
>
> (349–54, 361–64)

Twice Jesus' eyes are praised in language that bears an uncanny resemblance to Shakespeare's homoerotic sonnet 20,

"A woman's face with Nature's own hand painted." Shakespeare's beloved has

> An eye more bright than [women's], less false in rolling,
> Gilding the object whereupon it gazeth;

and is

> A man in hue all hues in his controlling.
>
> (5–7)[26]

For Southwell's Peter, Jesus' eyes "make thinges nobler then in native hew, . . . all but your selves in light excelling" (369, 397).[27] The homoeroticism is underscored by images of fecundity that are portrayed not merely scatologically, but anally. Peter reproaches himself:

> Is this the harvest of his sowing toile?
> Did *Christ* manure thy hart to breed him bryars?
>
> *   *   *
>
> No: no: the Marle that perjuries do yeeld,
> May spoyle a good, not fat a barraine field.

Peter's sin also seems to have been one of role reversal in the amorous exchange. In the context of the relationship between holy and erotic poetry he has established, Southwell's mention of the "court" of Caiaphas recalls his court(ship) of Jesus the divine lover and an eroticized, penetrative relationship. Peter laments,

> O, had I in that court much stronger bene:
> Or not so strong as first to enter in.
>
> (245–46)

Peter's sin is finally one of unfaithfulness or adultery to this true lover. His "hart," which should have been kept spotless and virginal for the holy lover Jesus, has been "deflowrde" (586) by heeding the servant girls' words.[28] Southwell uses the Passion narrative, then, as a context for the construction of a male, homosocial subjectivity, contrasting himself to false poets and linking Peter, Everyman and Catholic founder, with the true lover, Christ, across the bodies of debased women (servant girls, Eve, the inamorata of the sonnets). Identity is formed "between men" by fundamentally, as it were, distinguishing maleness from femaleness in the context of the Passion narrative.

The particular historical positioning Aemilia Lanyer brought to her *Salve Deus Rex Judaeorum* is more complex than Southwell's. Much has been made recently of Lanyer's Jewish origins through her father's family, the Bassanos (from Bassano del Grappa, near Venice).[29] This heritage is no doubt significant, but it is mediated by other religious and national positionings that inflected Lanyer's outlook. More formative in many ways than her father's origins would have been her mother's influence, not only because of the primacy of the mother in a young girl's life, but because her father died when Lanyer was seven. Her mother, Margaret Johnson (who was almost certainly Christian), lived until Lanyer was 18. Added to this is the likelihood that Lanyer spent at least some of her youth in the household of Susan Bertie, Countess of Kent, whose family was notable for the arch-Protestant politics that made them exiles during Mary's reign.[30] Further complicating the picture are the Roman Catholic roots of her husband's family, the Lanyers, who were also musicians like the Bassanos, who came to England, probably from Rouen, under Elizabeth, and whose given names — Innocent, Clement — read like a history of the popes.[31] Thus Lanyer was the product of multiple religious standpoints, none of which alone can define her particular religious positioning in the "Salve Deus." It is tempting to see her as pro-Jewish, but, while her Passion narrative is less antisemitic than Middleton's, it mentions the Jews more often than Southwell's, and more harshly.[32] I think it more accurate to call her pro-woman, but even that category is complicated by religious and, particularly, class issues: while she praises notably-Protestant women, she makes the Virgin Mary a principal player in the drama and identifies herself more adamantly and frequently with Christ than with her poetic assemblage of virtuous women. Instead of an overdetermined speaking subject, I would like, instead, to postulate Lanyer as a situated author, transforming and being transformed by the vortex of religious ideas that energized England in the sixteenth and seventeenth centuries and writing a self into existence through her poems.

Lanyer's "Salve Deus" is of interest not only because she constructs female subjectivity in contrast to male sinfulness, but for the way in which she subverts much of the oppressive potential of the narrative. That is, while Lanyer significantly substitutes the category "men" for "Jews" in her poem, men do not emerge from the poem so much as demonized but as sinners who, on account of their sin, do not have the right to lord it over women. While women are the focus of Lanyer's book, and the most holy person presented in the book is a woman — Margaret, Countess of Cumberland — neither Jews nor men as a group are damned. (Only Judas seems inescapably confined to hell because of his actions.) Indeed, Lanyer argues against the kind of divinely justified vengeance productive of persecution. Such behavior, she argues, is particularly abhorrent to Jesus. So the disciples' show of violence against the officials who come with Judas to arrest Jesus is contextualized by an analysis of the way decent people become persecutors. Jesus' enemies (Judas and the accusing Jews) are guilty, first, of rationalization: in them, "Falshood beares the shew of formall Right" (569). And violence born of objectifying, self-righteous hate is, for Lanyer, unchristian. So when Peter slashes off the ear of one of the soldiers, it "Offends [the] Lord, and is against the Lawes":

> So much [Jesus] hates Revenge, so farre from Hate,
> That he vouchsafes to heale, whom thou [Peter] dost wound;

*   *   *

Nay, to his foes, his mercies so abound,
That he in pitty doth thy will restraine,
And heales the hurt, and takes away the paine.

(600–02, 606–08)

Rather than using the false accusation of Jesus as an impetus for revenge against the Jews, the scene becomes instead an occasion for condemning revenge and violence.

This is not to say that the poem ceases to construct identity, but that her self-fashioning is more complex than the simple contrasts "Christian versus Jew" or "woman versus man." Lanyer's poem initially shifts the blame for Christ's death from a bigoted category — "Jews" — to the actions of individual men. Judas (not the Jews, as in Middleton's poem) enacts a kind of *felix culpa*: human beings lost their standing "by *Adams* fall" but are "rais'd by a *Judas* kisse" (259–60). All the disciples are wrong in claiming they will not desert Jesus, but "poore *Peter*, he was most too blame,/That thought above them all, by Faith to clime" (355–56). Only after the mitigated condemnation of the two disciples ("rais'd by a *Judas* kisse," "poore *Peter*") are the Jews introduced. They are called "Fooles" (495) and "Monsters" (497), but their sins are human:

How blinde were they could not discerne the Light!
How dull! If not to understand the truth,
How weake! If meekenesse overcame their might;
How stony hearted, if not mov'd to ruth:
How void of Pitie, and how full of Spight,
Gainst him that was the Lord of Light and Truth:
Here insolent Boldnesse checkt by Love and Grace,
Retires, and falls before our Makers face.

(505–12)

For Lanyer, the Jews are particularly misguided in their learning:

Yet could their learned Ignorance apprehend
No light of grace, to free themselves from blame:

> Zeale, Lawes, Religion, now they doe pretend
> Against the truth, untruths they seeke to frame:
> Now al their powres, their wits, their strengths, they bend
> Against one siely, weake, unarmed man,
> Who no resistance makes, though much he can.
>
> (545–52)

They are contrasted to Jesus, whom Lanyer characterizes as the incarnation of Wisdom (e.g., 694, 701). When Jesus/Wisdom finally speaks, he shows his divinity by eschewing revenge and violence, by refusing to condemn the Jews:

> Then with so mild a Majestie he spake,
> As they might easly know from whence he came,
> His harmelesse tongue doth no exceptions take,
> Nor Priests, nor People, meanes he now to blame;
> But answers Folly, for true Wisdomes sake . . . .
>
> (697–701)

In addition, Lanyer returns, in the agony in the garden scene, to a condemnation of all the disciples who fail to stay awake and pray with Jesus and who all desert him after his arrest. At that moment, they form a culpable category: "Though they protest they never will forsake him,/They do like men, when dangers overtake them" (631–32). Rather than postulating Jewish guilt to minimize Christian responsibility and, thus, construct Christian identity in the manner of Middleton, Lanyer has multiplied the guilt and demonized violence. There is no divinely ordained retribution or persecution in Lanyer's theology — against the Jews, or men, or any individual.

Further, Lanyer, unlike Middleton, does not portray the Jews as responsible for the condemnation and execution of Jesus. Instead, in contradiction to the gospel traditions, she places the blame on Pilate (where it no doubt significantly belonged). Pilate is blamed not, however, as a representative of Rome (as opposed to Jerusalem), but as a representative of men, and his guilt arises significantly because he fails to listen to his wife, who pleads for Jesus' life. And rather than constructing Jesus'

defense on his divinity or innocence, Pilate's wife context-
ualizes the error of Pilate's condemnation of Jesus in the Eden
narrative. This abrupt shift is poetically surprising, but
(theo)logically sound. The Christian tradition had seen Adam's
fault as one of uxoriousness: had he not listened to Eve, he
would not have sinned. This reading justified the silencing of
women in the Pastoral epistles and in the misogynist tradi-
tion that followed them. (Included in this tradition is, of course,
Southwell's "Saint Peters Complaint," where the condemna-
tion of Peter's heeding of the servant girls' words alludes to
Adam's fault.) But Lanyer shows that Pilate will err precisely
because he does not listen to his wife. The scene is a mirror of
the exchange between Adam and Eve and, thus, reverses for
Lanyer the relative guilt that had been assigned to Eve. Eve's
sin, imputed to all women, had allowed men "to over-rule us
all," says Pilate's wife, but Pilate's "indiscretion," imputed to
all men, "sets us free" (760–61). So while Pilate's ultimate con-
demnation of Jesus does allow Lanyer to blame men rather
than the Jews for the death of Jesus, and allows for the con-
struction of autonomous female identity, her theology does
not allow for the absolute othering of men. Rather, Pilate's
action restores an equilibrium that was disturbed in Eden: as
Mary's obedience was seen to correct Eve's disobedience, as
Jesus' saving actions repaired Adam's loss, so men's implica-
tion in Pilate's sin rescinds men's authority over women and
restores a gender balance. This is the context for Lanyer's
demand for equality:

> Then let us have our Libertie againe,
> And challendge to your selves no Sov'raigntie;
>
>   *   *   *
>
> Your fault beeing greater, why should you disdaine
> Our beeing your equals, free from tyranny?
> If one weake woman simply did offend,
> This sinne of yours, hath no excuse, nor end.
>
> (825–26, 829–32)

Like Southwell, Lanyer alters the subject/object dynamic in the Passion narrative to construct a gendered religious and poetic identity. She repeats accusations against the Jews but also accuses Peter, the disciples, and Pilate, significantly shifting the blame to men, who displace Jews as perpetrators of the crucifixion — and they are othered as coequals, not as subordinates. What effect her Jewish heritage might have had on these choices is difficult to say, though such self-knowledge may have made it impossible for her to portray the Jews as utterly inhuman. Nonetheless, a kind of thoughtless antisemitism is central to her portrayal; indeed, it is only in the context of a work like Middleton's that one can portray Lanyer's poem as moderate in this sense. One would have to credit her with a kind of Matthean prophetic voice — chastizing most harshly his own people for mistaking the identity of Jesus — to fit her negative portrayal of the Jews to her purported Jewish sense of identity, and nothing else in the text supports that reading. The ambient conversation about the "woman question" seems a more salient influence on her construction of subjectivity. Perhaps she shows herself, finally, to be more Protestant in her inclinations than Jewish, inclined to take seriously the contemporary injunctions of individual responsibility for individual salvation, working out a female subjectivity as she worked out a fit theology.

Lanyer's Passion narrative has recently been read in the context of Giles Fletcher's *Christ's Victorie and Triumph in Heaven, and Earth, over and after Death* (1610).[33] Janel Mueller has suggested that the two works share an analogous structure (*ottava rima* stanzas)[34] and patronage context, Fletcher making his suit to male patrons, and Lanyer, to female patrons of similar standing. For Mueller, these distinctions demonstrate, in part, Lanyer's "feminist poetics."[35] In this context, Mueller notes Fletcher's tendency to allegorize virtues (such as Mercy and Justice) as female, while Lanyer memorializes the virtues of real women like Margaret, Countess of Cumberland. The hagiography that developed around Fletcher's life resembles that tradition in the early memorials to George Herbert. Both were university scholars famous for their piety; after attending Cambridge and remaining there for several years as a "catechist," Fletcher was ordained and took a living in Suffolk "which is supposed to have hastened the period of his death":

> [H]e did not live long to reap the advantage of his preferment; the unhealthiness of the situation combined with the ignorance of his parishioners, to depress his spirits and exhaust his constitution; a lonely village in the maritime part of Suffolk, more than two hundred years ago, had few consolations to offer to one accustomed to the refined occupations of an University.[36]

The "refined occupations" of a university education are evident everywhere in Fletcher's poem, particularly in the characters from classical mythology that populate this biblical epic; indeed, the juxtaposition of Greek with Christian deities was disturbing to readers of earlier centuries.[37] The style, too, is explicitly imitative of Greek and Roman epics,[38] and Fletcher clearly means to establish poetic identity and authority in his appropriation of classical models. The shift from biblical to classical contexts nearly writes the Jews out of Fletcher's account. The crowds that clamor for Jesus' crucifixion are not identified as Jewish, but are rather called the "Fraile multitude" (31). And, when the sky darkens at the moment of Jesus' death, a Jew's response is portrayed sympathetically alongside those of a philosopher and the Roman centurion:

> The wise philosopher cried, all agast,
> "The God of Nature surely languishèd!"
> The sad Centurion cried out as fast,
> The Sonne of God, the Sonne of God was dead;
> The headlong Iew hung downe his pensiue head,
> And homewards far'd; and euer, as he went,
> He smote his brest, half desperately bent:
> The verie woods and beasts did seeme His death lament. (39)

In Fletcher's poem, guilt is instead assigned to Satan and to Judas (40–51).

More significant in the context of this discussion is the way that Fletcher fashions a self through the Passion narrative, again as in Southwell's, between men, across the identities, or, at least, the characters, of Mary Magdalene and Mary, the mother of Jesus. For Fletcher, this initiatory poetic moment occurs after the death of Jesus when Joseph of Arimathea provides the tomb for Jesus' body. Though the story of Joseph of Arimathea is, of course, biblical in origin (appearing in all four canonical gospels),[39] in the biblical accounts, Joseph's presence at the tomb is quickly superseded by that of Mary Magdalene and other women (sometimes named as Joanna, or Mary, the mother of James, or Salome), who are the most significant players in the denouement of the Passion narrative. But in Fletcher's poem, Joseph displaces the "shole/Of Maries" (54), initially indistinguishable from each other, as he laments the death of Jesus. At that moment, he becomes a model for poetic and religious subjectivity and is urged by the narrator (in an apostrophe reminiscent of pastoral poetry) to "Sing, then, O sing aloude, thou Arimathean swaine!" (53). Displacing Mary, the mother of Jesus, Joseph holds Jesus' limp body, evoking an image of the Pietà, and then kisses the corpse:

> . . . long he stood, in his faint arms vpholding
> The fairest spoile heau'n euer forfeited,
> With such a silent passion griefe vnfoulding
> That, had the sheete but on himselfe beene spread,
> He for the corse might haue been buried:
>
>   *   *   *
>
> At length (kissing His lipps before he spake,
> As if from thence he fetcht againe His ghost)
> To Mary thus, with teares, his silence brake:
> "Ah, woefull soule! What ioy in all our cost,
> When Him we hould, we haue alreadie lost? (54, 55)

After blazoning the healing powers of Christ's body (his eyes, his face, his feet, his hand, his lipps), Joseph wishes for exile and death. In this, he displaces Mary Magdalene, who, in the extra-biblical tradition, had become a hermit after Christ's death and was noted for her tears of sorrow and remorse.[40]

> Let mee, O let me neere some fountaine lie,
> That through the rocke heaues vp his sandie head;
> Or let me dwell vpon some mountaine high,
> Whose hollowe root and baser parts ar spread
> On fleeting waters, in his bowells bread,
> That I their streames, and they my teares may feed:
> Or, cloathèd in some hermit's ragged weed,
> Spend all my daies, in weeping for this cursèd deed. (62)

Fletcher's poetic identity and authority in this Passion narrative depends, then, on his figuration of Joseph as his antitype; Joseph, most faithful follower and poet, "sings" a poem about Jesus' death in Fletcher's poem about Jesus' death. The homoerotic connection between Joseph and Jesus relies on the co-option of extrabiblical traditions about both Mary Magdalene as holy lover and hermit and "the blessed Virgin" as Pietà. But, uniquely among the four poems I have discussed here, Fletcher's self-fashioning does not depend so much on othering as on displacement and effacement. It is not finally the contrast between Joseph and Mary Magdalene that constructs poetic vocation, but their likeness. Satan and his creature Judas bear the guilt (as, in "Christ's Victorie in Heaven," Satan bears responsibility for Adam's sin), but neither Jews, as in Middleton's account, nor women, as in Southwell's, nor men, as in Lanyer's, are othered to construct identity. Yet the context proves, again, to be productive of a poetic and religious self.

How, then, can we assess the significance of these authors' generically related yet very dissimilar poetic meditations? If we look for an answer in literary history and its byproduct, the canon, these four poems will not prove particularly revealing or illuminating and will remain footnotes to the biographies of major and minor poets — Middleton to Southwell, Southwell to Shakespeare, Fletcher to Milton — or exempla for revisionist literary scholarship reminiscent of Dr. Johnson's faint praise for the bipedal dog, as has partly been the case in Lanyer studies. But we mistake the context of these poems if we confine ourselves to a narrow vision of poetry and ignore the larger cultural and religious context within which they were written, including both public liturgy and private devotion. If seen as versions of a Passion narrative that was "performed" continuously in churches and homes throughout early modern England, the poems look different than if we see them as the oddities of a poetic corpus. In that larger cultural context, they reveal a spectrum of attitudes about nationality, religion, gender, and sexuality that the Passion narrative enabled because of its centrality to the Christian mythos and its long history as a producer of individual and corporate identities. The canon can illuminate. Like urban light pollution, it erases billions of dimmer stars and leaves us with a manageable set of constellations and bright suns. But it is sometimes interesting to travel to the desert, where darkness reveals the innumerable lights of the night sky and masks the relationships we thought we understood.

2 • "To Help Souls"
Recovering the Purpose of Southwell's Poetry and Prose

Scott R. Pilarz

Robert Southwell belongs to the first generation of Jesuits. He entered the Society of Jesus fewer than 20 years after the death of Ignatius Loyola, the Order's founder, and religious historians maintain that those present at or near the birth of a religious movement best understand its particular charism.[1] This makes Southwell a Jesuit's Jesuit and, therefore, problematizes scholarship on his life and work. This essay argues that these complications should be embraced in order to recover his English poetry and prose.

Southwell had been a Jesuit for eight years before he returned to England to write again in the language of his boyhood.[2] His long and carefully prescribed course of religious formation largely determined his approach to literature. Furthermore, Jesuit foundational documents, including but not limited to Ignatius Loyola's *Spiritual Exercises*, supply "the primary language for [his] model of Christian selfhood" (Shuger 9).[3] This model of selfhood subsumed his approach to authorship and needs to be contextualized for the sake of rediscovering the most fundamental aspects of his work. As a Jesuit, Southwell wrote to "help souls" through reconciliation, confirmation, and consolation.

Everard Mercurian, the superior general of the Jesuits from 1572 to 1580, gave his subjects specific orders when he missioned them to England, and none of these instructions touched on what Louis Martz describes as "the poor estate of English religious poetry" (180). Contrary to the arguments of Martz and critics writing after him, Southwell did not return home with the intention of "reform[ing] English poetry by bringing to it certain arts he had found flourishing on the Continent: the practice of religious meditation [i.e., the *Spiritual Exercises*], and the conversion of the methods of profane poetry to the service of God" (183). This literary reformation would happen later and only as a result of Southwell's prior understanding of what the first Jesuits called their "way of proceeding."[4] After considerable resistance based upon fears of what would happen to his men, Mercurian sent Jesuits to England "to confirm Catholics in their faith, to absolve the lapsed, [and] not to battle with the heretics" (Basset 40).[5] My reading of Southwell's poetry and prose will show that he adhered so closely to these instructions that his writing should be understood as an exercise in pious utilitarianism. He used literature to achieve the three ends prescribed by his religious superiors, and these specific goals fulfill the original purpose of the Society of Jesus.

Bernard Basset describes how Mercurian, "groping in the dark and not too certain of conditions in England," sent his men with "a list of simple and prudent rules . . . in their pockets":

> Their commission, as Mercurian set it out, must be wholly spiritual. . . . The missionaries were urged to avoid all controversy and politics. They were not to mention politics in their letters and must never, save in private and on urgent

occasions, join in conversations about the English Queen . . .
"They must so behave that all men must see that the only gain
they covet is that of souls." (40–41)[6]

As the primary purpose of the Society of Jesus, this "covet-
ing" of souls explains Southwell's motive for returning
home, as well as the various ministries he performed while in
England.[7] Everything else, including the ministry of the *Spiri-
tual Exercises* and producing literature, stands as secondary
for Southwell. After eight years of what he describes as "the
restrained and severe Course" of Jesuit formation aimed at
"victory over ourselves," Southwell understood this funda-
mental presupposition (*Supplication* 13).[8] Unfortunately, but
understandably, most of his biographers and critics have not.

To date, many scholars have stressed Southwell's "Jesuit-
ness," but in ways that do some injustice both to the poet and
his religious order. Southwell's motivation for writing has
everything to do with his understanding of the mission of the
Society of Jesus, and while the formative value of the *Spiri-
tual Exercises* and the pressures brought to bear by the Refor-
mation should not be underestimated in this regard, they
hardly account for all the energies that animate Southwell's
work. Issues unexplained by Loyola's *Exercises* or the Protes-
tant Reformation feature prominently in Southwell's poetry
and prose, but most readers have been unable to appreciate
this because they have worked without the benefit of recent
historical scholarship on the Jesuits.[9]

Louis Martz's *The Poetry of Meditation*, published in 1954,
marks the starting point in modern criticism of Southwell's
work. In response to his argument for the predominant influ-
ence on Southwell's verse of the meditative structure of
Loyola's *Exercises*, subsequent studies by Rosemond Tuve
(1961), Richard Strier (1978), Barbara Lewalski (1979), and F. W.
Brownlow (1996) have moved in other, but equally reductive,
directions. Tuve, for example, reads Southwell in the tradi-
tion of sacred parody as practiced by polemicists of every early

modern religious sort. Lewalski gives Southwell short shrift. To do otherwise would undermine her efforts to show that seventeenth century devotional poetry in England has more to do with native Protestant influences than with vestiges of continental Catholicism. Strier, too, discounts Southwell's importance, understanding him as a creature of the Counter-Reformation who paved the way for Crashaw and others to write poetry for the sake of "cultivating ecstasy" (37). Brownlow foregrounds Southwell's martyrdom, and in doing so stresses his "eccentricity and isolation." According to Brownlow, "Southwell made the decision, in some ways an extremely arrogant one, to be one of the absolutely excluded. He challenged his society to kill him . . . The effect, indeed the intention, of Southwell's work and life, was by violence to turn the world upside down in the spirit of the strongest gospel paradoxes and reversals" (xii–xiii). I do not dispute that Southwell wanted to conform his life to the pattern of the gospel, but I will argue that in his mind and art that pattern was refracted through a Jesuit lens, the dimensions of which need to be fully appreciated. Southwell may have been "isolated" and "excluded" from the perspective of Protestant Englishmen, but his poetry and prose place him at the center of the Society of Jesus. When asked who they were, Loyola and his first followers identified themselves as the *Compagnia di Gesu*, the Company of Jesus. Robert Southwell's writing reveals a company man.

According to its motto, *ad majorem Dei gloriam*, the Company of Jesus was founded to promote the greater glory of God. The number of times that this phrase appears in Jesuit foundational documents, however, pales in comparison to the more frequently used quotidian expression "to help souls" (O'Malley 18). This is news. Until recently, even Jesuits themselves labored under misconceptions about their original "way of proceeding." From the Order's inception, admirers and detractors alike have perennially confused its purpose because the

Society represents, from the start, a revolutionary way of exercising ministry in the church. As John O'Malley reports, early Jesuits constantly had to insist, "we are not monks." They needed to explain to themselves and others that, while members of monastic orders flee the company of other human beings, "the essence of the Jesuits was to *seek* their company in order to help them." Nothing was to stand in their way, and especially not the familiar trappings of medieval religious life. Jesuits did not chant the Office in choir, nor did they wear monastic garb or live in monasteries or convents.[10] According to Loyola, Jesuits must understand that "the world is our house." Jeronimo Nadal, the man to whom Loyola entrusted the instruction of Jesuits in their "way of proceeding," interpreted this to mean that there was a virtue in mobility. According to Nadal, "the principal and most characteristic dwelling for Jesuits is not the professed houses, but in journeyings." He declares that "the most perfect houses of the Society are the journeys of the professed, by which they diligently seek to gain for Christ the sheep that are perishing."[11] Southwell, while journeying between recusant houses, writes poetry and prose for his English flock precisely as a means of inhabiting his worldly, Jesuit "home." He seeks the company of readers for the sake of "confirm[ing] Catholics in their faith, absolv[ing] the lapsed, and not to battle with heretics" (Basset 33).

Documenting misinterpretations of the Jesuits can be entertaining, especially their demonization by early modern Englishmen, but it is more profitable for reading Southwell to follow O'Malley's efforts "to understand the early Jesuits as they understood themselves" (3). In doing so, it is especially necessary because of the Jesuits' controversial English mission to dispel the single most common misperception about the founding of the Society. As O'Malley puts it, "although the Society of Jesus would have had a much different history, it would have come into being even if the Reformation had not happened, and it cannot be defined primarily in relation to it." Moreover, "in many parts of the world, the direct impact of the Reformation on the Jesuits ranged from minimal to practically nonexistent" (17). Even in England, where the impact was considerable, Southwell and his fellow Jesuits "tended to understand the Reformation as primarily a pastoral problem": "They saw its fundamental causes and cures as related not so much to doctrinal issues as to the spiritual condition of the persons concerned, and they helped to perpetuate this interpretation, which correlated with their own understanding of what was most important in life" (O'Malley 16).[12] This insight illuminates Southwell's work. He writes as a pastor, not as a polemicist, and he is confident that his literary efforts will help souls by promoting reconciliation.

In several of his poems, Southwell reveals his preference for reconciliation to "battle" with reformers. Surprisingly, this preference even informs works on the Eucharist. Many of his contemporaries, Catholic and Protestant, came at Eucharistic issues with the intention of instigating arguments. But in "Mary Magdalene's Complaint at Christ's Death," for example, Southwell sees the conciliatory advantage of adapting the form of a lover's lament. In the first stanza of the poem, Mary wants to die since the source of her life has parted. Without Christ in her life, she "lives by meere extortion" (4). Southwell characteristically moves from this emotional opening to a more rational and meditative second stanza in which he makes analogies between "seely starres" that "must needes leave shining,/ When the sunne is shadowed" and "borrowed streames" that must "refraine their running,/ When head springs are hindered" (7–10). In the absence of Christ, Mary desires death, unless there exists some means by which Christ can be really present to her again: "Let me die or live thou in mee" (18). Lines 19–24 of the poem allude to controversies surrounding Christ's presence, or lack thereof, in the Eucharist, but the tone is far from antagonistic:

Where truth once was, and is not,
Shadowes are but vanitie:
Shewing want, that helpe they cannot:
Signes, not salves of miserie.
Paynted meate no hunger feedes,
Dying life each death exceedes.

Southwell could have Protestant churches in mind when he contemplates sites which were once home to truth. Like Mary Magdalene, he mourns the substitution of "shadowes" and "signes" for that which once gave life. But lamentation differs inherently in tone from most Reformation-era literature concerning Communion. This speaker's voice is amorous; it does not anathematize. The poem ends with a loving apostrophe to the spear that pierced the side of Christ. Catholic iconography connects this piercing with the sacraments of Baptism and Eucharist since Scripture reports that water and blood flowed from Christ's side (John 19.34). Southwell sees a paradox in this piercing. It deprives Christ of life, but the release of Christ's blood also allows for the possibility that Christ can remain with Mary: "Though my life though drav'st away,/ Maugre thee my love shall stay" (41–42). Southwell insists on the real presence of Christ to his followers through his blood, but he tempers this controversial assertion by the poem's pathos.

Given the contestatory attitudes of people on both sides of the Reformation divide, the reasonableness of Southwell's approach to the Eucharist should surprise us. Other Catholics were much less measured in their reactions to doctrinal challenges. As Peter Marshall reports,

> Confronted with growing evidence of disbelief in the real presence, some priests might be drawn to desperate measures to restore their credibility. In 1544 the London *Grey Friars' Chronicle* reported how a Kentish priest had been punished 'for cutting of his finger and making it bleed on the host at his mass for a false sacrifice,' a faked eucharistic miracle corresponding to the pattern familiar to the sermon literature and popular iconography of the middle ages. (75)

In responding to doubts about the Eucharist, Southwell, too, turns to the Middle Ages for his inspiration; but his solution relies more on good pastoral sense than on sham theatricality. In "A holy Hymne," entitled in the manuscripts, "St. Thomas of Aquinas Hymne. Read on Corpus Christi Day. Lauda Sion Salvatorem," Southwell translates and adapts traditional material in order to give it wider circulation. He points out how the feast was established for the purpose of celebrating the institution of the Eucharist at the Last Supper:

> A speciall theame of praise is read,
> A living and life giving bread
> Is on this day exhibited
> Which in the supper of our Lord,
> To twelve disciples at his bord,
> None doubted but was delivered.
>
> (7–12)

In arguing for the universal acceptance of what was "delivered" on Holy Thursday, Southwell avoids contemporary debates about Communion. Later in this long poem, he shows similar care when a priest performs the fraction rite during which the host is broken before reception:

> When the priest the hoast divideth,
> Know that in each part abideth
> All that the whole hoast covered,
> Form of bread not Christ is broken,
> Not of Christ but of his token
> Is state or stature altered.
>
> (55–60)

Southwell makes a typically conciliatory choice in describing this priestly action. The fraction rite was not controversial. Had Southwell wanted to provoke Protestants, he would have shown his priest elevating the host rather than simply dividing it. Debates raged over the post-consecration elevation of the bread and wine. According to Marshall, "the elevation of the host, once the epitome of concord, now came to symbolize

the divergence of religious attitudes" (974).[13] Southwell, fol-
lowing his superior's orders, does not want to foreground
that divergence.

"Content and Rich," a parody of Richard Dyer's "My Mind
to Me a Kingdom Is," perhaps best exemplifies Southwell's
conciliatory approach. Southwell writes,

> I wrastle not with rage,
> While furies flame doth burn:
> It is in vaine to stop the streame,
> Until the tide doth turn.
>
> But when the flame is out
> And ebbing wrath doth end:
> I turn a late enraged foe
> Into a quiet frend.

> (37–44)

While most of this poem responds line by line to Dyer's origi-
nal, these two stanzas concern matters all Southwell's own.
The speaker in Dyer's poem remains entirely self-absorbed.
Others are mentioned simply as points of comparison to
make the speaker's "bliss" all the more enviable. He "laugh[s]
not at another's loss," nor does he "grudge . . . at an other's
gaine" (31–32). Dyer has no interest in reconciliation, which
Southwell makes a major focus of "Content and Rich."[14] Un-
like Dyer, Southwell cannot be content until he befriends his
"late enraged foe."

This intention of befriending "a late enraged foe" also in-
forms one of Southwell's most carefully crafted prose works,
A Humble Supplication to Her Majestie. His appeal, ostensi-
bly written for Queen Elizabeth herself, responds to a 1591
"declaration of great troubles pretended against the Realme
by a number of Seminarie Priests and Jesuits." The precarious
political situation in the Netherlands, rumors of Spanish troops
assembling in Normandy, and the threat of a second Armada
occasioned the declaration. Elizabeth's Council introduced
new measures to repress the recusant population lest they be

tempted to join forces with potential invaders. Southwell's *Supplication* shows him at his conciliatory best. Instead of battling with heretics, he attempts to ingratiate himself with their recently excommunicated Queen.

The *Supplication* begins and ends with conventional courtly flattery, but the traditional language from the pen of a Catholic priest likely surprised sixteenth century readers. Without yielding any theological ground, Southwell petitions Elizabeth for clemency. She remains his "most mighty and most merciful, most feared and best beloved Princess" (1). In light of her "perfection in all Princely virtues," Southwell insists that she could never have countenanced "soe strange a Proclamation" filled with "Fictions" and "Counterfeit illusions" about her loyal Catholic subjects. It is equally impossible that she knows of the treatment of those subjects: "We presume that your maiestie seldome or never heareth the truth of our persecutions, your lenity and tendernesse being knowne to be soe professed and enemy to these Cruelties, that you would never permitt their Continuance, if they were expressed to your Highness as they are practiced upon us" (944).

After establishing this conciliatory tone, Southwell explains his mission to England in characteristically Jesuit terms. A natural love for his countrymen compels him "to winne soules" (4). For this end, and this end only, he and other Jesuits have been educated. The declaration that sparked Southwell's *Supplication* describes Jesuit colleges as "certaine receptacles made to live in, and there to be instructed in Schoole pointes of sedition" (Bald 60). Southwell corrects this by claiming that "nothing in those seminaryes is either intended or practiced, but the reliefe and good education of foresaken men, as from the stormes of our English shoare flie thither for a calmer Roade, till perfected in the Course of learning and vertue, they may returne to offer their blood for the recovery of souls" (5). The *Supplication* clarifies the issue of offering blood when Southwell explains how Jesuits will behave in the face of a foreign invasion. Instead of aiding and abetting the Spanish, "we doe assure your Maiestie, that what Army soever should come against you, we will rather yeald our brests to by broached by our Cuntrie swords then use our swords to th'effusion of our Cuntries bloud" (35). In response to the charge that he and his confreres are "Fugitives, Rebells, and Traytors," Southwell sums up his strategy and goal: "protesting upon our soules and salvations, and calling Allmighty god and his Angells for witnesses, . . . the whole and only intent of our coming into this Realme, is no other, but to labour for the salvation of soules, and in peaceable and quiet sort to confirme them in the auntient Catholique Faith in which their Forefathers lived and died these 1400 yeares" (11). When Southwell subsequently addresses Elizabeth as "gods annoynted" (33) and "your sacred self" (45), he dramatically confirms his own "peaceable" approach (33). He and other Jesuits, including the much maligned Robert Parsons, hope to "encline fury to Clemency, and rage to Compassion" (38).[15]

In describing recusants as "a bundle of broken reeds" who have "long enough been cut off from all Comfort"(45), Southwell informs readers of the *Supplication* why he needs to "confirm Catholics in their faith" and how he plans to do it. He will console them. When he arrives in England he realizes that his Catholic compatriots are "stinted to an endles taske of sorrows, growing in griefs as we grow in yeares, one misery overtaking another, as if every one were but an earnest for harder payment" (45). They need consolation, and he writes to meet their need. Martz correctly observes that Southwell felt discouraged by what he discovered upon his return to England, but his reaction had less to do with literature than with the conditions of the Catholic community. His pastoral response to their situation draws upon what he learned during the course of his Jesuit formation. He will confirm them in the faith by means of "consolation." Promoting consolation ranks preeminently among the hallmarks of Jesuit ministry, and Southwell shapes his poetry and prose according to this purpose. Loyola defines consolation in the *Exercises*:

> By consolation I mean what occurs when some interior motion is caused within the soul through which it comes to be inflamed with love of its Creator and Lord. As a result it can love no created thing on the face of the earth itself, but only in the creator of all of them. Similarly, this consolation is experienced when the soul sheds tears that move it to love for its lord — whether they are tears of grief for its own sins or about the Passion of our Lord, or about other matters directly ordered to his service and praise. Finally, I include under the word consolation every increase in faith, hope and charity, and every interior joy that calls and attracts one to heavenly things and to the salvation of one's soul, by bringing it tranquility and peace in its creator and Lord. (#316)

Southwell was surely familiar with this definition and with the importance of consolation in other foundational Jesuit documents. The *Formula of the Institute*, for example, lists "the spiritual consolation of all God's faithful" among the chief purposes for which the Society has been established (#1).

This clearly stated purpose inspires Southwell's earliest prose work, *The Epistle of Comfort*. In her introduction to *The Epistle*, Margaret Waugh compares Southwell's letter to Thomas More's *Dialogue of Comfort Against Tribulation*. While similar in title, the two works differ in "plan and execution": "St. Thomas More writes as a philosopher, musing and meditating in a heavenly manner of his fate; Southwell as a passionate pastor of souls" (xii).[16] He reveals his passion from the start when he writes about showing his "reverent affection" for recusants through these "Catholic, though broken, speeches" (4). With characteristic humility, Southwell likens himself to a "diseased physician" who "may prescribe some healthful physic" by enlarging "a few points which seem unto [him] the principal causes of consolation to those who suffer in God's quarrel" (4). Southwell suggests that Catholics can find consolation on account of their intimate relationship with Christ. He makes his pastoral appeal on the personal level. Rather than scoring doctrinal points, Southwell draws an analogy to the dynamics of friendship:

> The love of a mortal friend not only moves us but enforces us to love him again, and his perils for us make us eager for his perils for him, because thereby both our love to him is best witnessed and his love to us most confirmed. And shall not this love on an immortal well-wisher, who tendereth us more than we ourselves, and in all respects better deserveth to have his love countervailed: shall it not, I say, be able to inflame us with desire to suffer for him and testify our affection in the midst of our torments if need so require. (45)

In his reading of the *Epistle*, F. W. Brownlow describes Southwell as writing "without sorrow, regret, or sympathy" (34). He imagines the letter's primary recipient, the imprisoned Philip Arundel, as "the embodiment of the Southwellian man, his comfort a sheet of paper consigning him to the absolute as rigorously in its own way as his judges sentence" (34). Brownlow misses Southwell's appreciation of the potential of literature in relation to "the absolute." The "absolute," namely God, is, in Southwell's mind, the source of consolation; literature a possible means to it. As Southwell understands it, the sheet of paper upon which he writes can be transformed into a religious instrument.[17] Southwell admits the limitations of literature, recognizing that "neither the style nor the concept [of his *Epistle*] answereth to the weight and importance of the subject" (1). Nevertheless, he has confidence that his words on paper can cause "motions in the soul through which it can be inflamed with love." The only thing "rigorous" about Southwell's approach is the pressure he puts on himself to "labor" in "altering [his] style" so that his readers might experience "the full effect" of what he hopes will constitute an occasion of consolation (1).

Southwell's confidence that prose can mediate consolation is more than matched by his surety that poetry proves even more effective in moving souls. He turns to poetry, according to Josephine Evetts-Secker, precisely because he finds in verse a much needed "spiritual alchemy" (129). Poetic diction provides him with the means to recast the desolatory experiences of his audience. In his poetry Southwell not only presents "the mysterious paradox of finding life through death," but he also wants to "alter [his readers'] perception of reality, to mollify affliction by transforming it," so that they can "behold another truth and a more sublime reality" (129). Southwell distinguishes between poetry and prose in "To the Reader," arguing that "tis a sweete repose,/ With poets pleasing vaine to temper prose" (11–12). He describes recusants as "tyred spirits" who for "mirth must have a time" (6). The purpose of his "muses style," therefore, is to "delight" and "give sobrest countenance leave sometime to smyle" (2–3). Such delight is not superficial, nor should it be confused with enjoyment of the "profane conceits and fayning fits" so popular among his literary contemporaries. Southwell's poetry of consolation gives souls an opportunity to "take a breathing flight," but it stays grounded in "vertue" and finds expression in "measured wordes" (15–16). Southwell considers "the true use of this measured and footed stile" to have been best exemplified by "men of greatest Pietie, in matters of most devotion" (The Author to his loving cosin" 1–16). Old and New Testament authors, including Christ himself, provide Southwell with "a method to imitate," whereby he can promote worthy "affections" among his readers.

The specific affection that many of Southwell's poems cultivate, remorse, may strike modern readers as contrary to our concept of consolation. He wants his readers to feel remorse in preparation for sacramental confession. Along with confirming Catholics in their faith and avoiding controversies with reformers, Southwell had also been explicitly missioned to England to "absolve the lapsed." Some of his best known poems need to be recovered in terms of this characteristically Jesuit task. In all of their efforts to help souls, the founding members of the Society insisted that the sacrament of confession was "the centerpiece of Jesuit ministry" (O'Malley 20). It is not surprising, then, that it enjoys pride of place among the sacraments in Southwell's poems. As O'Malley observes, "for the Jesuits, Penance enjoyed . . . preeminence among the seven sacraments," and their confidence in the consoling power of penance was likely grounded in the experience of the *Spiritual Exercises*. The initial phase of this month-long retreat, made at least twice in the life of every Jesuit, climaxes with a confession of all the sins of one's life up to that point.[18] Given their own experience of the sacrament, "Jesuits consistently recommended it to others from all walks of life as the keystone and expression of their conversion," and they were quite specific about their priestly role in the consoling "drama of confession" (O'Malley 139). Jesuit confessors were instructed to "always incline in the more humane direction," and to fashion themselves as "vicars of the mild Christ" (142).

This image of a gentle God, deeply ingrained in Jesuit spirituality, manifests itself in Southwell's *Spiritual Exercises and Devotions*. In one entry he describes the consoling nature of his own relationship with God:

> If you love a friend so much, if he or she is so attractive that everything he asked of you, you would agree to; and if it is so sweet to sit and talk with him, describe your mishaps to him — then how much more should you betake yourself to God, the God of goodness, converse with him, show him your weakness and distress, for he has greater care of you than you have of yourself, indeed he is more intimately you than you are. (66)

Several of Southwell's poems, including the shorter of his two efforts entitled "Saint Peter's Complaynte," encourage readers to betake themselves to God in sacramental confession. Peter asks rhetorical questions which underscore his self-induced misery:

How can I live, that have my life deny'de?
What can I hope, that lost my hope in feare?
What trust to one that trewth it selfe defyde?
What good in him that did his God forsweare

(1–4)

Peter has forsworn his Lord out of fear; as a result, the church's "Chosen rocke" becomes "a pastor not to feed, but to betray" (24). Southwell reminds his readers that Peter is no ordinary penitent. He recounts the Apostle's great deeds and numbers the privileges granted to him by Christ, including the power to forgive sins: "I once designed Judge to lose and bynde/ Now pleade at mercyes bar as guilty thrall" (43–44). The model disciple must now become the model convert in need of consolation. Peter, who once had faith enough to confess that Jesus was Lord, must now find remorse enough to confess his sins:

O tongue, the first that did his godhedd sounde,
How couldst thou utter such detesting wordes,
That every word was to his hart a wounde,
And lawnc'd him deeper than a thowsand swords?

(61–64)

After examining his conscience and recognizing the gravity of his offenses, Peter is moved to deep "remorse" signaled by "tears." In hope of future comfort, Peters asks Jesus to "lett myldness temper . . . deserved hate" (70). Jesus proves a perfectly mild confessor, and Southwell's readers should take consolation in this example and seek to imitate it by cultivating remorse for their own sins.

A companion piece, "S. Peters remorse," reenforces the roles prescribed for penitent and priest. Again, the examination of a "selfe blaiming conscience" results in "streames of weeping eies" (2–4). These tears recall Loyola's definition of consolation. Peter models for Southwell's readers how motions can stir in a sinner's soul. He admits that fear has led him to "highest treasons," but he trusts that "mercy may relent and

temper justice rod" (24–25). The sinner reminds himself
and the reader that God is a "milde Lord" who can provide
"comfort":

> O milde and mighty Lord,
> Amend what is amisse:
> My sinne my soare, thy love my salve,
> Thy cure my comfort is.

(53–56)

Southwell's most frequently anthologized piece, "The Burn-
ing Babe," also stresses the mildness of Jesus in the act of
forgiveness. The speaker employs a traditional Ignatian "com-
position of place" to summon up images of a "newly borne"
Christ Child. Once the speaker sets the scene in vivid detail,
the "pretty babe" cries because "none approach to warm their
harts" (15). Were they to do so, the "fire" of his love would
reduce their "shame and scornes" to ashes. Jesus invites those
with "defiled souls" to approach him. He wants nothing else
but "to work them to their good" (26). The Christ Child mod-
els behavior prescribed for confessors, and the speaker learns
that his initial anxieties are groundless. He need not lift "a
fearful eye" at this consoling vision. Even the purifying fire
proves more comforting than harmful: "Mercie blowes on the
coales" (22). While perhaps constituting an instance of alterity
for us, writing a penitential poem to celebrate Christmas
makes sense for Southwell. He connects the comforting feast
of Christ's birth with a sacrament that also affords consola-
tion, and he establishes a similar relationship between con-
fession and Christ's death in "Sinnes heavie load." Here, the
speaker's gaze fixes on the way of the cross, and his report
foregrounds the dying Christ's kindness to sinners. The cen-
tral images of the poem all concern "falling." The sinner has
obviously fallen from grace, but Christ's fallings are more
literal. Southwell imagines the scene in relation to sacra-
mental confession. Again, Christ models behavior for future

confessors. They should follow Christ in refusing to be "severe," even when circumstances warrant such a reaction. If Christ could be kind while enduring excruciating pain, all the more must confessors avoid severity in a sacramental context. The speaker admits that the weight of his sins causes Christ to stumble, but he learns to be glad of it: "But had they not to earth thus pressed thee,/ Much more in hell would they have pestred me" (5–6).

After employing a stanza to apostrophize sin itself (13–18), the speaker speculates about sin's effects on him in the life to come: "Alas, if God himselfe sinke under sinne,/ What will become of man that dies therein?" (17–18). He draws a parallel between Christ's three literal falls on the *via dolorosa* and his three "falls" in the course of salvation history. The latter include Christ's descent into Mary's womb at the Incarnation (20), his harrowing "sathans cave" (32), and his second coming. All these "falls" are acts of love, the contemplation of which should increase the sinner's hope for consolation. The speaker points out how Christ treats those who are "the cause of [his] unrest." In contrast to God the Father, who was "often . . . severe" (27), Christ reveals himself as exceedingly kind to those who sin against him: "O loving Lord that so doost love the foe, as thus to kiss the ground where he doth goe" (23–24). In forgiving sins, Christ "seal'st a peace with a bleeding kiss" (28). Confessors, therefore, should imitate their "Milde Lord" in granting pardon to sinners even when it involves personal cost. Sinners can see that they have nothing to fear.

At least two of Southwell's poems which touch on the consoling quality of sacramental confession strike a note of urgency. Readers should not delay in seeking forgiveness. In "A phansie turned to a sinners complaint," Southwell's parody of Dyer's "A Fancy," the Jesuit turns the complaint of a spurned lover into a plea to sinners to confess while they can. The sinful speaker understands that his transgressions have not entirely blotted out the enduring power of grace. This grace, in fact, causes him a troubled conscience:

> Yet God's mist I remaine,
> By death, by wrong, by shame;
> I cannot blot out of my heart,
> The grace wrought in his name.
>
> (105–08)

He expresses remorse for his sins, admittedly adapting "the faining Poets stile" to "figure forth" his "greefe not fain'd" (146–49), and he worries that the time to repent is passing all too quickly. He fears that he will be found "Unworthy of reliefe/ That craved it too late" (69–70). The same worry surfaces in "Loss in delaies." Here, Southwell twists the *carpe diem* trope to make a case for confession. He employs imagery to describe the passing of time that rivals Marvell's in its oddity. While in "To His Coy Mistress" Marvell fixes on Time's masticating "slow-chapt power" (39–40), Southwell highlights his hairstyle:

> Time wears all his lockes before,
> Take thy hold upon his fore head,
> When he flies he turns no more,
> And behinde his scalpe is naked,
> Workes ajournd have many stayes,
> Long demurres breede new delaies.
>
> (13–18)

Southwell urges the sinner to seize the day, or the forelocks, as it were, and make a confession: "Happie man that soone doth knocke" (41). He ends by likening the consoling effects of confession to a "salve" (19).

This same urgency appears in Southwell's advice to his father, who had fallen away from the Roman Catholic church. One of Southwell's biographers, Christopher Devlin, notes that for Southwell, as well as for other English Jesuits, "the longing to bring spiritual help to his family played a great part in his vocation to an active [as opposed to monastic] order" (201).[19] In 1589, when the poet's father seemed close to death, Southwell wrote to him, urging him to return to the church by means of sacramental confession. He acknowledges his paradoxical position by writing that "He may be father to the soul that is a son to the body, and requite the benefit of his temporal life by reviving his parent from spiritual death" (*Triumphs* 42). After describing in no uncertain terms the proximity of his father's demise, he asks, "Why then do you not devote at least the small remnant and surplusage of these your latter days, procuring to make atonement with God, and to free your conscience from such corruption as by your schism and fall hath crept into it?" (50). Southwell acknowledges his father's dire straits, but does so in terms designed to underscore the consolation which confession will bring:

> Howsoever therefore the soft gales of your morning pleasures lulled you in slumbery fits; howsoever the violent heats of noon might awake affections; yet now, in the cool and calm of the evening, retire to a Christian rest and close up the day of your life with a clear sunset: that leaving all darkness behind you and carrying in your conscience the light of grace, you may escape the horror of eternal night, and pass from a mortal day to an everlasting morrow. (64)

Southwell mentions the threat of hell, but does not dwell on it. Instead, here, as in so many of his poems, the syntax and substance of his prose mean to console.

Unlike most twentieth century readers, Southwell's closest contemporaries appreciated the points set forth here. Even those outside the Society understood the context of his literary work and read that work in relation to his mission. One of his literary executors, John Trussell, introduced a 1596 printed edition of Southwell's *Triumphs Over Death* with some verses of his own, and his poems put Southwell's work in its proper Jesuit perspective. Trussell prefaces the book by greeting the nieces and nephews of Philip Howard, the original recipient of the meditation that follows:

To you succeeding hopes of mother's fame,
I dedicate this fruit of Southwell's quill.
He for your uncle's comfort first it writ:
I for your consolation print and send you it. (*Triumphs* xi)[20]

Trussle understands his efforts as a continuation of Southwell's ministry of consolation. Only after clarifying the purpose of Southwell's work does his publisher praise him for his literary achievement. He describes the author as "Our Second-Ciceronian Southwell" famous for "persuasive pithy argument" (xii).

Given Southwell's priorities as a Jesuit missionary, he would have appreciated his publisher putting first things first. When writing for mission, function takes precedence over form, and substance outweighs style. Southwell estimates that his literary work amounts to "a few course threads" meant to show "how well verse and vertue sute together" (The Author to his loving Cosen, 2. 25–27). In Southwell's mind, virtue remains preeminent. Verse, and prose as well, constitute means for virtue's advancement. His primary purpose remains the fulfillment of his mission: "confirm[ing] Catholics in their faith, absolv[ing] the lapsed, and not to battle with heretics." Recovering Southwell's work requires us to understand that he wrote for the sake of "helping souls."

3• Alabaster's "Ensigns" Sonnets

Calm Before the Storm

George Klawitter

It would be difficult to find a Renaissance poet of more religious discontinuity than William Alabaster. Born into a devout Protestant family in 1567, he became a recusant in 1597 after serving as Essex's chaplain on the expedition to Cadiz and coming into contact with Jesuits in Spain. Until 1610 he was an outspoken if not foolhardy apologist of his defection both in England and on the continent, but after a bout with the Inquisition, he fled from his quarters in Rome, headed for Amsterdam and vowed to write against the Jesuits. In 1611, however, while under house arrest in England, he recanted his apostasy from Rome and declared he would die a Roman Catholic. But by 1614 he had returned to Protestantism, was absolved publicly by a Westminster synod, was created a Doctor of Divinity by order of the king, and sailed into the remaining 26 years of his life with a prolific pen. In the early years of his turmoil (1597–1598), Alabaster wrote scores of religious sonnets, most of which were discovered in manuscript by Bertram Dobell at the turn of the twentieth century.

Louise Guiney printed six of the sonnets in *Recusant Poets* (1939) but died before her projected edition and biography were completed. In 1959 G. M. Story and Helen Gardner published an edition of the sonnets with an extended preface upgrading the DNB biography and explaining their editorial purpose for reordering the poems.

Very little has been written on Alabaster's poetry. Aside from the Story/Gardner edition and remarks by Martz in *The Meditative Poem* (where he reprints a dozen of the sonnets), only one article (Klawitter) has been devoted exclusively to the verses of this deserving poet. A few critics, however, have written sensitively on Alabaster in other contexts. Bell, for example, uses his sonnets as a contrastive touchstone for the less emotional rhetoric of Herbert, Herbert's poems betraying "none of Alabaster's polemical goals or theological anxiety" (225), and Ottenhoff focuses on Alabaster's need for "visualizing the typological emblem" (55). Both critics find Alabaster a foil for the greater voice of Herbert, and their essays, while appreciative of Alabaster, remain among the few to even address the poet's works. It is tempting to suspect that since Alabaster changed religious camps so frequently in his life, neither side over the centuries has ventured to champion his less than loyal soul's lyrics, but poems rise and fall on their own merit; e.g., the recusant Crashaw has always had his Protestant admirers. It would be equally tempting to suspect that Alabaster's late discovery accounts for his slight following, but Traherne was discovered no earlier, his rocket shooting high and remaining visible. I think it is probable that editorial decisions on Alabaster sequencing have contributed to his lack of popularity: an author's intention should not be second guessed by editors.

Forty years ago Story and Gardner used three primary manuscripts to reconstruct a thematic order for the sequences contained within the Alabaster corpus of 77 poems, but the attempt to make sense with such an order may have done more injustice to the poet than the two editors imagined. They explain away their tampering with manuscript sequence by saying, "If Alabaster were a major poet, this point might be of real interest and importance . . . but he is not a major poet, and an editor's aim should be to present his work in as interesting and attractive a form as possible" (xl). Their conflation of three manuscript traditions in order to arrive at an "attractive" form for the fourth grouping ("Upon the Ensigns of Christ's Crucifying") has been anything but gentle. From 13 poems in manuscript J they culled six, in spite of the fact that manuscript B follows the exact ordering of J and should therefore add some force to a kind of tradition in the stemma. From an earlier manuscript called O they pulled five poems to add to the six from J. Preserving only the first poem in its manuscript position, they then disjointed the sonnets in order to suit their editorial purpose. To achieve a smooth set of the poems numbered 24–34 in their edition, they had to rearrange two separate manuscript traditions. Using Story/Gardner numbers, J would read 24, 32, 25, 26, 33, 34. O would read 30, 31, 27, 28, 29. Moreover, following sonnet 24 three poems were removed to become 35, 36, and 37. Following sonnet 33 four poems were transferred to become 38, 39, 40, and 41. The seven extirpated become "Miscellaneous Sonnets" and are placed in Story/Gardner after the "Ensigns" sequence. Unfortunately, since theirs is the only complete edition of the poems, I am forced to use the Story/Gardner numbering throughout this article for the convenience of modern readers, even though the jumbling of the sonnet numbers may be at times confusing.

Part of the problem in the Story/Gardner decision arises from their misunderstanding of the title for the entire corpus, "Divine Meditations," a title John Payne Collier claimed headed an Alabaster manuscript lost circa 1843 by an editor of Henry King's poetry (Story xlviii). If the term "meditation" means a single sonnet, we have 77 separate meditations by Alabaster, and the editors could be justified in manipulating the order of the poems any which way they liked since each poem stands an island unit sufficient unto itself. But if the term "meditation" means a sequence of poems, the editors were wrong to shuffle the sonnets from three separate manuscripts, breaking up the sequences that date in manuscript as early as 1605, within a decade of the poems' having been completed. We have no holograph manuscript of the sequences, but we are better served by trying to read the poems in an order close to their original, believing that the order so transmitted to us may approximate the order in which the author either wrote them or intended to have them read. Alabaster was to live, in fact, 35 years after the O manuscript and, possibly even, the B were written. He never bothered to reorganize what he undoubtedly knew to be circulating among friends. Thus the manuscripts deserve more trust than they have been afforded in carrying Alabaster's meditations to a modern audience.

The term "meditation" refers to a religious process that contains several parts. The meditator begins by assuming a prayerful stance, then composes the self, quieting the soul. One then proceeds to paint in the imagination a scene from the life of Christ or one of the saints. This step is often called "composition of place." Next one relates the scene to one's own life and finally is moved to "pray." The final step of the process, emotive prayer, the climax of the entire meditation, is difficult to achieve without the stages that lead up to it. Devotional manuals teach the importance of the preliminary steps, and, although we call the entire proceeding "prayer" and refer to any one of its individual parts as "prayer," it is only in the finale, when the soul is moved to address God, that we recognize the highest form of prayer, an attempt to fuse a human soul with divinity. In their reordering of Alabaster's "Ensigns" sonnets, it seems that Story and Gardner conceived meditation simply as steps one and two: introduction and composition of place. By tearing sonnets 35 through

41 from their original splice points (in J and B) and placing
them as a separate "miscellaneous" group, the editors have
ignored the basics of the meditative method. Without the
quieting poems and the emotive poems, the "meditation" be-
comes merely a series of snapshots, paintings of the scene,
without the benefit of preliminary prayer, without the climax
of adequate preparation for human-divine fusion: "We must
also know, that the exercise of our Memory and Understand-
ing in Meditation, is ordained to the motion of our will, and
must therefore be used with such moderation as may serve
for the moving thereof, and no more, that so our Meditation
may be full of pious and good affections, not vaine and filled
with curiosities" (Dawson qtd. in Martz, *Meditative*, 13). In
other words, if the meditator gets too involved with the imagi-
native scene-painting, the proposed fruit of the process (a heart-
to-heart talk with God), may be ignored, and without the
prayerful conversation, the soul will never achieve what
Schoenfeldt finds in George Herbert's verse to be "artful
aggression against God" (157).

In Alabaster, the manipulation of God by the soul is less
evident than in Herbert because the Alabaster narrator is pros-
trate, overwhelmed with insignificance. Herbert's narrator,
more Protestant and stable than a vacillating recusant like
Alabaster's could hope to be, always seems to maintain a sense
of self-worth, an almost independent detachment from the
Almighty, a solemn presumption in God's loving care. Such
"detachment" must, however, be understood in a special sense.
It is not that Herbert can do without God: Herbert remains
essentially an orthodox poet, one who understands "his con-
ception of assurance as dependent wholly upon God's nature
and Word" (Strier 114). But there is in Herbert, nevertheless, a
comforting sense of righteous ease in God's presence that a
reader does not sense in Alabaster. The recusant Alabaster is
more anxious about his fate than is Herbert: knowing that his
fate depends upon divine beneficence, Alabaster follows a

deliberate process in sequencing his meditations, a process sadly fractured by Story/Gardner.

The original "Ensigns" sequence took the following form in manuscripts J and B:

> Introductory sponge sonnet (Story/Gardner #24)
> Quieting the soul (#35, #36, #37)
> Composition of place:
>   Christ Crucified 2 (#32)
>   Crown of Thorns 1 (#25)
>   Crown of Thorns 2 (#26)
>   Ego Sum Vitis (#33)
> Emotive prayer (#36, #39, #40, #41)
> Final colloquium with Christ Crucified (#34)

Each poem originally worked nicely to orchestrate the set toward a meditative climax, affording poetic closure to (what is more important for the faith experience) a spiritual exercise intended mystically to fuse the soul with God. The first sonnet in the sequence contains six metaphors in two sets, one set for the narrator, the other for Christ. For the former, the poet marshals his tongue, his tears, and his soul to signify a pen, ink, and the book wherein are written all his transgressions:

> O sweet and bitter monuments of pain,
> Bitter to Christ who all the pain endured,
> But sweet to me whose death my life procured,
> How shall I full express such loss, such gain?
> My tongue shall be my pen, mine eyes shall rain
> Tears for my ink, the place where I was cured
> Shall be my book, where, having all abjured,
> And calling heavens to record in that plain,
> Thus plainly will I write: no sin like mine.
> When I have done, do thou, Jesu divine,
> Take up the tart sponge of thy Passion
> And blot it forth; then be thy spirit the quill,
> Thy blood the ink, and with compassion
> Write thus upon my soul: thy Jesu still.

$$(1-14)$$

Of the three metaphors, two have both literal and figurative terms named (tongue = pen), (tears = ink); for the third, while "book" is stated, we are left to puzzle out whether "the place where I was cured" refers to the narrator's soul or possibly to his heart. The tone of the octave is abject: the poet humbles himself before God ("no sin like mine") as is customary at the beginning of a meditation: "Your soul having realized that she is in the presence of God, prostrates herself with profound reverence, acknowledging her unworthiness to appear before so sovereign a Majesty" (De Sales 79–80). Following the initial three metaphors is a transition metaphor, the sponge (for which the sonnet is named), acting as a hinge by which we are swung into the final three metaphors, two again having both literal and figurative terms expressed, one having only the literal term stated. Christ's spirit has become the new pen, his blood the ink for new jottings in the book of the narrator's soul.

Alabaster suppresses the figurative term in the final metaphor (book) just as he suppresses its counterpart (soul) in the octave. The balance is quite fine. Median to the two book-soul metaphors is the sponge, literally the vinegar sponge Christ was given to satisfy his "Sitio," but more importantly the sponge of the writing desk which Christ, as writer, uses to blot the narrator's sins preparatory to the accepting message, "thy Jesu still." Unlike the injunction to Astrophil, "look in thy heart and write," this prayer begs divine assistance, a plea typical at the outset of many meditations (see Dawson in Martz, *Meditative* 18). The sponge serves as an appropriate bridge to the Christ metaphors because it is imaginary, as are all of the six terms following it; that is, while the poet is in direct contact with his tongue, tears and soul, he transfers them into the writing implements on his desk (pen, ink, book), cross-indexes his blotting sponge (also visible) into the imaginary sponge of the Passion, and proceeds to elaborate Christ's writing instruments. But the sonnet does not come full cycle because we are never returned to the actual tools on the desk.

They are, after all, only a means to carry us into the figures of redemption, inaugurated by the sponge which in the poem is never a sponge tangible to the narrator. It may have lain on his desk, but only its biblical counterpart enters the poem. Alabaster calls it "tart," and the "tart sponge of the Passion" extends into a general reference for the entire sequence of Christ's sufferings which soak up humanity's continuous evils. Thus the opening sonnet is not a part of the "composition of place" phase in the meditative process but is rather a prologue to that process.

In the manuscripts, three poems follow the introductory sonnet and serve further to quiet the soul of the meditator. "Upon St. Augustine's Meditations" (Story/Gardner #35) recounts that the narrator is accustomed to retire with the saint's prayers so that his "thoughts are ravished with such high desire" that he leaves the earth. He hopes that a similar experience happens with his present meditation sequence:

> Where are we, Austin? Are the heavens come nigher,
> Or is my earthly soul aspired higher?
>
> (13–14)

Having readied himself for the extra-corporal event, the narrator raises a point of dogma in the next sonnet (Story/Gardner #36): if Christ's grace is a reward, does it merit more grace of itself? In Christ, the poet reasons, grace, merit, and reward are all "conjoined." The sonnet is flatly didactic, very much like the cool doctrines that medieval manuals of prayer posit as the bedrock for a meditation proper. The language is nonsensuous, rational, theological, but it is an integral part of the process, the foundation on which the emotional pillars of the meditation will rest. The third and final sonnet to quiet the soul is an apostrophe to the Virgin Mary who is addressed as the "graceful morning of eternal day." It is the narrator's last peaceful fortification before he faces the horrible realities of Christ's Passion.

Having quieted the soul, Alabaster proceeds to the *praeludia*, three steps in meditation that he fuses with the points of the exercise. Manuals of prayer are insistent upon the use of the three powers of memory, understanding, and free will, all of which are reflected in the Alabaster manuscript sequence as a triple wave aimed toward a final fusion with the divine. According to St. Frances de Sales, "After the action of the imagination, there follows the action of understanding . . . which [is] . . . made in order to stir up our affections toward God" (80). The memory is excited in sonnets 32 (Christ Crucified 2) and 25 (Crown of Thorns 1), the understanding in sonnet 26 (Crown of Thorns 2). The meditator requires memory again in 33 (*Ego Sum Vitis*), understanding in 38 (The Eternity). Finally the memory in sonnet 39 (To Christ 1) moves to understanding in 40 (To Christ 2) and culminates with the will activated in 41 ("Lo here I am"). The sequence ends with the colloquium of sonnet 34 (Christ Crucified 3).

The meditative activity known as "composition of place" requires the practitioner to recreate in the imagination some biblical or hagiographical drama. The details of Passion narratives are particularly rich for this exercise. Sonnet 32, the first of three Alabaster poems which focus on the cross itself, initiates a vine image which will figure in all three. It begins appropriately with chiasmus:

> Behold a cluster to itself a vine,
> Behold a vine extended in one cluster.
>
> (1–2)

The chiasmus emphasizes the image by double repetition of two terms within two lines. The grapes have grown upon the cross, and we realize they are Christ "whose nectar sweet the angels doth bedew." The poet enjoins himself to see the "purple blood" draining from the cluster, "with thorns, and whips, and nails, and spear diffused." Thus begins the "composition of place" phase of the prayer process, during which time the meditator works to charge up his emotional battery by focusing on the details of the scene. De Sales writes, "If you wish to meditate upon our Saviour on the cross, you will imagine yourself to be on Mount Calvary, and that you see there all that was done and said on the day of Passion" (80). The poet sees the instruments of torture, and he pictures himself drawing near to drink the life-giving grape-juice/blood, but of the four instruments of torture used in the Passion and named in line 10, only the crown of thorns will further the "composition of place."

Sonnet 25 ("Ay me, that thorns his royal head should wound") extends our visual appreciation of the crucifixion scene. Of the evangelists, only Matthew and Mark mention all three of the torture devices that Story/Gardner select for their sequence: crown of thorns, reed, spittle. Luke refers to none of them, John only to the crown. Both Matthew and Mark write of the three items in the same order, as we would expect of synoptic accounts, and Story/Gardner would have Alabaster devote poems to crown, reed, and spittle in the same order. However, holding to the gospel pattern causes a little havoc with the first crown of thorns sonnet because the primary setting in the octave is not Pilate's court but rather the encounter with the daughters of Jerusalem who stand along the Via Dolorosa. This choice for scene disjoints the chronology of the Passion sequence, which the modern editors were intent on preserving and which they carried out by balancing five poems on the humiliations suffered during the night with five poems on the crucified Saviour. But if the poet were to remain true to the gospel event, he could not have placed sonnet 25 after the reed and spitting poems because we would be thrust ahead in time, a sacrifice to chronology. If we read the first crown of thorns poem where it falls in the manuscripts, however, the time sequence does not become disjointed because the octave scene comes as a flashback. The first crucifixion poem positions the meditator facing the cross on

Calvary. He looks up at the head of the crucified Christ and sighs, "Ah me, that thorns his royal head should wound." The sense of the verb is present tense, but immediately the poet is reminded that the daughters of Jerusalem had seen and "scorned his diadem." "Scorned" leads Story/Gardner to suggest (51) that these are not the women of the Via Dolorosa but rather some "daughters of Zion" in the Canticle of Canticles. But the editors should have considered that "scorned" here probably means the women of Jerusalem were understandably hateful of what causes pain to their hero.

> Ay me, that thorns his royal head should wound,
> Which beams of majesty united stem.
> Is this the crown starred with the eastern gem,
> With which he deemed his glory so to abound
> That he invited to behold him crowned
> The lovely daughters of Jerusalem?
> They came and saw and scorned his diadem,
> Which was with dolours interpointed round.
> Then wherein doth that hidden glory rest,
> Which mortal dimness cannot apprehend?
> Was it the merit of his pain increased,
> Which he for purchase of the world did spend?
> It may be, but my thoughts cannot attain
> What pleasure 'tis to smart for others' gain.
>
> (1–14)

The verb tense indicates we are being taken to a memory of the Via Dolorosa while we actually remain rooted, facing the cross. Line 9 brings us back to the present: "Then wherein doth that hidden glory rest,/Which mortal dimness cannot apprehend." Story/Gardner's linear chronology, though following the gospel list of crown, reed, spittle, does not allow for a proper understanding of the time frame because Story/Gardner's daughters of Jerusalem are forced to precede the events at Pilate's court. Only by seeing the meditator at the cross throughout the sequence can we appreciate the flashback, and the manuscripts ordain this sequence, by beginning, not ending, the composition of place with a sonnet set on Calvary.

On the other hand, there is, of course, no need to explain a break in chronology beyond saying it suited the poet's purpose. For example, in a late fourteenth century poem, the chronology of the passion is not strictly followed: after the death of Christ, the poem turns back to Pilate's court:

> But now I dwelle and thou art gon;
> I-wis, I ne wot what I shal don.
> Writ his herte drury and drad,
> To-fore Pylat tho he was lad.

> (1493–96 in D'Evelyn 40)

Any attempt to rigorously enforce order on a meditation, treating it like a legal brief, ignores the dynamics of meditation because the mind is a "nimble spaniel" and capers where it will, the rigors of the meditative process notwithstanding. One does not become proficient at meditation on the first few tries: monks spend a lifetime honing the method. As the heart ponders one aspect of the Passion, it may very well be reminded of an earlier event. Thus the meditative poet may let allusion carry his narrative literally when the mood so moves him. The meditation poem has as its goal not storytelling, but movement of the will. To soften that faculty the meditator uses his imagination as well as his intellect, but it is a disciplined imagination that effects the best meditation. The control that comes with regular practice can then ensure that digressive forays of the mind be channelled to the ultimate value of the procedure. For example, theological quibbling can divert the process away from the heart (the movement of which is the real goal of prayer) to the ratiocination of the mind. Sometimes the niceties cannot be dismissed so easily. The first crown of thorns sonnet raises such a question that is best handled before the poet pushes too far into the sequence:

> . . . my thoughts cannot attain
> What pleasure 'tis to smart for others' gain.

(13–14)

Such a thought — that questions the very purpose of the Passion — illustrates the shuttling movement of actual meditation, the person in prayer shifting from imagination to understanding, from imagery to theology. The thought is best brought up early so that meditating can effect an answer: to save the problem until the end of the set might leave the meditator hanging. The answer, happily, comes close at hand in the companion sonnet (second crown poem), the imagery of which is more unified than that experienced in the first. It is, in fact, one of the most integrated poems in the series. We are told that humanity budded from the earth in Paradise like tall cedars, but postlapsarian people rise from a barren womb "as thorns in armed wise, / Darting the points of sin against the skies." The thorns are "Christ's coronal," but though crowned in grief, the people/thorns in heaven will become Christ's crown of glory: "He hath transformed us thorns from baser wood." Thus our "thorny sins" become "roseal virtues," Alabaster employing an adjective which suggests roses as a perfect and unexpected fulfillment of knotted, brutal vines. The adjective "roseal" is used in sonnet 37 which precedes sonnet 26 in manuscripts J and B. The use of an uncommon adjective in two sonnets does not mean they were necessarily written in a sequence, but repetition does pull the two poems close together for any reader who follows the order of the original sequence. Our memory having been aroused in the first crown of thorns sonnet, our understanding works toward resolution in the second.

The meditation swings back to the crucified Christ with sonnet 33, the second of the vine sonnets:

> Now that the midday heat doth scorch my shame
> With lightning of fond lust, I will retire
> Under this vine . . .

(1–3)

We are returned to the Christ-as-vine image and are ourselves
taking refuge under its leaves as a means of cooling our "law-
less flame." We have met those "leaves" before, in the second
poem of the sequence ("Upon St. Augustine's Meditation"),
and we have met there "heaven's crystal tier/With flame
unburnt," further evidence that the two sonnets belong in one
sequence. In the Augustine poem, the "leaves" are the pages
of Augustine's writing constellated in the "tier" of heaven. In
the second crucifixion sonnet, the "leaves" are the vine of
Christ "intertwist with love entire," and the "tier" of leaves
protects the narrator:

> And youthful vigor from the leaved tier,
> Doth stream upon my soul a new desire.
>
> (9–10)

The poet wonders how he was able to exist before he found
refuge under the Christ-vine, and, with his imagination-
memory heightened, his understanding flows into the theol-
ogy of sonnet 38 ("Eternity, the womb of things created") in
which he begs to know how eternity and time were tied to
each other. So ends the wave of the second meditative point,
but again we have not been swept into a colloquium of the
will with God. As St. Francis counsels, "If you do not find
anything to your liking in one of those considerations after
having dealt with it and tried it for a little while, pass on to
another" (82). Alabaster does just that.

The poet steps back for a third point with a memory son-
net, #39 ("See how the Sun unsettling doth uphold"). Just as
his first imagination sonnet drew a picture with "Behold" (#32),
this sonnet begins with "See." The primary images are the
sun and the "virgin morning," which figured earlier in the
final sonnet from the "presence of God" phase of the medita-
tion, a sonnet hailing the Virgin Mary. Here, however, the
focus is on Christ:

> See how the virgin morning doth unfold
> The golden cabin where he was enrolled;
> See how the Baptist with angelic wing
> Doth scatter crystal dew of true repenting,
> To bathe our eyes these glories to behold.
>
> (4–8)

It is not only Christ who is evoked in the scene, but the poet himself is brought into the heavenly setting where the cleansing showers can melt his heart, "may rain/Grace to mine eyes" (12–13). He senses that the path he must take is plainly in view.

Alabaster's sonnet 40 turns the understanding to accept God's movement within angels who supervise His works: denouncing heresy, scattering apostates, standing against Turks. The narrator knows the saints expect this motion of spirits, and he too can hope for it:

> In faith, in hope, and love they still attend thee,
> Lo here I am, Lord, whither wilt thou send me?
>
> (13–14)

The last line, reminiscent of the antiphon "Lord here I am, I come to do thy will," serves as the first line of the next sonnet, in which the poet wonders to which part of his soul he will be sent to discover his "commission": to the mind (line 4), to the will (7), or to the heart (12). The three sonnets which form the final wave of the meditation are not separate poems but thematically move from one into the other. They are one unit in the manuscripts and Story/Gardner preserve them as a unit in "Miscellaneous Sonnets," but it would make more sense to keep them in their original location, within the "Ensigns" group, because they are a necessary part of the sweep of the soul toward affective prayer.

That prayer is achieved in the final sonnet, #34 ("Now I have found thee, I will evermore/Embrace this standard where thou sitst above"). Christ is yet the vine upon the cross, but now the poet enjoins his heart to issue out its "two leaved door." The heart image comes directly from a sonnet Story/ Gardner wrested from its context, and the "leaved door" of that heart evokes the "leaves" of Augustine's book, also relegated beyond the sequence by its modern editors. What issues from the poet's heart is a vine, and this is his climactic solution to the meditation:

> O that I were transformed into love,
> And as a plant might spring upon this flower;
> Like wandering ivy or sweet honeysuckle,
> How would I with my twine about it buckle,
> And kiss his feet with my ambitious boughs,
> And climb along upon his sacred breast,
> And make a garland for his wounded brows.
> Lord, so I am if here my thoughts might rest.
>
> (7–14)

The image is not unlike that in Herrick's poem "The Vine," except the lust of Alabaster's sonnet is sacred, akin to the mystical indelicacies of Crashaw. Its sensuousness, however, occurs at precisely the right moment, that final point in the sequence where the soul is wafted into the "via unitiva," and the poet can hope to intertwine himself with Christ, leaf for leaf. It is possible, in fact, to read the "Ensigns" sequence as a path from "via purgativa," through "via illuminativa," to "via unitiva," the first group focusing on a sinner's vices (sonnets 24, 25, 26), the second on the planting of virtue (sonnets 33, 39, 40, 41), the third on union with God (sonnet 34). The excitement of this ultimate illumination of the sequence seems as vibrant as the raptures of Traherne, but Alabaster is more natural in his approach to ecstasy than is Traherne. For Alabaster, we witness a struggle borne out through a series of poems with nadirs as well as occasional lifts: in Traherne we are on a perpetual high from the beginning of a poem until its end and feel that we are not led to rapture so much as plunged into it. Alabaster conceives his rapture along the experience of most people: not saints, they must work toward rapture.

The "Ensigns" sequence ends in peace as the poet realizes his goal has been reached. The final line ("Lo here I am, Lord, whither wilt thou send me?") recalls the working of final lines in sonnets 40 and 41, further evidence that the poems should be left in their manuscript order:

> Lo here I am, Lord (#40)
> Lord I am here (#41)
> Lord so I am (#34)

Given the ardors of the meditation (after all, his Saviour has been crucified), the final solution is heroic (identification with the executed one), and such heroism merits what the poet originally requested: "Write thus upon my soul: thy Jesu still." So the poet ends his meditation with an appropriate word: "Lord so I am if here my thoughts might rest." It is both an ending rest and a refreshment. The sequence works, but wrenching poems from their intended order can have a disastrous effect on the energy that occurs not only within poems but also between poems. For example, Malpezzi has shown that Herbert's "flower" poem necessarily follows his "Cross" poem because the former must rest metaphorically at the foot of the cross, just as flowers so often do in crucifixion iconography (100). What is true for Herbert must be no less true for Alabaster, as minor a voice as he may be.

The Alabaster poems are a pause at the beginning of a turbulent period of some 15 years in the poet's life. As a preparation for the soul-searching to come, the allegiance to two faiths at various times, imprisonments in three countries, the examinations and cross-examinations by numerous prelates and clerics, these heartfelt verses were a first luster of the ardor that kept Alabaster formidable. They are both simple and complex, a mirror of his willing heart and his searching mind, fuel to sustain him through the trials that followed their creation. It is quite helpful today to read the Alabaster poems as an exercise that he may have used at a critical juncture in his life, to aid himself in sorting out the religious questions that were tearing him between two churches. As he inched toward Rome in 1596, he began to feel "a greater tendernes of harte towardes Christes Crosse and Passion than . . . the protestantes weare wont to feel," as he explains in chapter four of his autobiography (qtd. in Story/Gardner xii). The images of the suffering Christ that he identified with Roman piety worked themselves into the sonnets he penned between Easter of 1597 and Michaelmas of 1598. Any attempt to rearrange the order of these sonnets by modern editors does a disservice to a poet already too much at odds with his society and with his own soul. Once the original sequencing is returned to Alabaster's sonnets, he can be better appreciated for the singular voice that he is for the late Elizabethan lyric tradition. The influence of the Jesuits on his youthful soul is nowhere better illustrated than in his poetry, especially the intense involvement of the senses in initial stages of the meditation process, an involvement attributed to St. Ignatius as his unique contribution to the medieval style of meditating on the life of Christ (Martz, *Poetry* 78): we are to see, hear, smell, taste, feel the action we vividly summon into our imagination. Thus, for religious poets in certain eras, meditation lends itself to the creation of very fine poetry. As Martz has noted, "A meditative poem is a work that creates an interior drama of the mind: this dramatic action is usually (though not always) created by some form of self-address in which the mind grasps firmly a problem or situation deliberately evoked by the memory, brings it forward toward the full light of consciousness, and concludes with a moment of illumination when the speaker's self has, for a time, found an answer to its conflicts" (*Poetry* 330). With a craftsman like Alabaster, poetry becomes a tool of both aesthetics and religion: it is both an expression of his artistry and a grace-filled vehicle for his soul. Readers today can still recapture his exuberance and appreciate the singular effect that Ignatius's sensuous meditative method worked on the simple yet stunning Alabaster sonnets — when they are read in the order found in the early manuscripts.

4• Dreaming Authorship
Aemilia Lanyer and the Countess of Pembroke

Debra Rienstra

Twenty years after A. L. Rowse "discovered" Aemilia Lanyer's substantial, peculiar body of religious poetry, her work has recovered from its initial presentation as a Shakespeare-related curiosity to an established fixture in the sub-canon of early modern women's writing. Her *Salve Deus Rex Judaeorum* exemplifies literary culture of the early seventeenth century with its multiple-dedication scattershot at patronage, its deploying of scriptural authority, and its keen attentiveness to the social differential between author and audience. At the same time, however, Lanyer's work has made a glaringly illuminating addition to the canon exactly because it turns conventional practices forcefully on their heads. Her dedications circumvent gendered rhetorical strategies of the male, courtly suitor-author since both she and all her dedicatees are women. Her use of scriptural sources defies interpretive tradition, and mobilizes this defiance in a blatant critique of patriarchy and class structure itself — all the while hoping to benefit from the remainders of the system she decries.[1] One particularly interesting strain of Lanyer scholarship has attempted to answer the question, How does Lanyer, from her position of multiple social disadvantage, muster the courage to do this? Like her male counterparts on the fringes of court life — Spenser and Jonson make for especially apt comparison — she needed to find a means of entering "the psychomachia of writing performance," but she had to construct a feminine version of their masculine declarations.[2] Tracing Lanyer's strategies in this regard leads quickly to another recently recovered early modern woman poet: Mary Sidney Herbert, Countess of Pembroke.

Lanyer's dedicatory poem to Pembroke immediately suggests Pembroke's importance for Lanyer as a figure of feminine literary tradition. Lanyer reifies this tradition within her poem, then calls upon it to undergird her emerging authorship. The specific shape of Pembroke's precedence for Lanyer, however, turns out to be a rather complicated matter. Kari Boyd McBride and Wendy Wall have recently analyzed persuasively the relationship between Pembroke's and Lanyer's poetry. McBride connects Lanyer's dedicatory poem to pastoral conventions, describing Lanyer's anxiousness to legitimate not only female subjectivity in poetry, but, even more radically, the public presentation of this subjectivity through publication. She suggests that Pembroke becomes the poet Lanyer must "displace" in order to create for herself an Orphic narrative in which she establishes her poetic vocation on the "corpse/corpus" of the dead predecessor. Wendy Wall examines rhetorical strategies in the two poets' dedicatory poems, showing how Lanyer followed Pembroke, inverting the gendered language of mastery in presenting the body of the text through publication (Wall 310–30). Both of these perceptive essays usefully employ current critical interest in the rhetoric of the body. Neither, however, attends to the way in which the *content* of Lanyer's poetic project most pervasively reveals Pembroke's role in enabling Lanyer's writing performance.

Lanyer's volume is at heart an astonishingly radical exege-
sis of Scripture, one that lays bare the truth of Scripture that
had lain hidden, from her point of view, behind a centuries-
old veil of mean-spirited and misguided interpretation. This
ambitious task is not merely an act of loyalty to the sacred
text, or an attempt to write by ventriloquizing. Lanyer is
harnessing the most direct medium of authority in post-
Reformation England to valorize the humble, marginalized,
suffering, and feminine — where Lanyer persistently locates
herself. To access the power of this authority-source, Lanyer
had to wrest the privilege of interpretation away from the mas-
culine tradition and present an alternative interpretation. The
accuracy of her interpretation was, of course, essential. Thus
she challenges the Queen in her first dedicatory poem to judge
if "Eves Apologie," her most inflammatory exegetical perfor-
mance, "agree not with the Text" (76). But accuracy is not
enough; Lanyer needs to present some form of authorization
to interpret Scripture against tradition. Thus, any explanation
of Lanyer's strategies for establishing authorship must speak
not only to writing poems but also, even more urgently, to
exegeting Scripture. A stable, lyric subjectivity is necessary,
but not sufficient. Lanyer must justify the possibility that the
ability to circumvent traditional human (male) misprision and
speak Truth might indeed appear in a woman.[3] This is exactly
what Pembroke, author of the bulk of an innovative, schol-
arly metrical psalter, provides for Lanyer: a precedent for
female interpretive authority vis-à-vis the authoritative text.
But there is one further step. By publishing her volume, Lanyer
transformed an act of exegesis into a public polemic. To swing
the weight of divine approbation behind this move, Lanyer
had to claim not just a poetic vocation, but a *prophetic* voca-
tion. Here is where Pembroke's precedent is less apparent, but
equally crucial. Pembroke awakened Lanyer to the possibil-
ity of claiming the prophetic power of the Psalms by creating
a female, psalmic "I." This enabled Lanyer to move from the

more limited space in which Pembroke herself presented her exegetical work to the riskier sphere of publication. Lanyer's relationship to Pembroke, then, provides an example of how women poets, in a way parallel to male poets, create authorship by connection to a distinguished precedent. But because their poetry specifically involves deploying the authority of Scripture, the Pembroke-Lanyer connection also provides an instructive comparison for how authors of both genders negotiate the dangers and advantages of weaving the Text into their texts.

Pembroke as Imagined Mentor

> World-dwellers all give heede to what I saie,
> to all I speake, to rich, poore, high, and low;
> knowledg the subject is my hart conceaves,
> wisdome the wordes shall from my mouth proceed;
> which I will measure by melodious eare
> and ridled speech to tuned harp accord.
>
> (*Psalmes* 49.1–6)

The metrical psalms composed by Pembroke and her brother Philip Sidney came to be considered Pembroke's, even though her brother Philip initiated the project with his versions of the first 43 psalms.[4] After Philip's death, Pembroke edited his portion, completed the remaining 107 psalms over the course of several years, and circulated the complete work, *The Psalmes of David*, in manuscript.[5] The psalter was a magnificent accomplishment in a number of ways, as many of its contemporaries acknowledged,[6] but one of the most important dimensions of the volume for Lanyer was Pembroke's bold method of composition in "translating" the Psalms. The Sidney-Pembroke Psalter marked a critical transition in English religious poetry in the lyric mode. Rather than adhering as closely as possible within the loose confines of ballad meter to an English prose translation — as was the typical, deferent approach of mid- to late-sixteenth century English metrical psalmists — Sidney and Pembroke established a relationship of authority in tension with the text. Pembroke, especially, re-authors each psalm, drawing upon extensive study of commentaries and prose translations to recreate the emotional and imagistic contours of the original. Her psalms rearrange material, create rhetorical structures to define relationships among ideas left merely proximate in the Hebrew, intensify or insert images, and, in short, interpret and particularize the porousness of the psalm originals. Her translation of Psalm 111, for example, seems to drape her own passion for the work on the psalmist's basic framework:

> At home, abroad most willingly I will
> Bestow on god my praises uttmost skill:
> Chaunting his workes, workes of unmatched might,
> Deem'd so by them, who in their search delight.
>
> (*Psalmes* 111.1–4)

Instead of effacing herself before the sacred original, deliberately subsuming artistry to the "matter" as previous metrical psalmists did, Pembroke created speakers who exuberantly celebrate "uttmost skill" and originality in the singing of divine song. Far more than her predecessors in English, Pembroke's poetic subjectivity operates in collaboration with the authoritative text; she asserts her own stylistic ingenuity and meditative idiosyncracies upon and even against prose translations.[7] Donne remarks in his 1621 poem praising the *Psalmes* that Sidney and Pembroke as "David's successors, in holy zeal,/ In forms of joy and art do re-reveal" their scriptural originals.[8] To call them re-revelations places them on a plane of inspiration, and hence authority, equal to the originals. The *Psalmes* served, for poets of both sexes, as a transition from sixteenth century metrical psalm translations to the meditative, metaphysical religious poetry of the seventeenth century, still steeped in Scripture but embodying the lyric voice of the individual poet.

A further implication of Pembroke's work for Lanyer is that, by paraphrasing the Psalms, Pembroke found a location that could energize the feminine, lyric/prophetic "I." The biblical Psalms represent a vast range of moods and postures: repentance, jubilation, lament, praise, adoration, despair, as well as more polemic modes of vengeance, imprecation, and judgment. As a body of poetry, the Psalms model the same kind of crisscrossing mix of modes and genres that Lanyer created in her own complicated volume. More important, the Psalms merge the lyric, ritual, and prophetic modes.[9] Contemporary generic commentary on the Psalms widely acknowledges that David is both lyric poet and prophet, and that the Psalms are, of course, a book of resources for worship.[10] Overall, the Sidneys tend to shift the ritual-prophetic-lyric resources of the Psalms elegantly toward the lyric. Many psalms demonstrate an effort to enhance the lyric integrity of the poem: unifying apparently fragmented voices, smoothing transitions from one section to the next, and shaping a graceful music from the often rough-hewn English prose. However, as Pembroke's style often lends forcefulness and immediacy to the psalmic speakers, the more prophetic moments in the psalms (e.g., Psalm 49 quoted above) acquire an air of authority with a feminine shading.

The evidence of exegetical authority and the feminine prophetic voice can be observed by any reader through study of the *Psalmes*. But the question remains how Lanyer herself imagined Pembroke's importance. The answer is most readily available in Lanyer's dedicatory poem to Mary Sidney, "The Authors Dreame to the Ladie Marie, the Countesse Dowager of Pembroke." The poem gives no indication that Lanyer knew Pembroke personally, certainly not to the degree she claims to have known Margaret Clifford.[11] In fact, the speaker of the poem, representing Lanyer, observes a pastoral figure of Pembroke for much of the poem without knowing her identity. When the dream vision concludes, the speaker approaches the "real" Countess from a respectful distance. Nevertheless, the poem literally occupies a central position in Lanyer's full prefatory set, as the sixth of 11 pieces.[12] The form and length of the poem — a dream vision in 56 iambic pentamenter quatrains — are unique in her prefatory set. These observations serve as initial suggestions that Lanyer understood Pembroke to play a special role for her, an hypothesis that the poem as a whole supports.

Lanyer's speaker envisions a pastoral scene, in which she is seeking a certain unnamed "Lady whom *Minerva* chose" (3). Through the speaker's "eie of Reason" (6), she sees the lady, surrounded by the Muses and crowned by Fame. Other allegorical figures come to pay homage to the lady — Bellona, Dictina, and Aurora. The entire group then moves on to "That sacred Spring where Art and Nature striv'd" (81). The ladies (all present are female, except the god Morpheus, who is leading the speaker at a distance) take the role of goodnatured "umpiers" (85) and decide that Art and Nature should "for ever dwell,/In perfit unity by this matchlesse Spring./ . . . Equall in state, equall in dignitie,/ That unto others they might comfort give,/Rejoycing all with their sweet unitie" (89–96). The group are seated by the spring, where they "devise/ On holy hymnes" (115–16). They recall the *Psalmes* and agree

> Those holy Sonnets . . .
> With this most lovely Lady here to sing;
> That by her noble breasts sweet harmony,
> Their musicke might in eares of Angels ring.
>
> While saints like Swans about this silver brook
> Should *Hallalu-iah* sing continually,
> Writing her praises in th'eternall booke
> Of endlesse honour, true fames memorie.
>
> (121–28)

A note in the margin of this passage reads "The Psalms written newly by the Countesse Dowager of Penbrooke." There is no indication of a distinction between the biblical texts and

Pembroke's version of them; the Psalms are "written newly" by her, a phrase that effectively erases the "old versions" in a remarkable gesture, similar to Donne's, toward Pembroke's interpretive authority. At this point, the speaker requests the identity of this great lady, which Morpheus reveals in an eight-stanza encomium as "great *Penbrooke* hight by name,/ Sister to valiant *Sidney*" (137–38). The speaker then awakens, scolds Morpheus for leaving her just when she might have introduced herself, and determines that she "shall enjoy the selfe same sight" in her waking state as she did in her dream (191). She "to this Lady . . . will repaire,/ Presenting her the fruits of idle houres" (193–94). In the last five stanzas, the dream vision shifts into more conventional language of patronage, as the speaker addresses the Countess directly. The speaker offers her poem by several metaphorical means, "craving pardon for this bold attempt" (209) and inviting the Countess to "Receive him [i.e., Christ] here by my unworthy hand" (221).

The poem suggests by its genre that this famous lady whom Lanyer does not know nevertheless presides over Lanyer's imaginative world. She is the central figure in a pastoral, literary kingdom of women, just as Margaret Clifford will become the central figure (next to the dominant voice of Lanyer's speaker) in the earthly kingdom of heavenly-minded women created by Lanyer's work as a whole. Most important for Lanyer's creation of her own poetic persona, Pembroke provides the perfect model not only of a woman artist, but also a divinely sanctioned new-writer of Scripture. Her perfection is suggested in that the goddesses who attend Pembroke symbolize standard feminine virtues — Minerva, wisdom and chastity; Bellona, fortitude and wisdom; Dictina, chastity; and Aurora, beauty.[13] Morpheus testifies that the Countess exemplifies "virtue, wisedome, learning, dignity" (152), adding learning to the mix. This is a significant addition, since Lanyer is particularly concerned to celebrate learned women in her dedicatory verses. While learned women were still at this time considered exceptional to their sex and looked upon with nervous suspicion, learning might be a proper accomplishment for a noblewoman, so long as it was used to enhance her personal virtue and not to enter the world of male discourse — except through translating male voices.[14] Lanyer invokes this "learned and virtuous" formula for the Countess, but it is soon apparent that this Pembroke moves outside the zone of safety with her learning. She is not merely a pious translator, but a woman with a divinely inspired and sanctioned voice, a divine artist. Lanyer's presentation of the dream — Pembroke here recalls a term Philip Sidney used in his *Apology for Poetry* — a *vates*. Sidney defined this term first in reference to classical poets:

> Among the Romans a poet was called *vates*, which is as much as a diviner, fore-seer, or prophet, as by his conjoined words *vaticinium* and *vaticinari* is manifest: so heavenly a title did that excellent people bestow upon this heart-ravishing knowledge. (Sidney 98)

Immediately after this definition, Sidney "presume[s] a little further, to show the reasonablenes of this word *vates*" with the example of David as the divinely inspired poet (Sidney 98–99). Lanyer does not use Sidney's term, but in this pastoral world, the Muses and Graces wait upon this female David, and she leads the singing of angels and saints with "her noble breasts sweet harmony" (123). Lanyer depicts Pembroke as the first of a new kind of woman, one who has managed to harmonize the standard composite of the godly, virtuous woman with artistic mastery.

With the scene in which the ladies will that Nature and Art dwell in perfect unity, Lanyer subtly explores this classic tension to establish the deep superiority of the Countess as goddess-like singer. In defending her own voice to the queen in an earlier dedicatory poem, Lanyer acknowledges the suspicion with which her society regarded learned women —

particularly the ones who speak — by claiming that she her-
self is no scholar but writes simply from Nature:

> Not that I Learning to my selfe assume,
> Or that I would compare with any man:
> But as they are Scholers, and by Art do write,
> So Nature yeelds my Soule a sad delight.

(147–50)

She thus initially invokes the standard equation of women
with nature and the primitive, and men with civilization and
the artificial. But she goes on to defend the validity of her
voice by pointing out that Art springs from Nature, the
"Mother of Perfection" (152), in the first place. The impli-
cation is that hers is a more direct *imitatio* and therefore
superior, free from the negative connotations of the term
"artifice." In her own case, she mouths acceptance of the old
terms, while turning them to her advantage. When consider-
ing Pembroke, however, Lanyer affirms that the ideal is to
move beyond this Nature-Art dichotomy. In Lanyer's pastoral
world, by Pembroke's guidance, the ladies bring into harmony
Nature (feminine) and Art (masculine) by creating art in a femi-
nine voice. The scene suggests, then, if one can see past all
the pastoral trappings, that Pembroke's *Psalmes* make pos-
sible a female art superior to male art. The Sidney-Pembroke
Psalter itself stands as testimony to Pembroke's ability to har-
monize masculine and feminine voices, masculine and femi-
nine roles, Art and Nature. That this ideal harmony has at
last been achieved by a woman has powerful implications for
women's ability to surpass masculine tradition.

A few stanzas later, Lanyer expresses this rather subtly
implied declaration of Pembroke's superiority even more
explicitly, with a passage that must have pressed rather un-
comfortably against the cult of Philip Sidney. While the poem
frequently emphasizes Pembroke's eternal honor, both in
heaven and on earth, Morpheus's speech clearly presumes to
honor Pembroke before her brother Philip. After identifying

the mysterious dream-Pembroke as Sidney's sister and praising Sidney as the one who "Gives light to all that tread true paths of Fame" (139), Morpheus returns to "this faire earthly goddesse," declaring that

> In virtuous studies of Divinitie,
> Her pretious time continually doth spend.
>
> So that a Sister well shee may be deemd,
> To him that liv'd and di'd so nobly;
> And farre before him is to be esteemed
> For virtue, wisedome, learning, dignity.
>
> (145–52)

In composing this poem, Lanyer is shrewd enough to praise the brother whose praise is known to please Pembroke, but she does not refrain from emphatically setting Pembroke above him, even in the masculine field of learning. Pembroke has accomplished a unity of Nature and Art that no man, not even Sidney, was able to do. Perhaps Lanyer is implying that Pembroke surpassed her brother exactly because she completed his most "virtuous" project. Lanyer may be offering a corrective for the way in which praise of Pembroke is always overshadowed with praise of her brother — a phenomenon that Pembroke herself encouraged. But the passage is typical of Lanyer's gender configurations throughout the volume: women are central and men are marginalized, demonized, or excluded. Here, this applies even to the incomparable Sidney. In this female pastoral community, Astrophil may be highly honored, but he is not invited.

The next passage in Morpheus's speech further specifies Pembroke's role as an inspirer of divine lyric. Her "blessed spirit remaines," says Morpheus,

> Directing all by her immortall light,
> In this huge sea of sorrowes, griefes, and feares;
> With contemplation of Gods powrefull might,
> Shee fils the eies, the hearts, the tongues, the eares

Of after-comming ages, which shall reade
Her love, her zeale, her faith and pietie;
The faire impression of whose worthy deed,
Seales her pure soule unto the Deitie.

That both in Heav'n and Earth it may remaine,
Crownd with her Makers glory and his love.

(156–66)

Pembroke directs people through the troubles of earthly life with contemplations upon God that ravish the senses — her psalms. There is no attempt here to portray Pembroke's poetic endeavors as a safe, acceptable act of ventriloquism. And here is where the tentative suggestion that she is a Sidneian *vates* undergoes refinement. She is not a *vates* in the plain sense of *seer*, even a God-filled one, as Sidney seems to define that word in the *Apology*. Instead, in a way that would please Sidney for its emphasis on human creative initiative, she is clearly a *poietes*, a maker, working from the artistic impulses of her own mind.[15] Here the classical Nature/Art discussion takes on pronounced theological shading. Pembroke leads the pastoral virgins in "devising," or improvising, on holy hymns, and these heart-ravishing contemplations are wholly hers (Philip Sidney's role in their composition is conspicuously absent). While, like Donne in his poem praising the Sidney-Pembroke Psalter, Lanyer acknowledges that Pembroke's psalms offer a revelation of God and his "powrefull might" (she is in this sense a seer), Pembroke also receives glory herself. Ages hence will read *her* love, *her* zeal, *her* faith and piety. *She* is crowned with her Maker's glory. Further, her accomplishment, her art, is the very "worthy deed" that seals her intimacy with God. While Pembroke herself professed in her dedicatory poem to turn all praise for her work toward her brother and ultimately to God — she meant "to praise, not to aspire" — Lanyer revels in and celebrates the human achievement evident in the poems themselves. With regard to the question of inspiration, then, Lanyer has advanced beyond Sidney's sketchy treatment of the subject to combine the seer and the maker for religious poetry. Pembroke's voice is divinely sanctioned and inspired, yet she receives full creative credit for her poems. A model of virtue beyond reproach, Pembroke establishes the perfect fusion of Nature and Art, inspiration and initiative, in a woman's voice, earning eternal honor and God's special favor. She is to be esteemed even beyond her brother, the epitome of male virtue public, private, and literary. Thus, for Lanyer, this divinely sanctioned human achievement by a woman is absolutely vital: Pembroke makes possible the woman poet devising on Scripture. She opens the door, with the approval of God himself, to a female exegesis superior to its masculine rivals. Lanyer has hereby established for art what she will later establish for "reading" Christ and following the faith — that only women are capable of doing it right. However well Lanyer did or did not know Pembroke's *Psalmes*, she did recognize the theological implications of Pembroke's method.

The final section of the "Authors Dreame" features the peculiar disruption of the pastoral dream, and Lanyer's determination to overcome it. Within the pastoral narrative, Lanyer's speaker wakes up before she can present herself to the dream-figure of Pembroke. As with the edenic female pastoral community of Cooke-ham, this female eden, too, is fragile and frustratingly ephemeral. Nevertheless, the speaker is confident she can repair this disruption: "I know I shall enjoy the selfe same sight,/Thou [Morpheus] hast no powre my waking sprites to barre" (191–92). The speaker then proceeds to defy the inadequacy of the dream vision and work toward getting the job done in the waking world. The poem transforms into a plea for the real Pembroke to complete the broken dream, and seal the imagined mentorship with "grace," Lanyer's complex code-word for favor and real-world patronage. The dream becomes an offering of admiration and respect to which Lanyer wishes Pembroke to respond:

> And therefore, first I here present my Dreame,
> And next, invite her Honour to my feast.
>
> (205–06)

While the speaker acknowledges that Pembroke's art is beyond her own, she protests her worthiness as a follower, attempting to make her way into the waking-world Countess's circle, just as in her dream vision she placed herself on the edge of the Countess-nymph's virgin train.[16] She officially offers her poems to Pembroke using the same metaphorical threads that run through the entire work. She invites Pembroke to her feast, presents a "mirrour to her view" (210), and offers the poem as a means by which to meet Christ. Schnell argues at this point that the deference with which Lanyer positions her poetry in comparision to Pembroke's, her claim of unworthiness, is a paradoxical "claim to spiritual and epistemological superiority over the woman she would have as her patron" (92).[17] McBride also perceives Lanyer's paradoxical constructing of her own superiority here, pointing out that the Countess does not say a word in this pastoral dream. McBride interprets this silence in terms of pastoral convention; Lanyer is silencing her predecessor in order to make room for her own assertive voice — a voice that requires a large acoustic space indeed.[18] It is true that Lanyer's basic strategy throughout her volume is to turn her disadvantages into strengths. However, as McBride already admits, the critical difference between Lanyer's situation and other instances of poetic self-assertion against the deceased predecessor is that Pembroke is still alive. Lanyer solves this problem, McBride suggests, by "intimating" Pembroke's "symbolic death." I would offer, toward an alternative interpretation, that an even more crucial factor is Lanyer's desire for Pembroke's favor, preferably in this-worldly, material form. The dream-Pembroke's silence may therefore be interpreted as a gesture of respect for and deference to Pembroke's social and personal distance. Could Lanyer have presumed to place words in the mouth of a living woman who is by far her social and artistic superior? The poem uses pastoral conventions in an attempt to fit the aristocratic style of its central figure's poetic opus. But "The Authors Dreame" is still a dedicatory poem, designed to curry favor, delicately, from the actual Pembroke. Thus, the pastoral mode primarily operates to provide Lanyer with an elegant setting in which to enact Pembroke's role in Lanyer's imagination as the perfect conflation of artist and divinely ordained improviser, a model of the female poetic voice. She must illustrate Pembroke's imagined role before she can arrange for Pembroke to accept a version of this role in the waking world, a world which clearly matters urgently to Lanyer.

The Psalms and the Female "I"

> And call yee this to utter what is just,
> you that of justice hold the sov'raign throne?
> and call yee this to yeld, O sonnes of dust,
> to wronged brethren ev'ry man his own?
> O no: it is your long malicious will
> now to the world to make by practize known
> with whose oppression you the ballance fill,
> Just to your selves, indiffr'ent els to none.
> . . .
> O lett their brood, a brood of springing thornes,
> be by untymely rooting overthrowne
> er bushes waxt, they push with pricking hornes,
> as fruites yet greene are of by tempest blowne
> the good with gladnes this reveng shall see,
> and bath his feete in bloud of wicked one.
> while all shall say: the just rewarded be
> there is a god that carves to each his own.
>
> (*Psalmes* 58.1–8, 25–32)

Though Lanyer writes in her first dedicatory poem, the one to Queen Anne, that "A Womans writing of divinest things" is "seldome seene" (3–4), by 1611 this was not entirely true. Women writers had produced translations and other works on religious topics. But, as Susanne Woods remarks, for Lanyer in her recreation of the passion narrative to "revise fifteen hundred years of traditional commentary . . . is unheard of" (Lanyer xxxiv).[19] Before engaging in the main body of her exegetical work, her "radical unfolding of the passion,"[20] Lanyer begins with a pastiche of Psalm passages that further demonstrates her dependence on Pembroke's precedent of feminine exegesis, and exercises the feminine prophetic voice that Pembroke modeled. After nine initial stanzas addressing and praising the Countess of Cumberland, Lanyer merges her voice with the psalmist's in lines 57–144. The ensuing composite of Psalm passages praises God for his might and justice, especially when it involves punishing the wicked. Lanyer seems to have taken her references directly from the *Book of Common Prayer* Psalms, whose wording she follows quite closely in most instances. I found no direct verbal resemblances to the Sidney-Pembroke Psalter;[21] she is simply following Pembroke's more basic strategy of adopting the psalmic "I." She intertwines carefully selected passages to demonstrate emphatically that God favors the poor, weak, and suffering above the rich, strong, and proud. "He joyes the Meeke, and makes the Mightie sad,/ Pulls downe the Prowd, and doth the Humble reare," the speaker declares (75–76). Actually, this particular reference, while psalm-like, most closely resembles the song of Mary in Luke 1, and thereby co-opts a strong, biblical voice that is unambiguously female. Lanyer places the echo of Mary between references to Psalms 104 and 103.[22] Psalm 113.6, "He taketh up the simple out of the dust: and lifteth the poore out of the mire," appears in lines 123–24: "Unto the Meane he makes the Mightie bow,/ And raiseth up the Poore out of the dust." Lanyer finds psalmic imprecations especially useful for her purposes, including echoes of Psalms 55, 58, and 18:

> Froward are the ungodly from their berth,
> No sooner borne, but they doe goe astray;
> The Lord will roote them out from off the earth,
> And give them to their en'mies for a pray,
> As venemous as Serpents is their breath,
> With poysned lies to hurt in what they may
> The Innocent: who as a Dove shall flie
> Unto the Lord, that he his cause may trie. (113–20)
>
> . . . .
>
> That great *Jehova* King of heav'n and earth,
> Will raine downe fire and brimstone from above,
> Upon the wicked monsters in their berth
> That storme and rage at those whom he doth love.
>
> (137–40)

By creating this brief Psalm-composite in her text, Lanyer establishes a template of God's favor which she will place over the narratives examined in the rest of the poem. While she does not specifically identify the ungodly monsters or the protected righteous in these passages, the images she selects from the Psalms suggest how Lanyer's argument will proceed. From what she finds in Scripture, the venomous serpents are usually men, and the victimized doves, women. And although she apologizes for this Psalm passage as an unintentional digression, she also acknowledges by way of summary that it has laid a critical foundation for the rest of the poem. "Pardon (good Madame) though I have digrest," says the speaker, but this passage was necessary to establish God's

> speciall care on those whom he hath blest
> From wicked worldlings, how he set them free:
> And how such people he doth overthrow
> In all their waies, that they his powre may know.
>
> (147–52)

Lanyer draws an important initial reminder of how God views earthly dealings by redirecting streams of the inspired text to create a strong interpretive current.

Prophetic Vocation

> And I secure shall spend my happie tymes
> in my, though lowly, never-dying rymes,
> singing with praise the god that Jacob loveth.
> my princly care shall cropp ill-doers low,
> in glory plant, and make with glory grow
> who right approves, and doth what right approveth.
>
> (*Psalmes* 75.25–30)

The psalm-composite passage that opens the central poem of *Salve Deus* demonstrates that Lanyer has learned from Pembroke the power of the female, psalmic "I." Snaring the prophetic mode of the Psalms lays important exegetical groundwork for the ensuing re-reading of the passion story. But Lanyer's highly polemical purposes, along with her practical need to make herself known, require an even more emphatic declaration of her public, prophetic role. Establishing a precedent for the female artist-prophet was only the first step. She also had to declare that she was indeed responding to a divine calling.

In some instances, Lanyer's claims to a calling are caught up in the more conventional depictions of herself as the writer in service to the great personage. Thus, she tells the Countess of Cumberland toward the conclusion of the main poem that her purpose from birth, given her by the "Eternall powres," was to insure the Countess's everlasting fame:

> And knowe, when first into this world I came,
> This charge was giv'n me by th'Eternall powres,
> Th'everlasting Trophie of thy fame,
> To build and decke it with the sweetest flowres
> That virtue yeelds.
>
> (1457–61)

The Cookeham estate is special to her in part, Lanyer confesses, because there she received a confirmation of this call to service, this time from the Muses and Pallas:

> Farewell (sweet *Cooke-ham*) . . .
> where the Muses gave their full consent,
> I should have powre the virtuous to content:
> Where princely Palace will'd me to indite,
> The sacred Storie of the Soules delight.
>
> ("Cooke-ham" 1–6)

In other instances, however, this idea of service to the noble (the *virtuous* noble, she is always careful to note) falls away and only her calling is left. Complete versions of Lanyer's volume also include a brief prose paragraph on the last leaf, entitled "To the doubtfull Reader," where Lanyer explains that she received the title to her poem in a dream years before she wrote. She forgot about the dream until she had finished the poem, "when immediately it came into my remembrance." "[T]hinking it a significant token," she writes, "that I was appointed to performe this Worke, I gave the very same words I received in sleepe as the fittest Title I could devise for this Booke." The authorization for the work comes in dreamed form, beyond the jurisdiction of her human audience. Lanyer wishes to offer conventional gestures toward service by way of gaining patronage. But the anxiety in her dedicatory poems and her constant admonishing of her audience to virtue attests to her fear that these women's virtue and benevolence are not entirely reliable. Therefore, she wishes to bypass the implied authorization of her audience and establish herself as one of God's poets, according to Pembroke's example, thereby to "seale her pure soule unto the Deitie" and be "Crowned with her Makers glory and his love."

This need to declare her own prophetic calling reaffirms the importance of the dream-vision form of Lanyer's dedicatory poem to Pembroke. Numerous biblical narratives establish that the ecstatic vision or dream is the ritual form of prophetic calling. Moses' burning bush, Isaiah's live coal, Peter's sheet of unclean animals — those called by God to speak a harsh and contrary word of truth are commissioned through sometimes bizarre experiences of alternative perception.[23] In the late sixteenth century, this tradition was given more genteel expression in the notion of divine appointment to the poetic task, an idea gaining some currency among religious poets in England. Du Bartas's powerful and popular depiction of the Christian Muse, Urania, and her personal dream-visit to him impelled other poets to consider the possibility of claiming a divine calling to write religious poetry. Du Bartas adapted the classical muse Urania to figure the idea of inspiration, even command, from the Christian God for writing poetry.[24]

Lanyer's claims to poetic/prophetic vocation often use conventional, classical trappings — the muses, Pallas Athena — rather than Urania or an hebraic live-coal ritual. But the dream-vision form of Lanyer's "The Authors Dreame" can be seen as a tentative version of an ordaining vision she is attempting to construct for herself. The scene near the river Parnassus might have become an imagined passing of the prophetic mantle from Pembroke to Lanyer, if the two had met in the dream world. But Lanyer did not complete this manufactured transcendent experience; the dream is cut off. This disruption of the dream may speak to Lanyer's insecurities about her calling. Or, it may be a clever strategy for keeping Pembroke's mentorship from remaining purely imagined; after all, Pembroke is still alive in 1611 and could, presumably, help Lanyer "enjoy the selfe same sight" her dream created. By engineering the disruption, Lanyer creates a lack and invites Pembroke to fill it. The always practical-minded Lanyer is asking her Urania to bridge the imagined and the material with a prophetic anointing of her own devising.

The need for Pembroke's "grace" may have seemed all the more urgent to Lanyer as she was attempting to step beyond Pembroke's example. The real Pembroke stopped short of claiming a prophetic role for herself with her psalms. By "newly writing" the poems of the original lyric-prophet, Pembroke transposed the public voice of God's truth-singer into the female key. However, Pembroke left it to others to declare her poems "re-revelations." She herself carefully cultivated the impression that her psalms were a matter of private devotions, a bereaved woman's efforts to deal with the sorrowful vicissitudes of life. In her dedicatory poem to the *Psalmes*, "To the Angell spirit of the most excellent Sir Philip Sidney," Pembroke invokes the elegiac mode in legitimating her task. Her "penns impressions move/ the bleeding veines of never dying love" (79–80) for her brother, whom she asks to pardon her "presumption too too bold" (25). Even regarding her authority over Scripture, her dedicatory poem ritually denies what her psalms actually do. She assures God that she does not wish to aspire to "Theise sacred Hymmes thy Kinglie Prophet formed" (14). Pembroke made use of the printing press for other works, guiding her brother's and some of her own works to the press and thereby doing much to ease the "stigma of print" for the aristocratic author. But the text most crucial to Lanyer, her *Psalmes*, Pembroke withheld from print. Instead, she chose for the psalms the most prestigious and controllable form of publication — the beautifully rendered manuscript. From her position as a member of a powerful aristocratic family and the executor of her brother's reputation and poetic estate, Pembroke could navigate the conventions of print and manuscript publication and manage to distribute her psalms without risking a self-proclaimed prophetic calling.

For the more socially tenuous Lanyer, putting her manuscript where her call was and publishing *Salve Deus* in 1611 was obviously a huge gamble. Her choice to go to print represents, as Ann Baynes Coiro points out, an act of defiance against the system of patronage in which she was caught, a "rejection of her private role as a woman of service within a matriarchy" (373). Her position of simultaneous submission to and defiance of this system, and her gesture toward self-professionalization as a means of negotiating that entrapment, parallels Jonson with his 1616 *Workes*. But even Jonson, her approximate social peer, did not build his professional self on a claim to prophetic vocation. This is more, too, than her male counterparts in the mode of devotional lyric would attempt. For Donne and Herbert, as I demonstrate elsewhere, the shift in the relationship of the reader-poet to the sacred text that the Sidney-Pembroke Psalter represents was crucially enabling, but also a source of great anxiety.[25] Donne's anxiety in asserting a poetic subjectivity into the generic narrative of redemption distorts the psalmic-lyric precedent into a kind of mischievous bravado, a play-acted resistance to the humbling truth of free grace. Herbert's anxiety about "weaving the self into the sense" of his psalm-like collage of "spiritual conflicts" is most famously traced in his "Jordan" poems, but is apparent throughout *The Temple*. For them, the psalmic background of devotional verse marked out primarily a space for private struggle. Donne later found his public, divinely ordained vocation in the pulpit. Herbert cautiously imagined his vocation, but figured it as a cross carried in the presence of God. Any future reader who might thrust his heart into Herbert's lines would do so in a similar, private space. Fittingly, both Donne's and Herbert's religious lyrics were published only posthumously.

Herbert, Pembroke, even Donne, each had a more secure social footing on which to set up, in the early seventeenth century, the kind of public, divinely ordained poetic persona that Lanyer attempted. That she, with all the strikes against her, exhibited a more confident public ability to re-speak Scripture than better-established poets, fits the kind of inversion of good sense that permeates her work. Her very lack of likely qualification is exactly, in her mind, what justifies her audacity. In the long invocation section of the main poem, the speaker reassures herself that God's call bypasses every worldly qualification:

> But yet the Weaker thou doest seeme to be
> In Sexe, or Sence, the more his Glory shines,
> That doth infuze such powerfull Grace in thee,
> To shew thy Love in these few humble Lines.
>
> (289–92)

Lanyer may not have had the refined restraint of her imagined mentor, but she was merely driving Pembroke's example to its logical conclusion. Decades later, Milton would achieve what Lanyer attempted, masterfully sculpting his own prophetic/poetic persona. Unlike Lanyer, however, Milton seems to have been under the impression that, while he would suffer for his vocation, he was somehow qualified for it. Lanyer, by cleverly coopting her gender association with Pembroke and, at the same time, turning her social inferiority into a virtue, managed to dream her own authorship in 1611, unfolding the central narrative of Scripture in lines that "may no further stray,/ Than his most holy Spirit shall give me Light" so that not only "Heavens cleare eye," but "all the World may see" (301–07).

Appendix: Psalm References in Salve Deus Rex Judaeorum

The following is a list of references to the Psalms which I found in the psalm-composite passage of *Salve Deus Rex Judaeorum*. This passage stretches, in the title poem of the volume, from line 57 through 144. I used the *Book of Common Prayer* version of the Psalms to compare. Line numbers, taken from the Woods edition, are listed at left, with Psalm references opposite, listed by chapter and verse.

Line numbers	Psalm references
57–58	102.26
73–74	104.1–2
75–76	(Luke 1.52)
78	40.6, 106.2
79–80	103.12
81	18.10
82	102.25, 104.2
84	76.7, 130.3
85	44.21
86	25.11–12
87	104.1
88–91	104.3–4
95	97.5
97	104.3
98–100	18.11–14
103–04	15.1–2, 24.3–4
105–10	12.2, 57.5, 64.3
107–08	11.2
111–12	52.5–6
113–14	58.3–4
117	58.4
119–20	55.6
124	113.6
126–28	103.10, 17; 84.11
129–36	15.1–5, 24.3–4
138	18.8, 12
138–42	50.3–5, 83.15
143	75.9

5 • Aemilia Lanyer's "Description of Cooke-ham" as Devotional Lyric

Patrick Cook

Recent studies of "The Description of Cooke-ham," the concluding poem of *Salve Deus Rex Judaeorum*, have reclaimed Amelia Lanyer's priority in the generic tradition of the English country-house poem. Published in 1611, five years before the poem long taken to initiate the genre in England, Ben Jonson's "To Penshurst," "Cooke-ham" demonstrates its author's awareness of a poetic "kind" established by Martial, Horace and other Roman writers. But "Cooke-ham" locates itself within this generic heritage more by the conventions it excludes and revises than by those it imitates in a straightforward way.[1] Most notably absent is praise of the country estate's inevitably male owner, who is replaced by Lady Margaret Clifford, Countess of Cumberland, the center of an intimate female community that includes her daughter, Anne, and the poet herself, who at the time of the poem's represented actions were staying at a crown estate leased by the brother of Margaret's estranged husband (Lewalski, "The Lady of the Country-house poem," 265). Significant revisions include those worked upon the genre's emphasis on the generous hospitality provided by the lord from his manor's open hall and the closely related golden world motif of *sponte sua* whereby every subordinate on the estate, from plant to animal to human, provides itself or its services through his or her or its "own will" to complete the harmonious reciprocation that supports the hierarchical structure of the aristocratic world portrayed.[2] These changes constitute essential parts of the poem's revision of the genre's ideology away from the equation of virtue with ownership and lineage toward a more egalitarian "housing" of virtue in the inherent and practiced goodness of the Lady herself — "all delights did harbour in her breast" (8) — and of her daughter, "in whose faire breast true virtue then was hous'd" (96).[3]

While modern scholarship has made considerable progress in recovering the poem's place in its generic tradition, the by-now automatic classification of "Cooke-ham" as a country-house poem, and the consequent neglect of features not associated with the genre, have contributed to a failure to recognize this remarkable text's polyphonic richness, with the paradoxical result that finding a place in the canon for a woman's text long ignored has been accompanied by a failure to apply the kind of explicatory pressures to it that contemporary works by male writers have long received. This paper examines the poem's revision of country-house poem conventions in the light of another tradition flourishing at the time of its composition, the devotional lyric. Instead of celebrating the landowner's maintenance of a self-sustaining and harmonious estate, Lanyer offers us a portrait of Lady Clifford's piety through a meditative engagement with her own salvational history, using the idea of conversion through freely bestowed grace pervasive in Protestant religious lyric: she hails Cooke-ham as the place "where I first obtained/Grace from that

Grace where perfit Grace remain'd" (1–2).[4] The poem also dramatizes, in the associational manner of lyric, the affective oscillations of its speaker's spiritual condition and grafts onto its country-house framework a number of concerns and techniques of the great devotional lyrics of Donne, Herbert and Vaughan.

Lanyer's memorial clearing of a space in which a community of women can fashion themselves spiritually follows the contemplative itinerary of purgation, illumination, and union, a progression, traceable to early Christian writers, that Arthur Clements convincingly finds to organize many seventeenth century devotional lyrics.[5] Her radically feminist stance is nowhere more evident than in the fact that purgation, which detaches the self from worldly interests, is here principally a matter of removing inhibiting male presences. She replaces the men who, in country-house poems, limit women to the roles of chastely sustaining dynastic lineage and serving as part of nature's freely bestowed bounty, with both women and male biblical exemplars who can facilitate the subsequent stages of illumination and union. Freed from dynastic concerns, during their stay the women of Lady Clifford's retinue spend their time in meditation. This takes two forms. One is what W. T. Stace calls an "extrovertive" redirection of the mind, in which one uses one's senses to perceive "the multiplicity of external material objects . . . mystically transfigured so that the One, or the Unity shines through them" (*Mysticism and Philosophy*, 62). Landscape for the women is not, as in "To Penshurst" or "Upon Appleton House," a spatial embodiment of the owner's power and authority, but a contemplative opportunity, and one that in the discursive "now" of the poem, some time after their departure and separation, is no longer available. As Lanyer laments, "Never shall my sad eies againe behold/Those pleasures which my thoughts then did unfold" (9–10). This mental "unfolding" of perceptions takes place primarily from a panoramic prospect where, Lanyer recalls, addressing Lady Clifford, "thirteene shires appeared in all your sight" (73):

> What was there then but gave you all content,
> While you the time in meditaton spent,
> Of their Creators powre, which there you saw,
> In all his Creatures held a perfit Law.
> And in their beauties did you plaine descrie,
> His beauty, wisdome, grace, love, majestie.
>
> (75–80)[6]

The unfolding of unity in the Book of Nature from the observation of its features is accompanied, in the preferred Protestant manner, by meditation on Scripture that involves a fully sensual recreation of biblical scenes:

> In these sweet woods how often did you walke,
> With Christ and his Apostles there to talke;
> Placing his holy Writ in some faire tree,
> To meditate what you therein did see.
> With Moyses you did mount his holy Hill,
> To know his pleasure, and performe his Will.
> With lovely David you did often sing,
> His holy Hymnes to Heavens Eternall King.
> And in sweet musicke did your soule delight,
> To sound his pryses, morning, noone, and night.
> With blessed Joseph you did often feed
> Your pined brethren, when they stood in need.
>
> (81–92)

These typologically connected references perform several functions. The "often" repeated meditations evoke a timelessness that renders meditative removal from everyday temporality analogous to typology's identification of figures across the divides of biblical history. David, the psalmist, reminds us of Lady Clifford's recourse to biblical texts that were particular favorites of women, including Mary Sidney, to whom is addressed the longest dedicatory poem of Lanyer's collection.[7] Since the Book of Psalms "was widely recognized as the compendium par excellence of lyric poetry" (Lewalski, *Protestant Poetics*, 39), Lanyer here points to her own imitation of Lady Clifford's singing of psalms, setting herself forth as a *figura* of the biblical lyricist in her own devotional lyric, further emptying out the temporal distinctions that separate the speaker's now, the Lady's, and that of the biblical figures.[8]

The other biblical references possess a specific thematic implication that develops as we proceed through them, much as the typological meanings of Old Testament figures developed through their New Testament antitypes, though the chronology of the process is reversed. Joseph's story is picked up at the time of his greatest exaltation, when after being thrown in a pit he has risen to the position of Pharoah's governor and can feed the brothers who sold him into slavery. As Milton notes, the episode "illustrates how God brings good from evil" (*On Christian Doctrine*, 15.81).[9] The event represents the climax of a narrative, extending across Genesis 37–49, that begins with a dream in which Joseph views his brothers' sheaves bowing in obeisance to his own sheaves. The great Christian paradox of exaltation through humility adumbrated in the story through repeated acts of supplication and rising explains the relevance of Moses, who by submitting his will to his Lord's "mounts" to divine presence and reminds us that Christ's presence among his disciples represents the ultimate, kenotic example of the paradox.[10] At the same time, Joseph's story introduces the country-house theme of hospitality in the great hall, providing a biblical precedent for Lanyer's revision of the genre's convention of *sponte sua*:

> The very Hills right humbly did descend,
> When you to tread upon them did intend.
> And as you set your feete, they still did rise,
> Glad that they could receive so rich a prise.
>
> (35–38)

Rather than operating according to an economy of nature's free bounty set in reciprocal relation to the landowner's open board, an economy that in country-house poems throughout the seventeenth century naturalizes an ideology of hierarchy and exploitation, the poem offers a feminist utopics of rising through descent. This revision is consistent with the word-play that occurs when the poem most closely approaches the conventional *sponte sua*: "The swelling Bankes deliver'd all their pride" (43). The line invites us to see the stream yielding forth its abundance of fish *sponte sua* — a scene reminiscent of Jonson's "To Penshurst," where the eels, probably fresh-water lamprey commonly known as "pride," "leap on land/ Before the fisher, or into his hand" (37–38) — and, at the same time, to note that they are exalted through eliminating their superbia, just as the hills rise through their humble descent.[11]

The theme of exaltation through humility is a familiar one in seventeenth century poetry, but what makes "Cooke-ham" a devotional lyric rather than simply a narrative celebrating the Clifford retinue's pious activities is the incorporation of this theme into the speaker's mental processes. The poet sub-stitutes for the extrovertive and biblical meditation of the past an "introvertive" contemplation, whereby the meditator seeks "to plunge into the depths of his own [self]" (Stace, *Mysticism and Philosophy*, 62). To understand this aspect of the poem we must consider its complex narrative structure, which is organized around a series of carefully placed temporal mark-ers. After the introductory addresses to Cooke-ham (1–10) and Lady Clifford (11–16), we encounter a narrative, recov-ered through memory, of the Lady's arrival. This past-tense sequence of nature's enlivening response to her presence traces the estate's topography by beginning at the house (19) and ending at "that stately Tree,/Wherein such goodly Prospects you did see" (54), reversing (what will become) the usual move-ment of the country-house poem from exterior to interior. As the lyric voice proceeds along this itinerary, observing pieces and inhabitants of the landscape arranged in no mappable order, it proceeds as well from a specific remembered event into the timeless unity that is the meditator's goal. From what we might call the "historical" event of fixing up the estate — "The House receiv'd all ornaments to grace it" (19) —, we move into a landscape where temporal progression is undermined by the paradisal absence of seasons ("The Trees with leaves, with fruits, with flowers clad" 23) — and by the slippage from simple past tenses to, beginning at line 47, "would" constructions indicating repeated actions: "the pretty birds would oft come" (47), little creatures "would come abroad" (50) and "would runne away" (52). This growing timelessness accompanies the narrator's increasing immersion into the landscape. "Now let me come unto that stately Tree" (53), she says to herself, where the "now" is the past recovered meditatively in its full sensual presence and the speaker is no less approaching the stately tree than Lady Clifford was walking with Christ and his apostles. In modern narratological terms, the poetic voice slides from the position of an heterodiegetic narrator outside the situation being recounted to that of a homodiegetic narrator within it.[12]

The Christian *via contemplativa* is supported in the poem by a more historically specific practice. The meditator applying the techniques popularized by Ignatius Loyola and the Jesuits but, as Louis Martz has shown, still popular in Protestant England, "imagines a scene vividly, as if it were taking place in his presence, analyzes the subject, and stirs up emotions appropriate to the scene or event or personal spiritual situation" (Lewalski, *Protestant Poetics*, 149). With the speaker's arrival in memory at the tree, this section of the poem sheds its last vestige of temporal progression. It has developed into a full-fledged "composition of place" and now proceeds to analysis as it lingers around the tree: the speaker who near the beginning of the section noted that "all things else did hold like similies" (21) now does her own holding by means of similes. Drawing on the kind of traditional emblematics favored in Protestant meditation, the speaker finds the tree, which has replaced the now marginal hall of the country house as the site of action, first an "Oake that did in height his fellowes passe" (55), with the emphasis on height asserting its cosmic nature and forecasting the reward of exaltation available to the humble.[13] The oak is then compared to a "comely cedar straight and tall,/Whose beauteous stature far exceeded all" (57–58), as the analyzing mind discerns the quality of beauty. Finally we learn that the tree

> Would like a Palme tree spread his armes abroad:
> Desirous that you should there make abode:
> Whose faire greene leaves much like a comely vaile,
> Defended Phebus when he would assaile.
>
> (61–64)

"The righteous shall flourish like the palm tree," writes the psalmist, providing a biblical gloss on a tree that traditionally stands as an emblem of female chastity.[14] Even as it retains its masculine modifier, the horizontally embracing and vertically shading tree grows increasingly feminized, until with the idea of "abiding" it has been transformed into an appropriately feminist replacement for the domain of male *virtus*: the great hall of the country house, which remains unvisited, relegated to the poem's margins.

As the tree similes progressively add affect to analysis, the speaker fully achieves the final, affective stage by recalling how often the Lady (and presumably the speaker with her) would come to where she is "now," producing a kind of contemplative union with her cherished patron. The union of poet and Lady is furthered as the meditating-into-presence speaker, in a *mise-en-abyme* effect, proceeds to picture the Lady herself engaged in the repeated biblical meditations-into-presence. Her own meditation both contains the Lady's and is in a sense merged with it, as both have entered the same timeless space and are performing equivalent actions. But now the presence of male biblical exemplars appears to produce an unfortunate association. A hostile male presence has hovered about the edges of the poem. It appeared most openly when the Lady assumed the figure of Diana:

> The little creatures in the Burrough by
> Would come abroad to sport them in your eye;
> Yet fearefull of the Bowe in your fair hand,
> Would runne away when you did make a stand.
>
> (49–52)

This is the very image of successful purgation, with Diana not defensively imitating the intrusive violence of Actaeon, but maintaining her difference from his representatives in the poem by merely standing — in the personal allegory Margaret Clifford asserting her legal "standing" in litigation with her hostile husband. The leaves of the central oak create pastoral shade, but the fact that they "defended Phebus when he would assaile" reminds us that the benevolent sun that embraced the crystal streams (27–28) can shift valence, transforming the scene from one of pastoral *otium* to one of Ovidian rape, a context that might have been passed over as we encountered "Philomela and her sundry leyes" (31), which were, of course, the result of a sexual assault. Christ, Moses, and David facilitate the speaker's continuing meditative immersion, but for some reason, perhaps the inclusion of the wicked brothers that the allusion requires, or perhaps the too-near approach to the country-house poem's hospitality theme and the ideology that theme supports, the story of Joseph precipitates the speaker's return to the less joyous present. An association that invites but ultimately frustrates our analysis turns her attention toward Anne Clifford, whose engagement to be married may have occasioned the departure from this paradise of women:

> And that sweet Lady sprung from Clifford's race,
> Of noble Bedfords blood, faire steame of Grace;

To honourable Dorset now espows'd,
In whose faire breast true virtue then was hous'd.
Oh what delight did my weake spirits find
In those pure parts of her well framed mind:
And yet it grieves me that I cannot be
Neere unto her. . . .

(93–99)[15]

As the subject of dynastic lineage intrudes and the females are assigned identity only through the names of the father and husband, a "now" intrudes that is very distinct from the "then" of Anne's virtue. The vision collapses and the poem modulates into lament.

Contemplative vision, though it leads in Christian tradition to union in the timeless realm, is always transient, since the self that must be purged to gain this vision inevitably, like anything repressed, returns. The tension between a true self realizable only briefly and an illusional self that must live in the world is pervasive in seventeenth century devotional verse. As Arthur Clements writes:

> This central paradox of gain through loss, of life through death, embodies a traditional distinction important to understanding so much in Donne, Herbert, and Vaughan: the distinction between the outward and inward man, Greek *psyche* and *pneuma*, Hebrew *nephesh* and *ruach*, the man "himself" and the divine supra-individual Being. (*Poetry and Contemplation*, 11)

The distinction, I am arguing, is also important to understanding "Cooke-ham," which focuses upon an exemplary "Phoenix" (44), a familiar symbol of life through death. Lanyer now introduces another conventional figure easily linked to the paradox. Blaming "Unconstant Fortune," "Who casts us downe into so low a frame" (103–04), for the separation of herself from the Clifford women, she offers a polysemic pronouncement on "love,/In which, the lowest alwayes are above" (109–10). Lanyer's editor Susanne Woods paraphrases the lines as "the lower born are more devoted to the high than the reverse"

(134). That is certainly a meaning relevant to the self as psyche, the social creature who has regained dominance within the speaker at this point, but for the self as *pneuma* the Christian paradox prevails, and Fortune's lowering represents the male-assigned lower status of the female that enabled the original experience at Cooke-ham and its recovery in the poem. What for the psyche is a negative subjection of gender and class can become for the *pneuma* an opportunity for spiritual growth.

It is significant that the point where higher and lower selves can find divergent meanings in the high/low paradox is also the point in the poem where the speaker displays the greatest self-division:

> But whither am I carried in conceit?
> My wit too weake to conster of the great.
> Why not? although we are but borne of earth,
> We may behold the Heavens, despising death;
> And loving heaven that is so farre above,
> May in the end vouchsafe us entire love.
>
> (111–16)

A confusion of agency registered in the passive voice and dialogue within the self issues in the renewed realization that lowness and death have their rewards. This insight initiates the poem's second move into meditation, as focus on Anne Clifford, whose married future shattered the previous vision, now provides a context for recovery. The description of Anne's activities as "former sports,/So farre from being touched by ill reports" (119–20) marks another purgation of male influence. The speaker now works herself into a narrative of Lady Clifford's departure that closely mirrors the earlier narrative of arrival, to the point where line 191 repeats line 45 precisely. The section is filled with sorrow as nature dies into wintry sterility, but it also reenergizes the poet's contemplative faculties. Returning imaginatively to the fair tree, the speaker achieves another union with the Lady: "To this faire tree, taking me by the hand,/You did repeat the pleasures which had past" (162–63). The Lady joins the speaker repeating the past by becoming a similar speaker repeating the past, and both are repeating the pleasures which were "past" in another sense, since the union of the departure section repeats that of the arrival section. The Lady's final gesture is to kiss the stately tree, an act that the speaker transforms into the richly traditional union of souls through a kiss by repeating another pleasure which had passed: she kisses the tree herself, "bereaving" it of the Lady's kiss.[16] Her admission that "Yet this great wrong I never could repent" (174) colors the scene as a Fall and expulsion from the garden, but the enhancement it affords to the speaker's immersion in the scene suggests that this is a Fortunate Fall consistent with the poem's pervasive thematics of gain through loss.

As the narrative moves from the tree to the house (201), temporal markers again manifest a shift into the timelessness of meditation. Nature's sorrowful decline begins in the past tense, but, with the appearance of another "now" (186) and a string of present tense verbs, the speaker seems momentarily to reenter this past until past-tense description resumes in line 195, though "did now" of line 200 briefly reintroduces the effect even as it follows a convention of past-tense narration. The second meditative section ends without the abrupt intrusion of a negative association, suggesting that through repetition the poet is acquiring mastery over the process. And not merely mastery, but exclusive mastery, as Lanyer concludes her radically feminist book somewhat problematically with an imitation of the way male poets had long asserted primacy in their Oedipal struggle with influential literary forefathers. As Nature mourns, the birds "warble forth sorrow, and their own dismay" (188). Philomela, the image of the woman poet enabled by male oppression at first imitates them, turning her song of praise into a "mournefull Ditty" (189). But she exceeds them by drowning "in dead sleepe" (190). Similarly silenced is a cognate Ovidian figure, Echo, who "wonted to reply/To our last words, did now for sorrow die" (199–200). Having eliminated her competitors in the realm of female song, Lanyer announces her mastery in the concluding valediction with three emphatic first person pronouns:

> This last farewell to Cooke-ham here I give,
> When I am dead thy name in this may live,
> Wherein I have perform'd her noble hest,
> Whose virtues lodge in my unworthy breast,
> And ever shall, so long as life remaines,
> Tying my heart to her by those rich chaines.
>
> (205–10)

The Lady's virtue has passed from the estate, where it was located at the beginning — "Farewell (sweet Place) where Virtue then did rest" (7) — to the poet's breast, as the meditation completes the transfer of action from the external world to the internal, from the country-house poem, we might say, to the devotional lyric. The image of rich chains continues the word-play that has repeatedly explored the paradoxes of meditative presence and absence. The hearts are united across distance, linked by a filament of continuing presence. But accompanying the notions of linkage across distance and secure internalization is a notion of imprisonment, and therefore of separation, implicit in "chaines." The poet is reminding us that it is only through the psyche's containment and absence that the pneuma can abide in the supra-individual realm where contemplative union occurs. And the Lady's virtue will remain within her throughout absence, always available for the meditative recovery that absence enables.

If Lanyer's silencing of rival voices marks a limit to her inclusionary, feminist poetics, and perhaps expresses the "profound ambivalence" that Lisa Schnell finds in her "notion of female community" ("So Great a Difference" 29), another gesture made in "Cooke-ham" runs counter to this exclusionary practice, as Lanyer's dual role as "poet-priest" (McGrath, "Let us Have Our Libertie" 342) undergoes revision. Throughout

Salve Deus Rex Judaeorum the poems themselves are presented as Eucharistic offerings, with the implication that the poet is herself a priest administering the communion to the readers whom she invites to her textual feast. The idea is most fully developed in the opening poem "To the Queen's most Excellent Majestie":

> For here I have prepared my Paschal Lambe,
> The figure of that living Sacrifice;
> Who dying, all th'infernall powres orecame,
> That we with him t'Eternite might rise:
> This pretious Passeover feed upon, O queene,
> Let your faire Virtues in my Glasse be seene.
>
> (85–90)[17]

Already syncretic in its equation of the Jewish Passover and Christian communion, the passage draws as well upon the contemporary Protestant debate that sought a satisfactory replacement for the Roman doctrine of transubstantiation. Rejecting both Luther's belief in consubstantiation, which denied the co-presence of bread and wine with body and blood, and Zwingli's denial of Christ's presence, Anglicans developed the doctrine of "virtualism" whereby the "communicant receives together with the elements the virtue or power of the body and blood of Christ" (Davies, *Worship and Theology in England*, 1.83).[18] The metaphor of the mirror complicates the Eucharistic message, allowing the virtue to be something returned to the reader as she feasts on the poet's paschal lamb, to be both internally renewed and externally bestowed. Elsewhere Lanyer both praises her reader's virtue and portrays her poems as the promoter of and context for it, most notably in "To all vertuous Ladies in generall," where Virtue's book "where she inroules/Those high deserts that Majestie commends" (4–5) figures the book of poems similarly enrolling its readers. As this line of imagery is brought to a close in "Cooke-ham," Lady Clifford is numbered among the "virtuous" (4) visiting Cooke-ham, the "(sweet place) where Virtue then did rest" (7). When her "virtues" come to lodge in the poet's un-worthy breast, the carefully maintained ambiguity of virtue's location in relation to the poet and her reader is finally resolved. As Lanyer asserts her primacy in women's poetry, she also assigns to Lady Clifford the priestly role she claimed throughout the collection. In becoming a humble communi-cant, she rises to her poetic vocation.

6• Drummond's Artistry in the *Flowres of Sion*

Robert C. Evans

Many arguments can be made for recovering the work of heretofore neglected writers, particularly those, such as William Drummond of Hawthornden, who enjoyed a significantly higher reputation in their own period than they do at present. The works of such writers can be studied, for instance, because of their historical significance, including the light they shed on the aesthetic tastes and intellectual trends of their day. Or such works can be explored in sociological terms, as reflections of such issues as the cultural status of authors, the changing functions of the "author" category, the documented or implied role of readers, the influence of the writer on (or his indebtedness to) other writers, and the whole complicated question of literary reception. Or such neglected works can be scrutinized from an ideological perspective — for what they can tell us about how the author's culture (and our own) responded (and responds) to such issues as gender, class, power, race, and national or ethnic discrimination.

All these matters are inherently important and deserve

attention, but an issue likely to be of even more immediate concern to nonprofessional readers (that is, to those not paid, forced, or otherwise driven to study antiquarian texts) is altogether simpler: do these bones live? Does the work of a poet such as Drummond, in other words, reflect sufficient skill in the use of language and sufficient relevance to timeless human concerns to repay current or continued attention? Did Drummond possess enough talent in the manipulation of diction, imagery, metaphor, meter, rhyme, and all the other elements of poetic art to make his poems still worth reading *as poems*? Did he possess sufficient insight into (or curiosity about) the kinds of basic issues that interest most humans at some point in their lives, such as the meaning of life, the puzzle of death, desires for happiness, fears of pain, hatred of evil, or love of beauty and goodness (however we choose to define those loaded nouns)? No poet, no matter how historically interesting, is ever likely to be fully recovered unless we feel that his or her words merit attention *as words* — as examples of linguistic skill and formal craftsmanship. Can a poet like Drummond pass this basic test? Does he deserve our attention because of his poetic talent? Or is he of interest — if at all—mainly for other reasons? These are the kinds of questions I seek to raise and address.

I

Just as Ben Jonson's literary reputation might be even greater if he had not been a contemporary of Shakespeare, so Drummond's might be greater if he had never played host to Jonson in 1618/19. Jonson apparently never realized that Drummond was keeping detailed notes of their many talks, but these *Conversations* provide one of our best sources of information about the life and opinions of any early modern poet. Because Jonson, however, often emerges from these records as a bit conceited, Jonsonians often have denigrated

Drummond, both as a man and as a poet. In this latter judg-
ment they have some proper precedent, for Jonson himself,
with his characteristic bluntness, told Drummond in the *Con-*
versations that the latter's verses

> were all good, especiallie my Epitaph of the Prince save that
> they smelled too much of yᵉ schooles and were not after the
> Fancie of ye tyme. for a child sayes he may writte after the
> fashion of yᵉ Greekes & latine verses jn running. yett that he
> wished to please the King, that piece of Forth-Feasting had been
> his owne. (1:135)

Probably, in dismissing Drummond's poetry in this way,
Jonson was thinking mainly of the love poems, which do in-
deed have a familiar if not unpleasant air. Aside from their
debts to the Greek and Latin precedents Jonson mentions, the
love poems also recall many continental and native English
models, particularly the sonnets of Sir Philip Sidney. Drum-
mond's love poetry would probably be much more widely
respected and read today if he had only lived half a century
sooner. His love poems are good, but they do seem old-fash-
ioned when compared, say, to Donne's.[1]

A different argument can be made, however, about Drum-
mond's religious verse. Whereas the love poems often do seem
to be competently rehearsing many familiar tactics, the reli-
gious poems frequently have the capacity to startle, intrigue,
and move. Although these sacred works are themselves in-
debted to continental models (especially Marino), they seem
far fresher than the obviously Petrarchan love verse. Indeed
Drummond's religious poems, I will argue, deserve much more
detailed and respectful attention than they have yet received.
They merit repeated close readings.[2]

In these works, Drummond shows himself adept at using
a wide variety of tactics and techniques in quite effective
ways. In these religious poems he draws on many of the
best resources of the best poets and poetry, including puns,
word-play, inversions, alternating line-lengths, balanced

phrasing, startling juxtapositions, lively apostrophes, paradox, delay, arresting conceits, sudden shifts and reversals, clever sound effects, subtle connotations, apt concluding words, a fine sense of drama, a tone of spontaneity, striking or charming imagery, effective use of monosyllabic words, strong verbs, apt concluding terms, and memorable and often surprising final couplets. The religious poems are alive in ways that seem less often true of the secular verse; certainly they deserve more attention than they have yet received.

II

Most of Drummond's religious poetry was published in a volume issued in 1623 and entitled *Flowres of Sion, or Spirituall Poems*. Earlier versions of some of these works had been published before, in a volume containing secular verse, but *Flowres* (reprinted, with revisions, in 1630) represents the core of Drummond's achievement as a religious writer. Drummond uses various verse forms, from short madrigals to lengthy songs, but it seems best to focus here on the short poems, especially the sonnets. These works provide the best opportunities to discuss the poet's craft in some detail and quantity. It is that craft, after all, that finally makes Drummond or any other poet worth reading, and it is through close attention to Drummond's artistry that we may be able to demonstrate how an imitative poet can still be significantly original.[3]

The opening poem of the *Flowres* volume seems as good a place as any to begin. It displays many of the characteristic traits and strengths of Drummond's religious verse.[4]

> THE INSTABILITIE OF MORTALL GLORIE
> Triumphant Arches, Statues crown'd with Bayes,
> Proud Obeliskes, Tombes of vastest Frame,
> Colosses, brasen *Atlases* of Fame,
> Phanes vainelie builded to vaine Idols praise;
> States, which unsatiate Mindes in blood doe raise,
> From the Crosse-starres unto the Articke Teame,

Alas! and what wee write to keepe our Name,
Like Spiders Caules are made the sport of Dayes:
All onely constant is in constant Change,
What done is, is undone, and when undone,
Into some other figure it doth range,
Thus moves the restlesse World beneath the Moone:
 Wherefore (my Minde) above Time, Motion, Place,
 Thee raise, and Steppes, not reach'd by Nature trace. (88)

Various features help make this poem effective. These in-
clude the word-play with "brasen" (simultaneously suggesting
something literally made of brass; something figuratively
impudent, shameless, and self-assertive; and something cre-
ated during the long-dead age of brass); as well as the punning
on "vainelie" and "vaine" (suggesting both pride and futility —
and thereby encapsulating an important theme of the entire
poem). Also effective are the heavy assonance (depending
mainly on long "a" sounds) in the first five lines; the subtle
reminder (in l. 5) of the specifically human cost of abstract
political ambition; the clever juxtaposition of mental and
physical in the reference to "States, which unsatiate Mindes
in blood doe raise" (l. 5); and the abrupt, brief, and emotional
interruption of "Alas!" (l. 7). The poem is furthermore
strengthened by the sudden implication that both writer and
reader are themselves involved in the follies the poem has
thus far catalogued from a distance (l. 7), and also by the way
in which line 8 (the end of the sonnet's octave) not only sud-
denly ends the lengthy list, but also reenacts the very process
of abrupt destruction that is the poem's central theme. Just as
spiders' webs (or "Caules") can be swept away with one blow,
so line 8 sweeps away everything listed in the preceding seven
lines. Paradoxically, of course, this destructive gesture actu-
ally completes and fulfills the structure of the opening sec-
tion of Drummond's sonnet.

 When the sonnet shifts from octave to sestet, we find even
more to admire, including the repetition of "constant" in l. 9
(a repetition that thereby enacts the word's meaning); the

emphasis on such encompassing and exclusive words as "All" and "onely" (l. 9), and the further word-play on "done" in l. 10 (its sudden shifts, combined with repetition, suggesting the very combination of stasis and change that is the poem's main theme). Similarly effective are the possibly reflexive pun on "figure" (perhaps suggesting Drummond's awareness of his own use of rhetorical figures) in l. 11; the appropriate rhyme of "Change" and "range" (appropriate since the two words not only sound alike but carry the same connotations; ll. 9 and 11); and the assonance of "moves" and "Moon" (l. 12). Likewise, the poem benefits from such features as the subtle shift from sestet-structure to couplet-form in lines 13–14; the narrowing focus on the speaker himself in the last two lines (as he personally internalizes the lesson he also teaches); and the implied opposition between the tempered "Minde" of l. 13 and the "unsatiate Mindes" of l. 5. Equally intriguing are the strong but paradoxical emphasis on delayed verbs in the final line (paradoxical since "raise" and "trace" both suggest a movement to get beyond movement); the subtle hint of upward (i.e., heavenly; spiritual) motion implied by "Steppes" (l. 14); and, finally, the implication, suggested by the word "trace," that the most profitable kind of movement follows a spiritual pattern already set by countless others.

Just as this first sonnet of the *Flowres of Sion* volume displays considerable poetic skill, so does the book's first madrigal. Even the brevity of this poem is appropriate to its subject:

THE PERMANENCIE OF LIFE
Life a right shadow is,
For if it long appeare,
Then it is spent, and Deathes long Night drawes neare;
Shadowes are moving, light,
And is there ought so moving as is this?
When it is most in Sight,
It steales away, and none can tell how, where,
So neere our Cradles to our Coffines are. (89; italics in original)

Part of the poem's effectiveness depends on its movements from line to line and on sudden juxtapositions. The opening line, for instance, already carries some paradoxical force, for although it asserts that life is merely a "shadow" (this one word negatively coloring or over-shadowing the other four), "Life" is still the first, emphatic word and the literal syntactical subject. That subject continues to dominate line 2 and the first three words of line 3, only to be abruptly cancelled (or literally finished) by the strong verb "spent," after which a new clause begins and a new subject — "Deathes long night" — enters the poem. Appropriately, the line mentioning this "long night" is metrically the longest so far and is also graphically the longest of the entire poem. With line 4 Drummond begins to offer a new definition, this time of "Shadowes," that both balances and reverses the different definition already offered in line 1, while the abrupt abutment contained in the phrase "moving, light" mimicks the very quickness these words describe. Sudden juxtaposition of a different sort is emphasized in the shift from line 6 ("When it is most in Sight") to line 7 ("It steales away"), while the startling, brief joining of "how, where" at the end of that line enacts the very haste it describes. The similarly surprising conjunction of "Cradles" and "Coffines" in the last line again catches us offguard, and then this poem on the brevity of life suddenly ends. In the final line, though, Drummond not only shifts (in the references to cradles and coffins) from abstract to extremely concrete imagery but also, by doubly emphasizing "our," reminds us that the poem's previously generalized musings personally implicate both him and us. All in all, the poem is a short but highly polished performance — a credit to its author's skill.

Similarly skillful is the fifth sonnet of *Flowres of Sion*, in which the overtly religious (and specifically Christian) tone of the volume first begins to assert itself:

NATURE MUST YEELDE TO GRACE
Too long I followed have on fond Desire,
And too long painted on deluding Streames,
Too long refreshment sought in burning Fire,
Runne after Joyes which to my Soule were Blames;
Ah! when I had what most I did admire,
And prov'd of Lifes delightes the last extreames,
I found all but a Rose hedg'd with a Bryer,
A nought, a thought, a show of Golden Dreames.
Hence-foorth on Thee (mine onlie Good) I thinke,
For onelie Thou canst grant what I doe crave,
Thy Nailes my Pennes shall bee, thy Blood mine Inke,
Thy winding-sheete my Paper, Studie Grave:
 And till that Soule from Bodie parted bee,
 No hope I have, but onelie onelie Thee. (90–91)

Once again Drummond shows himself adept at using various poetic techniques. These include the anaphora of "Too long," in which the very repetition reinforces the words' meaning; the elongated assonance of those same words, with their stretched-out "o's"; the word-play on "fond" (suggesting both "amorous" and "foolish"); the separate paradoxical force of lines 2, 3, and 4; and the memorable image — suggesting futility — of attempting to paint on streams (l. 2). Also effective are the clever juxtaposition of "deluding Streames" and "burning Fire" (ll. 2–3); the meaningful ambiguity of that same "burning Fire" (which implies both erotic passion and its potentially hellish torments); and the appropriately sudden shift to the metrically emphasized verb "Runne" at the start of line 4. Meanwhile, the poem also benefits from the even more emphatic "Ah!" that begins line 5 (suggesting, among other possibilities, regret, frustration, and sudden realization); the skillful placement of "last extreames" at the very end of line 6; and the almost trivializing but appropriately trivial sound-effects of "A nought, a thought" (l. 8) with which the octave ends.

When Drummond shifts to the sonnet's sestet, however, a

new syntactical subject and a new force enter the poem. No
longer is the emphasis on "I" (as it had been explicitly in ll. 1,
5, and 7 and, implicitly, throughout the octave); now the stress
shifts instead to "Thee" (l. 9), "Thou" (l. 10), "Thy" (ll. 11–
12), and then again, quite forcefully, to "Thee" as the very
final word (l. 14). Similarly, the octave's emphasis on the words
"too long" is now replaced by the sestet's emphasis on the
word "onelie" (ll. 9, 10, 14). Suddenly, too, Drummond's lan-
guage becomes much less abstract. The octave had mentioned
broad concepts, such as "Desire," "Joyes," "Soule," "Lifes
delightes," and also its "last extreames" (ll. 1, 4, 6). In the
sestet, however, the figurative language becomes almost
shockingly concrete and "conceited." Drummond now shifts
to the kind of diction we expect from Donne or the other
metaphysicals, as if references to the incarnate Christ demand
a full-bodied rhetoric: "Thy Nailes my Pennes shall bee, thy
Blood mine Inke,/Thy winding-sheete my Paper, Studie
Grave" (ll. 11–12). Each of these clauses becomes increasingly
compressed, until we can't be quite sure whether the enig-
matic last one — "Studie Grave" — means "my subject of study
becomes your grave," or whether it means "your grave be-
comes the figurative place where I think and write," or whether
it means "the crucifixion is now the subject of my grave
(i.e., serious) study." The very brevity of the phrase forces
us to pause and puzzle out its meaning, but the quick shifts
from one metaphor to the next in lines 11–12 give those
lines an energy appropriately lacking in the more leisurely
paced movement through the four alternatives already offered
in lines 1–4.

Meanwhile, the reference to "Soule" in line 13 looks back
to the use of that same word in line 4 (thereby linking octave
and sestet), while the splendid alliteration ("hope," "have")
and assonance ("No," "hope," "onelie," "onelie") of the final
line lend it superbly memorable force. Even Drummond's
play on the double "onelie" is meaningful and not merely

decorative, since the repetition can suggest both powerful emotion and rational discrimination (by implying the meaning, "only you, who are unique and self-sufficient"). Finally, the fact that the poem ends with "Thee" — in Drummond's day a more familiar and intimate word than the more formal "you" — suggests both the special status and the disarming approachability of God. The earlier, somewhat abstract reference to God as the speaker's "onelie Good" (l. 9) here gives way to the more tender, more personal "onelie Thee." Once more Drummond demonstrates a mastery of words to convey both thought and feeling. The final line, meanwhile, is both an optimistic affirmation of faith and a somewhat pleading confession of utter dependence.

In a subsequent sonnet from *Flowres of Sion*, Drummond deals not with the crucifixion but with the nativity. As with Milton's later, more famous treatment of the same subject — which may in fact have been influenced by Drummond (see Davies, *SLJ* 1985) — the poem tries to convey a strong sense of the presence (or present-ness) of the event as well as its world-historical implications:

> THE ANGELS FOR THE NATIVITIE OF OUR LORD
> Runne (Sheepheards) run where *Bethleme* blest appeares,
> Wee bring the best of newes, be not dismay'd,
> A Saviour there is borne, more olde than yeares,
> Amidst Heavens rolling hights this Earth who stay'd;
> In a poore Cotage Inn'd, a Virgine Maide
> A weakling did him beare, who all upbeares,
> There is hee poorelie swadl'd, in a Manger lai'd,
> To whom too narrow Swadlings are our Spheares:
> Runne (Sheepheards) runne, and solemnize his Birth,
> This is that Night, no, Day growne great with Blisse,
> In which the power of *Sathan* broken is,
> In Heaven bee glorie, Peace unto the Earth.
> Thus singing through the Aire the Angels swame,
> And Cope of Starres re-echoed the same. (92)

Once more Drummond demonstrates his poetic skill, includ-
ing his use of the heavily accented (and then repeated) verb
"Runne" in the poem's first syllable (which immediately cre-
ates a strong sense of energy while also provoking our curios-
ity); his playing with assonance in *"Bethleme,"* "blest," and
"best" (ll. 1–2); and his subtle suggestion that the gospel is
not merely good news but the very "best of newes" (l. 2). Also
effective are his fine use of abrupt juxtaposition and paradox
in the two halves of line 3; his further refinement of such
paradox through the implication that the newborn babe is lit-
erally and not just figuratively "more olde than yeares" (i.e.,
older than time itself); and his implied contrast between mo-
tion and stasis in the words "rolling" and "stay'd" (l. 4). Simi-
larly, the poem benefits from his ambiguous reference, in line
6, to a "weakling" (since it is not immediately clear whether
the term refers to Mary or to Jesus); his play on "beare" and
"upbeares" (l. 6); his juxtaposition of apparent weakness and
true strength in lines 7–8; his return (at the beginning of the
sestet) to the phrasing with which the octave itself had begun
(l. 9); and his suggestion of energy and spontaneity in the phrase
"Night, no, Day" (l. 10). The poem is likewise strengthened
by Drummond's subtle play on the idea of pregnancy in the
reference to a "Day growne great with Blisse" (l. 10); his jux-
taposition of creation and destruction in the shift from line
10 to line 11; and his effective use of balance in the subjects
and structure of line 12.

As usual, Drummond here also makes effective use of his
sonnet's final couplet: he pulls back from the immediate event;
comments on the angels' singing (which the poem implicitly
associates with his own lyricism here); offers a wonderfully
understated image of the bodiless angels needing to swim
through "Aire" that seems as substantial and resistant to them
as water does to us; and puns when referring to the "Cope"
of stars (since "cope" could simultaneously imply a kind of

religious cape, a vault or canopy of heaven, or a vast expanse or firmament). Finally, he plays a subtle sound-game by making the verb "re-echoed" a four-syllable word, so that it mimes the very action it describes. In short, Drummond breathes life into a very conventional religious subject by treating it with talent rather than merely going through a series of conventional motions.

Much the same might be said of a later sonnet, a kind of companion piece to the poem just discussed:

> TO THE ANGELS FOR THE PASSION
> Come forth, come forth, yee blest triumphing Bands,
> Faire Citizens of that immortall Towne,
> Come see that King which all this All commands,
> Now (overcharg'd with Love) die for his owne;
> Looke on those Nailes which pierce his Feete and Hands,
> What a sharp Diademe his Browes doth crowne?
> Behold his pallid Face, his Eyes which sowne,
> And what a Throng of Theeves him mocking stands.
> Come forth yee empyrean Troupes, come forth,
> Preserve this sacred Blood that Earth adornes,
> Those liquid Roses gather off his Thornes,
> O! to bee lost they bee of too much worth:
>
>   1   2   3   1   2   3
> For streams, Juice, Balm they are, which quench, kils, charms
>   1   2   3   1   2   3
> Of God, Death, Hel, the wrath, the life, the harmes.

As in his sonnet on the nativity, Drummond here makes effective use of verbs in the first positions of many lines, thus giving the poem a great sense of energy, urgency, and force. Most of these verbs occur in alternating odd-numbered lines (ll. 1, 3, 5, 7, 9). Significantly, however, when that pattern *is* broken (in line 10, which begins with the verb "Preserve"), the shift in structure accompanies a shift in sense: until line 10 the angels have been summoned mainly as witnesses, but in that line they are suddenly urged to take an active role as preservers of Christ's blood, which (in an especially striking image) is depicted as "liquid roses" (l. 11). Yet the poem also takes advantage of other intriguing shifts and contrasts, as in the counterpointed images of the angels as "blest triumphing Bands" (a fairly conventional description; l. 1) and as "Citizens of that immortall Towne" (a less predictable metaphor whose simplicity is worthy of Herbert; l. 2); or in the play on "all" and "All" in l. 3; or in the sound effects of "Come see" (which begins line 3) and "commands" (which ends it). Similarly effective are the abruptness with which the catalogue of Christ's powers in the first three-and-a-half lines ends with the reference to his willingness to "die for his owne" (l. 4), and also the way the next four lines (ll. 5–8), which emphasize Christ's sufferings, are counterpointed with the first four, which emphasized his glory. Even language that might at first seem imprecise (such as the reference to the "*Throng* of Theeves" [l. 8; emphasis added] where we might expect a reference merely to the famous condemned pair) seems justified on reflection (since all those who participated in Christ's crucifixion were "Theeves" in the broadest sense).

Finally, though, what makes this poem especially memorable is the *tour-de-force* of the concluding couplet: clearly Drummond is playing with notions of the Trinity by offering a four-fold catalogue of three interlinked words, but this ending seems more than a trick or a bit of self-indulgent wit. Instead, these lines with their clotted monosyllables help enact, rather than simply describe, the rich, viscous significance of Christ's blood. The lines make the reader pause, read more slowly, think and meditate, and carefully puzzle out the meaning of each combination of terms. The "liquid Roses" of Christ's blood become (simultaneously) the streams that quench the wrath of God; the juice that kills the life of death (an idea full of paradoxes); and the balm that charms the harms of hell. Even now, however, the poetic richness of the lines is not exhausted, for our final impression of the poem as we move through it, word-by-word, is of the paradoxical richness embedded in the alternating meanings of the final six syllables: "the wrath, the life, the harmes." "Harmes" is literally Drummond's last word, but the dark overtones of that noun have already (appropriately enough) been cancelled out by the verb that long before precedes it. If this poem seems baroque, it is baroque in the best sense. Elaboration here is more than decorative; instead, it works to enrich the poem's meaning.

One might argue, of course, that since this poem — like so much of Drummond's poetry — derives from another author's original model (in this case a sonnet by Marino), Drummond is therefore a merely derivative writer whose verse lacks originality and whose writing thus lacks merit. Such an argument, however, would apply to much Renaissance literature (which was deeply rooted in the theory and practice of imitation and even translation) and would diminish the standing of many English authors — including Wyatt, Howard, Sidney, Shakespeare, Donne, and Jonson, to name a few. What matters when dealing with a talented writer is not so much whether he or she relies on prior sources but rather how that writer uses them. Clearly Drummond is no Shakespeare; he may not even be a Howard; but he does seem a writer of some talent whose skill deserves further study and appreciation, not dismissal for being "derivative."

Consider, for instance, one of his most undeniably derivative poems, a madrigal sometimes entitled "THE WORLD A GAME":

> The world a Hunting is,
> *The Pray poore Man, the* Nimrod *fierce is Death,*
> His speedie Grei-hounds are,
> Lust, sicknesse, Envie, Care,
> Strife that neere falles amisse,
> With all those ills which haunt us while wee breath.
> Now, if (by chance) wee flie
> Of these the eager Chase,
> *Old Age with stealing Pace,*

Castes up his Nets, and there wee panting die. (109; italics in original)

This, one could argue, is a "direct translation" of a madrigal by the Italian writer Valerio Belli:

> Questo mondo è una caccia, è cacciatrice
> La Morte vincitrice:
> I veltri suoi rapaci
> Sono cure mordaci,
> E morbi, e mal, da cui cacciati siamo:
> E se talhor fuggiamo,
> Vecchiezza sua compagna,
> Ci prende ne la regna. (Jack, *Italian Influence*, 122)

Compare, however, Drummond's "translation" with the following (much more literal) prose rendering by Ronald D.S. Jack (from *Italian Influence* 122):

> This world is a hunt, and the hunter is Death, the conqueror; his rapacious hounds are cruel cares, diseases and troubles, by which we are hunted. And if sometimes we flee, old age, his companion, catches us in the net.

Part of the success, subtlety, and originality of Drummond's poem becomes apparent precisely when we contrast it with its Italian original. Consider, for example, Drummond's opening line, which juxtaposes the static noun *"world"* and the more active gerund *"hunting."* The force of Drummond's line is amplified even more, however, by its final emphasis on the verb *"is,"* and this sense of energy is also increased by the conjunction of *"a"* and *"hunting"*: the combination sounds almost like an archaic verb-form: *"a-hunting."* Drummond, in short, gives us a more dynamic line than Marino — an impression also enhanced by his line's greater brevity. This is not to say that Drummond's phrasing is necessarily better (although in this case I think it *is*); it is only to say that his phrasing is sufficiently different to make both his line and his larger poem no "mere" translations.[5]

Other differences between the original and the "translation"
also seem worth noting. Thus it is Drummond who adds
(in l. 2) the alliterative, empathetic, and even self-reflective
reference to "*poore Man*" as the "*Pray*" of Death, and it is
Drummond who brings in the biblical allusion to "Nimrod"
(with all of its accompanying connotations). Drummond also
gives his second line a neatly balanced structure lacking in
the original, just as he mentions "*Grei-hounds*" (appropriate
both because of their color and their speed) rather than refer-
ring more generically to "hounds." He also increases the num-
ber of the hounds from three to five, using the lengthened
catalogue of nouns (in ll. 4–5) not only to give his poem a
more emphatic sense of the world's troubles but also to play,
paradoxically, with the idea of a chaotic force ("*Strife*") that is
also terrifyingly accurate ("*that neere falles amisse*"). In addi-
tion, Drummond modifies the list of nouns so that they de-
pict human beings not only as the victims of evils (as in
Marino's "cruel cares, diseases and troubles") but also as their
self-destructive causes (especially in the reference to "*Lust*,"
but also in the references to "*Envie*," "*care*," and "*Strife*").
Drummond's lines thus imply, much more clearly than
Marino's, our own sinful responsibility for many of our
troubles — a fact that interestingly complicates the meaning
of his poem. No longer are humans merely the poor, pitiable
prey of Death; now we are partly ourselves to blame for his
success as a hunter (partly because we are hunters ourselves).

Drummond's next line (l. 6) resembles the fifth line of
Marino's poem because of its effective length, but Drummond's
line, typically, is also a bit more specific. Drummond further-
more adds (in l. 8) the reference to "*chance*" (which makes
the possibility of fleeing Death seem literally more chancey
by making it seem merely a lucky accident); and he addition-
ally supplies the reference to the malevolently "*eager Chace*,"
so that lines 7 and 8 are counterpointed in subject, sound, and
emphasis, one stressing flight, the other pursuit. Moreover,

he also characteristically appends an extra line, thereby achieving not only added force but also structural balance. His reference to the personified *"Old Age,"* along with the clever ambiguity of *"stealing"* (i.e., both slow and deceptively pilfering) and the appropriate noun *"Pace"* (which already implies measured, deliberate steps) all help give his poem a distinctive resonance and help make it more than a simple "translation." Finally, Drummond's last line is much more powerful and specific than Marino's original (partly because of its length): *"Castes up"* (with its accented second syllable) is an effectively energetic verb, while the final two words (*"panting die"*) seem appropriate in every way — especially in connotation and placement.

The point of this detailed comparison and contrast of the two poems is not to argue that Drummond is the better poet or even that Drummond in this case has written the better poem. Rather, the point is simply to demonstrate that these *are* different poems, and that our appreciation of Drummond's skill and originality as a writer can often be enhanced rather than diminished by looking closely at his so-called "translations."

III

Full appreciation of Drummond's literary merit — especially as a writer of religious verse — would of course require detailed examination of many individual poems, but these few examples at least suggest that his religious poetry does deserve much fuller scrutiny. Nearly every poem he wrote reveals skill and craft of one sort or another, and it may be useful, in closing, to review some of the best individual features of his artistry. The first ten sonnets of the *Flowres of Sion* luckily provide a convenient (and conveniently arbitrary) sampling, although in surveying these poems I will ignore the works I have already discussed at length.

Drummond's literary talent is especially apparent in *Sonnet ii*, for instance — particularly in the poem's effectively brief, abrupt conclusion (with its punning reference to the "ends" — i.e., both the goals and deaths — "wee toyle for heere below"), as well as in the nicely delayed introduction of "wisest Death" (ll. 13–14). In *Sonnet iii* (entitled "NO TRUST IN TYME"), moreover, Drummond cleverly makes the adverb "lingringlie" the longest word in its line (and one of the longest in the whole poem [l. 1]). Later in the same lyric, he adroitly juxtaposes the two halves of line four when describing how a flower, "As high as it did raise, bowes low the head." Here the sudden switch from "raise" to "bowes" subtly mimicks the argument of the entire work. Juxtapostion is also deftly employed in *Sonnet iv*, especially in the use of "wearie" and "fast" in line 1 and in the sudden abutment of "Tempest" and "Harbour" in line 2. In addition, *Sonnet iv* also plays with paradox by asserting that the light of the senses blinds the mind (l. 10), while the poem as a whole ends adeptly with two words: "silent Grave" (l. 14). Indeed, Drummond is often quite clever in the ways he ends poems, as in the concluding couplet of *Sonnet vi*, where the word "Or" (l. 13) momentarily tricks us by falsely suggesting a possible shift in argument; but l. 14 once again reiterates the poem's main argument (this time with final force) while also placing the word "Margine" in a literally marginal position.

Meanwhile, the opening line of *Sonnet vii* displays another important feature of Drummond's literary skill — his manipulation of rhetorical devices, in this case antimetabole ("The Grief was common, common were the Cryes"). The ensuing line, however, uses juxtaposition once more, this time to disrupt the neat pattern the first line had suggested and thereby to extend the catalogue of sufferings: "Teares, Sobbes, and Groanes of that afflicted Traine." Finally, in the poem's couplet Drummond deftly uses enjambment, describing how "God of a Virgines wombe / Was borne," while also making the verb in the final clause ("and those false Deities strooke dombe") appropriately ambiguous, since it can be read as either active *or* passive (or both). "Dombe," moreover, seems exactly the right concluding word for this poem, especially since the term can simultaneously imply shock, stupidity, and silence. Effective for different reasons, however, is the final couplet of *Sonnet ix*, which dexterously links the prosaic ("Before the Babe, the Sheepheardes bow'd on knees") and the mystical ("And Springes ranne Nectar, Honey dropt from Trees").

As even this brief survey should suggest, Drummond's verse provides much evidence of the kind of skillful craftsmanship that ultimately makes any poet worth reading. Many of his most characteristic techniques come together in *Sonnet x*, entitled "AMAZEMENT AT THE INCARNATION OF GOD" — a poem which may be taken as one final illustration of his religious art and artistry.

> To spread the azure Canopie of Heaven,
> And make it twinkle with those spangs of Gold,
> To stay this weightie masse of Earth so even,
> That it should all, and nought should it up-hold;
> To give strange motions to the Planets seven,
> Or Jove to make so meeke, or Mars so bold,
> To temper what is moist, dry, hote, and cold,
> Of all their Jarres that sweete accords are given:
> Lord, to thy Wisedome nought is, nor thy Might;
> But that thou shouldst (thy Glorie laid aside)
> Come meanelie in mortalitie to bide,
> And die for those deserv'd eternall plight,
>   A wonder is so farre above our wit,
>   That Angels stand amaz'd to muse on it. (93)

Here the heavy use of anaphora ("To . . . To . . . To . . . To . . .") not only emphasizes the poem's verbs (thus adding to its considerable energy) but also contributes to the highly effective suspended syntax, in which the crucial subject of all the verbs (the noun "Lord") is delayed until line nine — that is, until the very end of the poem's octave and the very beginning of its final movement. Even after that central word is reached, however, the syntax of the poem still continues, all revolving around and depending on the centrally significant word "Lord," until we realize that the entire sonnet is one long sentence. The poem's structure thus replicates the phenomenon it describes: a universe in which everything depends on (and depends from) God — a creation in which everything leads toward and proceeds from its Creator.

As in George Herbert's famous poem "Prayer (I)," the sonnet's long, constantly accumulating syntax makes the work a structural *tour-de-force*, and if we feel somewhat breathless when we finish the sonnet, that feeling seems entirely appropriate to the "AMAZEMENT" the poem both describes and seeks to evoke. In ways both large and small, moreover, Drummond here combines a sense of uncertainty and surprise (as in the suspended syntax, or in the lovely paradox expressed in l. 4, or in the almost chaotic rush of adjectives in l. 7) with a sense of order and control (as in the parallel structure of each pair of the first eight lines, or in the balanced phrasing of l. 6 or l. 8, or in the pairing of "Wisedom" and "Might" in l. 9). In other words, the sonnet (like the universe), seems pulled in all directions; its forces are both centrifugal and centripetal, its movements both upward and downward (especially in the sestet), with the Lord (and the *word* "Lord") as the ultimate source of coherence. Here too, as in other poems, Drummond plays not simply with meanings but with sounds, as in the appropriate alliteration of "meanelie" and "mortalitie" or the more shocking assonance of "bide" and "die" (ll. 11–12). By the end of the work, when Drummond finally leaves us with an image of the angels who "stand amazed to muse" not simply on God's works but on his mercy, we feel almost forced by the poem's power to share their reaction. The final words thus invite the very response they describe.

As this poem and as many others demonstrate, Drummond is a "minor" poet only in the sense that all poets except the vcry best are "minor": not every writer can be a Chaucer, Shakespeare, or Milton, and there is much honor in being a Surrey, a Drayton, or even a Drummond. The latter's verse will seem uninteresting only to those who fail to take a closer look — the sort of look it has been the main purpose of this paper to encourage.

7 • William Austin, Poet of Anglianism

Kate Narveson

Recent attempts to recover a fuller sense of the seventeenth century religious landscape in England force us to ask whether anyone actively liked the church as established. While laying to rest the Victorian ectoplasm of pious Dr. Donne and saintly Mr. Herbert, high church Anglicans, revisionists tend to evoke in its place a picture in which early Stuart believers were either the Calvinist godly (more or less puritan, Scripture-centered evangelicals, all for putting down alehouses, grudgingly conformable to the established church) or anti-Calvinists (sacramentalist and ceremonialist, in favor of Laud's "innovations" and nervous of lay initiative).[1] But the "Calvinist/anti-Calvinist" (or Herbert/Herrick) alternative has proven unhelpful in placing Donne's piety, nor, with its picture of discontent from both sides, does it tell us much about those who might have liked the early Stuart Church of England.[2] The case of William Austin — member of Lincoln's Inn, antiquary, devotionalist, poet — provides a valuable picture of that third alternative. His works indicate that it was possible to be at once a firm Protestant and well-read in patristic, medieval, and contemporary Roman Catholic writers, to enjoy an active social life and conversation with men of letters, to appreciate church music and art, to embrace the traditions, worship, and festivals of the established church, and to be deeply devout — without being either Puritan or anti-Calvinist.

In this article I will make two related arguments. First, in keeping with the intent of this volume to recover the early Stuart religious landscape, I will explore how Austin's prose meditations and devotional poetry indicate that the cultivation of an informed faith through devotional exercises, more than the pursuit of theological precision through disputation, was at the heart of religious practice among believers actively committed to the established church. Austin's works help us to recover a world in which men and women not only attended sermons, contributed to the parish funds, and served as churchwardens but also gathered outside public worship to share their attempts to kindle a lively faith. The first part of this article will consider Austin's life and prose meditations in order to provide a snapshot of that world. The subsequent examination of Austin's poems will build on that recovery in order to further the other purpose of this volume, discovery. Those poems are more than cultural curiosities, they are fine examples of early Stuart religious verse in their own right. When viewed as part of the society of devotion sketched in the first half, they indicate how central to a devotional life was the act of shaping one's devotion into forms that could move, instruct and delight one's companions. Further, they importantly expand our sense of Protestant poetry's generic possibilities beyond the lyric forms most often discussed. The second half of this article will introduce Austin's poetry.

Recovering Austin's Devotional World

Austin, 1587–1633/4, was called to the bar at Lincoln's Inn in 1611 (*Black Book* 141). He lived in Southwark, where he was friends with Edward Alleyn, John Donne's son-in-law. Alleyn, according to his diary, dined frequently with Austin, sent gifts to Austin's wife and mother, and attended the baptism of one of Austin's children (Young 2:59 *et passim*). At one of Alleyn's dinners, Sir Thomas and Lady Grymes and Constance Donne were present along with Austin. Austin was well off. Both he and his mother gave expensive gifts to St. Saviour's Church. Austin's funeral monument, still standing, reflects not only wealth but learning and piety. Angels in classical poses, holding agricultural implements, flank pilasters crowned by a cornice; between the pilasters another angel stands on a rock, pointing up at a sun bearing the motto *Sol Justitia*. On the cornice is the motto *Vos estis dei agricultura*. A stream representing the sacraments flows from the rock; beneath stands a sheaf of corn, with the motto *Si non moriatur, non reviviscit*, and a snake, emblem of the snake Moses lifted up in the wilderness, a type of Christ. The rock is inscribed *Petra erat Xtus*. In the monument's overall effect, classical form is thoroughly governed by Christian content (Taylor 82).

Austin's dedication to literature broadly understood is further testified by his translation of Cicero's *Cato Maior* and his composition of an antimisogynist treatise, *Haec Homo*, which draws from Agrippa, Pliny, Bede, Martial, Josephus, and Spenser, among others. Both were published posthumously. Austin was involved in a plan to establish a "Royal Academy of Literature" to revive the society of antiquaries that had gathered around Cotton, Spelman, and Camden. Proposed by Edmund Bolton, a recusant writer and projector, the society was to be composed of "persons culled from out of the most able and most famous lay-gentlemen of England" (*Archaeologia* 140). The list of those who were to be members includes George Chapman, Kenelm Digby, Michael Drayton, Ben Jonson, Inigo Jones, Toby Matthew, Endymion Porter, John Selden, and Henry Wotton. The proposal was close to realization when James I died, and it died with him, despite attempts to interest Charles (*Archaeologia* 138–47).

Austin's inclusion is not the only indication that he associated with London's men of letters. In his *Devotionis Augustinianae Flamma or Certayne Devout, Godly, & Learned Meditations*, he refers to "my worthy friend, the learned Selden" (220), and also mentions Sir Edward Spencer, probably the author of a translation of Boethius and the Edward Spenser [sic] who entered Lincoln's Inn in 1613 (181, *Admission Register 162*). In 1620 Austin was a co-trustee for Dulwich College, Alleyn's foundation (Young 2:50). Austin's poems are praised in a letter by James Howell, the letter-writer and would-be Son of Ben, who includes a rapturous letter in *Epistolae Ho-Elianae*, urging Austin to publish his verses (211).

From these associations, we form a picture of Austin's circle and inclinations. His associates were men of letters, interested in antiquity and moral philosophy. Austin reads medieval manuscripts in the Tower of London (*Meditations* 221); he shows wide learning and progressive ideas in his antimisogynist treatise. None of his circle (allowing for Selden's erastianism) were hostile to religion. Indeed, Howell's letters often strike a pious note while Alleyn's establishment of Dulwich school was exactly the kind of godly work that was encouraged by Protestant conceptions of almsdeeds. But, as is most clear in the case of Selden, wide reading led to a sense of the extent to which religious customs vary over time and space, a sense that resulted less in relativism than in an inclination to point out where practices reflected past interests or superstitions that could now be seen as such and corrected.[3] Clearly, Austin felt no reluctance to read Roman Catholic works; he is especially fond of the popular life of Christ by the fourteenth century monk Ludolph of Saxony. But Austin reads with a critical eye, welcoming useful insights but rejecting what, as a Protestant, he felt to be folly. Durandus, for instance, provides Austin a critic lodged within the popish church who can be cited against the invocation of saints (*Meditations* 216).

In such intellectual interests, attitudes, and associates, the "contented conformity" that I would argue Austin shared with

Donne begins to appear. Austin's meditations, published by his widow in 1635, give us further clues to his piety and ecclesial loyalties. The meditations are in effect lay sermons, beginning with "A Meditation for our Ladie-Daie 1621, which this yeere fell on Palme-Sundaie" and concluding with a meditation titled "the Authors owne funerall, made upon Himselfe."[4] One meditation is on Psalm 16, one an "essay of tutelar angels," the others on Lent, Good Friday, and Pentecost, and on the Nativity, Ascension, and Sts. Thomas, Michael, Matthew, and Bartholomew, feast days recognized in the *Book of Common Prayer.* These choices of topic mark Austin as someone who embraced the established church, since to observe the festivals it retained is to signal one's distance from Puritan reservations. Austin also distances himself from Puritanism insofar as he condemns singularity and separation. On the other hand, he does not share the Laudian hesitation to voice strong disapproval of such Roman Catholic practices as invocation of the saints (Milton 67). Austin condemns the practice as both foolish and impious (*Meditations* 216). Austin's meditations confirm that he shared many standard Protestant prejudices against Romish religion: it was idolatrous (especially in prayers to the saints) and superstitious (Austin ridicules pilgrimages); it supported sterile monasticism and work's righteousness, and arrogated to itself the authority that belonged to God's word (23, 36, 68–70, 179, 184, 224–25).

The essentially Reformed nature of Austin's piety appears in his lively sense of mutual edification as a duty of lay people. His meditations were written for "private" devotion only in the sense that such exercises were outside the public worship of the church, because they address a group, using the first-person plural. They do not, though, seem to have been intended for the standard household devotion, for Austin refers more than once to his society, brotherhood, or "Consanguinity" as his audience, and he extols the benefit of "enflaming each other mutually" (36).[5] The meditation for Bartholomew's Day especially develops this theme. Austin declares that "Bartholmew [sic] . . . is a Saint, that (by being an Apostle) is become the fitter Patron for a Society. For thereby, he was a Man, that was of a Society, himselfe . . . that particular-Society pickt out from the rest, (the twelve Apostles) which was of Christs owne making." Austin is careful, therefore, to defend special fellowships:

> Let no man (then) that shall see some few honest men draw together into one Societie, for the stirring up of Charitie and Devotion (two principall ends of Societie) thinke them proud Separatists, that affect singularitie and faction. For such Societies are not Separations, from the great Congregation; but parts of it, and (as it were) so many Under-schooles; wherein good men, doe but practise, and exercise (in private) that love, which they owe, and will be ever ready to put to the whole Church in generall. (226)

This stress on the way that godly fellowship can keep the fire of devotion alive has generally been seen as a hallmark of puritanism, and one of Laud's ways of discouraging lay piety outside the control of the church was to forbid gatherings of ten or more people not of the same household "to read, preach, or expound" (Davies 69). In defending special devotional societies yet distancing them from Puritanism, Austin's work is valuable as evidence that there could be godly of the "hotter sort" among anti-Puritan conformists. In a Donnean passage, Austin takes the Apostles as evidence that Christ loves societies, explaining that Christ "is a Conjunction." "He is the (ET) betweene Alpha and Omega: the (ET) betweene God and Man: the (ET) between Priest and Sacrifice, uniting all in himselfe" (*Meditations* 225). Indeed, Austin continues in a passage reminiscent of Donne's fifth meditation in the *Devotions upon Emergent Occasions*, "So well God loves Conjunctions; that hee would have no good-thing, to be alone. . . . So well hee loves Society, as hee loves his owne-Being. For the very Godhead, is a society; a Trinity of Persons, in Unity of Essence" (225).

Austin is also close to Donne in his constellation of ideas about public worship. Both value prayer in the congregation (Johnson 307, Sherwood 183–86). While one may fast and pray in one's own chamber and God will hear, "yet, much-more, will he heare, when two or three be gathered together, in his Name; and, will bee most mercifull, when (the *Vis Unita*,) the Congregations of his people show, (like the roarings of the Sea) up to the altar. And that, in his House; which he calls the House of Prayer, and made, to that purpose" (*Meditations* 148). This position opposes two perceived abuses. First, the church is the fittest place for public prayer, "and not, in places of Separation; or of Faction; or private Conventicles." Second, prayer and preaching must be balanced. Quoting an unidentified source, Austin notes that the congregation should "continue both praying and praising God (as the Lyturgie of the Church hath taught them) longer, then they doe; before the Sermon: Which (often) takes up more time in teaching us, that wee must and ought to pray; then it gives us to pray in. But . . . God, hath called his house, the house of prayer" (148). At the same time, Austin saw the clergy as "Ministers of Jesus Christ: who is the Word. And, they must minister the Word" (69). The emphasis by both Donne and Austin is on the proper balance and valuation of preaching, private devotion, and public prayer.[6]

A final piece in this cluster of interests and attitudes that characterizes a committed conformity is the way Austin approaches church customs such as fasting in Lent or marking festivals such as Pentecost. In both cases, Austin points to "their practice and example in all ages" but notes also that "it is no Command from Christ," and therefore we do not observe such days like the Jews the Sabbath, "nor, with more strictnesse, then the Church or Magistrate (for, Christian conveniency) hath commanded" (146). Of fasting at Lent he argues that "when a Custome of the Church, is knowne to be so ancient, general; and nothing (in the old, or New Law) against it, it growes (it selfe) to be a Law" (100). This desire that people would observe what has always been done reflects an attempt to preserve the status quo while resisting challenges from the left and the right to underpin their practices with dogmatic "strictness." We can see a similar desire in the moderate Calvinist Daniel Featley, chaplain to Archbishop Abbot and then Charles I, and in George Herbert's "Lent."[7]

While clearly non-Puritan, Austin should not therefore be seen as part of the Caroline reaction against what has been seen as the Jacobean consensus. Austin's mother, Lady Joyce Clark, bestowed on their parish church an elaborate altar rail and Austin seconded his mother's gift with a silver chalice and platter. But Julian Davies has shown that desire to rebuild altar rails was not confined to Laudians (209–10). There is no Laudian eucharistic focus in Austin's meditations, and they seem to have been undertaken with a sense of the value of a laity well-read in theology, called to cultivate devotion through the explication of scripture, and dedicated to mutual edification. Austin exhorts his audience: "let us, by learning divine and high Mysteries, and Revealing them to our Brethren (for their Edification) become like Archangels" (257). Laudians, on the other hand, centered devotion around the ceremonies of the church, supplemented by daily devotions such as those in John Cosin's *Collection of Private Devotions* (1626). That lay people like Austin who published meditations would be conscious of clerical disapproval is evident in *An Apologie for Lay-mens Writing in Divinity* (1642), by Sir Richard Baker, a friend of Donne's.

While many details of this picture indicate that Austin and Donne may have moved in overlapping circles, it is less important to demonstrate a connection than to insist that in their religious sensibility the two men shared much. Even if there was only a tenuous personal connection, Austin is interesting for the evidence his work provides that Donne, while remarkable, was perhaps not so singular in his piety as he is often represented, and that we need to be alert to the existence of a committed conformist piety. Austin's case suggests that it was quite possible for a devout lay person in the 1620s to be both a typical Jacobean Protestant, with a comfortable anti-popish bias, a concern for fellowship in edification, and a Scripture-centered devotion, and to be interested in the church fabric and in patristic and later Roman Catholic writings. Like Sir John Hayward, like Sir Richard Baker, two other lay men of letters who also wrote passionately devout meditations, Austin represents a segment of early Stuart piety too little recognized: those genuinely content with the established church, whose piety was confidently enough settled within it that they could draw on Roman Catholic writers without signaling any discontent with their own well-reformed church. Like Donne, such men had a taste for art and for church music, and they valued the eloquence they saw in Scripture as part of its character as God's word (*Meditations* 23, 224). It is among believers who embraced the resources of language that we find attempts to press poetry into the service of devotion, and I will turn to Austin's poetry next.

Poet of "Anglianism"

Austin's poems voice a piety in some ways akin to what we see in the religious verse of Donne and Herbert. His poems on the passion are able to express bondage to sin with a force reminiscent of the "Holy Sonnets" and yet place that agonized self-knowledge within the context of Christ's grace with more subtlety and assurance than Donne achieved. His epicedium upon himself articulates the value he places on art, yet, unlike Herbert, he can comfortably renounce its ultimate importance with an urbanity that attests Austin's familiarity with the polished verse of Ben Jonson. Sharing with

Donne and Herbert both wit and scripturalism, Austin develops his themes at greater length and with some debt to Spenser in his extended metaphors. Yet he does not fall into the shapelessness that plagues the work of devotional poets like Nicholas Breton or Alice Sutcliffe. Thus, while participating in a familiar world of religious lyrics, Austin's poems are a distinctive contribution to Protestant poetics.

Austin circulated his poems among his friends, for James Howell sends thanks "for that excellent Poem you sent me upon the Passion of Christ." He adds "surely you were possess'd with a very strong Spirit when you penn'd it. . . . [A]ll the while I was perusing it, it committed holy rapes upon my Soul; methought I felt my heart melting within my breast" (211). Howell's comment suggests that a central purpose of religious poetry was to share one's fervor with others and to move them, reminding us that devotional feeling was not expected to be a private and distinctive subjectivity but a participation in the shared patterns of Christian experience. The poems that Austin wrote to capture this experience were included by his widow in four sets interspersed among her husband's meditations. The sets follow the suitable meditation, so that there is a poem titled "In Aurora Annunciationis" following a meditation on Lady-Day, and carols following the meditation on Christmas Day. Three poems on the passion and two contemplating death round out the number; I will focus primarily on these.

Except for the carols, Austin's poems are either octosyllabic or pentameter couplets, ranging from 32 to 126 lines, with the couplet generally the unit of sense. Austin is a reasonably skillful versifier. He does not pad his lines and there is little awkwardness of stress but at the same time his verse is neither leaden nor monotonous. His first poem for Good Friday, a version of the Complaint of Christ poem, will serve to illustrate:

O Man! Looke what Paine, for Thee,
Willingly I take on Mee:
See, my Bodie scourged round,
That It seemes but all, one wound:
Hanging-up twixt Earth, and Skie,
Mock'd, and scorned by All, goes by.
See my Armes, stretch'd wide, and open,
And my Sinewes torne, and broken:
While sharpe Nailes with bitter pang,
Rend my pale-Hands, where I hang:
Which Mine-owne-Waight doth not teare,
But thy waightie Sinne, I beare. . . .
View my Feete; and see my Side
Pierc'd, and ploughd with Furrowes wide.

(1–18)

The subject, as Rosemond Tuve has shown, is traditional, but the handling pithy and swift enough to capture the well-known scene effectively (24). Medieval versions usually give a stanza to each incident of the scourging, the nailing to the cross — and to each part of the body — the open arms, the feet, the side — developing one by one the traditionally associated meanings, as distinct topics. Austin, however, develops an overall unifying conceit. Most of the poem evokes the scene: See my bodie . . . see my arms . . . view my feet. But the viewer is in fact exhorted to look not so much upon the physical torment as its significance: "Oh Man! Looke what Paine for Thee/ Willingly I take on Me." Thus the first main clause is "See my bodie . . . hanging-up twixt earth and skie," with the scourging and mocking not treated as separate events but as dependent clauses, part of the full impact of seeing that torn body. Similarly, the second main clause, "See my Armes," incorporates both Christ's open embrace and the weight of human sin that tears his hands.

Austin's poem is not simply competent versifying, but gives evidence of a shaping imagination able to see a poem as a whole. His evocation of scene continues with eight lines on the mocking crowd, and then concludes:

This I beare, for Thine-amisse,
Was there ever Paine, like this?
Yes: and I doe most-feare, that:
Lest, thou Man should'st prove Ingrate.
Now thou dost but make Me smart,
But (in that) Thou kill'st my Heart.

(29–34)

This closing sets Austin's poem apart from its medieval pre-
cedents, which tend not to develop logically but to grow by
accretion of stanza and refrain ("was there ever pain like
mine"). Austin recasts the form as a unified whole that builds
to a climax in the form of a witty turn. In his treatment the
initial scene-setting takes on a larger purpose, to set up this
theological contrast between temporal, physical pain and the
true death-giving pain of humankind's ingratitude. The vivid-
ness of the evocation of the earthly pain and humiliation serves
to heighten the impact of the final couplet, which jolts read-
ers out of the contemplation of a past event into their own
immediate involvement as potential murderers of not just of
Christ's body but of his heart. The close also marks the poem
as Protestant, focused not so much on the historical cruci-
fixion as on its soteriological significance.

The construction of a poem around a conceit marks one
"metaphysical" element in Austin's poetry. In general, Austin's
conceits are rarely farfetched, and his imagery is as close to
Herbert as to Donne. And though the world his poems evoke
is usually less domestic than that in Herbert's lyrics, none-
theless Austin, like Herbert, has a gift for treating the abstrac-
tions of doctrine as everyday realities. This is most clear in
his second poem for Good Friday, which I'll therefore treat in
some detail.

This poem, his most interesting, is structured around the
implements of the Passion, often the focus for medieval medi-
tations. I have, however, found no precedent for its central
conceit: the poet describes in detail how he is crucified by the
world on the cross of fleshly temptations when he should be

crucified to the world by Christ. The poem could be seen as a
meditation (the narration of his crucifixion by the world) fol-
lowed by a prayer (that Christ crucify him to the world), of
about equal length. The speaker opens with an appeal to Christ:

> O Thou! That on the Crosse, for Me hast di'de!
> Heare now; and send me not away deni'de.
> See; I am gone a-stray, and am at losse
> When I should follow Thee, and beare thy Crosse.
>
> (1–4)

Instead, he finds his life a sinful parody of Christ's passion,
from the scourge to the burden of the cross to the *via dolorosa*,
the crown of thorns, the affixing of the hands and feet, the
sponge of gall, the lance that pierced his side, the mocking,
and the tomb, each implement becoming in the world's hands
a fleshly parody. Rather than scourging, "My Sinnes, when
they should strike, stroke with their hands," and "from thy
Paths, they turne my erring Feete." Then, instead of "thy yoke,
thy Burthen-sweete,"

> . . . mine-owne-Flesh begins
> To over-load my soule, prest downe with Sinnes
> (His heavie-load) the whole-waight of the World:
> And on the top of all this Packs [sic], sits Hee;
> On which my ghostly Enemie hath hurld
> O wretched Man! Who shall deliver Mee?
> When to the World, I crucified should bee
> The World hath crucified mee, unto Thee.
>
> (9–16)

The allegorical but homely narrative, with the Enemy not only
overloading this poor beast of burden with the whole world of
sin but perching on top, and the speaker's tone, loving, plead-
ing, and self-accusing toward Christ, clear-eyed yet compas-
sionate toward his sinful self — these remind us of Herbert.
To note resemblance is not to argue influence. Austin prob-
ably wrote in the 1620s; Howell's letter commending his
poems is dated 1628. Protestant scripturalism with its ready

stock of homely metaphors (straying from the path, Christ's yoke) is the obvious seedbed for this manner of describing a spiritual condition in physical terms. Further, Austin's casting of this condition as a narrative may reflect not only his central conceit, contrasting his crucifixion with Christ's, but also his familiarity with Spenser.[8]

Spenserian touches are evident in the section that follows. Having introduced the crucifixion conceit, Austin notes in the margins each implement of the passion as he describes its worldly parody:

Via   Along a down-steep broad way, strew'd with flowers,
         Shee drives mee gently to her wanton Bowers.
Crux   And (for a Crosse) stretched on her Bed, I lye,
         (Softer then Downe, blowne with Prosperity:)
         Whose height, is Pride; whose Depth, Hels farther Coast:
         Whose Bredth, is life: whose length, a Span at most.

                                        (17–22)

But if there is something of Spenser in the allegorizing and in the wanton bowers and seductress World, Austin gives the poem a metaphysical flavor with the sudden excursion into expansive abstractions of the sort that excite Donne's imagination. The World's bed/cross suddenly soars to the heights of Pride. It is planted not just in Hell but on Hell's farther Coast, wide as life — and, with a sudden "metaphysical" shift of perspective, brief as a span.

Another similarity to the Donne of the "Holy Sonnets" appears in the next two couplets:

Spinae When I should weare thy Piercing Wreathe of Thornes;
         My head, with wanton-Roses she adorns.
         And clings me to Her, with Embrace so loving,
         That (but Thou plucke Me thence) there is no mooving.

                                        (23–26)

Like Donne, Austin's self-description is accompanied by expostulation, reminding Christ of the speaker's dependence, his utter imprisonment by sin. Like Donne and Herbert, the

speaker describes being imprisoned by the goods and pleasures
of this world and yet perceives those worldly goods as fetters
and as empty shows, maintaining a double perspective:

Manuum	For, stead of piercing Nailes, She fills my Hands
	With the vaine-sinful-use of Coyne and Lands.
	Which, though I spread my Armes wide, to receive,
	They'l through my Hands at List, and nothing leave.
Pedum	My ready Feete, lest they should run thy Way,
	She fixes downe, in sinful-Mire and Clay.
	My Minds swift Feete, that faine thy Pathes would know,
	Shee nailes to Earth, with Thoughts most base and low.
Fel	In stead of Gall, and Sponge (to hide Her malice)
	She reaches wine in Babylonish Chalice;
Spongia	Whose golden shew, and sweete-taste, stirres up Mirth
	Able t'expunge all Goodnesse from the Earth.
Lancea	My Sides She Pierces with sharpe-Jests and Toies;
	Whence flowes a Streame of laughter, and vain-Joyes;
	Which my fond Soule, in Ruddy-Mirth doeth dye.
	And, when I thus am lifted-up on high,
Suffragium	In stead of those should mock my Sinnes with Shame
	Her Parasites (about Me) lowd proclaime
	My seeming Sparkes of Goodnesse. Jesu see
	The World hath Crucified Me (thus) to Thee.

(27–46)

If even the mind's swift feet are nailed to earth, we could ask
how the poet can recognize so fully his plight, but the stance
is quite typical of devotional "soliloquies" in which the soul
laments the Pauline doubleness of experience under which
the regenerate person feels utterly in bondage to sin and yet
longs for the freedom afforded by Christ. From this perspec-
tive, true joy is not found in the superficial humor of "sharpe-
jests and toys," the kind of "Ruddy-Mirth" based in ridicule,
not joy.[9] Nor is there true fellowship. This crucifixion by the
World comes full circle, ending in parasitic flattery where it
began with the stroking hands of his sins.

The second half of the poem repeats the use of the imple-
ments to narrate a Passion, this time a prayed-for crucifixion
of the believer to the world by Christ:

> Redeeme Me (Saviour) while I yet have Breath,
> And let Me not goe laughing (thus) to Death.
Flagellum   Thou, that thy Temple, with a Whip, didst purge
> So (wounding) cure Mee, if Thou please: and Scourge
> These Robbers from Me.
>
> (49–53)

The horrific prodigality of going laughing to death, the sense that he is in bondage to his own self-destructive folly, are reminiscent of Donne's sense of his own perversity in the "Holy Sonnets." As in the sonnets' violent imaginings of the need for divine force (rape, battering, burning) and in the scourging that burns off the sinner's rust in "Good Friday 1613," the poet can only envision freedom from sin' s bondage through purgative violence, the paradox of the wounds that cure. The apparent masochism is as much a longing to feel deeply, to experience faith as something inescapably tangible, something that renders impossible that inattentive levity of daily existence that Protestant preachers called "security."[10]

Donne's "Holy Sonnets" rarely advance beyond the desperate cry for divine violence to the sort of loving appeal common in Herbert's lyric. Austin does achieve something like Herbert's intimacy of address to Christ in his prayer that he be rightly crucified. He begs "impose thy Yoke (I pray;)/Load-Me againe; and set Me in thy-way" that he may "know the Love of Thee, which is exprest/By laying thy sweet-Crosse, where Thou lov'st best." However, Herbert's piety is almost exclusively private, focused solely on the speaker and God, or looking at the world as the storehouse of emblems for that relationship. Austin's poem encompasses the sense of Christian community found in Donne's sermons, if not his religious lyrics. Like Donne, Austin regards self as on a continuum with neighbor, and is compelled by an idea of holy emulation:

Spinae   But give Me (first) Compunction for my Sinne:
> Next, Sorrow; for Will State, my Neighbours in:
> Lastly, a Zealous-Goad of Emulation,
> To doe what's right before Thee; and so fashion

> (Of these-three-piercing-Twigs) a Crowne of Thorne
> For Me, as Thou, (and all thy Saints,) have worne.
>
> (67–72)

Donne's sermons are set apart from much evangelical preach-
ing in the early Stuart period, with its primary stress on
personal regeneration, by just this ability to intertwine com-
punction for self, compassion for neighbor, and emulation
of the examples present in Christian tradition. Austin sums
up the consequence of this passion in a particularly Donnean
manner:

> *Affixio*   Then Naile my Hands, and Feet, and make them tarry;
> That I (thy Servant) may thy-Image carry,
> And every day Thine, and My-Sufferings mix,
> Untill I grow a perfect Crucifix.
>
> (73–76)

Like Donne in "The Crosse," Austin offers a radical transform-
ation and self-application of the Roman Catholic crucifix.

I have considered only a little over half of "Christo Sal-
vatori," but it is enough to show that Austin's religious dis-
position shares a good deal with Donne's. Like Donne, Austin
exhibits his committed conformity in embracing but treating
freely older traditions of Christian devotion and poetic, and
in putting those resources to the service of a reformed sense
of the ongoing struggle between carnal and spiritual selves.
Austin's devotion, unlike much puritan piety, does not linger
in potentially isolating self-examination but situates the poet
within the universal Christian predicament just as Austin's
prose meditations found expression in his "confraternity"
of fellow believers. At the same time, while resembling Donne,
Austin creates his own poetic voice and style. I will conclude
by discussing the final set of poems in Austin's volume,
entitled "The Authors Epicedium, made by himself, upon
himselfe." In these poems as well we will find elements
reminiscent of Austin's contemporary London men of letters

and a devotional outlook at times akin to Donne's, yet a whole that is not derivative but coherently, at times wittily, accomplished.

Austin's "epicedium" consists of two poems, one on Job 17.1, "sepulchrum mihi super est," the other on Job 17.13, *"sepulchrum domus mea est."* The first poses the question, "Shall there be Nothing left me, but a Grave?" and begins by rebuking flesh and blood for "her" reluctance to acknowledge this. "Why, he asks his 'foolish-flesh' it shak'st thou at this?":

> Shrink'st thou from That, which thy best-Physicke is:
> Thou art Earth-borne; From thence, thou did'st descend,
> And here (growne sicke by sin) thou canst not mend;
> Till, toward thy Native Countrey, thou repaire,
> And draw (by Meditation) that-cold-Aire.
>
> (16–20)

The conceit and procedure are mildly reminiscent of Donne's *First Anniversary*, with its proposition that meditation on something removed from the earth may prove a physic for sin-sickness. And parts of Austin's prosecution of this conceit use the same dramatic sort of metaphor:

> Change but this Aire, and thinke upon thine End:
> Thy Sinne will lessen, and thy Soule will mend.
> For, as at Sea, (When clouds-put-out the Stars;
> When winds from Heaven; and Waves, from Earth, make Wars;
> And mad-brain'd-Saylors, all the Decks ore-whelme)
> The Pilot (sadly sitting at the Helme)
> Better-directs the Ship, Where It should goe,
> Then all their wild Endeavours can: Ev'n so,
> (When through the Worlds darke Stormes, to Heaven we tend[)]
> One quiet Pilot (sitting at the end)
> One thought of Death, our Course more right doth guide,
> Then all the Vaine-works of our Life beside.
>
> (21–32)

Austin's metaphor evokes the frantic and fruitless activity familiar from Donne's satires but in a Protestant devotional context that sees ordinary life as "Vaine-works." Austin drives home this extended metaphor with a briefer but more violent conceit that contrasts the soul-threatening distraction of earthly thoughts with the healthy contemplation of death:

> These Thoughts will make those (which our Soules-Blood quaff,
> Like Horse-leeches) strow'd ore with dust, fall-off.
>
> (33–34)

The metaphor is wonderfully apt, drawing together the medical conceit and the dust of mortality that, strewn on leech-like worldly thoughts, cause them to shrivel. Having set out the reasons for contemplation on death, Austin's poem then turns away from this dramatic imagery to urbane lines more akin to Horace's satires. The poet opens the second section with a general observation on human nature: "It ever hath belong'd to Mortall-wights,/That severall-heads take severall-delights." He then brings the observation down to the personal level, declaring:

> I joy in three; which few can discommend,
> And most, desire, next to a Constant Friend.
> And these, are they, that draw me most-along:
> A well-writ Booke; a Picture, and a Song.
> As for my Wealth, (in which some take delight)
> I got it not; Nor, doe I of It write.
> But of those-Things, Indeavour brought me to,
> I some-what know, and some-what can I doe.
>
> (47–54)

The handling of the couplet is smoother, more in the manner of Jonson, with its neatly balanced parallel clauses. Austin paints an attractive picture of a sophisticated, cultivated man, yet in writing of his three loves, he also becomes a gentle moralist, in the tradition of *tempus fugit*:

> But will they stay with Me? Oh no, alas,
> They were belov'd long-time, before I was:

> And when their Lovers dy'de, they thriv'd, and spread,
> Nor will they goe with Me, when I am dead.
> Some learned-Friend (perhaps) may, on my Herse
> Scatter some Lines; and strew the Cloth with Verse.
> Painting (perchance) may gild some Flag, or Banner,
> And sticke it on my Coffin for mine Honor.
> Musicke may sing my Dirge: and tell all Eares
> I love'd that Art, which now their Senses heares.
>
> (57–66)

But none of those things will tarry with him when the funeral ends. Further, adding a note of social criticism, Austin points out that the things that other men prize will no more accompany their owners to the grave. He evokes the consternation grim death brings:

> Will Beautie goe? Will Strength, in Death appeare?
> Will Honour, or proud-Riches tarry there?
> They All say, No. For, let grim-Death draw neare,
> Beautie lookes pale, and Strength doth faint with feare.
> There's little Wealth, or pride in naked-Bones;
> And Honour sits on Cushions; not Cold-Stones.
> Nay; aske our Friends, (that when We are in health
> Would die for love of us (or for our-Wealth)
> Marke what they set their hands to; view it well;
> [Your Friend, till death:] But once-dead; Fare-you-well.
>
> (73–82)

This shift to gentle irony, with its reminder of the folly of placing too much stock in transient things, is fitting given its addressee, the self. In its ease of manner and the way it captures the common stock of social intercourse, it reminds us of J. B. Leishman's observation that what linked Donne and Jonson was a commitment to colloquial rather than aureate diction (20). The observation of common social practice continues in the next lines:

> Nought then will tarry, but the Grave. For Note,
> How of a man new dead, Men talke by Rote.

This, was his Wife (saies one:) That, was his Land:
This, was his Friend: That, was his Building, and
This, was his Wealth; That, was his chiefest Blisse;
And Thus they talke a-while, of what was his.
But, walke the Church-yard; and thou there shalt have
Report (till Doomes-day) say; This, is his Grave.

(83–90)

The speaker is clearly one who engaged in human society and knows its ways, as Herbert exhibits his knowledge of "the ways of honour" in "The Pearl." Austin's conclusion, though, is not that he loves God despite the world's attractions. Rather, his considerations lead him to conclude if, then, this is the way of the world, "why should I therefore strive, to get such-Things?" Yet, as social critic, he notes that the closer we get to death, the more we clasp the world to us:

For dying-Men will graspe at All they see,
While they can see: When Sense failes, fare-well All;
The worlds too-heavy then; they let it fail.
Though we are Borne, Clutch-fisted:
When we die We spread our Palmes, and let the World slip by.

(102–06)

The final letting-go is natural, inevitable and oddly gentle, as the hands relax their grasping and the world slips away. Austin concludes by asking:

Since all I want here, God gives; and I have;
What can I more-expect now, but my Grave?
O cease my Flesh, for ought else to contest,
Sepulchrum Mihi solum super-est.

(109–12)

There is none of the world-hating so often characteristic of the genre here; Austin does not try to make the world distasteful. Indeed, because his meditation pays attention to what he finds good (music, friends, painting, literature), his final claim that "all I want here, God gives; and I have" sounds less like an argumentative proposition intended to refute the flesh's claims than a quiet retrospective judgment of his life. "What can I more expect now?" in this context seems the reasonable question of a man who recognizes the blessedness of his life but also its transience.

By ending here, Austin avoids the anxieties that for Donne attend the moment of death: the anxiety about judgment, the uncertainty about where the body and soul shall rest (Friedman 76). On its own, Austin's first epicedium could be a piece of classical moralism, showing the folly of grasping at ephemeral earthly goods. He turns to the second, Christian half of the equation in the second poem, which contrasts the grave with the courts of the Lord's house. There Austin once again echoes Donne, meditating that "the Wombe was (first) my Grave: Whence since I rose,/My Body (Grave-like) doth my Soule enclose" (15–16). So too his bed, with a carved tester like a funeral monument, and his very house, are like graves. And we make our bodies graves: "Creatures of sea, and Land, we in-us bury;/And at their-Funerals, are Blithe and Merry" (33–34). This more grotesque sense of the mutability of flesh leads to a contemplation of the sleep of the grave, where the forces of weather cannot touch the body, which will rise, refreshed and "cheerefully inclined" as from sleep, when the last Trump blows. But the adjectives — blithe, merry, cheerful — indicate that mutability does not trouble Austin. His vision is, ultimately, itself cheerfully inclined, participating in the comedic spirit behind the Christian view of the grave: "This House is of such fashion,/The Tenant ne're shall pay for Reparation" (77–78).

Taken together, the two poems of Austin's epicedium reflect an unstrained piety, without, perhaps, the kind of zeal that we associate with puritanism, fueled by an urgent sense of the need to battle the pervasive forces of Satan and carnality. Austin's is another sort of zeal, a thorough-going confidence that salvation provides the true perspective-glass for looking at ordinary life. He does not rip up his heart in pursuit of its devious ways; rather, he takes as a given his sinfulness and in that light explores Christ's passion and its consequences in freeing him from heedless carnality or fear of the grave. Certainly he feels the flesh's inclination toward earthly gratification and longs to feel faith equally strongly, but Austin does not demonize the body so much as he sees it as a slightly clamorous, none-too-enlightened companion who must be lectured to.

That urge to lecture, to rehearse Reformed soteriology and Christian duty in a way that touches the affections, unifies Austin's devotional output, both in verse and prose. Like Donne the preacher, he gives himself over to unpacking what lies enfolded in a verse of Scripture, but unlike Donne the divine poet, he is not anxious and perplexed. What to believe is not the issue, but rather how to express it passionately and vividly, in the Good Friday poems, or with a realism alternately philosophical, mildly satiric, and cheerful, in the epicedium. Austin's devotion expresses a piety thoroughly Protestant in its preoccupation with an experiential grasp of doctrine, and it is that foundation that lets him draw comfortably on medieval traditions. Above all, it is a confident piety.

This piety flourished during a brief stretch in the development of the Church of England when a basically Reformed doctrine and the liturgical and ecclesial compromises of the Elizabethan reformation were comfortably in place, and before the revisionary implications of Caroline religious policies re-polarized lay piety. Leah Marcus has shown us the politicization that colored Jonson's or Herrick's perception of religion. Whether we call them avant garde conformists or Laudians, their piety involved a sense that religion's role was being abused politically or destroyed as a social force, a sense to be expected among those whose piety is marginalized. Austin's poetry, or Donne's, is insulated from such political concerns: with their piety that of the established church, they were freer to focus on personal piety, on the struggle to conform the heart and the life to the religion of England. Julian

Davies has suggested that we can follow Thomas Harrab, who, writing in 1616, declared, "I call the religion of England Anglianisme, because it among the rest hath no one especial author, but is set forth by the Prince and Parliament" (Davies 5). Davies points out that the strength of the Jacobean church lay in the involvement lay people felt in its functioning. Austin's meditations, his participation in a society of lawyers who met to explicate Scripture and enflame one another's piety, and his poetry, all give credence to what Davies and I argue, that among early Stuart English Protestants there was a third alternative to puritan conformity and avant garde conformity, a conformity committed to the faith and worship of the established church that can be called Anglianism. As a poet of Anglianism, Austin deserves recognition.

8• Patrick Cary's Education of the Senses

Sean McDowell

The slim manuscript of religious verse by Patrick Cary (1623/ 24–1657) has inspired little modern scholarship for some of the same reasons that have caused other noncanonical writers to be neglected. Yet while not as popular as even William Drummond (see Robert Evans's essay), Cary can teach us about seventeenth century ideas of the human mind and about sclf-fashioning within the religious lyric tradition. Cary's verse is important in our understanding of the religious lyric for two reasons. First, its size and character call into question some of our habits of critical classification, and second, its focus on the senses suggests a model for how first-person religious lyrics generally present the creation and consecration of the self. Cary's religious verse consists of 13 poems — a little more than one fourth of his poetic canon. This percentage places him in good company. Other major and minor religious poets, such as Henry Constable, John Donne, William Habington, and Andrew Marvell, to name a few, wrote more secular poems than religious ones. But in contrast to these poets, whose reputations derive as much or perhaps more from their secular work, Cary is known primarily as a religious lyricist and very recently as a minor emblem book writer, a description that rests both on his religious poems and on a newly discovered manuscript of an emblem book.[1]

Interestingly, this evaluation seems to run counter to Cary's own final estimation of his work. Unlike fellow religious lyricists — Constable, Herbert, and Vaughan, for example — who eventually abandoned the profane muse for a Christian one, Cary's career as a poet moved in the opposite direction. Sister Veronica Delany, Cary's modern editor, argues convincingly that Cary composed his secular poems after his return from France to England in 1650, which places their composition several months after the writing of the religious verse.[2] Cary converted back to Protestantism in 1651, and so when Lucy Tomkins requested that he write out his poems in that same year, he placed more value on his secular poems. He copied them first, gave them a title (*Triviall Ballades*), and kept working with them. In 1652–53, he converted 13 of them into an emblem book (the Brotherton manuscript) by supplying each with an epigrammatic couplet and an emblematic picture of his own making — no small task. His divine poems, meanwhile, were written out in 1652, left untitled, and then left untouched, remnants of an earlier life that Cary had left behind. Despite these facts and their import, however, we tend to speak of the poet today, if we speak of him at all, foremost as a religious lyricist.

This description results partly from our perceptions of the quality of his work: we often consider his religious verse better poetry than his secular verse. Indeed, it is hard to contradict the validity of this judgement. Cary's "Triolets," for example, is more innovative and more interesting than many of his occasional ballads, which were written to be sung to various popular tunes. The same may be said for his other religious poems as well. But more significantly, this valuing also owes to the drama of Cary's life story. The religious poems are the culmination of a spiritual quest that included a conversion to Catholicism and ended in a failed three-and-a-half-month attempt at being a Benedictine novice. The story may be related briefly: at age 13, Patrick and his younger brother, Henry, were smuggled out of England by agents of their mother, Elizabeth Cary, whose Catholic views clashed with the Protestant inclinations of her eldest son, Lucius, second Lord Falkland and the boys' guardian at Great Tew.[3] For the next two years, the boys stayed in a monastic school in Paris. Then, in 1638, Patrick journeyed to Rome to seek a living. On the way, he was caught up in the religious fervor of his traveling companions and vowed that at some point in his life he would become a Benedictine monk. In Rome, his fortunes were tenuous. He subsisted as best he could while trying to procure a living from the Catholic Church. Under the patronage of Pope Urban VIII, he was given incomes from an abbey and a priory, along with other pensions. Unfortunately for Cary, though, these benefices were temporary; soon after the accession of Innocent X as pope in 1644, Cary lost these livings and was back where he started six years before. Somehow he managed to hang on in Rome for another three years without a steady income, then abandoned the city entirely and returned to Paris in 1647, where he continued to search for patronage. By 1650, his options seemed to have run out, and he followed the example of his younger brother, Henry, by entering a Benedictine monastery, thus fulfilling his earlier vow. There, at St. Gregory's Priory in Douai, amidst the hardships of his novitiate, he composed his religious poems.

The entire story is filled with financial and emotional hardships, all deriving from the poet's decision to remain true to his Catholicism. It matters little that Cary eventually switched church loyalties the following year: at the time that he wrote the religious poems, his one desire was to remain faithful to

his vow, and to do so, he undertook to reorient his life from
the pursuit of preferment in society to the study of God's
service.

The story of a would-be monk struggling to write religious
poems that incorporate forms and devices of courtly love po-
etry (Delany remarks that Cary was the first "Englishman to
use the triolet") is enough to capture the imagination (Cary
lxxvi). But before it captures mine too much, I am reminded
of Donne criticism cautioning against the indiscriminate use
of biography in interpreting poetry. In recent Donne studies,
biography — taking the form of a search for Anne Donne in
such poems as "The good-morrow" and "A Valediction for-
bidding mourning" — has been made to support Donne's be-
lief in "mutual love" and thus trump charges of misogyny.
But as Judith Scherer Herz explains, "for all the vaunted mu-
tuality of Donne's so-called serious love lyrics, there is nearly
the complete absence of another" (Herz 139). The "She" in
Donne's poems, Herz reminds us, "is our fiction," a fact we
sometimes lose sight of. Speaking more broadly of suspect uses
of biography, John T. Shawcross claims that "The good-mor-
row," "The Sunne Rising," "The Canonization," "Twicknam
garden," "Valediction of the booke," "The Exstasie," "The
undertaking," and "The Primrose" all have been suspiciously
yoked to biography at one time or another. He stresses, how-
ever, that some poems do have valid biographical readings. In
fact, such readings are sometimes necessary in our recovery
of "poetic intention," if we correctly contextualize biographi-
cal considerations and recognize that for every "personal" read-
ing of Donne's (or anyone else's) poems, we acknowledge the
possibility of an "impersonal" reading as well.

Rather than weed biography from the consideration of Cary's
poems, or labor hopelessly to attach specific poems to spe-
cific events during Cary's novitiate, I wish to capitalize on
these compositional circumstances to develop a pattern of self-
consecration that paradigmatically applies to seventeenth

century religious lyricism generally. Like the meditations on the Passion that Kari McBride discusses in her essay, Cary also participates in self-fashioning but of a different type. The character of his verse and, in particular, its emphasis on managing the senses suggest that poetry was part of his larger spiritual program, and the resulting close connection between actual spiritual training and its poetic rendering, between the novice Cary and the lyric "I," establishes a trajectory of self-definition that many religious lyrics follow, though rarely so explicitly. As Cary sought to consecrate his life, his poetry enacts the consecration of the self through the direction and correction of the will and the reorganization of desires, values, aspirations, and ideals. The initial step in this process concerns the speaker's taking charge of the senses, and the central gesture of Cary's religious poems is to educate the senses, to redirect them so they function in accordance with God's will. Only this redirection can effect the profound psychological changes that living religiously required. The pattern mirrors what Cary experienced personally, as he struggled with the worldly renunciations demanded by his Benedictine calling. And it establishes the larger psychological narrative within which so many first-person religious lyrics function as episodes.

To apprehend how Cary's educational paradigm was supposed to work, we require a precise, historically situated description of how the senses, the mind, and the affections were thought to function in those circles in which Cary (and other religious poets) traveled.[4] Cary's education of the senses depends on ideas about the proper functioning of the soul in a Christian universe and the theory that managing the five senses is an important way to marshal one's inner passions. The senses figure prominently in most Protestant and Catholic works on faculty psychology; but the conclusions of Richard Brathwaite, an Anglican, in *Essaies Vpon the Five Senses* (1620) are especially instructive in reading Cary's poems because of their clarity and because of Brathwaite's insistence about the spiritual *benefits* of the senses.[5] One must have a positive view of the senses if one follows a devotional program that treats material objects as *visible* signs signifying *invisible* Christian truths. Cary's poems suggest his worldly renunciations in the monastery presupposed this metaphysics.

Like many of his contemporaries, Brathwaite (1588–1673) believes the senses exist as gateways between the seductive diversity of the world and the often tempestuous parts of the human soul. The senses are "organs of weale or woe," in that like all instruments, they are indifferent in themselves and can be exercised for good or bad purposes (Brathwaite A3). This idea is not new; it goes back as far as Aristotle and can be found in some of the church fathers. Unlike Christians who favor strict asceticism over any kind of sensual indulgence, however, Brathwaite believes the senses can edify the soul and further spiritual good: "though the *fiue Sences* (as that deuout *Barnard* observeth) be those *fiue gates*, by which the world doth besiege vs, the Deuill doth tempt vs, and the flesh ensnare vs; yet in euery one of these, if rightly employed, is there a peculiar good and benefit redounding to the comfort of the soule, no lesse than to the auaile and vtilitie of the bodie" (57–58). Rather than deny the profound psychological influence of perceived objects, the reader should retune the senses so that they function as God intended them to. Brathwaite dedicates his five essays to illustrating how this realignment might be accomplished, each essay devoted to a different sense.

In the simplest terms, Brathwaite thinks the "eye" of the body, by which he means all the senses, must be made to serve the "eye" of the soul. While this task may appear impossible because our postlapsarian depravity causes us to be highly susceptible to the allure of worldly objects and delights, it can be accomplished if the senses are properly ordered. Ideas about ordering the senses derive from faculty psychology and its mapping of the human mind. Brathwaite does not present a full map of human faculties, and so we must turn to other writers for help in explaining his ideas. For the most part, Catholic and Anglican writers agreed about the composition and arrangement of faculties, though Puritans disagreed with Catholics in the degree of their distrust of the senses. For example, Nicolas Coeffeteau (1574–1623), a Dominican bishop, and Edward Reynolds (1599–1676), the moderate Anglican Bishop of Norwich, both arrange the parts of the soul in roughly the same way.[6] The soul consists of three *"degrees of* Soules" that become more rarefied in proportion to their cosmic importance: the "Vegetaiue" soul (responsible for growth, nourishment, and reproduction), the "Sensitiue" soul (responsible for empirical knowledge, physical desires, and movement), and the "Reasonable" soul (responsible for the other souls and the higher forms of knowledge and desire) (Coeffeteau 9). Although the rational soul is the most important (Reynolds, in fact, considers it the only part to survive death), it is inherently blind to material reality. It relies on the sensitive soul to gather, initially process, and relay empirical information, then carry out its commands. The sensitive soul gathers information with the five senses (its exterior powers) and then judges, conveys, and stores it with three interior powers — common sense, imagination, and memory (14–22). The imagination sends the forms of sense information to the understanding, one of the rational soul's two parts, which abstracts the information, compares it to universal truths, and instructs the will — the "Queene" of the soul — in the proper course of action (28). The understanding is the chief advisor because its essence is divine. For this reason, Coeffeteau, Reynolds, and Brathwaite consider it the most important faculty because only it can interpret sense information against the pressing spiritual demands of existence. For Brathwaite, the understanding, if "rightly seated," is like a "wise Pylot" who saves the ship "from splitting, mannaging all things with a prouident respect" for "what may come after" (Brathwaite 32).

The trouble comes in "rightly seating" the understanding. If the will had only the understanding to advise it, virtuous conduct would be easy. Every sensation would be analyzed with the end of creation in view, and the most laudable actions would follow. But the will, sometimes called "reason," also must deal with the passions of the soul — those turbulent internal forces that often arise as direct, unpremeditated responses to external stimuli and become tremendously difficult to control.[7] These, along with the external temptations inspiring them, are the co-conspirators in humanity's fallen state. Their influence on the will leads to immoral behavior that exacerbates the separation between the soul and God. The passions mainly exist in the natural appetite of the sensitive soul, subdivided into the "Irascible" part and the "Concupiscible" part. Some psychologists situate these parts in the heart because they think the heart is a storehouse for the passions, which travel like vapors throughout the body to create physical motion, relate important information to the soul's various parts, and generally react to what the senses communicate. In the irascible part reside the violent passions, most notably anger, ire, and indignation. This part wishes to secure honor and advantage and is characteristically aggressive in pursuit of these goals. Additionally, it is quick to perceive insults and prosecute perceived injustices: Brathwaite writes that its "prayer-booke" is revenge (38). The concupiscible part, meanwhile, is associated with covetousness and ambition, and if allowed to control behavior, it will encourage thievery, miserdom, dishonesty, and overreaching. Obviously, both parts have the capacity to corrupt individuals and those they encounter. Herein lies the spiritual danger: a person must successfully manage the passions to live truly as a Christian.

At this point, a discrepancy between the above model and some modern accounts of seventeenth century psychology should be noted because it could affect the way we read Brathwaite's characterization of the senses. The discrepancy emerges in seeing the relations between reason (the angelic, immortal side) and the passions (the bestial, human side) as entirely antagonistic. The will, corrupted by the Fall, is continually besieged by internal, animalistic forces, and it wins morally when it succeeds in failing to act on them. This view suggests that renouncing or repressing the passions is the way to sound moral conduct, a strongly Neoplatonic attitude that throughout much of the history of Christianity has informed many strands of Western asceticism. Many Anglican and Catholic writers, however, do not espouse this inherent disavowal of the passions, which they consider unrealistic. Occasionally, they display some ascetic tendencies — at one point, in fact, Brathwaite expresses the wish to become "dead to the world." But this remark must be considered against his larger purpose: to demonstrate how sensations can operate as pointers to God, if considered properly. Brathwaite, Coeffeteau, Reynolds, and others do not advocate a purgation of the passions — the *via negativa* — but a realignment and control of them through the right use of the senses, the mediators between the external world and the soul.[8] Destructive passions, like envy, must be restrained because allowing such passions to direct reason transforms humans into beasts. But love, too, is a passion, and so is joy, and these must be nurtured for the soul to be elevated heavenward. Negative passions are potentially constructive as well. For instance, anger, the facilitator of much violence, becomes useful for the Christian if it leads to zealousness for God and the abhorrence of sin. Similarly, the same covetousness that reduces a person to a thief can become "heauenly" if the person covets "righteousness, sobrietie, temperance, yea all the vertues which confer to humane perfection" (Brathwaite 41–42). The passions, for

Brathwaite, are matters of one's point of view, and to tap their productive potential, one must cultivate the most advantageous point of view, literally and figuratively.

In plain terms, Christians should subjugate the senses to the rational faculties. They accomplish this feat by attempting to steer their sensory focus: by determining what stimuli their senses fixate on and, in this way, influencing the passions produced internally. Obviously, no one can exert complete control over what the eyes see or do not see, or what the ears hear or do not hear: the world is too much filled with white noise and other distractions. But if Christians become more selective about the stimuli to which they devote attention, they can take advantage of the homeopathic relationship between the external world and their souls. They can prevent the senses from becoming enslaved to external objects that disturb the soul and instead use external stimuli to edify the soul. Admittedly, this sensual reordering sounds too idealistic to be practically useful, and Brathwaite is particularly vague in his description of the spiritual use of touch and taste. But we gain an idea of what he means in his discussions of sight, hearing, and smell. The Christian should use each of these senses meditatively, first, by focusing only on the objects that do not produce harmful passions; and second, by speculating on how these stimuli might be connected to, or reminiscent of, God, Christ, or divine truths. The correct use of hearing, for instance, entails seeking out and absorbing good advice, which seasons the understanding and contributes to the "minde's comfort" by instilling the "*Melodie of heauen*" (26–27). Conversely, harmful hearing consists of listening to gossip, flattery, slander, and lies and then acting on them in some way, either by spreading them or inflicting some form of harm on another person. In a parallel way, one's sense of smell makes the body susceptible to injurious vapors, but it also "confers" many "delights" to the mind and body: the flowers, shoots, and other harbingers of Spring vivify the concept of God's mercy because of the correspondence between Spring and the Resurrection.

The same logic obtains for the other senses, as Brathwaite describes in a poem, "The heauenly Exercise of the *fiue Sences* couched in a diuine Poem":

> Let *eye, eare, touch, tast, smell*, let euery *Sence*,
> Employ it selfe to praise *his* prouidence,
> Who gaue an *eye* to see; but why was't giuen?
> To guide our feet on earth, our soules to heauen.
> An *Eare* to heare; but what? not rests o'th'tune,
> Vaine or prophane, but melodie diuine.
> A *touch* to feele; but what? griefes of our brother,
> And t'haue a *fellow feeling* one of other.
> A *tast* to relish; what? mans soueraigne blisse,
> "*Come taste and see the Lord how Sweet he is!*
> A *smell* to breath; and what? flowers that afford
> All choice content, the *odours* of *his* word.
> "If our *fiue Sences* thus employed be,
> "We may our Sauiour *smell, tast, touch, heare, see.* (116)

The movement here is similar to the application of the senses in Ignatian, Salesian, and other forms of spiritual meditation.[9] The main difference between, say, Ignatian meditation, which George Klawitter usefully examines in Alabaster's "Ensigns" sonnets, and what Brathwaite proposes is that Brathwaite is not speaking of the sensory exploration of an imagined scene (i.e., Calvary at the time of the Crucifixion) but of sensory engagement with the everyday world. God should never be far from one's thoughts; everyday objects function as signs leading to God, but only for the properly attuned Christian.

The odds do not favor Cary's direct knowledge of Brathwaite's treatise or of some of the others. Significantly, though, all of these writers develop ideas that were widespread in their cultures and all assume a similar understanding of the spiritual dimensions of sensory experience. Indeed, we find in Cary's divine poems a sustained effort to educate the senses in much the same way that Brathwaite describes — by wedding them to virtue. Through this education, Cary articulates a newly consecrated self, a once worldly self tempered to become more godly.

Cary's divine poems are loosely organized in a sequence whose progression initially is difficult to discern. The sequence begins with "Triolets," which Delany cites as evidence that Cary composed the divine poems just before or shortly after he entered his novitiate (Cary lxx–lxxi). This poem is important because it establishes Cary's goal of effecting the psychological change that will bring him closer to God. It begins with a bold farewell to the "snares" of the world:

> 1. Worldly Designes, Feares, Hopes, farwell!
> Farwell all earthly Joyes and Cares!
> On nobler Thoughts my soule shall dwell,
> Wordly Designes, Feares, Hopes, farwell!
> Att quiett, in my peacefull Cell
> I'le thincke on God, free from your snares;
> Worldly Designes, Feares, Hopes farwell!
> Farwell all earthly Joyes and Cares.
>
> (1–8)

The speaker vows to renounce worldly investment for his "peacefull Cell" and so immediately contrasts "nobler Thoughts" with emotions predicated on earthly contexts. The juxtaposition of thoughts with fears, hopes, joys, and cares seems to indicate a subordination of affect to reason, a move we might expect in a monastic setting. A similar valuing occurs in the second stanza, where the speaker pledges to turn away from "Riches," "Power," and "Pleasures" (all understood as worldly) and toward the fulfillment of God's Law, another expected turn. So far, the first two stanzas lead us to suspect a wholly ascetic approach to the religious life — a retreat from the world, a shift toward contemplation, a purgation of the passions in accordance with God's Law. But Cary modifies this view slightly in the third and final stanza, which is crucial for understanding the poems that follow:

3. Yes (my Deare Lord!) I've found itt soe;
Noe Joyes but Thine are purely sweet:
Other Delights come mixt with woe,
Yes (my Deare Lord!) I've found itt soe.
Pleasure att Courts is but in Show,
With true content in Cells wee meete;
Yes (my Deare Lord!) I've found itt soe,
Noe Joyes but Thine are purely sweet.

                                                    (17–24)

In these lines, we discover that this form of asceticism does not entail a purgation of passions, as we might expect. This religious life has joys, its most attractive feature. The speaker's task is to learn how to acquire these joys. The tone of the poem has become rapturous; three times the speaker exclaims parenthetically, "my Deare Lord!", evidence of a heightened emotional state. The religious life includes an effort to consecrate certain passions, to make them holy, to discover "Joyes" that are "purely sweet" and not "mixt with woe," like the heavily qualified delights described in volumes of courtly songs and sonnets. The last four lines echo poems about the clandestine meetings of lovers, and the last line, "Noe Joyes but Thine are purely sweet," by itself could fit into a great many love poems of the period, as well as many other Catholic ones.

Because it favors a substitution of productive passions for harmful passions rather than the complete purgation of passions, the last stanza suggests an inner reorientation similar to what Brathwaite and others propose. Not surprisingly, in the following poems, we learn that the process begins with the education of the poet's senses, beginning with sight, often considered the highest sense. Seeing, we remember from Brathwaite, is the quickest way to stir or allay the passions. It follows, then, that any reorientation of the soul must begin with this sense.

The difference between Catholic and Calvinist views of sight (and the senses generally) centers mainly on the degree of trust placed on people's ability to gain control. Catholics, like Wright and Coeffeteau, acknowledge the dangers of misguided seeing, but rather than deny the importance of sight, they prescribe rules for its proper use. *Guided* sight has an incredible power to stir and hence manipulate the passions. As a result, seeing often figures prominently in Catholic devotion because ordering the passions strengthens the soul's virtue. Conversely, strict Calvinists never fully abandon their distrust of sight under any conditions. They fear sight because they consider the sense irrevocably corrupted and deceiving.[10] Brathwaite and Reynolds, though Anglican, lean toward the Catholic view: when used naturally — that is, when subordinated to the authority of reason — sight, like the other senses, can further the soul's development.

In the two poems following "Triolets," Cary also treats sight as beneficial. In "O that I had wings like a Dove," he explores true and false seeing in spatial terms that resonate with stories about the creation of Adam. Brathwaite, for instance, remarks that the eyes are endowed with muscles for directing them upward rather than downward, an ability which makes the eyes ideal for expressing thanksgiving. And in *Paradise Lost*, the first action of Milton's Adam is to turn his "wond'ring Eyes" "Straight toward Heav'n" (8.257). Cary's speaker, though, reports that he once gazed upward at something else: the "pompe of Kings" (4). Raised by "Ambition," he once "wish'd for wings" so he could "draw neare" to regal splendor (1–7). But now he believes "those Joyes" that once entranced him were really "Bubbles" or "Glow-wormes" that shone brightly only "When that wee/Blinded bee/By darck Follye's stupid Night" (8–14). This recognition leads to another about earthly joys:

> 4. But a nobler Light I spy,
> Much more hye
> Then That Sun which shines i'th'Sky:
> Since itt's sight, all earthly Things

I detest;
There to rest
Give, o Give mee the Dove's wings!

(22–28)

The joys he mistakenly thought were above him are actually
beneath him. Instead of gazing on them, he should direct his
attention to a much higher and "nobler" light, the Sun, and as
soon as he does so, he detests "all earthly Things." The bubbles
that once caught him explode because his perceptions have
changed. He now can see them correctly, as they really are.
Moreover, he now can fix his vision on its proper object, the
"nobler Light," which causes him to desire another set of
wings — those of the dove, a symbol for Christ and peace. He
still has aspirations of flying above his current status; only
now they accord with God's will.

"*Servire Deo, Regnare est*" (To Serve God is to be King), the
second poem on sight, develops a similar leveling of hierar-
chies. It begins on a note of incredulity: "Are These the Things
I sighed for soe, before?" the speaker asks,

For want of These, did I complayne of Fate?
Itt cannot bee. Sure there was Somewhat more
That I saw then, and priz'd att a true rate;
Or a strange Dullnesse had obscured my Sight,
And even rotten wood glitters i'th'Night.

(1–6)

With his newly reoriented sight, the speaker realizes his mis-
taken estimation of worldly things. Formerly, his eyes were
"dimme," and he admits the "Folly" of having valued what
was truly ugly (7–12). From his current vantage point, though,
precious gems are "but *Sparckling Froth*" and gold, "but *guilt
Clay*" (17–18). The changes in his estimation of worldly things
do not stop with valuables. The alteration in the speaker's
ability to see extends also to other earthly hierarchies and
results in a complete leveling of distinctions between high

and low. Ants and bees are on the same level as human beings in their corporal significance (stanza four), and those misguided aspirants who would seek power or wealth will find, if they "looke downe on them," that "*Kings* in *Thrones*, as well as *Graves*/Are but poore *Wormes*, enslav'd to vilest *Sence*" (26–28). The only true rulers on earth are those who seek God and live according to virtue.

The ideas expressed in these poems are seventeenth century commonplaces, not very instructive in themselves. Worth noticing, however, is Cary's heavy reliance on the physical sense of sight as a means of attaining a true vision of the world, one that accords with Christian truths and values perception within a divine cosmology. The first three of Cary's religious poems establish that the eye directs us on earth and should direct us toward heaven. In other words, the eye of the body should be subordinate to the eye of the soul. The next step in the consecration of the self is to extend this revaluing to the other senses and thereby take charge of the passions of the soul, which Cary begins to do in the next poem, "Whilst I beheld the necke o'th'*Dove*." In this six-stanza poem, one stanza is devoted to each sense and attempts to correct the perception of each sense by undercutting an image or object normally considered pleasing. Thus, the beauty of the dove is revealed as arbitrary because God could have given the raven the dove's coloring; the nightingale complains that her singing lacks melody; the rose's fragrance really belongs to God, not the flower; the sweetness of honey could have been "Gall" if God so willed; and the softness of a swan's down likewise exists because of God's choice. In each of these stanzas, the spiritual danger is to locate the source of sensual pleasures in the object, rather than its Creator, and to enjoy the objects for themselves, rather than for what they represent. The poem attempts to awaken an awareness of this truth, which the final stanza underscores:

> 6. *All Creatures* then, confesse to *God*
> That th'owe him all, but I.
> My *Senses* find
> True, what my *Mind*
> *Would* still, oft *does* deny.
> Hence *Pride*! out of my soule!
> O're itt Thou shalt noe more controule;
> I'le learne this *Lesson*, and escape the Rod:
> *I too, have all from* GOD.

(46–54)

When properly ordered, the senses are truer than the mind because they can contribute to this recognition, whereas reason might be unable to arrive at it unassisted. As we discover in the later poems, the mind's misapprehension of the truths the senses can reveal is caused by the psychological power of the passions, which Cary's speaker attempts to bring under control.

The last nine of Cary's poems are not as tightly grouped thematically as the first four. Cary moves from explicating the processes and insights of the senses to restoring order to the passions. In *"Crux Via Caelorum"* (The Cross is the Way to Heaven), the speaker attempts to mitigate the temptations created by *"Restraint," "Griefe," "Feare,"* and the *"Cold"* by pointing out cases of individuals who suffer more for lesser purposes than God's service. *"Crucifixus pro Nobis"* ("Crucifixion for Us"), like Robert Southwell's meditations on the Crucifixion, attempts to stir feelings of love and repentance through an emphatic recreation of Christ's life and sacrifice for humanity.[11] *"Fallax, et Instabilis"* (The Deceptive and Unstable) discourses on the constant mutability of worldly things and cautions readers to

> 3. Lett None then fix his heart
> Uppon such trifling toyes;
> But seeke some object out,
> Whose change Hee n'ere may doubt;
> There, let Him place his Joyes.

(27–31)

The reader should not be led to "trifling toyes" by his heart, which represents the passions, but should instead direct his "Joyes" to the one constant, God. While not explicitly about the passions, *"Nulla Fides"* (Non-Existent Faith), the following poem, emphasizes the precariousness of corporal life and establishes a context for the next poem, *"Stulte, hac nocte animam tuam repetunt a te"* (Fool, this night your soul shall be claimed from you), Cary's most complete description of psychological disorder and its effects:

> 1. What use has Hee made of his Soule
> Who (still on Vices bent)
> N'ere strove his *Passions* to controule;
> But, hum'ring them, his Life has spent?
> Pray tell mee, if I can
> Call such a very *Thing* as that is, *Man?*
> For since that just as *Sense* has bidde
> Itt *doe,* or *leave;* Itt *wrought,* or *ceas't;*
> And would not heare when *Reason* chidde,
> Or her commands reguard the least;
> Itt might have liv'd e'ene as Itt did,
> And yett have beene a *Beast.*
> 2. Had Itt a *Lyon* beene; Just soe
> Itt would roare out, and fume:
> Were Itt a *Peacocke,* Itt would goe
> Just thus, admiring itt's owne Plume:
> Or if Itt were a *Goate;*
> Thus, onely on base pleasures Itt would dote.
> More then this *Thing,* the ravenous *Hogge*
> Searches not, where his gutts to fill;
> Nor att a Stranger's Hound, the *Dogge*
> O'th'House more snarle or *envy* will;
> Then this odde *Thing* (though apt to cogge)
> Repine att Others still.
> 3. The *Crow,* that hoardes up all she finds;
> The *Ant,* that still takes paynes;
> Doe nothing more, then Hee who minds
> But how to fill his Baggs with *Gaynes.*
> The *Snayle,* & *Sluggerd* bee
> Within alike; tho'in shape They disagree.
> Call not that *Thing* then, *Man;* even as

> Thou wouldst not injure by the same
> *MAN*, who like *God* created was;
> *GOD*, who for *Man's* sake, *Man* became;
> But, since soe much o'th'*Beast* Itt has,
> Call Itt, by Itt's owne Name.
>
>   (1–36)

Cary's argument here is identical to Brathwaite's: people not in control of their passions, people with disordered souls, are no longer human; instead, they are beasts. This degradation occurs because the senses roam without the guidance of the will and exacerbate feelings of anger, pride, lust, gluttony, envy, covetousness, and sloth (all figured as creatures). When this happens, *"Man"* no longer deserves the name or its prelapsarian connection to God's image. One should call a beast what it is, a beast.

By now, this line of thinking should sound familiar. Christians gain control of themselves through their control of the senses, an act of will. Cary's advice to Christians (and to himself) is, "Open thy selfe, and then looke in" (*"Dirige via meas Domine"* 1). External objects, when perceived from a religious perspective, can reinforce love and lessen pride and despair. Only through such intense self-scrutiny can Christians remove the obstacles posed by their sinful natures and dedicate themselves to God. The rest of Cary's poems continue to explore these themes.

Joseph Hall writes that "Only Christianity" has the "power" to restrain the passions because "with our second birth" Christianity "gives us a new nature: so that now, if excesse of passions bee naturall to us as men, order of them is naturall to us as Christians" (Hall 100). We see in Cary's divine poems a pattern for the creation of this new nature, and this self-consecration applies to other seventeenth century religious poems, particularly those written in first-person. This pattern emerges from a set of realizations. First, the nonreligious speaker learns of his or her fallen state and its consequences.

He or she has forgotten his or her role as God's servant, has turned away from God, and is a slave to the passions and worldly objects in themselves. The materialistic fixation creates false hierarchies that are reinforced by the five senses and the passions they inspire. To change this state of affairs, the person must educate the senses so that they reveal — not obscure — the true nature of human existence in a Christian universe. Then, the Christian must consecrate the self in light of this realization, placing faith in God, renouncing false hierarchies and worldly lures, and restoring order to the disordered parts of the soul. This new order is not devoid of passion but encourages those passions that lead to spiritual good. After the senses are made to pursue virtue, and the passions no longer interfere, the Christian can live with the goal of immortality in mind.

Undoubtedly, the education of the senses outlined here has points of contact with the poetry of meditation described by Louis L. Martz, Anthony Raspa, Anthony Low, and numerous others. It is especially helpful in explaining what we mean by "meditative" in those poems that do not follow the structures of well-defined meditative or devotional practices but do reference psychological processes nonetheless. Virtually every seventeenth century religious lyricist at one time or another assesses the turmoil of the spiritual life in terms of the passions and the reorientation of the senses, and virtually every religious lyricist attempts to counter spiritual distress by enacting the consecration of the self. At the end of Donne's "A Hymne to Christ, at the Authors last going into Germany," for example, the speaker's "Divorce to All" necessitates his removal of himself from the "sight" of temptations because this is the only way "To see God only" and "to scape stormy dayes," by which he means days filled with psychological strife (22–28). Many of Herbert's poems about spiritual distress ("Giddinesse", "Nature", "Sinnes round", "Deniall", the "Affliction" poems, etc.) similarly rely on references to the passions and the dire effects of misapplied sensation to depict internal disorder. Vaughan's explorations of nature presuppose that the senses aid the soul in learning about transcendence. Marvell also values sensory experience in a similar way in his consecration of pastoralism. And the list goes on. Unfortunately, the educational paradigm is frequently not as explicit in the work of canonical poets and becomes hard to recognize. Donne, Herbert, Vaughan, and others invest themselves in the same sort of sensory education and consecration of the self that Cary found personally and poetically necessary. But without Cary's example and the psychological background Cary relies on, their efforts appear more abstruse than they really are. Cary's contribution to the religious lyric tradition cannot be called major, though it can be missed. Cary's 13 religious poems place emphasis on one of the most fundamental problems of religious experience: how to live spiritually in the alluring material world. His poems develop a simple, honest solution to the problem, one that possesses a great deal of explanatory value for reading the work of other poets, both canonical and less well-known. For this reason, his work does not deserve the almost complete obscurity with which it has been greeted for more than 300 years.

9• *Penseroso* Triptych
"Eliza," An Collins, Elizabeth Major

Patricia Demers

Sir Anthony Van Dyck's canvas, "Charles I in Three Positions," supplies an emblematic entry to my discussion of three little-known poets of the Commonwealth. Its iconic significance, adaptability as a way of seeing one subject in at least three ways, and associations with contemporary politics and intrigue make the portrait an instructive parallel to an examination of three women as historically positioned subjectivities grappling with issues of selfhood, loss, and corruption. Completed in 1636 and dispatched to Bernini in Rome with the commission from Henrietta Maria, a commission authorized by Pope Urban VIII, that the sculptor carve, in Charles's own words, *"il Nostro Rittratto in Marmo"* [our portrait in marble] (Millar, *Age*, 63), Van Dyck's penetrating study of different temperaments as well as angles struck Bernini with what he recorded as "something of funest and unhappy which the countenance of that Excellent Prince foreboded" (Evelyn 335). Designated as "now rare," "funest" means "causing, portending death or

evil" (OED). The royal couple admired Bernini's marble, re-
ceived at Oatlands in the following year (though ultimately
lost in the Whitehall fire of 1698), for its "likenesse and nere
resemblance . . . to the King's countenance" (Millar, *Age*, 63).

Presenting its subject in profile, frontally and in three-quar-
ter view, with three differently colored doublets, and creat-
ing dramatic contrasts between the blues and greys of the sky
and the warm sienna shadows around the heads (Millar, *Van
Dyck*, 65), this portrait, "combining majesty with a melan-
choly that seems to presage the King's eventual martyrdom"
(Starkey, "The Real Image," 18), also has the quality of being
"eerily modern in its fluid feeling for how one individual, even
a kingly individual, can change depending upon one's perspec-
tive" (Stevens, "Master of the Grand Manner," 112). Although
"no image has had a greater impact on historical perceptions
of the king's character and hence of opinions about the nature
of his personal rule than this painting" (Wheelock, *Van Dyck
Paintings*, 288), many viewers reject the interpretation of
mopish melancholy in Charles's "unfocused and contempla-
tive" gaze (Brown, *Van Dyck*, 176). Roy Strong, convinced the
explanation is a retrospective one, draws attention to accounts
of Charles's "smiles not sorrow" (Strong, *Charles I on Horse-
back*, 33–34). Christopher Brown comments on the aura "of
royal grandeur" (176), Arthur Wheelock, on "the mystique of
divinity" (290), and Graham Parry, on Van Dyck's other fa-
mous canvases of Charles[1] as "an active and enterprising, . . .
a stirring, watchful monarch in charge of events" ("Van Dyck
and the Caroline Court Poets" 249–50). Certainly other trip-
tychal studies, Lorenzo Lotto's portrait of a jeweller in three
positions and Philippe de Champaigne's of Cardinal Richelieu
with its "arrogant swish of silk" (Starkey 18), may have served
as inspiration or competitive goad to Van Dyck. But the
uniquely Caroline response to the artist's closeness to the King
and assumed collusion in papal plans to return England to
the Catholic fold was the Puritan criticism of attempts "to

seduce the King himself with Pictures, Antiquities, Images &
other vanities brought from Rome" (Brown 174–76). The bio-
graphical, diplomatic, and sacramental import of the depic-
tion makes it a source of continuing intepretive exercises.

This painting of a famous subject, however, has not yet been
linked to three obscure women who wrote in the aftermath of
the regicide in the 1650s. I believe there are compelling rea-
sons to pursue relationships between ways of seeing Charles
and of seeing "Eliza," An Collins, and Elizabeth Major as
unique — though connected — subjectivities. With the trip-
tychs of Lotto, Champaigne, and Van Dyck himself, viewing
strategies can range from collapsing the side panels into the
center and focusing on hinging details to panning from left to
right, tracing the adjustments, shifts, and transpositions. Be-
cause information about the author of *Eliza's Babes*, Collins,
and Major is so sparse, it would be impossible to try to match
the detail of Van Dyck's oils, his small grisaille portraits, or
his pen and sepia studies. Perhaps the closest analogy, allow-
ing for a necessary blurring of outline, is with his black chalk
sketches on blue paper. Like the eerie modernity of Van
Dyck's portrait, the apprehension and spiritual abjection of
these women can readily engage and, at times, challenge
our post-modern sensibilities. Of course, unlike Van Dyck's
portrait, they call for recovery and, in a sense, preliminary
examination.

And what of Milton's companion piece? "Sober, steadfast,
and demure" ("Il Penseroso" l. 32), "Eliza," Collins, and Ma-
jor were all acquainted with "a sad Leaden downward cast"
(l. 143) and retired from "Day's garish eye" (l. 141). Having walked
"the studious Cloister's pale" (156), they were also numbered
among the privileged "11 per cent of women" (Spufford, "First
Steps in Literacy," 409) who could read *and* write, the con-
junction demarcating significant differences in class and
opportunity.[2] Likely from gentry or merchant/tradesmen
families, where through factors of birth or residence they also

knew London, they can thereby be identified as "members of the fully literate minority" (Cressy, "Literacy in pre-industrial England," 239). The Bible and the physiologically suffering self provide their meditative texts, which themselves testify to "the porosity of private and public spheres" (Schwoerer, "Women's public political voice," 58). Yet they were not unaware or unappreciative of jocund merriment and what Collins terms "spirituall Mirth" ("Another Song exciting to Spirituall Mirth" 50). Their poems are not point-for-point Miltonic studies in contrast nor, to move from doubles back to triples, do they share much with the middle ground of the Handelian pastiche, *Il Moderato*.[3] *Penseroso* rules, in the sense that Marc Berley explicates Milton's depiction of "the condition of waiting," the poet's "relation to divine harmony" and "wait for Christ, for redemption" ("Milton's Earthy Grossness" 155), and in the sense that they share with Milton the idea Eugene Cunnar has described as "the moral burden of artistic choice" ("*Ut Pictura Poesis*" 95).

"Eliza," Collins, and Major experience religious melancholy, a designation in need of some specificity and comparative positioning. Often disconsolate and abject, in Julia Kristeva's taxonomy of being "excluded" and disturbing "identity, system, order" (*Powers of Horror* 2, 4), these early modern women fashion an idiosyncratic faith that sustains and buoys their burdened and occasionally aphasic spirits in ways emphasizing their distance from the *jouissance* and material *négativité* of feminist psychoanalysis. Importantly, they never succumb to despair or unorderable cognitive chaos; nor do they add to the ranks of the Dantesque "woeful people who have lost the good of the intellect" in the "city of grief" (*Inferno*, 3.22–23). Because it dwells in so many shadows and seems so detached from postmodern, post-Christian patterns, the melancholy they instantiate requires attentive reconstruction. Among the "psychological symptoms" they share with the "disturbed patients" treated by the seventeenth century astrological

physician Richard Napier are a religious preoccupation, call-
ing on God, inability to pray, doubt of salvation, sadness, fear-
fulness, and weeping (MacDonald, *Mystical Bedlam*, 244).
Significantly, in the gender-specific tabulation of cases pre-
pared by Michael MacDonald, Napier's women patients
showed higher instances of each of these symptoms.

Melancholy becomes what Judith Anderson, in her study
by the same name, would call a word that matters, a "frozen"
(7) word whose meanings must be thawed. Anderson explores
both Plutarchan and Rabelaisian senses of "frozen," through
the *Moralia's* account of the fate of Plato's writings and the
delayed perception of the meaning, when "people heard in
the summer what they had said to one another in the winter"
(1. 418–21), and through Rabelais's revisiting of the fable in *Le
Quart Livre*, when Pantagruel throws on the deck "whole
handsful of frozen words" which are "warmed between [their]
hands . . . [and] melted like snow" (569). The retold fables
intimate the partiality, historical contingency, and material
consequences of a single, fixed, or frozen understanding of
melancholy. Several explorations of melancholia as figured by
male artists in the early modern period exist. In scanning the
melancholy landscapes in Montaigne, Bacon, and Burton, as
well as Milton and Browne, William Engel reminds us that
"writing was the prerogative of the melancholy man" (*Map-
ping Mortality* 116); he concentrates on the "ontotheological
construction and prospect" (3) of death as displayed through
"the aesthetic of anamnesis," by which he includes the var-
ied "disposition of fragments drawn from the common store-
house of inventions" (229). Representations of melancholy
have "potent psychological effects to this day" (418), as John
Moffitt notes, in "Who is the Old Man in the Golden Hel-
met?," his study of the relief decorations on the antique hel-
met in "the modified, or iconographically reduced, portrait of
Saturn" (426), attributed to the school of Rembrandt (c. 1650).
Lynn Enterline looks at the "ever labile fantasies of male

melancholia" (*The Tears of Narcissus* 309) as an index of the early modern sorrow of "the self's recurrent alienation from itself" (305).

Yet despite the surge of critical interest in early modern women's writing, no extensive study of female melancholia has appeared.[4] Is melancholia a gendered concept? Were expressive, transformative opportunities available to women within the confines of established or contestatory belief communities? Did social turbulence affect or promote spiritual sadness and yearning? What characteristics distinguished the poetic, meditative autobiographies of these religious women from the political activism of others? This essay attempts to address such issues.

The inward, inherently performative, though solitary, religious melancholy of "Eliza," Collins, and Major is the product of unique sensiblities and defining cultural circumstances. It is quite distinct in dimension, voice, and recognition from such Shakespearean portraits as Jaques's double dose of sucking "melancholy out of a song, as a weasel sucks eggs" (*As You Like It*, 2.6.13), Falstaff's ironic gaming to be "as melancholy as a gib cat or lugg'd bear" (*I Henry IV*, 1.2.82), and Hamlet's dismissal of visual "trappings" as "forms, moods, shows of grief" (*Hamlet*, 1.2.82). Their devotional temperament is also removed from the humoral psychology of melancholy, whether in the Aristotelian grid of cold and dry atrabiliousness or with the admixture of "the Platonic conception of frenzy" (Klibansky, *Saturn and Melancholy*, 17).

While some readers discern in Milton's introduction of the advocate of "divinest" (l. 12) Melancholy "the positive and, as it were, spiritual values ascribed to Melancholy" (Klibansky 229), I want to insist on a specifically religious form of melancholy that goes well beyond "heightened self-awareness."[5] Although Burton inveighed at length against "solitariness, fasting and that melancholy humour" as "the causes of all hermits' illusions" (Burton 3.343), he also discussed the real, if rarely experienced, benefits in "sobriety and contemplation join[ing] our souls to God," and cited Erasmus and Bonaventure to corroborate: "'Ecstasis is a taste of future happiness, by which we are united unto God'; 'a divine melancholy, a spiritual wing,' Bonaventure terms it, to lift us up to heaven" (343).[6] Pascal viewed melancholy as a sign of lost innocence, referring to the sense of "void" and "infinite abyss" rhetorically in *Pensées*, written during the 1650s. "What does this greed and helplessness proclaim," he asked, "except that there was once within us true happiness of which all that now remains is the outline and empty trace?" (52). Almost two centuries later Kierkegaard's philosophical and religious writing explored the idea of religious melancholy in a distinctly Pascalian rather than Burtonian sense, thus transforming theology into "an anthropology of self-knowledge" (Ferguson, *Melancholy and the Critique of Modernity*, 217); in For *Self-Examination/Judge for Yourself!*, Kierkegaard depicted the moment of nakedness and intoxication, in which the "sensible, sagacious and level-headed" are abandoned, as "being before God" and "totally com[ing] to oneself in the transparency of soberness" (106). Sobriety, which may appear to be its opposite to unaffected observers, and eschatological insight are two salient features of the religious melancholy of "Eliza," Collins, and Major. Kristeva herself would recognize their sadness, their spiritual *tristitia*, as "mystical, . . . as a means toward paradoxical knowledge of divine truth" (*Black Sun* 8).

Certainly these women had just cause for wanting to transcend their situation. All suffered emotional or physiological pain. With grieving acceptance "Eliza" addresses the Lord about the death of her brother: "A Brother and a friend was he,/But much more thou wilt be to me" ("Upon the losse of my Brother" 38).[7] A similar resignation colours her otherworldly response to marriage and preference for the relatively painless birth of her poetry to the delivery of human offspring.

> Lord! if thou hast ordain'd for me,
> That I on earth must married be:
> As often I have been foretold,
> Be not thy will, by me contrould.
> And if my heart thou dost incline
> Children to have, Lord make them thine,
> Or never let't be said they'r mine.
> I shall not like what's not divine.
> I no ambition have for earth,
> My thoughts are of a higher birth.
> The Souls sweet Babes, do bring no pain,
> And they immortalize the name. ("On Marriage" 42)

Although her husband proves very sympathetic, "As if of heaven, he were elect," and she sees herself removed from the plight of most wives who "live in strife" ("The Change" 43–44), she returns to the matter of progeny quite insistently in comparing her intellectual offerings "to a Lady that bragg'd of her Children":

> Thine doth delight in nought but sin,
> My Babes work is, to praise heav'ns King.
> Thine bring both sorrow, pain and fear,
> Mine banish from me dreadfull care. (55)

The perils of pregnancy were real for early modern women; the increasing number of English funerary monuments featuring mothers and babies and of prayers devoted especially to women in labour[8] point directly to the imminence of death in childbirth.

Collins and Major disclose other physiological torments. Collins's references to her physical debility, though oblique, are more succinct than "Eliza's". "Restrained from bodily employments," "enforced . . . to a retired Course of life" ("To the Reader"), "[b]eing through weakness to the house confin'd" ("Preface"), she admits but refuses to dwell on chronic ill health:

Even in my Cradle did my Crosses breed,
And so grew up with me, unto this day,
. . .
'Twere to no end, but altogether vain,
My several crosses namely to express,
To rub the scar would but encrease the pain,
And words of pitty would no griefe release.

("The Discourse" 4–5)

The autobiographical information gleaned mainly from the opening of the verse portion of Major's work reveals that her mother died in Major's infancy, that she was brought up until age 15 by "a godly and careful father," that after 10 years of either service or tutelage (or both) in "a great and honorable family" Major was crippled and forced to return home, where she wasted time and money with dissolute companions who "pretended skill in lameness" (*Sin and Mercy* h2–h3).

Eliza's Babes: or the Virgins-Offering. Being Divine Poems, and Meditations (1652); An Collins's *Divine Songs and Meditacions (1653)*; and Elizabeth Major's *Honey on the Rod: or a comfortable Contemplation for one in Affliction with sundry Poems on several Subjects (1656)* appeared in the space of five tumultuous years following the regicide and the defeat at Worcester. On the one hand, it is easy to dismiss these private, devotional documents as entirely unconnected with the public realm: with a two-year war with the Netherlands (1652–54) and English victories at Channel (1652) and Texel (1653) and defeat at Dungeness (1652); with the business of successive Rump, Barebones, and Protectorate Parliaments (1653–56); with the pacification of Ireland through the Cromwellian Act of Settlement (1652) and the readmission of Jews to England (1655); with the installation of Cromwell as Lord Protector (1653) and forcible pledges of loyalty called "Engagement" and "Recognition" (1654); and with the collapse of La Fronde (1653), the abdication of Christina of Sweden (1653), the start of another war with Spain (1655), and the capture of a Spanish treasure fleet at Cadiz (1656). One chronicler of this "chaotic political scene" has indicated that it moved from fragmentation to shattering, ushering in "true anarchy — a multiplicity of ideologies and a total lack of political direction" (Skerpan, *The Rhetoric of Politics*, 157).

On the other hand, it is worth considering how the very turbulence of these times, as Lois Schwoerer argues, moved women "to speak out" (61). Although she mentions none of this paper's trio and attends to the political voices of Katherine Chidley, Elizabeth Poole, Mary Howgill, Mary Cary Rande, and Hester Biddle, she suggests reasons for their "violation of normative rules of conduct" (61) that apply equally to women's political commentary and meditative poetry: "religion animated and empowered women, giving them confidence and a sense of responsibility" (61) and women's social origins and roles in the family economy "helped them escape the full weight of the restrictions mandated by ideal female behavior" (62). *In Unbridled Spirits: Women of the English Revolution: 1640–1660*, Stevie Davies chronicles the radical spirits of female Separatist dissenters, Leveller activists, and Quaker missionaries engaged in "petitioning, marching, agitating, producing, and dispersing subversive books" (73); but Davies also registers an awareness of women's indoctrination "in a culture of female guilt," where their souls experienced a "familiar Reformation dilemma, in the binary world of a God whose embrace inexplicably gave way to the ice of his absence or the fire of his wrath" (39–40).

Yet because the work of "Eliza," Collins, and Major concerns mainly an eschatological rather than a political economy, is it also necessary to pause to weigh the appropriateness of the criterion that their poetry would reflect these circumambient conditions? Debora Shuger offers the plausible reading that domestic, political, and sacred hierarchies "mirror and participate in one another" in complex ways (*Habits of Thought* 255). In addressing these hidden ligatures and the fact that "inwardness is itself shaped by culture," she proposes, "The public character of language guarantees that the relation between 'inside' and 'outside' more resembles a Möbius strip than nesting boxes" (254). Kristeva reminds us that the space of the abject is "braided, woven, ambivalent" (*Powers of Horror* 10), while Engel addresses the importance of what the author and reader already know, as melancholic texts open up "a space from within which we can consider the place we occupy every day, between the visible and the invisible worlds" (233). By contrast, Elaine Hobby's sustained treatment of "Eliza," Collins, and Major stresses their political as distinct from theological situation, presenting them as dutiful, confined, passive women, faithfully promoting "highly restrictive ideologies" and "an analysed self-policing which vindicates the fetters of feminine duty" (*Virtue of Necessity* 54, 74).

As I read "Eliza," Collins, and Major, the culture of violence and chaos they inhabited, where the fates of occlusion, neglect, and retirement had been assigned to them, and the theological inculcation of guilt did not heighten feelings of neediness and powerlessness. Not as prisoners of affect but as builders of poignant, therapeutic catharses, they produced work whose "prosodic economy, interaction of characters, and implicit symbolism constitute a very faithful semiological representation of [their] battle with symbolic collapse" (Kristeva, *Black Sun*, 24). I think it is as important to disentangle stereotypes of melancholy as passive and impotent in a consideration of the work of these women as it is to allow for the reading of inscrutably divine majesty and, perhaps, doomed foreboding in Van Dyck's portrait of Charles. These women promote the private space of the inward, "pneumatic self" (Shuger 257), where "Eliza" experiences the curing and drawing out of "that distemper" and "tormenting," "unrulie" passions ("On Earthly Love" 66) to be free to declare "So though on earth, I as in heaven shall be" ("The Heart" 30), where An Collins proclaims that "blessed beames my mind eradiates, . . . / And so . . . communicates/Celestiall health to ev'ry faculty" ("The Discourse" 8) and prizes "internall ornaments, . . ./ Though all things pleasing outward sense/Should utterly forsake [me]" ("A Song declaring that a Christian may finde tru Love only where tru Grace is" 39), and where Elizabeth Major anticipates liberation as she implores "unlink my heart," "unfix me, Lord, from earth," and "from thick clay unclog my drossy heart" (*Honey on the Rod* 182).

Each of these authors produced a single work through which we glean whatever information we have about her. There are great differences in this triptych: the psychological dynamics of their connections to family, community and state realities are clearly perceptible, and so is the theocentric emotionality by which they assume agency and subjectivity in their writing, by which they form the repetitive rhythms of their verse into uniquely "frugal musicality" (Kristeva, *Black Sun*, 33).

Speculating that "Eliza" may have "come from a dispossessed Royalist family" of "Calvinist sentiments,"[9] the editors of *Kissing the Rod* draw an affiliation between her and Collins and Major, "two other religious women poets who would adopt the metaphor of literary babies to excuse their pride in their work" (Greer *et al.* 142, 144). Although "Eliza's" evocation of the humility topos is clear in the reference to her "frail pencell" ("To my Sister, S.S." 28), equally apparent is her assertiveness in declaring "publique thankes" and in commending her babes' health and attire: "you want none of your limbs, and your cloaths are of rich materials" ("To the Reader"). Self-possession — comparable to that of a prophetic mission — delineates this authorial persona, especially in laughing detractors "to scorne":

> And now I dare not say, I am an ignorant woman, and unfit to write, for if thou wilt declare thy goodness and thy mercy by weak and contemptible means, who can resist thy will. My

> gracious God, I will be now so farre from being unwilling to doe it, that I will not rest till I have done it, for in all ages thou wilt not leave thy selfe without a witnesse of thy mercy and goodnesse to thy children, and therefore I will send out my words to speak thy praise, and as thou hast made them comfort to some troubled mindes, so I wish they may be to more, when they shall see the truth of thy mercifull dealing with me, and how thou hast made me so happy in this world, as my heart can wish. ("The Support" 75)

Integral to such happiness has been "Eliza's" mother, whom she commends as a "souldier" of Christ who "used her authority by love, to bring her children under the obedience of that Generall, whom she serv'd, and to make me love him in my childhood, whom her experience had taught to love and admire" ("The invincible Souldier" 79). She also addresses poems to two sisters, identified only by initials, and a "bill of thanks" to a preacher, "Mr. C" (47–48), for his instruction.

As for having a voice in the public sphere, "Eliza" is the most assertive of the trio, addressing verses to Charles I advising him not to "affright" her Babes "with war" and to "be not too rigid" ("To the King. writ, 1644" 23), to his sister Elizabeth, Queen of Bohemia, in admiration, and to Cromwell, whose virtue she challenges to an equity match:

> But why doe I complain of thee?
> 'Cause thou art the rod that scourgeth mee?
> But if a good child I will bee,
> I'le kiss the Rod, and honour thee;
> And if thou'rt vertuous as 'tis sed,
> Thou'lt have the glory when thou'rt dead.
>
> ("To General Cromwell" 54)

Her promise to be "a good child" is not really as regressive or infantilizing as it might at first sound; obedience is predicated on Cromwell's ability to "whip . . . the Lawyer from his fee" and "Free us from . . . Laws Tyranny." Without doubt "Eliza's" voice is the least melancholic and most assured. Depicting herself "sett free from thrall" and "fild . . . with contemplation" ("The Triumph" 6), "cur'd of the plague of [her] own heart" ("My Redemption acknowledged" 88) and en route to the "blessed Tabernacle of security" ("Security in Danger" 100), she rhapsodizes about being "unwrapt" from the "robes of earth" ("Luke 20.36. In that world they shall be equall to the Angels" 20).

With An Collins we move to a more intimate, certainly more discursively present, acknowledgement of Melancholy as an instructive, elevating state. Sorrow serves "as springing raine/To ripen fruits, indowments of the minde" ("The Preface" B). When her mind, "scorched with distracting care," seeks the shade "which fruitlesse Trees, false fear, dispair/And melancholy made," she feels strengthened and confident in this bleakness: "Sith I enjoy the Spring,/Though Sesterns dry I find" ("A Song Expressing their happinesse who have Communion with Christ" 28, 29). Seeking the retired shade of Melancholy is one thing, but resigning oneself to "excessive worldly Griefe" ("Another Song" 61) is unacceptable in Collins's theology. Such a state "devouers" the soul "and spovles the activenesse of all Powers" ("Another Song" 61), as "sad Discontent and Murmors" cause the creature to destest "all delight":

> His Wits by sottish Folly
> Are ruinated quite
>   ("Another Song exciting to Spirituall Mirth" 51)

Collins's engagement with the Cromwellian Protectorate, proclaimed in the year of her publication, is critical, for she devotes two lengthy songs to the topic. Recalling prefatory images about "the scum of frothy braines/Perhaps extracted from old Heresies,/New form'd with Glosses to deceive the eyes" and the perverseness of "a spider generacion" whose "touch occasions deprivacion" ("The Preface" A3, B), she holds forth against the false interpretation of Scripture and the "Losse of lightsom Liberty," and prophesies the end of this "new Babell":

Prophanesse must be fully grown,
And such as it defend
Must be ruind or overthrown,
And to their place defend,
The Sonns of strife their force must cease,
Having fulfild their crime,
And then the Son of wished peace
Our Horizon will clime.

> ("A Song composed in time of the Civill Warr,
> when the wicked did much insult over the godly" 66)

Elizabeth Hageman sees "radical" potential in Collins; "what is on the surface an 'innocuous' spiritual autobiography may in fact be a book offering political inspiration to those who share her religious beliefs" ("Women's poetry in early modern Britain" 195). Sidney Gottlieb, who introduces Collins as "no mere statue of Patience," finds "much evidence of her boldness and engagement in public issues throughout the volume" (*An Collins* x). *Kissing the Rod*'s editors maintain that Collins was "devoutly anti-Calvinist, if not actually a Catholic" because of her "belief in the innate attraction of the soul to goodness" (148, 154), while Eugene Cunnar posits that her "Protestant theology" was "influenced by Calvinism" ("An Collins" 49). True, she is the least preoccupied with the mire of sin and peccant fallibility. She is also the most accomplished of these poets, devising the 103 stanzas of "The Discourse" in rhyme royal with appended biblical glosses, ballad stanzas, sestets and octaves, and creating original, if not experimental, metaphors, as in the image of the wind that "sweetly our soules refrigerates" ("This song sheweth that God is the strength of his People, whence they have support and comfort" 54) — a usage not included in the three pre-1660 examples of "refrigerate" cited in the OED.[10]

Beyond the indirect endorsement of the Protectorate through Joseph Caryl's licensing[11] and the text's overall ethical imperative to resist surrounding corruption, *Honey on the Rod* contains no specific or oblique reference to national events occurring at the time of the inner experiences related. Having "unmasked" (h5) sin and confessed herself "a long and a perverse wanderer" (26), Elizabeth Major catalogues her own inconstancy and vulnerability without apparent sense of progress through this private, intensely felt exploration of sin, sorrow, and self; she dispenses with most particularities to concentrate on interior dialogues between Soul and Consolation and Soul and Eccho about overarching issues of worthiness and correction. In this circular, recursive narrative, her torment is real and all the more compelling for its nonpatternable untidiness, the competing flashes of buoyancy and melancholy upending any program of spiritual progress and revisiting, complicating the surety of such linearity. Major is alert to the multifariousness of the rod, presenting it as a cordial and corrective, according to the requirements of the situation and her own disposition — dejected, obstinate, amenable, grateful. In arguing "A Particular Application of the Book of Jonah" she casts herself ("alas for I do *Nineveh* out-sin") as the principal impediment to the merciful efficacy, the instructive cordial, of the rod:

> . . . unless he send
> A rod me to prevent, then for a time
> I may observe his will; but if my minde
> He's pleas'd to cross, I'le grumble, fret, nay cry,
> And in that passion of him wish to die:
> My nature's grown so bold, that I with him
> Dare expostulate, nay plead it is no sin
> To wish not to be, rather then to lie
> Under his rod; no, sooner let me die;
> If he in mercy me my errors tell,
> My answer is, I know that I do well;
> I sin and grieve thee, still thou wilt be kind,
> Wilt mercy shew, though oft against my minde. (209)

Major not only does not shrink from pain, as the frequent associations of the trope of the rod with wounds, darts, and imprisonment witness, she also uses metaphorical language to call for demonstrative, appropriative, genuinely rough intervention. Acknowledging that "the filthy keeping of the cabinet may soil the Jewel," she anticipates "a hard pollishing before it come to a right lustre" (90). She solicits God, "husbandman to thy own purchased seed," to "break up this fallow ground of [her] heart" (159–60). In addition to emptying her heart "of all dross" (164), divine intervention will "unclog" (182) and "unglue [her] heart from earthen pleasures" (196). She seeks God as much to counteract evil, "which like A Christmas Box, till brok't has been,/Can't vent the treasure that's inclos'd within" (179), as to celebrate her forecasted reclamation, by decking her "naked soul . . . like the Kings daughter, which/That beauty hath that's truly called such" (170). For the willing, patient recipient, such apparel remains mysterious and unmerited:

> I tell thee, O my soul, none can express
> The glorious beauty of this robe of his;
> How cure and cloth, and all from him is free;
> Believe and wait, is all that's done by thee. (198)

In her poetic catalog of the sources of deadly sins, her rehearsal of the ages of man, and the initial and terminal acrostics highlighting her name, Major recalls, revisits and reconstructs her life. Neither placidness nor passivity characterizes the purposefully open-ended argument with herself about the seductiveness of sin and gift of submission. With a candour reminiscent of Paul's admission (Romans 7.14–15), she confesses, "When I would good, then evil shews his face,/ The good I leave, the evil I embrace" (198). A similar paradox informs her plea for "the gift of a submitting spirit":

> O order then my changes, that a good day
> Make me not to presume, nor yet delay
> Hasting to thee; nor let a bad day cast
> Me in dispair, but to thy mercies haste. (210)

She strives to create her own consolation through language, fulfilling Ben Jonson's "requisite" of "imitation" as a creature "that feeds with an appetite, and hath a stomach to concoct, divide and turn all into nourishment, . . . turn all into honey" (86).

How might we read this triptych of chalk sketches? Since only "Eliza" married and none bore children, "Eliza," Collins, and Major confound the domestic stereotype of the godly housekeeper; they substantiate Patricia Crawford's efficient debunking of the suggestion that "the godly woman was the successfully socialised woman" (*Women and Religion in England* 4). Songs are their children, as Collins's re-working of the *hortus conclusus* with an emphasis on the specialty of intellectual parturition indicates:

> Yet as a garden is my mind enclosed fast
> Being to safety so confind from storm and blast
> Apt to produce a fruit most rare,
> That is not common with every woman
> That fruitfull are.
>
> ("Another Song" 57)

To extend Gottlieb's summation of Collins to include the trio, they are all "autobiographer[s] of a self both tremulous and assured, suffering and singing, in the midst of spiritual and physical, public and personal pressures" (xiii). In addition to illustrating that "there is no imagination that is not, overtly or secretly, melancholy" (Kristeva, *Black Sun*, 6), they exemplify the Pauline mystery of the "powerlessness of the godly" (Corns, *Uncloistered Virtue*, 305) through the frequency of lapses into rebellion and momentary hopelessness.

This trio also propagates enticingly unresolved paradoxes about the conditions of women's writing in the Commonwealth. They share an initial reluctance to publish dissolved by an insistence on catechetical utility, a coexisting humility topos and impressive spiritual poise, a quest of hope and comfort through the recounting of torment, and reliance on the Bible and the suffering, articulate self as the complete evidentiary ground of testimony. This genuinely remarkable balance of humility and doubt with productivity and confidence underlines my disagreement with Lois Schwoerer's observation that "excessive self-deprecation seems to signal a female writer" (71). Although she speaks of "sectarian women devalu[ing] themselves" (71), I find evidence of precisely the opposite kinetic, propulsive conviction (of both fallibility and, proleptically, redemption) in the work of these meditative poets.

As for genres, only Collins trusts solely to poetry — with the exception of her brief address to the "Christian Reader." In light of her experimentation with a range of poetic forms and her exhortation to be "soberly merry" ("A Song demonstrating The Vanities of Earthly Things" 40), Collins could serve, in one viewing plan, as the center panel into which the occasionally forced and awkwardly enjambed couplets of "Eliza" and Major might turn. Panning for sisterly, if not denominational, similarities is another strategy. Each voices heated opposition to carnality. "Eliza" upbraids "a Lady unfaithfull" who "wantonize[s]" unseen since "your wanton lovers actions hate the light" ("To a Lady unfaithfull" 40). Collins compares "carnall merth" to lightning "For as a flash it hastes and soon is gon" ("The Discourse" 8). Although specific examples "would taint a modest tongue," Major is convinced that England "doth Sodom pass in sins" ("On Immodesty" 175). I find their opposition to lasciviousness much more than "a justification for female celibacy" (Hobby 62); it argues for a determination not to be commodified in a phallogocentric patriarchy.

The common religious, praising nature of their work needs to be addressed, too. For all their exploration and reconstruction of individual struggles, their probing and renunciation of a unique self, and the particularity with which they pledge "engagement" and "recognition" elsewhere, "Eliza," Collins, and Major participate in the great tradition of devotional writing as a gift returned. When "Eliza" tells her "sisters,"

> Looke on these Babes as none of mine,
> For they were but brought forth by me;
> But look on them, as they are Divine,
> Proceeding from Divinity (sig. A^v),

she is working within the same tradition of poetic offering to the Creator as, a generation earlier, George Herbert had invoked in his "dedication" to *The Temple*:

> Lord, my first fruits present themselves to thee;
> Yet not mine neither: for from thee they came,
> And must return. Accept of them and me,
> And make us strive, who shall sing best thy name. (5)

Instead of concentrating on their "purported passivity" and inability "to resist being used by God to his greater glory" (Hobby 57, 55), I think the complex fullness of the triptych's creaturely, filial response deserves to be heard and felt. "Eliza," Collins, and Major all cast shadows on the fragility of the self which is, as Kristeva observes, "hardly dissociated from the other" (Kristeva, *Black Sun*, 5). However, Kristeva concludes that this "shadow of despair" is cast "precisely by the loss of that essential other." Defying, challenging, transforming *loss*, these poets of the Commonwealth conduct a valiant search. Moreover, they enter into conversation with biblical pericopes about sought after perfection and omnipresent corruption, situating themselves at that Pauline boundary where what has been sown in dishonour and weakness will be raised in glory and power (1 Corinthians 15.42).

10• Eyes on the Prize

The Search for Personal Space and Stability Through Religious Devotion in *Eliza's Babes*[1]

Michael Rex

Toward the end of his publishing career, Laurence Blaiklock published an octavo collection of religious verse and prose meditations by a lady who refused to give her name. The book was published in June, 1652 as *Eliza's Babes: or the Virgins-Offering. Being Divine Poems, and Meditations* written "by a lady, who onely desires to advance the glory of God, and not her own."[2] This volume contains: a one page dedication to "My Sisters," a 4–page prose dedication to the reader, 59 pages of poetry, and 43 pages of prose meditations. The title page, dedication pages and the last page in the volume all contain rather elaborate marginal decorations. "Eliza's" book negotiates an interesting place in mid-seventeenth century English women's writings, not only because of its social, political, and publicational contexts, but also through the issues she approaches within her poetry and prose. These issues shed new or refocused light on the ways ordinary people made sense out of the chaotic world of the English Civil War.

Specifically, Eliza writes about social, political, religious, and personal issues, all in the terms of religious devotion. While Eliza seems to be writing in a faith influenced by what Anthony Milton terms moderate Protestantism, she does not define her theology in clearcut terms (Milton 15–18). She uses elements of Catholicism, Calvinism, and Anglicanism without admitting or attempting to reconcile the differences between those theologies. As Margaret Ezell suggests in *Writing Women's Literary History*, women writers, especially those publishing in the print medium, and their publications often do not fit neatly into theological, literary, or canonical spaces. (Ezell, *Writing Women's* 132–38). Eliza not only challenges our modern conceptions of seventeenth century women and religious writers, but she uses the commandment of God, much like Anna Trapnel, Margaret Fell, and the Lady Culross do, as a justification for her appearance in print. *Eliza's Babes* creates a new personal world out of the confusion of the physical world in the hopes of achieving stability through a close, matrimonial relationship with Christ.

The years of Charles I's personal rule (1629–1640) sowed the seeds of revolution (L. Smith 232–34). Archbishop Laud's crackdown on Puritans, other religious dissenters, and even moderate Protestants; the crown's unstable and illegal financial practices; and Charles's inability or unwillingness to explain himself to the Parliamentary elite raised their anger to a fever pitch (L. Smith 235–37). These tempers were inflamed by members of the Long Parliament and eventually led to civil war. It is in this period and with these conflicts that Eliza wrote most of her poetry. Some of Eliza's poetry and prose deal with specific events in her own life caused by the political situation. She writes of her joy at seeing Elizabeth, sister of Charles I, in the poem "To the Queen of Bohemia." Given that Elizabeth was in exile in Holland in the early 1650s, Eliza's poem suggests that she herself had fled England after the execution of Charles I (Greer 142). Another poem, "To General Cromwell," suggests that she was dispossessed of her estate and might have gone to Holland instead of facing persecution at home (Greer 144). The likelihood that she fled England with the court of Henrietta Maria seems slight in view of her stance against Catholicism. In one of her prose meditations, "The Support," Eliza states that she would have willingly submitted to martyrdom: "if the contrary Religion (which then too much abounded) had prevail'd, I then might have offered up my life in flames, with devotion to manifest my love to thee" (*Eliza's Babes* 74). Her own political situation seems tenuous at best. "Security in Danger" provides a thinly veiled description of Eliza's actual situation. She states that she is secure in the knowledge of God's love, but she describes a scene of physical danger:

> [F]or thou Lord onely makest me dwell in safety. I will not be afraid, of ten thousand of people, that should beset me round about; for seeing it hath pleas'd thee to let me be in a Kingdome of division . . . I am now in a place of peace, yet for ought I know I might tomorrow be incompased with ten thousand enemies . . . then let not me be afraid of them, for thou canst preserve me. (99–100)

Eliza sees no safety or stability in her physical world. Only through her relationship with God can she have peace.[3]

Several general assumptions about Eliza can be drawn from her poetry and prose. The title page states that Eliza is a lady and probably of the aristocracy. Her poems, "To a friend at Court," "To the King, writ, 1644," and "To the Queen of Bohemiah," suggest that she had some connection with the royal court; and "The Souls Peace" suggests that she was criticized for supporting Charles I: "if I have been thought too mean to speake in the praise of an earthly King; My God, I cannot but confess myself too mean, too ignorant to speake of, and in the praise of the Majesty of Heaven" (*Eliza's Babes*

73). Apparently Eliza, her two sisters (S. G. and S. S.) and her brother (who died young) were raised by their mother, after her father's death, in a devout household (*Eliza's Babes* 79). These slim facts are all we know for certain about the author.

There are four specific areas that I want to examine in *Eliza's Babes*. These include her problems and religious justification for publishing her work versus keeping it in a more limited manuscript circulation, her use of what Barbara Lewalski, in *Protestant Poetics and the 17th Century Religious Lyric*, calls the Protestant poetic or meditative methodology, her social, and political commentary.

In her preface "To the Reader," Eliza states quite clearly her reasons for writing and more importantly, her reasons for publishing. Although the majority of published women's writings in this period was religious (Ezell, *Writing Women's* 58–59), there was still a cultural reluctance to publish in the print medium (Hobby 54). As Wendy Wall states in *The Imprint of Gender*, this reluctance was not gender specific, but based more on class distinctions and the perception that the publishing market resembled a place of "social deterioration and sexual scandal" (Wall 16). The "Preface," which she states proliferated in early printed books, was the writer's way of combating this class prejudice and offered reasons for using the print medium (Wall 173). In her preface, Eliza equates the act of having her work printed with Christ's very public death. She sees publishing, as Elaine Hobby states, as a "Christian Act" (Hobby 55). Eliza uses Christianity as a way to justify her action of publishing.

Eliza obviously saw her work as following in the footsteps of George Herbert's *The Temple*. Helen Wilcox makes the argument that many writers of religious lyric modeled their collections on Herbert, even in their titles such as *Steps to the Temple*, and *The Synagogue* ("Curious Frame" 20–21). Eliza's title evokes this same idea of the body of religious poems as a type of personal, spiritual church. Specifically, "offerings" are made at a church or temple. The words "virgin's" and "babes" evoke other extremely personal, religious images. These images deal with the Virgin Mary, who, like Eliza, was the bride of God. In Mark's gospel, Mary brought an offering of two turtle doves to the temple after Christ's birth in accordance with the law, which involved the presentation of the child (babe) to God. Not only does Eliza call her verses "babes," but she also presents and dedicates them to God. In addition, Eliza writes three poems, one titled "The Virgins Offering," another "To my Doves," and the poem at the end of the collection where she tells her doves to fly.

In "The Virgins Offering," Eliza speaks specifically of the Virgin Mary and sees herself as almost equal to the mother of Christ. She compares her own two doves, which are her verses, to those of Mary, but then agrees that Mary's sacrifice of her son was the more important offering:

> With thee, blest Virgin, I would bring
> An Offering, to please my King . . .
> These two small Turtles now of mine,
> To him, I do present with thine.
>
> (1–8)

By framing her verses as sacrificial doves equal to those given by Christ's mother, Eliza endorses the idea of equality among Christians. She also shows that her verses themselves are her offering to her God. She dedicates her verses or babes to God and sees them coming from Him, from the Divine: "Looke on these Babes as none of mine, For they were but brought forth by me; But look on them, as they are Divine, Proceeding from Divinity" (*Eliza's Babes*, "Sisters" A1).

In calling her collection of verse and prose "babes," Eliza follows a well established tradition. Wendy Wall suggests that the feminization of printed texts by male authors led to the use of the childbirth metaphor (Wall 181). Eliza flirts with a type of voyeurism by offering her specifically female readers a glimpse into a divine marriage. She puts the emphasis on the divine nature of her "babes" in order to preserve her social modesty. By framing her work as the product of a divine union, Eliza allows herself to enter the social sphere while remaining "enclosed within [her] home" (Wall 280).

In "To the Reader," Eliza lays out her reasons for printing her work. In doing this, she deals with several problems involving not only publishing, but also publishing *as a woman.* Eliza's fear of hostile reaction is justified, since many people viewed print publication by a woman as an unwomanly act (Wall 277–81). Women were instructed to be obedient, silent, and chaste, and the act of publishing violated these ideas (Beilin 4). Furthermore, even reformed Protestantism, which claimed to be a "better" religion for women, seems to limit and confine the roles for women even more than either Roman Catholicism or High-Church Anglicanism (Crawford 42–43). As men gained more authority as "priests in their own homes," women were restricted to more domestic roles; and writing for publication, which took a woman outside of her family, was considered a violation of both religious and social codes (Crawford 42).

Eliza counters these expected arguments by evoking three traditions: not seeking fame for herself, answering the call of the Lord, and attempting to educate others morally. Eliza seeks to deflect her fame in several ways. She does not use her real name, stresses her social rank as that of a lady, and states that her only reason for publishing is "to advance the glory of God." The first two strategies were common to both male and female writers of the period (Wall 173). In the preface she emphatically states that any glory or fame belongs to God and not to the poet:

> I therefore sent them abroad; for such a strict union is there betwixt my deare God and me, that his glory is mine, and mine is his . . . the Prince of eternall glory had affianced me to himselfe; and that is my glory. (A3)

Her role as a poet in the poem "Of Poetry," and a prose medi-
tation "The Support," implies that all inspiration and fame
come from the total surrender to the will of God (Hobby 55).
Further justification for printing her work comes from her
denial of agency for their dissemination. Although it was com-
mon for writers to deny that they wished to see their work in
print, Eliza is rather ambiguous as to just who the agent is
(Wall 174). Her phrase, "it was suggested to my consideration,"
which occurs in the first paragraph, denies action for herself,
yet it does not name the agent specifically (*Eliza's Babes* A2).
Who suggested that she publish her work? Did her husband,
either her earthly or divine husband, make the suggestion? Or
as Wall suggests, in her discussion of William Percy and George
Pettie, is this simply a conventional disclaimer? Given the
rest of "To the Reader" and the fact that this disclaimer comes
so early in the preface, I believe that Eliza is simply deflecting
any potential criticism away from herself.

Eliza also justifies her publishing by stating that she is re-
sponding to the call of the Lord. Her argument rests on the
idea that Christ commanded her and gave her the power to
create this work. She says that she is working only for the
Kingdom of Heaven, striving to bring everyone into the fold.
In this section, Eliza is almost preaching a sermon, extolling
the benefits of a personal relationship with Christ. Acting as
the mouthpiece of God, publishing her work becomes the act
of following his commandments. This type of response to God
is characteristic of the language of seventeenth century devo-
tional poetry (Wilcox, "Exploring" 86):

> I would have you love him, and him to love you all. I being his
> *must do*, as he will have me: and methinks, *he directs me* to
> tell you, that you shall never bee happy on Earth, nor glorious
> in Heaven, if you doe not love him, above all earthly things.
> More, *I must tell you*, that if you will dedicate to his service,
> and present into his hands, your wealth, witt, spirit, youth,
> beauty, he will give you wealth, if less, more usefull: your witt

more pure, your spirit more high . . . and returne them again for eternity. (A4) [italics mine]

Eliza is playing the active role of a preacher of the Word and I think it is this idea that undermines Hobby's reading that Eliza is advocating a passive role in the religious experience (Hobby 55–56). While Eliza states that she is speaking through the power of God and that can seem passive, what she is doing is indeed active. Eliza acts through her passivity and, as Wilcox points out, this passivity is characteristic of the "female aesthetic" found in the majority of religious verse of this period (Wilcox, "Exploring" 86). Eliza goes even further in a prose devotion called "The Support" by insisting that God has given her both the will and the authority to write: "And now I dare not say, I am an ignorant woman, and unfit to write, for if thou wilt declare thy goodness, and thy mercy by weak and contemptible means [using a woman], who can resist thy will" (*Eliza's Babes* 75).

In her third justification for publishing, Eliza draws on the socially acceptable role of woman author as motherly advisor.[4] Following the lead of women like Elizabeth Joceline — *The Mothers Legacie to her unborn Child* (1624), Frances Aburgavennie — *Praiers* (1582), Elizabeth Crashawe — *The Honour of Vertue* (1620), and Elizabeth Grymeston — *Miscelanae, Meditations, Memoratives* (1604), Eliza sees her work as a gathering together of advice to help improve others:

> But rising one day, from my Devotions, it was suggested to my consideration, that those desires [to publish her work] were not given me, to be kept in private, to my self, but for the good of others. (A3)

Eliza justified her very public act of publishing her work by saying "that these Babes of mine should be sent into the world" (A3). While she uses many of the common strategies for overcoming social condemnation such as publishing anonymously, deflecting agency, and pleading youth, Eliza's authority rests mainly on her relationship with God. It is through this divine union that she finds the power, the will, and the ability to act.

In her poetry, Eliza uses what Barbara Lewalski names the method of Protestant meditation (*Protestant Poetics* 147–48). Eliza's meditations, particularly the early ones, function as an order of religious service operating in a didactic mode. While Eliza uses a structure similar to an Ignatian meditation, she grounds her poetry in moderate Protestant theology. The first eight poems of *Eliza's Babes* illustrate both her structure and theology. She begins with The Word as her focal point and develops her poetic authority through an examination of her personal relationship with her personal God, quoting from Psalm 56: "In God (I will praise His word),/In the Lord (I will praise His word)." This Scripture sets the tone for the entire work. Psalm 56 is a "Prayer for Relief from Tormentors." The choice of this particular Psalm has a twofold meaning: since Eliza is using this sequence to establish her "right" to poetry, she is, perhaps, attempting to silence her critics (tormentors) and, throughout the entire collection, she is concerned with the individual's ability to create and preserve personal stability in a chaotic world.

Eliza uses a more Calvinistic devotion to The Word as a guide and as a source of personal salvation and inspiration. "I Glory in the word of God . . . All you that goodness doe disdaine/Goe; read not here" (1–2). These lines, from the first poem in the collection, illustrate Eliza's point of view. Much like "Superliminare," the opening of the second part of George Herbert's *The Temple*, Eliza admonishes those who do not want to participate in these spiritual exercises to leave. Unlike Herbert, Eliza is almost nasty about her rejection of the unfaithful. Her voice is not the kind, teacherly voice that is evident in Herbert's work; she simply does not care about the unfaithful:

> Goe; read not here:
> And if you doe; I tell you plaine,
> I doe not care.

For why? above your reach my soul is plac'st,
And your odd words shall not my minde distaste.

(6–10)

Her glory and relationship with God have placed her above
this world and outside of its problems. Eliza seems to be writ-
ing to women who are searching for a type of stability in their
own lives and offers them her method of achieving that
stability.

She moves from a focus on The Word through a series of
poems, "The Invocation," "The Request," "The Answer,"
"Anguish," and "Of Submission" (I), dealing with what Louis
Martz calls "the threefold Image of God: memory, understand-
ing [and] will," and struggling with the issue of how she can
achieve a state of Grace (56).

In "The Invocation," Eliza states that her inspiration, con-
tent, and ability to write come from her relationship with God.
She calls God her "sweet Companion," and "From thee, this
gift, I did receive" (5–7). Her created world is based on thoughts
of Heaven and a desire to reside with the godhead. Eliza's de-
sire to live only in the light of God and to ignore the physical
world is a trait common to much of the devotional literature
of the period (Wilcox, "Exploring" 81).

The poems "The Request" and "The Answer" build up
Eliza's vision of her own new world. She asks God for protec-
tion, happiness, and guidance. She takes an active role in call-
ing on the Lord to grant her requests; she almost orders God:

Come sweet Spirit expell my fear,
Assure me that thou hast a care . . .
That thy Spirit shall me direct,
And that thy power shall me protect.

("The Request" 1–6)

Eliza does not ask in a humble way, but almost speaks as if
these gifts are her right because she serves God. This com-
manding attitude continues where the poet suggests that God's

ability to fulfill her demands is linked with her ability to desire God's love:

> His Spirit much thou dost desire,
> His Spirit much he will inspire.
> What thou desirest, that shall be,
> Thou hast thy wishes granted thee.
>
> ("The Answer" 1–4)

These are not the words of a penitent sinner; the speaker continues to ask God for the ability to overcome the perils of the physical world and to think only on Heavenly things. In a later portion of the poem, the speaker reflects on the misery of separation from God. Eliza experiments with the emotions of joy and misery found in much devotional literature (Wilcox, "Exploring" 83–84). She realizes the great joy of union with God: "It is the injoying of thy Spirit,/That makes my soul here, true joy inherit," while at the same time expresses the sorrow of separation: "On Earth a while I must tormented be,/ Because that sin, too much abides in me" ("The Answer" 13–14: 11–12). By the end of the poem, Eliza's soul reunites with God and her world seems more secure.

This security, in the speaker's view, is only temporary. "Anguish," the next poem in the series, shows that Eliza's physical world still encroaches upon her self-created world and threatens her stable relationship with God. She pleads with God to save her from the "vaine pleaures" of the world. In the physical world around her, there is no stability. Folly, vice, and death are the rewards of the physical life, and yet, these forces tempt the speaker away from the security which she finds in holy service:

> From this distraction, Lord my poor soul bring, . . .
> For this distemper doth my soul affright;
> My Lord, it takes from me, all my delight,
> And pleasure that I had, in serving thee . . .
> No comfort can I find, but endless paine.
>
> (1, 3–5, 8)

The speaker's world is shaken by the forces of sin and the only way to restore stability seems to be utter devotion to God's service. This is a type of passivity and a withdrawal from the world that is more a functioning of religious lyric in general, than the female specific reading that Hobby gives it (Hobby 59). Eliza attempts to provide stability to her own life on her own terms, and at the end of "Anguish" she almost tries to bargain with God:

> But in thy service, if I pleasure take,
> And thy sweet word my whole delight do make
> That word doth still my drooping soul assure,
> That for the best it shall be all to me,
> If patiently I doe awaite on thee.
>
> (13–17)

She is saying that if she devotes her life to God, this will earn her salvation. However, Eliza does not accept this idea. In the later poems of the sequence, she shows how the idea of earning salvation is futile and impossible.

It is only in "Of Submission" (I)[5] that the speaker realizes that she can do nothing on her own; her sins are too great, her love of the world is too strong, and her ability to overcome temptation is too weak. The opening lines of this poem show that the speaker realizes that she cannot earn Grace; it is a gift from God. "What comes to me, Lord comes from thee?/ Nought comes to me, but comes from thee" (1–2). Eliza is advocating, in this poetic sequence, coming to a state of Grace through submission to the will of God, and she ends this series of poems with "The Only Comforter" where the speaker is reveling in a state of Grace and the power of God. Eliza is also showing that only through complete devotion can an individual achieve personal stability.

While the majority of Eliza's poems deal with this kind of search for stability through a close relationship with God, there are four poems, in particular, that I want to examine in the context of Eliza's building of her own world.

"The Triumph," an early poem in the collection, describes Eliza's view of the "New Jerusalem." Her picture of Heaven is fairly standard: the streets are paved with gold; the walls are brighter than any jewels found on earth; and the city is populated by choirs of angels. What is interesting is how Eliza treats this image and her role in it. The opening of the poem makes a direct contrast to the England in which Eliza was living. She describes Heaven as:

> . . . a glorious Nation,
> Which triumphantly doe sing,
> Praise and glory to their King.
> No darkness, nor no dolefull night,
> Obscures their Vision of delight,
> No noise doth interrupt their voice.
>
> (6–11)

Eliza suggests that the physical world is full of noise, darkness, and night in the thralldom from which God freed the speaker in the poem's first lines.

Eliza's treatment of the Bride of Christ contributes to the creation of her new world. While her description of the Bride is somewhat traditional — she is called "Fresh, fair and beauteous . . . Like Orient Pearl she doth appear" (44–46) — the poet does not speak of the Bride as the Church. Throughout the entire poem she [the Bride] is treated as an individual while Christians are either "The ancient Martyrs Crown'd with gold" or "The blessed Saints [who] sit safe and sure" (58, 62). The image of Christ's bride is striking because, in her preface, Eliza states that she is the wife of Christ and that these poems are her children by him. So the Bride becomes, at the same time, both the Church as a whole and the individual Christian. The poet is both observer and player. This is the world that Eliza envisions and through the grace of God, she plans to experience it as much as she can until her death when she will enter it in reality. The poem speaks of security and safety. The saints are "safe and sure" and the martyred Christians are triumphant. Eliza is showing that only through God can this type of stability be achieved.

"The flight" carries this idea even further. Instead of just envisioning this new world, Eliza has actually gone there. The speaker clearly states that Eliza is no longer part of the physical world:

> Eliza for, aske now not here,
> She's gone to heaven, to meet her Peer.
> For since her Lord, on earth was dead,
> What tarry here! she'd not, she sed [said] . . .
> And so to us she bid adieu,
> But prov'd herself a lover true.
>
> (1–8)

The ambiguity of which Lord she is talking about in line 3 adds to her rejection of the physical world. Since Eliza does not differentiate between her husband, her king, or even Christ in the form of man, she collapses all physical realities into one and then rejects that combined physical being. By rejecting the physical world, the speaker suggests that Eliza is on the same level as God and through her rejection of the world has proved her faith and trust in him.

In "Christ's Kingdom," the speaker creates the kingdom of God within herself and there chooses to live. She is able to do so because God has departed from Heaven and come directly to her:

> With you blest Angels, I must sing,
> That brought the news of heav'ns great King
> That from bright Heaven awhile did part,
> To raise his Kingdom with my heart.
>
> (1–4)

Eliza gives her readers the message that through God's intervention and a direct personal relationship with him, a new world is at hand. For Eliza, the new world is not only the after-life in Heaven, but here on the physical earth. Her relationship with God removes the strife, sin, darkness, and fear that had possessed the speaker. In exchange for these worldly things, he gives her light, "sweet joy and peace" (21). This is exactly the kind of stability that Eliza seeks, and, given the chaotic situation in England at this time, it seems likely that she is trying to show her readers how to achieve this same type of stability.

Eliza's concern for other Christians and how others can achieve the peace and stability that she has found is evident in the poem "Comfort in Temptations and Afflictions." In this poem, Eliza states that Christ can provide both physical and spiritual comfort and protection.

> Come Christians that so [a]mazed bee
> At earths events, O come and see
> What cause there is for your dismay,
> When God takes care for you each day.
>
> (1–4)

She then lists all the evils that faith in Christ can overcome: imprisonment, war, sickness, and even death itself. Nothing in the world can be trusted and it is the concern with the world and its evils that can disrupt the Christian heart.

> Let not your hearts here troubled be,
> For if you do beleeve on me [Christ] . . .
> Then sith heav'ns King can safe you keep,
> There is no cause for you to weep.
>
> (9–10, 23–24)

As in her other poems, Eliza insists on a personal devout relationship between the individual and God. Only this relationship can provide the protection and comfort described throughout the work.

Perhaps Eliza's best statement on the relationship between the individual and God is the prose meditation "The Temple." In this meditation, the speaker questions the idea of the Holy Ghost dwelling within the individual and the relationship between God and the individual works. She opens by saying that she is an unfit vessel for God and that she cannot imagine how the Holy Ghost could live within her. She proceeds through the idea of God's love and that if she loves God, he has said that he will dwell within her and create his throne in her heart. The meditation is laced with uncertainty as Eliza addresses how her life should express her relationship with God:

> give me then thy assistance, that no proud imagination, for my own greatness, may arise to disthrone thee, and make the[e] distaste that habitation; but be thou in my heart, ever attended by sweet humility and humble obedience.

(93)

This "sweet humility and humble obedience" also show that Eliza follows a Calvinist influenced Protestantism in her idea of works. She sees good works coming only from her obedience to God and that he allows her to perform these works. The things that Eliza asks for can be seen as the foundations of the world she wishes to create for herself and the antithesis of the real world around her. She asks God for selflessness, humility, and the ability to avoid murder, vanity, and slanderous speech. She links each of these attributes to a part of her own body and asks God to inhabit her completely so that "all the members of my body be imployed in thy service" (93). It is through this complete surrender and utter devotion to God that the speaker attains her desire of Heaven on Earth.

Throughout her religious poetry and prose, Eliza exhibits most of the predominant features of the seventeenth century religious lyric collections as described by both Barbara Lewalski and Helen Wilcox. She grounds her meditations thoroughly in scripture; investigates her relationship with Christ; and examines how everyday objects like swans, doves, and sunrises express God's given truths (Lewalski, *Protestant Poetics*, 155). She uses what Wilcox calls "the language of devotion," to deny her own creative power, giving all the agency to God, and to create her own world where she could live in security and stability. While her experimentation with form and her ability to create metaphors is not equal to those of George Herbert, Andrew Marvell, An Collins, or Elizabeth Major, she apparently believed that she had something to offer her society, particularly women. Her poetry reveals a strong Christian faith and advocates an active submission to the love and power of God.

Although the majority of her poetry and prose are specifically religious in both subject and tone, Eliza does exhibit a form of the eclecticism that Achsah Guibbory finds in Robert Herrick's *Hesperides*. Guibbory suggests that Herrick intentionally saw his collection as religious verse and that he strove to expand what is considered religious devotion ("Enlarging the Limits" 30–31). While Eliza has nothing that compares with Herrick's "Corinna's Going A-Maying" or the Julia poems, nor does she attempt to blur the lines between the pagan and the Christian; she does include several poems on more secular subjects both social and political. Her social works concern mainly the family: raising children, relationships between siblings, and marriage. Her political writings include poems to several political figures and writings on the political structure as a whole.

In the first part of "The Invincible Soldier," Eliza discusses her own childhood under the rubric of military training. She was raised by her mother who worked to provide her children with a Christian education. Eliza's use of military language is striking. She sees the proper way of life as training for membership in the army of the Lord. Her mother:

> . . . was happy in being a Soldier of thine, used her authority by love, to bring her children under the obedience of that Generall, whom she serv'd, and to make me love him in my child hood . . . inforc'd me to read his Royal story, wherein I might see his victorious conquest. (79)

Even though Eliza says that her mother used love to teach her children about Christ, this use of military terms is unsettling for a discussion of child rearing given the less strident theories on the same subject expressed in contemporary works by other women writers such as Elizabeth Countess of Lincoln and Elizabeth Joceline. It does fit with the overall theme of the essay, which describes the speaker as a full warrior of God, capable of defeating all enemies, but since this is one of only a few places where Eliza discusses physical children, I find this view of childhood disturbing. Yet, even here, Eliza discusses her childhood as an act of God: she is given to these parents as a conscious act of the Lord. Both the speaker and her parents completely submit themselves to God's will and in return they all become active soldiers in the war against God's enemies.

Her poem "To a Lady that Bragg'd of her Children," shows that Eliza did not relish the idea of childbirth. She sees physical children as a source of pain and sin. Real children "bring both sorrow, pain and fear,/Mine banish from me dreadfull care" (9–10). Her children are her writings and these babes "praise heav'ns King" (8). This fear or dislike of physical children becomes more important in the light of her other "family" poems. Eliza writes poems to both of her sisters and two poems about her brother, but there are no poems about her own children, if she indeed had any. These poems come after her marriage poems, an order which suggests that, perhaps, it was this aspect of marriage that she disliked most. Her divine marriage causes no such problems. For Eliza, all physical children are born from sin and she would rather avoid the entire question.

In a sequence of seven poems, Eliza discusses the idea of an earthly marriage and the problems she sees in the social contract of marriage. In an earlier poem "The Bride," Eliza defines herself as the bride of Christ and rejects the idea of an earthly marriage. She sees earthly marriage as a kind of slavery and wants no part of it. The speaker says that she is "Not here to live a slavish life,/ In being to the world a wife" (3–4).

Instead, she sees herself as the bride of Christ, suggesting that Christ died for her love and that she is predestined to be his wife and not an earthly one:

> For that great Prince prepar'd a bride,
> That for my love on earth here dy'd.
> Why not I then earths thraldom scorn,
> [illegible word] for heavens Prince I here was born?
>
> (7–10)

In this poem, Eliza uses the metaphor of the Bride of Christ to mean both the Church and the individual, while at the same time obscuring the line between the physical world and the spiritual one. She justifies her rejection of an earthly marriage by combining her salvation as a Christian with a legal, binding marriage to the godhead.

Unfortunately for Eliza, social pressures and realities force her into a marriage. In "On Marriage" Eliza questions society's reasons for her to marry. She exhibits a streak of independence in not wanting to marry and a legitimate fear of childbirth:

> I no ambition have for earth,
> My thoughts are of a higher birth.
> The Souls sweet Babes, [her poetry] do bring no pain,
> And they immortalize the name.
>
> (9–12)

Even though she does not wish to marry and is afraid of having children, the speaker resigns herself to follow God's will.

In the next poem, "The Gift," however, the poet turns the tables; she is angry with God and cannot understand why he has given her away. She questions the power of prayer and her own faith in God:

> My Lord, hast thou given me away?
> Did I on earth, for a gift stay?
> Hath he by prayer of thee gain'd me,
> Who was so strictly knit to thee.
>
> (1–4)

In the rest of the poem, the speaker insists that she will remain true to God, even if He will not be true to her, and that her husband will possess just her body and not her love, mind, or being. She sees herself as just on loan from her divine marriage. In viewing marriage as only the subjection of the body, Eliza is able to preserve her identity and retain limited control over her life (Hobby 59).

Three poems which follow "The Gift," "The Choice of my Friend," "The Change," and "Not a Husband," alternate between addresses to her fiancé and to God. Those poems addressed to her fiancé warn him that he will never possess her and that her religious devotion and her faith in her Christ will preserve her identity as Eliza. She specifically tells him, in "The Choice of my Friend," that she did not choose him for any earthly reasons. This poem shows the speaker in probably her most active voice. She has chosen the man to be her husband: "I did chuse thee,/Cause thou aspir'st to heaven with mee" (1–2); she tells him to explain her choice to the world: "Pray tell the world" (1); and she has told God what kind of man she wanted, since she was obligated to marry: "Thus with heaven, I did decree/That such a one my friend should be" (7–8). She chooses this particular man because he matches her in her devotion to God. Since he is as devoted to God as she is, Eliza can still believe that she is free and not enthralled by marriage, as the speaker in "The Bride" believed she would become.

The other poem addressed to her fiancé, "Not a Husband," warns him that he will not be able to interfere with her spiritual life. She states that she is already fully devoted to God and while she is not unhappy in her earthly life, he must realize that he comes second to God.

> To heaven's great prince I must away,
> No love on earth here must me stay.
> He lent me but awhile to you,
> And now I must bid you adieu.

(13–16)

Eliza retains her independence even in the face of both soci-
etal and family pressures to marry. This independence, like
the stability of her earlier poems, comes only through her
devotion to and love for God.

The poem addressed to God, "The Change," praises God
for his ability to look out for the speaker. In "The Change,"
she rejoices in the choice God made for her in the person of
her husband. Through God's love, she can see that being mar-
ried is not bad if one allows God to do the choosing. She voices
the concerns she previously held about marriage and credits
God for the change in her attitude:

> Great God!
> How hast thou chang'd my thoughts in me,
> For when I thought to be a wife,
> I then did think troubled to be
> Because I saw most live in strife.

(1–5)

These lines reflect Eliza's former attitude toward marriage,
apparently based on her observations in society. While echo-
ing the sentiments in "The Bride," she negotiates a way for
women to survive such an earthly marriage. By surrendering
her will to God's choice, she not only avoids the slavery she
sees in other marriages, but she is also freed from her worldly
obligations and can spend more time in the praise of God. She
can do this because her husband "take[s] all trouble quite from
me,/ that earths possession here doth bring" (10–11).

The last two poems on marriage are both addressed to her
husband, and in "To my Husband," she expresses her love for
him through her love of God, while in "My Second Part,"
which is several pages later, she gives herself the right to sepa-
rate from her husband if his devotion to God wavers.

"To My Husband" speaks with a loving and poignant
tone. The speaker tells her husband that she does not want
him to mourn her after her death because she is gone to a
better place.

> Then let no blacks be worne for me,
> Not in a Ring my dear by thee.
> But this bright Diamond, let it be
> Worn in remembrance of me.
> And when it sparkes in your eye,
> Think 'tis my shadow passeth by.
>
> (3–8)

By saying that she will remember him even after death, she is granting him the greatest gift that she can bestow. She is putting her love for her husband on a similar level with her love for God. She is still exerting her independence by describing her wishes for her husband in the event of her death: she tells him where she wants to be buried, how she wants him to act, asks him to remember that she is going to Glory, and that she will see him in Paradise. She reminds him that these are promises that he made to her and that just as God will keep his promise of salvation and paradise, so must her husband keep the promises that he made.

This loving concern for her husband's grief is completely absent in "My Second Part." In this poem, the speaker addresses both God and her husband, restating her whole argument against marriage, but admits that she has been happy in her own. Problems occur, though, when the devotion to God weakens. Eliza seems to be speaking about all marriages and that wives must remember that even if their husbands stray, God will never abandon them:

> For should our Husbands love fixt be
> Upon some others, not on thee,
> Heavens Prince will never thee forsake,
> But still his darling will thee make.
> And should he of thee careless bee
> Heavens Prince, he will more carefull bee.
>
> (19–24)

Eliza seems to be creating a plan for dealing with a bad marriage. Whether she is including herself in this description is hard to tell, but her faith in God is constant throughout. She reminds her readers that through the power of God they can survive. In all her marriage poems, Eliza creates a new definition of the wifely role (Hobby 59). She advocates a complete devotion to God and faith that he will do what is best; he will provide either a good, devout Christian husband or the ability to survive in the relationship with a bad one. But faith in God's love and power is paramount.

This faith in the stabilizing power of God is also prominent in Eliza's political writings. In all of these writings, Eliza addresses the political situation of the times and reflects on how these political actions can affect the individual and her sense of identity and stability. In "To the King," the speaker advises King Charles to emulate Christ as "that Prince of might/ Who is the Prince of peace behight" (5–6). She also pleads with the king to make peace with Parliament and warns him that he might, if he continues in his actions, lose his kingdom and by extension totally disrupt the lives of everyone in the country. Eliza emphasizes her role as teacher by sending her verses to him and reminding him that Christ "by yeelding won the field" (9). Her desire for real political stability is voiced in the last lines of the poem:

> . . . you peace to bring.
> A Kingdome I'de not have you leave,
> But rather three reform'd receive.
> All bliss and peace I wish you,
> Let us in peace, your presence view.
>
> (14–18)

Eliza still advocates putting the individual self, whether king or commoner, under the direct control of God as the only means to peace and stability.

Eliza's other political writings all appear to come after the execution of Charles. In her poem "To General Cromwell," Eliza addresses different issues than in her other political writings. She admits that Cromwell now has the authority that was once the king's, but she also gives him the authority of God and father. He has "[t]he Sword of God" and the right to chastise her as if she were a child (1). She draws on the image in Proverbs 29 of the rod as the instrument of instruction:

> But why doe I, complain of thee?
> 'Cause thou'rt the rod that scourthgeth mee?
> But if a good child I will bee,
> I'le kiss the Rod, and honour thee.
>
> (3–6)

Eliza then gives Cromwell the mandate of Heaven, but warns him that he must be virtuous if he is to succeed. The second part of the poem asks Cromwell to continue his scourging of the nation. The speaker asks for relief from lawyers and the enforcement of bad laws. She sees these laws as tyranny which Cromwell, as a virtuous man, must destroy since he destroyed the earlier tyranny of the king. Exactly what Eliza's legal problems are is uncertain, but Germaine Greer believes that they involved either the confiscation of her own estate or her husband's property (Greer 144).

The poem "God's Prerogative" directly addresses the execution of the king and creates a bewildering situation for the speaker. She knows that it is within God's prerogative to remove a king, but she still does not understand it:

> Lord, shall I grudge at thy just will,
> Or shall I question thy great skill
> And think the world thou dost not rule
> As thou art wont; peace silly fool.
>
> (1–4)

By calling herself a fool, Eliza rejects the idea that people can know the mind of God. She realizes that God still controls the world even if the entire political situation has fallen apart. Again, she advocates submission to God's will, expressed in Parliament's victory over the king, but warns that without God, any political system will fail:

> Then let me Lord myself submit
> To what thy wisdom seeth fit.
> Sith no authority can be
> But what appointed is by thee.

(17–20)

The speaker explicitly states that God is the agent that sanctions political power and that God can just as easily remove the "new" government as he did the royal government.

Eliza deals with the ideas of Christianity and kingship in the essay, "The Royal Gods." Here she equates divinity with royalty only through God's choosing. The king himself has no right or power to rule without God. Eliza directly states that earthly kings cannot think or be thought of as having power in and of themselves:

> And shall not wee, who know from whom and by whom Kings reigne, think our Princes to be as they are [en]stil'd by that great King, who set them to reign for him? God forbid, but that we should so think of them, and they of themselves. (71)

Eliza does not defend the Divine Right of Kings, but rather allows kings to rule as long as they act as God acted to protect the Israelites in the Wilderness (71). She insists that all kings must emulate Christ in every way: protecting the weak, punishing the evil, and granting mercy. Eliza also insists that they have no right to exempt themselves from the punishment of their peers; for just like Christ, "They must die like men." (72).

Eliza's essay "The Royal Priest-hood" is almost bizarre in its political implications. She argues against the treatment of women in a hostile and angry tone. She states that living by faith erases any differences between all groups in society: between men and women, between kings and commoners, and between the clergy and the congregation:

> Peace! Present now no more to . . . that I am a creature of a weaker sex, a woman. For my God! . . . I must live by faith, and faith makes things to come as present . . . then thou wilt make all thy people as Kings and Priests, Kings are men and men are Kings; and Souls have no sex. (100)

For Eliza, the ideal political world is one that makes no distinction between people. She states that by closing "the eyes of my Soul, to mortality" and not opening them "but to eternity," she can create and live in this ideal world where all people are equal (100). She can survive in the mortal world by the power of her faith in God. She denies the physical world with its gender, class, and religious differences, and instead focuses on the spiritual world. Her vision of the spiritual world is one of triumph through the power of God. By his power, Eliza enters Heaven in a chariot where she "shall reigne with him for all eternity, and never more desire to change" (101). She sees this new world as the only answer to her real world full of strife, sin, and instability. Of course, the only way to achieve this world is the total submission of the individual will and desire to the control of God. Only when she has become God's willing "unworthy servant" will he grant her this mercy. She becomes, in this one action, servant, king, and priest.

Throughout her poetry and prose, Eliza attempts to provide a way to spiritual independence and stability. She uses moderate Protestant tenets of faith, influenced in part by Calvinist theology and Catholic imagery, to develop her personal relationship with God. Through the power of Christ nothing can threaten her: political upheaval, social chaos, and an unwanted marriage are the crucibles that she must endure, but it is her strength in her faith that allows her to triumph over the evils of this world. Eliza believed that she had a right and a duty to share her hard-found knowledge with her fellow Christians. In the end, nothing of this world, not politics, society, friends, lovers, nor husbands, can provide true independence, space, and stability. Only through the utter devotion and submission to the love and faith of God can these things be received. The prize is the neverending union with Christ, the Prince of Peace.

11 • An Collins

The Tradition of the Religious Lyric, Modified or Corrected?

Ann Hurley

An Collins is a philosophical, even didactic, poet, less interested in creating an arresting image or immediacy of narrative voice than in crafting a plain style suitable for the specific mix of exaltation and reflection that marks her verse.[1] As such she scarcely stands out in the seventeenth century meditative tradition as we have been taught to describe it, defined by figures like Donne, Herbert, Vaughan and Traherne and derived, on the one hand, from a courtly, largely European and Catholic, tradition emphasizing the graphically vivid participation in heroic scenes like the Crucifixion and, on the other, from the Protestant tradition of the anguished confrontation of a single human soul with God. Neither criterion, the graphic nor the immediate, serves us well when responding to the poetry of a poet like Collins.

Nevertheless, I would like to argue, we should not approach Collins simply as a secondary or minor poet. Rather, as critics, it is more to our advantage to use Collins's poetry as an occasion for extending our understanding of the practice of English meditative poetry in the seventeenth century, establishing new criteria of evaluation that include a sensitivity to the didactic voice and to the moods and methods that sustain it. Secondly, as scholars, we can also come to appreciate a poet who alerts us to a greater range of meditative poetry than we have heretofore considered and who, even more valuably, may lead us to revise our current narrative of the history of seventeenth century poetry, its origins, its forms, and its most skillful practitioners.

Accordingly, with these goals in view, I propose first to describe Collins's poetry which, now existing in a single volume from what must have been originally a fairly small single printing, has rarely appeared in print since 1653.[2] Second, I will make some suggestions about where Collins fits in the tradition of the religious lyric and, more pertinently, how our rediscovery of her verse may reshape our understanding of that tradition. While it will ultimately be of significant scholarly value to situate Collins's verse among its probable influences and to make some educated historical inferences about religious circles or individuals she might have had contact with, in this initial essay I am primarily concerned with bringing her verse to the attention of a scholarly audience and with offering some suggestions about directions that further study might take.

An Collins is known to us only through the one remaining volume of her poetry, the *Divine Songs and Meditacions* (printed by R. Bishop, 1653, STC II 177:1), currently located in the Huntington Library and noted in 1815, when it was first mentioned in print, as "so rare as to be probably unique" (Griffith, 67). The volume is described by Sidney Gottlieb, editor of the recent (1996) reprint of Collins's verse, as a small octavo, page size (cropped) of 136 by 83 mm, bound in thick brown polished calf, with 102 pages of text. It consists of a brief poetic "Preface," a long philosophical verse "Discourse," several "Songs," and five "Meditacions." The verse itself implies a practiced poet, particularly skillful in handling metrics. Its metrical schemes vary from rhyme royal to a variety of stanzaic patterns, some innovative and some derived from the traditional forms associated with songs, ballads, and translations and imitations of the Psalms. Of Collins herself we know nothing: neither her dates, nor family situation, nor even when during her life she actually composed these poems.

Collins's verse has been described as "spiritual autobiography" (Cunnar 51) and it is that, but her "Preface" suggests that she herself saw her volume primarily as a record of Protestant doctrine, particularly as this was animated and made relevant through its activating force in her own life. In this intention she is consistent with Protestant poetic practice, which endorsed the application of the scriptures to the spiritual situation of the individual.[3] Indeed, as we shall see, there is some suggestion that Collins felt that in describing, in print, her own response to scripture, she was completing God's task by making His effects known. Taking to heart the urgings of Athanasius (reprinted in the Matthew Parker *Psalter* and cited by Lewalski 234) that the reader of psalms "singeth to God those woordes as his very own words and Petitions," in her dedicatory epistle, "To the Reader," Collins is direct about her purpose, not simply in writing but in publishing her verse: "it was the manifestacion of Divine Truth, or rather the Truth it self, that reduced my mind to a peacefull temper, and spirituall calmnesse, taking up my thoughts for Theologicall employments," she writes. She continues, "Witnesse hereof, this Discourse, Songs and Meditacions, following; which I have set forth (as I trust) for the benifit, and comfort of others, Cheifly [sic] those Christians who are of disconsolat Spirits, who may perceive herein, the Faithfullnesse, Love, & Tender Compassionatnesse of God to his people, in that according to his gracious Promise, *He doth not leave nor forsake them. Heb. 13.5. But causeth all things to work for theyr good. Rom. 8.2"* (1).

The poems that follow document in considerable detail the implications of this position. Much of their matter has to do with Protestant doctrine as Collins experiences it both intellectually and emotionally. Her emphasis on certain aspects of Calvinism, particularly the doctrines of the elect and of original sin, is clear, but her modification of some of the harsher aspects of those doctrines suggests that she is expressing a mainstream form of Protestantism, rejecting too narrow a definition of "the elect" while avoiding the dangers of Arminianism. Throughout the volume, Collins's emphasis on doctrine, however, is that of means rather than of end. Clearly she sees an informed understanding of the church's teachings as one of the avenues toward the faith that she chiefly celebrates. The other avenue is Scripture. In "The Preface" she specifically rejects sudden revelation as a false means to truth, rebuking those attracted by "every new device that seemes to shine" (l. 3). "Rather," she says, "with the Saints I doe rejoyce,/ When God appeares to his in Gospel-voyce" (ll. 76–77). Repeatedly she emphasizes her role, not as one who interprets scripture but as one who brings its vivifying force on the human soul into focus. The distinction is important since, in contrast to some of her predecessors (George Herbert, for example), Collins cites scripture directly, rather than appropriating it into the narrative voice of the poem. She also follows prose traditions in listing the relevant scriptural verse in the margins of her verse. Quite clearly, Collins's selected medium of poetry, as opposed to the theological treatise, for example, reflects her desire to inspire rather than instruct her readers. It was, she tells us, her "morning exercise/The fruits of intellectuals to vent, / In Songs or counterfets of Poesies, . . . haveing therein found no small content" ("The Preface" ll. 8–11), and in her letter "To the Reader," she confesses that she is "affected to Poetry." "The thing it self [writing poetry] appeared unto me so amiable, as that it enflamed my faculties, to put forth themselvs, in a practise so pleasing" (1).

Although her "morning exercise" of writing was evidently spontaneous, the arrangement of the verse selected for her *Divine Songs and Meditacions* is quite clearly a calculated one, and the reader is apparently expected to move sequentially through the collection rather than sampling at random. Beginning with "The Preface," we are given an overview of what is to come, then led immediately into the doctrinal center of Collins's poetic experience with "The Discourse." The poems that follow this central piece, first the "Songs" and then the five "Meditacions," are evidently designed as, respectively, casual and then formal exemplifications of the moods and spiritual states that result from the kind of religious experience "The Discourse" details. It is important, then, to follow Collins's directions and begin a close study of her work with "The Preface."

This poem, in 19 stanzas, graphically conveys its importance not only through its use of the formal metrical pattern of rhyme royal, but also through the selection of an italic type font. In keeping with her emphasis on Scripture, Collins also invokes formality through biblical reference, setting her prefatory remarks within two important biblical texts, Revelation 6, which she paraphrases as God "opening the Seales successively" (l. 19) and Isaiah 40.11, which she renders as describing how Christ "himselfe . . . doth the weaker lead; He to his bosum will his Lambs collect,/And gently those that feeble are direct" (47–49). In so doing, she directs her readers' experience of her poems to follow the pattern of her own successively ecstatic experience of, first, the miracle of God's grace and then the greater miracle of its sustained repetition. This movement — emphasizing the necessarily successive nature of religious experiences in keeping with both scriptural promise and human experience — governs the organization of the poems to follow.

"The Preface" does give us some incidental autobiographical information, but this is immediately integrated within the larger pattern of the successively incremental expansion of religious experience. For example, Collins opens her poem with an oblique reference to a physical disability, possibly occurring suddenly, which apparently exempted her permanently from the domestic preoccupations which had earlier filled her mind: "Being through weakness to the house confin'd,/My mentall powers seeming long to steep,/were summond up, by want of wakeing mind/Their wonted course of exercise to keep" (1–4). But she quickly moves on to set her own history within the larger context of God's "history" as implied by Scripture, seeing her own physical disability simply as an instance of trials suffered at the hands of the wrathful Old Testament God and her spiritual ecstasies as correlative with New Testament mercies. Here her emphasis, conveyed through conventional biblical images of rain and harvest, is less on the process by which God works (hence the conventional imagery) than on the particular nature of the "vertue" that is his product as realized in her. The potency of that virtue is the "matter" of the poems to follow:

> So sorrow serv'd but as a springing raine
> To ripen fruits, indowments of the minde,
> Who thereby did abillitie attaine
> To send forth flowers, of so rare a kinde,
> Which wither not by force of sun or Winde:
> Retaining vertue in their operacions,
> Which are the matter of these Meditacions.

(106–12)

One of the few critics to engage Collins's poetry, Thomas Healy, uses verses from "The Preface" as a point of comparison with George Herbert's "Jordan I" to instance the differences

between the male poet's resources of a classical education and
a courtly audience and the female poetic stance when deprived
of those resources (49–52).[4] Yet it is pertinent to our under-
standing of her poetry that Collins does not position herself
against other poets but against a different order of religious
experience. She writes, she says, in opposition to those reli-
gious enthusiasts who "hanker after Novelties," instead of
seeing "Divine Truth" as located in a progressively more in-
formed human response to the Gospel. The "ground of Truth,"
she says, lies in the full experiencing of "Gospel," and it is
cumulative: ". . . who time past with present will compare/
Shall find more mysteries unfolded are,/So that they may who
have right informacion/More plainly shew the path-way to
Salvacion" (88–91). In short, the ground of authority for Collins
is the progressive unfolding of God's plan, and her writing
is empowered by it; gifts of a classical education or a poetic
ancestry are beside the point.

"The Discourse," Collins's central poem, begins by reca-
pitulating some of the points made in "The Preface." For us,
the most immediately interesting detail is the second auto-
biographical reference, which implies either that at least a
portion of Collins's disability may have been congenital or
that she was prey to a recurrent form of depression: "Even in
my Cradle did my Crosses breed/. . . Which of my selfe, I
never could alay,/Nor yet their multiplying brood destroy,/
For one distemper could no sooner dy, / But many others would
his roome supply" (57–63). This time she expands at some
length on her own inability to address her depression and on
the passing nature of the few solutions she found: "All mocions
of delight were soon defast, /. . . They quickly were disperced
every one,/Whereat my minde it self would much torment,/
Vpon the rack of restless discontent" (66–70).

Her recovery is not sudden. It began, she tells us, with an
intuitive awareness of a need which is at first misdirected,
"through ignorance of better exercise," to the reading of

"plesant histories." It is at this point that grace is unexpectedly granted to her — "The Sun of righteousness reveald his light / Vnto my soul" (124–25) — and she rejects secular literature and turns her attention to the reading of scripture, which at last supplies the "matter" for her mind and soul "to feed upon."

The central purpose of "The Discourse," however, is not simply to record a spiritual epiphany but rather to fully impress the reader with both the demanding and the fulfilling nature of the life that Collins has chosen. It is this theme to which she gives her greatest sustained attention throughout the poems to follow and which is, I would argue, her central contribution to the examination of what follows from faith. Spiritual ecstatic experience, she points out, is no more lasting than its secular equivalents. It must be supplemented by rigorous self-instruction: "holy Zeal . . . must with knowledg dwell,/For without [the] other, neither can do well" (202–04). From this point on, "The Discourse" is annotated with scriptural reference, demonstrating that Collins's pursuit of the "grounds of true Religion" was serious and complete. It was also far-ranging, as the remainder of this poem is given to a compressed and succinct, yet inclusive, discussion of Protestant doctrine, Old Testament Christian history and the mysteries of New Testament true faith. Collins's compression and elucidation of these points is impressive as she succeeds not only in instructing her readers, but also in holding our interest by weaving her personal experience through her explication of doctrine.

The doctrine as Collins expresses it is generally Protestant, but, parenthetically, it may be premature to attempt to establish exactly what variant of mid-seventeenth century Protestantism until we have more biographical evidence of her.[5] She is careful to tell us, for example, that of God "I frame no Image in mind,/But I conceive him by his properties" (240–41) and her order of proceeding is conventional, moving from an exploration and discussion of each person of the Trinity, directly to several verses on the topic of original sin and its consequences for humankind, and then into a discussion of the role played by Christ in our salvation. Context, cause, and solution are so deftly described that a reader can easily overlook Collins's skills of selection and compression unless one pauses to recall the sources she is probably working with and the centuries of discussion she is alluding to.

The latter part of this long poem, the discussion of faith, is the most personal, yet Collins is careful to give the greater part of her attention to those critical doctrinal distinctions which are essential for individual salvation, thus bringing the personal and doctrinal into harmony. "Christs sufferings are sufficient for to free,/All men from wo and endlesse misery" (365–66) she observes. Yet, and for her this is an emotional as well as an intellectual point, "all men have not faith, and therfore be,/ Vnlikely to have benefit thereby" (367–68). Faith is critical, she emphasizes, not only to one's eventual salvation but also to one's daily life. And it is not achieved simply by wishing; instead it is "wrought," "hammered" out, distilled from a nuanced understanding of God's "Law," especially the ten commandments, which in Collins's rendition are each presented not prescriptively but experientially.

Collins goes to considerable effort to define faith ("a Grace which doth the soul refine,/Wrought by the Holy Ghost-in contrite hearts" 372–73) and is explicitly Protestant in describing its essential role in human salvation ("thereby only are we justified . . . and thereby only are we sanctified" 569–71; and it is God "whose grace it is that justifies;/And not our works," 578–79). Her greatest attention, however, is given to the precise nature of sustained faith, its successive stages and its progressive growth. Her emphasis here is, as she stresses in the line just quoted, not on "our works," in the Church of England sense of "good deeds," but on the slowly garnered understanding that faith, while often interrupted in this mortal life, can be depended upon to return. Thus, "there are," she tells us, "divers measures or degrees/Of Saving Faith" (526–27). At the first stage, the individual knows of "inward bliss" (530) yet cannot feel the "full assurance" that such bliss will be granted to him. At the second stage, he gains confidence by moving from awareness of a need for faith to the realization that, it is God's will, not human desire, that prompts that need. After this critical juncture "On God he waites, and for an answer staies" (539). From this point on, "his Soul it faints not, nor his Spirit tires,/Although he be delayd yet still he praies" (537–38), confident that "He hath the Spirit of his Saviour dear" (542) and "where his Spirit is there Christ resides" (545). Although Collins uses the masculine pronoun here, the reader will recall the opening of "The Discourse" when Collins described her own experience of moving from felt need to increasingly confident practice, to the blessings of "full assurance" and will understand that this generalized discussion arises as much from the poet's own experience as from the "worn and old" (710) standards of Protestant instruction. Thus, although this central poem concludes on a general note, the reader is invited to hear Collins's individual voice through the "Songs" and "Meditacions" that, following, exemplify the spiritual states correlative to these theoretical positions.

The first of these spiritual states, appropriate to one who suffered physical and emotional pain, is the product of the conquest of melancholy. It is captured in the first "Song," titled "A Song expresing their happinesse who have Communion with Christ." This poem, one of the longer songs, uses a combination of conventional biblical images with an innovative metrical pattern to both persuade and induce a spiritual state of relaxed (not ecstatic) grace. The conventional biblical language, drawn from a mix of passages from Corinthians, Ephesians, Galatians and the Gospel of John (all cited in the margins of the text), is used to describe the successive stages through which the soul moves in her progression from melancholy to grace. Here the pivot point is the text from Isaiah (54.5), "Who formed thee is thine," which Collins uses to investigate the paradoxically reciprocal connection between the God who both made and died for the human soul and that soul that both is possessed by and possesses God. Intriguingly, the "Song"' does not conclude with the resolution of the paradox. The stanza following the one exploring the mysterious union of maker and made does resolve that mystery by opening with the line "in our Vnion with the Lord alone,/ Consists our happinesse" (33–34) and by concluding with "Through Christ that strengthens me/No thing is hard I see/ But what perform I may" (46–48). Yet this is not the concluding stanza of the poem, although it might logically be so. Instead, Collins continues by remaining more true to experience than to logic as she goes on to acknowledge what she herself must surely have known firsthand, that grace in this mortal life lapses. The soul is thus counseled again, and visited by Christ again, until the last stage of "happinesse [through] Communion with Christ" is reached — not the stage of ecstatic union but rather the stage of confident ("firm") trust that grace, once extended, will never be permanently withdrawn. The spiritual state celebrated in this song, then is not ecstasy but confident acceptance, genuine "Communion" as the title confirms.

As the other songs reiterate, ecstasy is not a goal to be pursued but a stage on the way to the real goal, "comfort," and this point seems to be the essential human truth which Collins seeks to convey to her readers. Where the matter of her verse might be repetitive, however, the meter is not, and, as the editors of *Kissing the Rod (153)* have pointed out, Collins, like other imitators of the Psalms and similarly song-like sections of the Bible (e.g. the Song of Solomon or Ecclesiastes), often selected complex song forms, variants on ballads or on more formal rhyme schemes (like rhyme royal), for her verse. Her comment, already cited, from her "Letter to the Reader," that she was "affected to Poetry," a "practise so pleasing," is thus confirmed by this section of her lyrical verse.

Collins's volume concludes with five "Meditacions" and a last poem titled "Verses on the twelvth chapter of Ecclesiastes." These evidently differ from the "Songs" in that they present the distilled essence of Collins's personal theology, those spiritual truths upon which she could rely. As a group they have more formal unity than do the songs because they are written in couplets, rather than displaying the more varied patterns of rhyme and meter found in the preceding verses. Yet while they display less range and variety in both form and content than do the "Songs," they nevertheless assert greater confidence. The opening line of the second "Meditacion" provides the theme for them all: "The storm of Anguish being over-blown/To praise Gods mercies now I may have space" (70).

"Praise" for Collins is still didactic in form, however. The third "Meditacion" is representative, counseling patience yet reminding the reader of Collins's own hard-won awareness that patience and passivity are not the same. The poem opens with the counsel,"Faint not my Soule, but wait thou on the Lord." It then develops more fully the point that faith, for Collins a form of "praise" because it is a return to God, is exercised not simply by waiting but is also displayed through the study of Scripture: ". . . then my Soule, the Lord thy Porcion be/Delight in his Word and sacred Covenants/Wherby his Graces are conveyed to thee,/As Earnests of divine inheritance" (49–52).

The study of "Word and Covenants" through Scripture is efficacious not in a vaguely generalized but in a quite specific way, a point made in both the first and fourth "Meditacions." In the first, Collins describes the effect of the moment of original sin on the spiritual faculties:

The Understanding, Will, Affections cleare,
Each part of Soule and Body instantly
Losing their purity, corrupted were.

(26–28)

In the fourth "Meditacion," she describes how the penitent
soul, touched by grace, humbled and washed by contrition,
and strengthened through the study of Scripture will experi-
ence Christ as a "Restorative," who will make the "Under-
standing apprehend," and who will "affect the Will/As it
forsaketh that which cannot fill," until, finally,

The over-flowings of this grace divine,
To goodnesse the affections will encline,
Turning the hasty current of thy love
From things below, unto those things above.

(26–29)

Terms like "understanding," "will," "affections," then, as well
as "faith," "grace," "restored," "sanctified" have very specific
meanings for Collins. As we have seen, they blend established
Protestant doctrine with individual experience so that they
receive the stress of active contribution and become infused
with Collins's own determination to sustain the faith offered
through the unexpected grace of God. It is out of these mean-
ings, the "over-flowings" from the line above, that she con-
structs her poems.

The concluding poem, the versified paraphrase of chapter
12 of Ecclesiastes, appears as a kind of coda after the "Medi-
tacions" have concluded. Initially, Collins stays fairly close
to the text, her first seven stanzas corresponding more or less
directly with their biblical source. Stanzas 8 through 13 are,
however, as Collins acknowledges, a digression as she com-
ments with reference to Ecc. 12.7 — "and the spirit shall
return unto God who gave it" — on the controversy over whe-
ther the soul dies with the body, a heresy (in Collins's view)
articulated by some. She vigorously disagrees here, and her

disagreement is of interest to us chiefly for her reasons in opposing this belief. There is, she says, no support for it in Scripture: ". . . they have no Scripture . . ./Save what they wrest unto theyr own Perdicion" (ll. 61–62). Collins thus leaves her readers with a reminder of how closely her own faith and poetic practice are grounded in Scripture, a point of some significance as we turn now from describing Collins's poetry to assessing her place in the literary tradition of the religious lyric.

Traditionally, those scholars who have traced the evolution of the religious lyric in English Renaissance poetry have seen its formal properties as drawn from secular verse (sonnet, song, verse letter) and its religious matter as increasingly Protestant, though by way of adaptations from continental and Catholic, Augustinian and Ignatian, practices.[6] Those poets most frequently labeled as "major" — Donne, Herbert, Crashaw, Marvell, Vaughan and Traherne[7] — command respect for their wit and irony, for their skill with imagery, and for their control of narrative voice. Moreover, their handling of scripture and doctrinal materials is usually praised precisely for its skillful integration with that voice. George Herbert's "The Collar" is one such example of the traditional seventeenth century religious lyric.

A moment's reflection will underscore how different this poem is from what we find in Collins. In Herbert's poem, doctrine (the unexpected, undeserved gift of grace) and scripture (Matthew 11.29–30) are digested into the narrative; the persona, a courtier turned cleric, appeals to an essentially masculine experience; the reader is unacknowledged, placed offstage in a bystander position; the speaker and poet are clearly distinguished from each other, and the poem is vigorously non-didactic, dramatizing, not telling, its point. Behind it lie techniques we have been well-trained to locate: rhetorical traditions from university exercises, plays on the double vocabulary of the secular and sacred worlds ("collar," "suit," "cordial fruit," "wine," "crown," etc.), the manipulation of syntax to convey the agitations of unexamined speech so that the listener knows more than the persona and thus undergoes the self-congratualtory experience of realizing where the re-counted spiritual experience is headed before the speaker does. The poem is thus the product of a particular tradition, to the techniques of which we as twentieth century readers have been trained to respond.

An Collins's verse is quite different, and for some readers may suffer in contrast. Yet one earlier seventeenth century voice, describing some religious lyrics at least partially writ-ten by a woman, is worth hearing more attentively. That voice is Donne's, and the verse he speaks of is Mary Sidney's trans-lations of the psalms. In his verses titled "Upon the transla-tions of the Psalms by Sir Philip Sidney, and The Countesse of Pembroke his sister," Donne comments of the Sidneys, "They tell us why, and teach us how to sing" (Shawcross 388–90). A careful reading of Donne's poem makes clear that he defines that "why" and "how" in ways which do not quite accord with the view of the English religious lyric as we are currently describing it. To begin with, Donne designates the Sidneys' poems as valuable not in spite of the fact that they are translations but precisely *because* they are translations, "songs" through which "heavens high holy Muse" who once "Whisper'd to *David*" now speak. As "*Davids* Successors," the Sidneys have been divinely selected, marked with "holy zeal," so that the Psalms "are become so well attyrd" in English as they have been in French and Italian before. Thus it is not originality or innovation that Donne celebrates. It is divine selection, expressed in "formes of joy and art." Our own bias, in favor of what the Sidneys might have seen as an ego-centric originality, is difficult to see through, and even the most astute critics sound a note of struggle when selecting these materials for discussion and seem anxious to justify them on the increasingly narrowed grounds of literary merit which sometimes seems dangerously close to being reduced to narrative voice.[8] If translations and paraphrases of biblical texts are more frequently seen as historical rather than literary matter, the explication of doctrine is deemed even less worthy. Thus An Collins's subject matter, the vivifying force of Protestant doctrine on the struggling human soul, may well have excluded her, to date, from the standard lists of major religious lyric poets of the seventeenth century.

Yet if we listen to Donne and consider the implications of his praise, that the English religious lyric has at least part of its origins in translation and in poetry rooted in scripture, then our attention is directed toward a body of poetry which has also not been acknowledged in standard undergraduate courses, the body of religious poetry written by women. It is thus possible that the religious lyric may be being denied part of its true heritage because translation, particularly insofar as it plays a part in the tradition of the English religious lyric, was the one area that did not exclude women writers. It is only recently, in fact, that Mary Sidney, who was responsible for the larger share in the Sidney Psalms, has begun to receive the credit she deserves.[9] Thus, a second revision of our understanding of the tradition of the English religious lyric is prompted by Collins's poetry, suggesting that we might explore further translations of the Psalms and other biblical poetic texts, especially those done by women. Increasingly, I suspect, if we do so, we will find the tradition of the religious lyric refocused in ways that may correct some of the impressions we are currently working with.

It may well be that some of this refocusing will include greater attention to those features of verse we have just been noting in Collins's poetry, especially those which so directly contrast with Herbert's verse: attention to doctrine as subject matter; attention to the speaker's spiritual state, unmediated by a persona; greater stress on the listeners as an intended, not inadvertent, audience with shared concerns; verse that is woven from departures from and returns to acknowledged, rather than digested, biblical sources; greater attention to subtle ranges of tone, especially in its modulations from reflection to exaltation and back again; and greater attention to the role of metrics in the creation of such variations in tone.

At the very least, for the undergraduate reader, An Collins's verse provides a useful introduction to Protestant doctrine; more tellingly, for us as scholars and critics, it also extends our definition of the poetics of the English religious lyric, as An Collins, like Mary Sidney before her, teaches us "why" and "how" to sing.

12 • "It is a lovely bonne I make to thee"

Mary Carey's "abortive Birth" as Recuperative Religious Lyric

Donna J. Long

I have to much case to feare, my condetion dismall, senc the light of thy grace in me is by my abomenations become darcknes, O how greate then is my darcknes . . .
from *The Private Diary of Elizabeth, Countess of Mordaunt*

Maire Mullins introduces *Religion and Literature*'s special issue on women, spirituality, and writing, by observing that "[n]aming one's relationship to the sacred both empowers and is empowering" (1). It is, Mullins continues, "the crucial and most difficult first step for women writers" (2). The Countess of Mordaunt, from whose seventeenth century prose diary I take my epigraph, provides one example of the possible repercussion of "naming" that relationship. Her paradoxical empowerment through self-degrading humility is a familiar trope, but it is by no means the only possible approach to constructing a relationship between one's sense of self and God. Mary

Carey, another seventeenth century woman with arguably greater reason to despair than had the Countess, discovers a sense of herself as precious in relation to the sacred. In elegies for two infant sons and for a miscarriage, Carey recovers an "empowered" maternal body. In the poem, "Upon ye Sight of my abortive Birth ye 31th: of December 1657," Carey equates her miscarriage with the deaths of five other children and employs many of the conventions we recognize as belonging to the elegy. Yet the poem is also a religious lyric, in which Carey engages a wide range of doctrine and negotiates biblical tropes.[1] The poem demands that we recognize not only early modern women's appropriation and critique of religious doctrine, but their investment in it as well. Following Mullins, we may see Carey's poem as a "difficult first step," in which she explores the tensions inherent in writing as a mother and a mourner, and as a "godly woman" whose sacrifices cause her to question God. Carey is moved to engage God, to "name" her relationship with God, in response to her grief over the many deaths she has weathered. Claiming the complex emotions of the religious lyric as her own, Carey seeks to find, as Paul phrases it in Romans 12.6, her "gifts . . . according to the grace that is given unto us," or her value in relation to the sacred. In this essay I want to explore how Carey's interpretations of the Word enable her recuperation of subjectivity, or, to put it another way, how the lyric exploration of religious conviction enables Carey to value the capacity for childbearing as a gift given both to her and by her.

Women's Writing and Sacred Belief

As the editors of this collection rightly observe, the writing of women and other "minor" writers of seventeenth century religious lyric enables us to better understand canonical works. The "silent neglect" of texts by women and others, whether a result of their perceived inferiority to canonical works or the individual writer's gender or small *oeuvre*, is being remedied, as this collection makes clear. While appreciative of the religious lyric as an art form, scholars are asking different questions: for example, what experiences moved women to write, what cultural discourses allowed them a voice, and how did their voices in turn affect those discourses. That early modern women's writing is largely religious in content is now a commonplace. The 1985 collection *Silent But for the Word* asserts as much in its title, and, in her introduction to the volume, Margaret Hannay notes, "women were permitted to break the rule of silence only to demonstrate their religious devotion" (4), while "women who ignored the limits of female discourse [were] herded back within their proper boundaries" (5). While extant texts suggest sixteenth century women were more often translators of male-authored texts than generators of "original" writing, in the seventeenth century women increasingly began to "author" their own works.[2] Whether translated or "original," women's writing is characteristically infused with scriptural authority.

This omnipresent religiosity paradoxically has led scholars to assume, and consequently to demote, religious conviction in favor of a concerted effort to discover something "in addition to" that investment.[3] Elaine Beilin has argued that "private prayers" were an acceptable genre for women, "perhaps because of the illusion that [the woman writing] was absent from the work" (*Redeeming Eve* 87). Avra Kouffman has observed that spiritual diarists like Lady Mary Rich, writing in a sanctioned genre which constrained subjectivity, "consciously attempted to copy the models" in Christian guidebooks (Kouffman 13). Clearly female piety cannot be taken for granted: as both Beilin's and Kouffman's syntax intimates, there is often more than meets the eye in even overtly religious genres. In an introductory essay for *Order and Disorder in Early Modern England*, Anthony Fletcher's and John Stevenson's focus on social status demonstrates the complexity of early modern piety. They argue, "The mass of the people were never persuaded to see life's travails in terms of the workings of God's providence or to accept the link between sin and misfortune that was so central to protestant theology" (23). The fine distinctions made by Fletcher and Stevenson potentially pertain to rituals surrounding childbearing. Like the "rural populace" Fletcher and Stevenson discuss, mothers and midwives "took from the church and its rituals what they wanted" (9). For example, prayer augmented rather than replaced other childbirth rituals.[4] The pious sensibility we typically posit for the literate gentlewoman commingled with popular culture at the childbed — when even she relied on a midwife's knowledge and skill to bring her safely through labor.

On the other hand, respecting and consequently foregrounding the religious conviction of early modern women provides crucial insight into their experiences. Women's roles in the religious turmoil of the period were significant, if not always as well-chronicled as the roles of male figures of rank. In *Godly People: Essays on English Protestantism and Puritanism*, Patrick Collinson notes that historians "have . . . long recognised that the staunchest and most zealous recusants were often women," and "the same observation was often made of the more fervent Protestants by their contemporaries" (274). Alicia Ostriker similarly observes that women have always been a part of Christianity's "anti-institutional" history, "in Christian martyrology, in the lives of the female saints, in women's conversion narratives" (13). As these observations imply, there was also a deep schism in women's representation in religious terms, beginning with Eve and Mary. Richard Hooker believed that "women [were] naturally 'propense and inclinable to holiness'" (Collinson 274), while the recusant Mary Ward wrote of meeting "'a Father'" who claimed "'he would not for a thousand worlds be a woman, because he thought that a woman could not apprehend God'" (Crawford 1). The contradiction between female piety and depravity abounds in early modern texts and is inherent in Christian ideology. Protestantism allowed women spiritual equality but presumed physical and intellectual inferiority to men. Active piety and passive femininity were ill-fitting dual ideals for women which made religious expression, like writing religious verse, always already a kind of oxymoronic act.

As form and fodder for poetry, religious faith was of particular relevance in the seventeenth century, as has been well documented.[5] The Protestant emphasis on scripture and the individual's relationship with God provided the faithful with example and impetus. In "Cleared by Faith," John Augustine notes the legitimation of poetry as a scriptural form came from "Reformed Protestants [who] recognized the literary qualities of the Bible and argued that these qualities established an authoritative precedent for the use of poetry elsewhere" (18). When poetry was based in Scripture, however, it was agreed that it must be "rightly understood to 'exactlie agree with the word of God'" (21). With the Bible as the ultimate source of the religious lyric, Helen Wilcox reasons, "it is no wonder that the poets were intimidated as well as justified by this sense of the standing of their poetic mode" ("Curious" 22).[6] That poets did take license on occasion is clear enough, even though it meant running a risk of placing "one's own work above that of God."[7]

The shared historical moment and its crisis of faith are overarching elements of the religious lyric as a genre. The "freedom" to define one's own relationship with God was not unproblematic, and treatises instructing the faithful in religious meditation were available to English readers in hundreds of editions by 1600 (Martz 5). The literary qualities of the Bible as a poetic influence can be coupled, therefore, with what Louis Martz has identified as the "meditative" mode in the religious lyric. Martz's evidence that meditative "exercises" closely correspond with works by Donne, Herbert, Vaughan, Southwell, Crashaw, and others, is significant for religious women poets of the period as well. Martz argues that "the common practice of certain methods of religious meditation" allows us to recognize "Donne's originality, not as a meteoric burst," not as springing from his exceptional genius, "but as part of a normal, central tendency of religious life" (2). As Martz disburdens Donne of his role as sole influence to a generation, so we are invited to disburden the writing woman from her "exceptional" label and make room for recognizing women as full participants within the culture. If these "methods" are, as Martz demonstrates, found not only in the work of important male poets of the period, but also in the widely-disseminated treatises to religious meditation, that women employ them in their own poems is not surprising.[8]

Many characteristics of the religious lyric are, at first glance, gender-neutral. Among meditative methods, "an acute self-consciousness that shows itself in minute analysis of mood and motives; a conversational tone and . . . language that is 'as a rule simple and pure'" (Martz 2), are found in male- and female-authored religious lyric, as are an "intensely verbal sense of God" and the overall "'objective' of honoring God" ("Curious" 12, 24). But there are also discernible gendered aspects of the genre. Hannay has argued that the Psalms provided Anne Lok and Mary Sidney with "opportunity for individual meditation" ("Wisdome" 66).[9] Michael Schoenfeldt has shown how Amelia Lanyer's devotional verse "converts the traditional materials [of the religious lyric] into a specifically female genre" (216). The religious lyric combines for the woman writer the authority of scripture with the stimulation of prosody. The first provides a right to write, while the latter propels an exploration of the subconscious. The examples of Sidney, Lok, and Lanyer allow us to submit that the religious lyric invites distinctions along gender lines. Wilcox, in examining the devotional writing of a number of early modern women (including Mary Carey), concludes the wide variety of forms and approaches found in their work results in

> two significant effects. On the one hand, there is an inten-
> sification of the speaker's vulnerability through the parallels
> between the inscribed feminized soul and the prescribed
> situation of woman . . . . On the other hand, . . . the soul's right
> to praise, to sue for grace, or to discover layers of selfhood offers
> a freedom to the speaker that is all the more notable when the
> voice is female ("Soule" 14).

A woman wrote in the gap between her desire to profess her
faith (often signified as a duty) and her desire to meet the cul-
tural measure of ideal femininity which elided silence with
virtue and speech with whoredom.[10] In fact, the diverse ways
in which early modern women negotiated this gulf speak to
the depth of their faith, to their creativity, and to the reality of
the gulf itself.[11]

Elegiac Conventions and Sacred Belief

In "True State Within: Women's elegy 1640–1700" Kate Lilley
points out that "women's contribution to elegy, public or oth-
erwise, has . . . been steadily overlooked in generic histories"
(214 *n13*), and thus the definitive characteristics of elegy have
been culled from male authors. Most of the extant elegies by
mothers partially employ the genre's characteristics, as de-
fined by studies of male-authored elegy: unconditional accept-
ance of a loss as God's will and even a source of pleasure;
condemnation of grief as impious; death as God's "due"; and
assurances that patience, humility, and faith will be rewarded
with healthy children.[12] G. W. Pigman notes that both men
and women were admonished not to mourn the dead, and the
bereaved were reminded that *their* sin caused the virtuous
deceased to be taken by God (18). The theological foundation
of these elegiac conventions permeated the culture at large.

Whether participating as poets or not, men and women in
the period were enjoined by religious doctrine to cope with
grief over loss. "Providence" provided the bereaved with some

explanation for what surely must have seemed at times like overwhelming hardship. Patricia Crawford notes, "A concept of 'Providence' helped women to make sense of the accidents in their personal lives. They thanked God when they or their families escaped illnesses or death . . . " (83).[13] Pigman, citing only male poets, argues that grief became more acceptable during the seventeenth century (27–39). I want to suggest a slightly different point of view: while men may have been allowed greater expression of grief, as Pigman maintains, women may have been more consistently instructed to repress grief, to accept God's will, and to avoid "self-indulgence." Because women were considered less able to control their passions, they were believed to be more susceptible to grief.[14] In addition to anxiety over grief as a sin, Anne Laurence notes the beliefs that the emotion "could send people mad" or even prove fatal (75–76). It is significant as well that an inspirational work for women like the *Monument for Matrons* included many prayers for safe pregnancy and thanksgiving for successful childbirth but have no like orison for childloss, an oversight which further suggests women had to work through grief on their own.[15]

Faced as they were with often multiple deaths, early modern mothers' investment in such belief systems is understandable. However, investment in a system of belief does not preclude the potential for, even the necessity of, negotiating the terms of that system. As often as particularly mothers' elegies achieve the ideal of submission, the poems negotiate, or revise, conventions, enabling an expression of grief beyond what the culture deemed appropriate and perhaps beyond what the poet anticipated. Like religious lyrics by women, elegies by women are significant for their prosodic experimentation. In mothers' elegies, prosody often reveals an uneasy balancing act between conscious subjectivity (evidenced by realistic and autobiographical approaches to the loss) and elegiac conventions which deny subjectivity (evidenced by submission to God's will and consolation, typically signified by acknowledging the deceased is with God). In some elegies by mothers, the recuperation of subjectivity, evidenced by the value placed on maternal capacity and nurture, is achieved. Women's elegies, particularly those for children, reveal a complex engagement with religious doctrine and provide us with new insight into how the genre is gendered.

Given Lilley's observation that "[e]legy makes up a conspicuous part of women's poetic production in the seventeenth century" (72), the scarcity of scholarship on women's elegy is surprising.[16] One explanation for this dearth may be the tendency of scholarship ultimately to degrade the contribution of early modern women to the genre by reading their elegies primarily through a canonical lens.[17] Celeste Schenck, who wrote one of the earliest essays on women's elegy, and Melissa Zeiger, whose recent book *Beyond Consolation* devotes a chapter to women's elegy, each touch briefly on seventeenth century elegy. Schenck finds, "Early female elegists deplore their own inadequacies rather than the patriarchal constraints of the form" and "seem . . . not to trust [themselves] with the task of elegy" (14). Zeiger argues the palpable "anxiety and frustration" in response to "compulsions of social and religious decorum" in elegies by early modern women have contributed to their consistently "minor" status (62). Lilley begins to lead us from these dark woods. Recognizing that women claim a right and a duty to elegize, Lilley argues, if they question their "ability to write," they also question "the decorum and efficacy of the genre itself" (83). In mothers' elegies in particular, Lilley concludes, the "relation and access to strategies of consolation" and to the "specific literary practice" of elegy "is *troped* as inherently flawed" (72, 86; my emphasis). Every early modern woman's relationship to literary conventions was sometimes rocky, but that she resisted and revised those conventions speaks not to her failings as a poet but to her strengths.

What enables early modern women to engage the conventions of elegy so powerfully is their recourse to religious faith, perhaps the most significant of their "strategies of consolation." The work on Anne Bradstreet's poetry also bodes well for her sisters across the water. The strong Puritan current running through Bradstreet's verse originally flowed from England's shores, and Bradstreet's elegiac modes have resonance for English women elegists as well. In "'Mouth Put in the Dust': Personal Authority and Biblical Resonance in Anne Bradstreet's Grief Poems," Eileen Razzari Elrod demonstrates how Bradstreet "derived her sense of authority from the biblical texts she regularly heard, read, memorized, and meditated upon" (36). In poems for the "untimely" deaths of her three grandchildren and her daughter-in-law, "Bradstreet presents two opposing ideas — that of a good, sovereign God and that of her immediate experience [of loss] — and holds them in tension" (Elrod 42, 43). It is faith that enables Bradstreet to feel "rage and bewilderment" without giving in to despair: "The poet's sense of herself as speaking within a biblical tradition enabled her to voice her authentic experiences as a woman, as a suffering, perplexed, even angry Puritan" (36, 52). I find in this tension, as Elrod does, the possibility for the recuperation of women's experiences as mothers, mourners, poets, Christians.

The negotiation of faith in the face of loss produces a specifically female "poetics of tension," born of a continuing social repression of "immoderate" grief and a need to express grief. The term "poetics of tension" is Stanley Fish's, from his essay on George Herbert; however, I use it with a difference. In Fish's reading, Herbert conscientiously creates tension, as his persona first resists the Christian doctrine that all things are framed and informed by God's word and then inevitably "lets go" of any claim to "independence" (157). Women were also aware of the doctrine of the primacy of God's will; the difference is that the tension in their poems comes unbidden, that it happens because the conventions of elegy and of grief expression cannot contain their experience. These tensions suggest, too, that women were changing how they related to their children, to poetry, and to themselves.

What were the dynamics of the mother-child relationship that influenced how women grieved? It is the case that what looks to us like potentially nonaffective behavior — employing a wet-nurse, leaving an infant with a nurse while traveling, reporting a child's injury or death in a matter-of-fact tone — did not necessarily signify as nonaffective behavior in the period. In "The Good Death in Seventeenth-Century England," Lucinda Beier cites Elizabeth Joceline's comment in *The Mother's Legacy to her Unborn Child* that her pregnancy was "as then travelling with death itself" (52), and Joceline was and is held up as a loving mother. In the seventeenth century, a boundary between affective and nonaffective mothering is clearly drawn only at cases of infanticide or abandonment, which are called "unnatural," though today we may recognize extenuating circumstances.[18] The primacy of one's relationship with God was arguably more relevant to the early modern period than to our own, and it shaped parent-child relationships. God's will, God's ultimate "ownership" of children (who are always only "lent" to parents), and God's demand to be loved before anyone — including one's child — were surely powerful incitements for constructing particular relationships to children and to childloss.

We read with anguish, or perhaps awe, accounts of parents burying child after child, scarcely able to imagine like losses, and Lawrence Stone's argument that parents consciously avoided affective relationships with especially infants seems plausible (83). Beier notes, "Infants, young children, child-bearing women, and the elderly . . . were so at risk that mention of the age group or category itself was sufficient explanation of the cause of death . . . without recognising as necessary further diagnoses or descriptions of symptoms" (44). Kouffman observes of Mary Rich's diary, "One feels . . . that death is always hovering over the shoulder of the Stuart woman, as those around her fall prey to the very high infant mortality rate, incurable disease, fires, and wars" (15). Nonetheless, as the vigorous response to Stone's argument has shown, there is as much evidence for what we consider affective behavior as there is for what may appear to us as nonaffective behavior.[19] While an individual woman's desire for children and affection for them may seem to belie Stone's argument, expressions of affection and grief in the period are not so singular.[20] A woman who believes that a child's death is the result of her sin takes on a relatively greater burden than the loss of a child. Nor is this burden necessarily gender-specific: the seventeenth century minister Ralph Josselin "felt that his own life and the lives of his family members were virtual hostages dependent upon his piety and virtue," and he considered illnesses contracted or avoided "as a kind of barometric reading of how well he stood in God's favour" (Beier 52). If one believes in the child's salvation but nonetheless accepts responsibility for its death, the expression of grief is as much about God's displeasure as about childloss.

A child's death implicated a God-fearing woman's spiritual health (the inability to become pregnant carried the same implication), and her submission to God's will becomes a kind of exoneration. In print, submission and consolation can look like no grief at all, but they are, rather, distinct forms of grief expression. Achieving submission relieved guilt over the loss and restored some sense of worth for the bereaved, while consolation provided an explanation for what would otherwise seem an arbitrary and far more cruel experience of loss.

We can recognize some early modern women's apparently "easy" acceptance of childloss-as-God's-will as simply a different approach to grief. But in doing so we must also recognize that affective relationships are constructed by the same doctrine: children are valued as signs of God's grace and to love them is to love God. The mother-child relationship in the period is, in fact, a love triangle.

Mary Carey and the Recuperative Religious Lyric

A Calvinist by conversion, Carey's sure sense of her "right to praise, to sue for grace," to recall Wilcox, is evident in her *Meditations*, a diary of prose and poetry. In one prose meditation, "A commemoration of the love of God the Father, Son and Holy Ghost," Carey imagines Satan's charge that she has often "want[ed] the light of God's countenance" (48). She responds with a typical appreciation of her experience: "my want of inward peace made me search the cause; and a true search is a great advantage. It made me know myself" (49). Much of what we know of Carey's life is from her *Meditations*. The daughter of Sir John Jackson of Berwick, Carey was probably born between 1608–1612. She first married Pelham Carey, the son of Henry, fourth Lord Hunsdon, and, according to Carey's account, her life with Pelham was "'frivolous'" and much time was spent "'in Carding, Dice, Dancing, Masquing, Dressing, vaine Companye, going to Plays, following Fashions, & ye like'" (Greer 155). There is some indication in Carey's correspondence that one child survived from her first marriage (Greer 155), but by 1643 Carey was a widow (Blain, et al., 178). She may have met her second husband, George Payler (or Taylor, as he is named in the Meynell edition), when he was garrisoned at Berwick, the home of her family, in 1642. They were married, and by July 1644 Carey was pregnant. This was one of at least eight pregnancies (the eighth ending in the miscarriage described in the poem, "Upon ye Sight of my abortive Birth"), but only two children with Payler, Nathaniel and Bethia, lived to adulthood. Carey moved about with Payler as he fulfilled his duties as a parliamentary paymaster, with most of her time spent in the south of England. Carey outlived both her husband and her son, and was named executor of their estates. She died in 1680.

We have one poem by Carey's husband on childloss and three by Carey. While Payler's poem empathizes with his wife's grief, his first two lines — "Dear wife, let's learne to get that Skill,/Of free Submission to God's holy Will" — chide her for excessive feeling (*Rod* 157). As Payler's poem makes clear, mourning had specific boundaries. In her husband's view, Carey is overstepping those boundaries by failing to freely submit to God's will. In Carey's poem on her miscarriage, several attempts at submission and consolation are frustrated by the depth of her grief, and Carey closes the poem demanding that God act to sustain her faith.[21] For Carey, God's grace is signified by full-term pregnancy, and her consolation for this loss comes not so much because the child is with God but because she created the child for God. What Carey values, at least as she expresses her values in her poem, is God's grace as evidenced by a living child. Carey's relationship with her children is synonymous with her relationship to God. She interprets the miscarriage in part as a warning to love her two living children more, and in part as punishment for her own sin. When grief over the loss of her children — this one in miscarriage and five others — cannot be contained by conventional elegy, Carey's desire to achieve submission and consolation leads to a radical revision of those tropes. Calvinist doctrine, wherein the individual is incapable of not sinning, is reenvisioned by Carey as her individual sin juxtaposed against the perfect grace of her body.

Carey's prosodic shaping of the poem enables her to negotiate the grief she feels over childloss and over her own loss of God's good will. Her use of the present tense provides the poem

with immediacy and "realistic" imagery and tone, as well as
a "plain" style which would have been appropriate both to
her sex and to her Calvinism. In 46 heroic couplets, Carey
employs a wide range of feminine, masculine and slant rhyme
in varying end-stopped and enjambed lines. She uses caesura
freely, often in conjunction with internal slant rhyme that
further works to deemphasize masculine end-rhymes and
provides the poem with lyric movement. Other linguistic
resources which make the poem formally and narratively
sophisticated include balanced syntactical phrases and log-
ical units of time and action. Carey makes effective use of
repetition of key words like "nothing" and "quickening"
which suggest a need for "conscientious meditation" on sub-
mission, and, by implication, the depth of her grief, and four
other word choices — "frute," "expectation," "presents" and
"miscarrie" — that reflect consideration of connotative and
double meanings.

Carey's overt and covert negotiation of biblical tropes and
rhetorical strategies ultimately leads to her recuperation of
maternal power and spiritual assurance. Carey cites 37 bibli-
cal verses from the Psalms to Revelation. The poem employs
meditative elements, including a dialogue with God. Yet Carey
deviates from the meditative mode in one significant respect:
that she specifically dates her miscarriage, includes her ma-
ternal history, and names her two living children, strongly
suggests that hers is not an imagined event but a "medita-
tion" on an actual miscarriage. While male poets did include
realistic and personal experience in their poems, Carey's rela-
tionship between physical experience and spiritual wellbeing
in this poem is intensified.[22] Covert, or seemingly subcon-
scious, elements in the poem include feminine rhetorical
strategies, insofar as we characterize women's tendency to
apologize for or anticipate criticism of their writing as
gendered. These strategies, which produce a tone of submis-
sion in the poem, are countered by moments of resistance

to submission as Carey expresses taboo emotions — shock, anxiety, and rage — in response to her miscarriage.

The threat of losing a child, if not the actual experience of it, was an ever-present aspect of early modern motherhood. Carey's rendering of her experience of miscarriage provides us with insight into the relationships women had with their living and deceased children, and with their own bodies. We learn in the poem that of eight pregnancies (including the miscarriage) only two children are living. Many mothers' elegies claim, as Lilley observes, that "[m]aternal severance may be healed only by death" (90); Carey discovers in her miscarriage, in her desire for children, and in her body, metaphorically and literally, her potential for a state of grace. Carey's source of consolation, finally, is not the fetus's salvation nor the promise of her own death but her "own definition of motherhood outside established discourse" (Finzi viii), or, in Carey's case, her own interpretation of the established discourse of Scripture. Carey makes a distinction between miscarrying and taking a child to term, even if the child dies soon after. She chooses to believe that her full-term and miscarried children are all "saved," or numbered among the "elect," but the more significant distinction Carey makes among her living children, children who died soon after birth, and miscarriage is for herself: her ability to carry a child to term is a sign of her spiritual well-being, while miscarriage signals all is not right between herself and God. (Carey's poems on childloss for two infant sons reveal similar tensions and so belie her distinction in "abortive Birth.") By defining her spirituality in the physical act of childbearing, Carey privileges her biological role as a means for recuperating subjectivity.

Hannay highlights another example of an early modern woman reclaiming maternal value in Mary Sidney's version of Psalm 51, verse 5 ("Wisdome" 73). Sidney's Psalm 51 contains the inevitability of original sin through being born of woman, the main thrust of the psalm, but also values the recuperative power of maternal love: "My mother, loe! when I began to be,/Conceaving me, with me did sinne conceave:/ And as with living heate she cherisht me,/... My trewand soule in thy hid schoole hath learned" (Rathmell 120). Hannay notes how "Sidney picks up the metaphor of heat used in Calvin's explanation that 'we be cherished & kept warme in sin, as long as we lye hid in the bowels of our mothers'" and envisions the possibility of "the womb itself [as] a place where God imparts knowledge" (73). Carey similarly reenvisions and reclaims maternal power, as she negotiates conventions of mourning and elegy.

Carey's straightforward title, "Upon ye Sight of my abortive Birth ye 31th: of December 1657," and her address to the fetus in the first stanza, "What birth is this; a poore despissed creature?/A little Embrio; voyd of life, and feature" (1–2), make abundantly clear that Carey writes about a real, physical, female experience. Carey will use childbirth as metaphor in the poem, but her opening image leaves little room for reading her "Embrio" as other than tangible, constituting a wholly female employment of the image. Carey's impulse in the second stanza to recall her maternity history suggests the importance she places on her experience of pregnancy, childbirth and childloss. It seems a safe assumption that Carey's poem was written for — at most — readers familiar with her history. However, how Carey values pregnancy and childbirth, and, consequently, how she understands childloss, allow us to recognize the complex dynamics women brought to these experiences.

Early in the poem, Carey praises God in order to render her miscarriage acceptable; she refers to her previous childloss as "great wisedome," and asserts, "This [loss] is no lesse [wise]: ye same God hath it donne;/submits my hart, thats better than a sonne" (7–10). Carey emphasizes her submission to God's will by making submission synonymous with miscarriage: it is "better than a sonne" (10). From a specifically Calvinist orientation, Carey's allegiance to God over a "sonne" may be a *double entendre,* meaning both a literal male child and Jesus, although she ultimately finds assurance — and authority — in Christ's sacrifice. The next stanza continues the thread of submission imagery, but the thread is "knotted" with heavy punctuation, revealing that although Carey submits to His will, it is not easy: "In giveing; taking; stroking; striking still;/ his Glorie & my good; is. his. my will" (11–12). Carey's use of periods — "is. his. my will" — makes her struggle aurally and visually concrete. Her list of God's actions reflects as well the arbitrary God of Calvin's theology.[23] Following this stanza, Carey reiterates the primacy of God in her life: "In that then; this now; both good God most mild,/his will's more deare to me; then any Child" (13-14). Such reiteration suggests her need to conscientiously meditate on this idea and thus her conflicted feelings over the miscarriage.

Carey initially resists grief by allowing submission to God's will — the appropriate reaction to childloss — to be her primary emotion. Following these high-tension lines, she constructs a typical consolatory moment but, atypically, does not end her poem here:

> I also joy, that God hath gain'd one more;
> To Praise him in the heavens; then was before:
> And that this babe (as well as all the rest,)
> since 't had a soule, shalbe for ever blest:
> That I'm made Instrumentall; to both thes;
> God's praise, babes blesse; it highly doth me please:
>
> (15–20)

There is consolation — even joy — in knowing this soul is saved, while her conviction that she provides service to God *as a woman* is reiterated, and provides us with evidence of an early source of female esteem, as well as a source of consolation specific to women and distinct from conventional grief expression. (The contradiction is that in Calvinist doctrine no "act" will make one more or less likely to be saved.)

Nonetheless, Carey's attempt at consolation fails or, we might say, is "aborted," and, in this necessary revision of elegiac convention, the depth of her grief is signaled. She is unable to end her poem because she is not consoled.

Carey's resistance at this moment in her poem is to submission, and it takes the form of an unconscious, or covert, negotiation of convention. Carey's simile comparing God's act (the miscarriage) with "limners draw[ing] dead shadds" suggests her ambivalence. In her analogy, God provides Carey with only an "Embrio . . . voyd of life, and feature" in order to "teach" her to appreciate his skill as evidenced by her two living children, just as painters use rough sketches to sell prospective buyers on their skills, which they will not fully employ unless they know a painting is sold. Though Carey praises God's wisdom, her choice of the morbid "dead shadds" as the comparative image suggests an unconscious anger over this loss of another child.

Carey next questions why she miscarried: "May be the Lord lookes for more thankfulnesse,/and highe esteeme for [of] those I doe posesse" (21–22). We can find evidence of "sincere" grief in Carey's representation of the miscarriage as a punishment. If the loss was unimportant she would not question, as she does, "why [God] tooke in hand his rodd" (34), nor, presumably, be moved to write the poem at all.[24] Carey's recognition that she is on dangerous ground, doctrinally speaking, is made clear when she is careful to show submission, as though simply desiring to know may be misconstrued as not submissive enough: "what is the thinge amisse/I faine would learne; whilst I ye rod do kisse" (36).[25] Following Micah 6.9, Carey's scriptural source, she "acknowledges [God's] majesty" in this event (376), rather than assume a more quotidian explanation such as a fright or exposure to a bad smell, just two of many "explanations" for miscarriage in the period.[26] More significantly, we can recognize Carey's negotiation of grief when she discovers consolation for the miscarriage in the form of her living children. They provide evidence of her own election:

So doth my God; in this, as all things; wise;
by my dead formlesse babe; teach me to prise:
My living prety payre; Nat: & Bethia;
the Childrene deare, (God yett lends to Maria:)
Praisd be his name; thes two's full Compensation:
For all thats gone; & yt in Expectation:

(25–30)

Carey's term "Expectation" puns on pregnancy and suggests
that "thes two" make more children probable, which leads to
a subtle pronouncement that God has caused her enough pain:
"if heere in God hath fulfill'd his Will,/his hand-maides
pleassed, Compleatly happy still" (31–32). Carey makes her
happiness contingent on God's "Will," but "if" qualifies her
acceptance of His will. Carey demands that God be "fulfill'd"
with what he has already taken. Recognizing her literal sacri-
fice as worthy, she refigures tropes characteristic of canonical
religious lyric in a way that foregrounds her sex. In the reli-
gious verse of "poets from Donne to Traherne" Wilcox finds
"an acute consciousness of their weakness and the consequent
need to be broken in order to succeed" ("Curious" 11, 26).
Carey does not anticipate "be[ing] broken," nor does she
desire it: she has already sacrificed so much.

Carey accepts responsibility for the miscarriage in a dia-
logue with God, where he chastises her for her devotional
"dead frute" (39). A Calvinist emphasis on individual con-
science is apparent in Carey's lines, "Methinkes I heare Gods
voyce, this is thy [the] sinne;/And Conscience justifies ye same
within" (37–38). Carey's location of her conscience "within"
parallels the site of fetal nurture; thus "conscience" for Carey
may be read as spiritual and physical, just as she represents
her relationship with God. Carey's God explains that his "re-
turns" (dead children) only suit her "presents" (40) to him.
These presents, cataloged in the poem, include duties, prayers,
praises, hearing, reading, "Conference," meditation, and "act-
ing graces & . . . Conversation" (43–44), and are "the principle
spiritual exercises of Calvinism" (Greer 162).[27] Carey's choice

of the noun "presents" echoes her signification of a child as gift and as a member of the elect for God, but also as a sign of election for a mother. According to Beth Fisken, "God as portrayed by [Mary Sidney's] psalmist's prophetic voice is familiar and plainspoken, often brusque and impatient with human foibles" (170). Like Sidney's God, Carey's is impatient, capable even of insult: "thou'rt Cause of Mourning, not of Immitation" (46), he tells her. The sting of this remark is hardly soothed by recognizing that Carey herself wrote this dialogue and suggests, again, the dual burden childloss placed on women in the period.

In responding to God's impatience, Carey reinterprets Hebrews 12.6. The preface to Hebrews 12, "1 Heb doeth not onely by the examples of the Fathers before recited, exhort them to patience and constancie, 3 but also by the example of Christ. 11 *That the chastenings of God can not bee rightly judged by the outward sense of our flesh*" (114; emphasis added), is made to correspond to Carey's recuperation of the physical, as she uses sensuous adjectives — "lively," "sweet" and "sharpe" — to describe her response to His consternation. Her ecstatic response suggests the attainment of grace and even sexual pleasure, with "o" marking a moment of high emotion, "Lively: o do't, thy mercyes are most sweet;/Chastisements sharpe; & all ye meanes that's meet" (49–50). However, Carey does not consistently employ the familiar representation of the supplicant as a lover in relation to God. Her vision of her relation to God is less lover than servant (32), daughter (51), or nurse as, even in the midst of her ecstatic closure, she promises him, "It is a lovely bonne I make to thee" (81). The OED defines "bonne" as "Good; also sb. a nurse i.e., 'good woman'. a good girl; ? a novice. A (French) nursemaid" (247). Carey's specific citation, Hebrews 12.6, "For whom the Lord loveth, he chasteneth: and he scourgeth every sonne that he receiveth" (114v), enables Carey to "feel" God's displeasure as the sign of His love. Carey further appropriates the Scripture to the extent that it specifies a "sonne"; though a "daughter," she revels in God's chastisement as proof of His love and of her election.

While the dialogue with God is a familiar trope, here Carey not only compels God to chastise, she compels His forgiveness as well: "Mend now my Child, & lively frute bring me;/ so thou advantag'd much by this wilt be" (51–52). The doubling of "frute" as devotion and promise of pregnancy allows Carey to recuperate herself by recognizing her capacity for nurture as a sign of grace.

Following God's forgiveness, Carey conscientiously submits to God's will. The repetition of "nothing" to describe herself suggests that submission requires a rejection of subjectivity:

> In Christ forgive; & henceforth I will be
> what, Nothing Lord; but what thou makest mee;
> I am nought, have nought, can doe nought but sinne;
> as my Experience saith, for I'ave ben in:
> Severall Condissions, tryalls great and many;
> in all I find my nothingnesse; not any
> Thing doe I owne but sinne; Christ is my all;
> that I doe want, can crave; or ever shall:
>
> (55–62)

Having acknowledged twice that her children are not her own, Carey conscientiously gives up ownership of every thing but sin, claiming "this union [with Christ] is my only happynesse" (66), even as her relative specificity in "Experience," "Condissions," and "tryalls" suggests "real life" references. Carey's (re)turn to the desire for pregnancy is signaled by a linguistic turn, or volta, in the next line: "But lord since I'm a Child by mercy free;/Lett me by filiall frutes much honnor thee" (67–68). In literalizing the sign of God's grace as healthy children and making healthy children God's will and not her own, Carey employs typical tropes of submission. But she radically reverses the familiar biblical idea of testing and ordeal by making her faith contingent upon God's provision of "frute," rather than the other way around. The promise of salvation through Christ, coupled with her own ability to bear children, em-boldens her. She claims her "lineage," "I'm a branch of the vine" (Christ), and demands that God respond: "purge me therfore;/father, more frute to bring, then heeretofore" (69–70), as has been promised in John 15.2. Carey does not, perhaps tellingly, contemplate the first clause of John 15.2, "Every branch that beareth not fruite in me, he taketh away" (52). Rather, she warns: "Lett not my hart, (as doth my wombe) miscarrie;/but precious meanes received, lett it [faith/ child] tarie;/Till it be form'd; of Gosple shape, & sute;/my meanes, my mercyes, & be pleasant frute" (73–6). Carey demands, subtly, that God act to retain her faith, and this theme is present throughout the final lines of the poem. As Wilcox has noted in discussing Carey's elegy for her son, Robert, "[t]he ability to hold her own with God is Mary Carey's outstanding quality" ("Soule" 22).

Carey knows the scope of acceptable grief expression, and she knows the elegiac tropes; that she revises them suggests their inadequacy for containing her emotions.[28] While Carey self-consciously "accepts" God's will, she nonetheless expresses a range of emotions, including anger, that we recognize as familiar steps in the grief process but that were not condoned in the early modern period. The poem's closure, striking for the sustained ecstatic voice with which Carey "beggs" for God's grace, suggests in part discomfort with her grief but also a recuperation of her self: she is consoled for her sin, if not for the losses she has suffered. Carey's investment in Scripture and faith is revealed in her closure, as she works to make all the tangents she has explored fitting for God's sight and her own sake. Crawford has suggested feminist scholars in particular have been slow to take up religious women's writing because "it seems as if the godly woman was the successfully socialised woman" and therefore an "unexciting" prospect for study (4). Carey is a "successfully socialised" woman whose very godliness makes her an exciting study. She takes her godliness seriously enough to struggle with it.

For Carey, God's grace is both physical and metaphysical: literally, "quickening," repeated six times in seven lines, means pregnancy; metaphysically, it is the "secret operation of the Spirit" as Calvin phrased it (Boulger 20).[29] Additional support for a literal reading of physical desire is found in Carey's plea that God "let the Presence of thy spirit deare,/be wittnessed by his fruts; lett them appeare" (85–86). Carey's use of the pronouns "thy" and "his" allows the fruits of her body, in the form of children, to be both a sign of her election and her husband's "fruts." This is the first time in the poem that her husband has been (potentially) visible, and his emergence signals a shift in the final three stanzas to a subject position embodying silence, obedience, and a humility reminiscent of the Countess of Mordaunt. Taken another way, as the grammar of the line implies in part the "fruts" of God, Carey reverses her earlier metaphor, lines 51–52, when her devotion is signified as fruit. According to James Boulger, the "mystery" of God's arbitrary mercy and signs of election were never defined by Calvin: "To know that one is called, and is therefore one of the elect, one must experience the secret operation of the Spirit, for no mere exercise of intellect or will can bring about assurance of calling or election" (29). This is a significant statement for women as it makes election theoretically accessible to anyone, although there was a numerical "cap" on election. Carey evaluates and values her difference as a woman and interprets her specifically female capacity for conception as the sign of her election. If we may read the female body as grace, pregnancy as gift, we have in Carey an example of a redemption of Eve and the residual influence of Catholicism's veneration of Mary.[30]

Carey's poem presents us with a wealth of critical issues to explore — mothering, grief, and religious faith among them. My focus here recognizes that the "religious lyric" is not only comprised of complex and even contradictory poetic modes and theologies, but is also a genre that provided women with means to explore and express their complex and even contradictory subject positions. While male poets express a desire for the spiritual realm and find physicality a weakness and a liability, Carey's religious lyric must recognize her status as a woman. Her maternal body signifies her spiritual assurance, her "chosen" status. Given the largely negative cultural signification of women's bodies, Carey's is a remarkable revision. Rather than feel dismay or shame over her female distance from the spiritual state, Carey discovers and recovers "God's will" in her very sex and so revises the often negative stereotype into a "God-given" quality. Herein lies the power of the religious lyric for Mary Carey.

13• Felicity Incarnate
Rediscovering Thomas Traherne

Barry Spurr

I

Thomas Traherne (1637–74), a priest-poet in the tradition of John Donne and George Herbert, is at least as remarkable for the idiosyncrasy of his subject matter and his inimitable expression, as for the more conventional aspects of seventeenth century spirituality which his lyrics (in the *Poems* and *Thanksgivings*) and prose meditations (in *The Centuries*) reveal.

Belonging (with Richard Crashaw and Henry Vaughan) to the second generation of the poets of meditation, Traherne, like them,

> had the misfortune to come abroad into the World, in the late disordered Times when the Foundations were cast down, and this excellent Church laid in the dust, and dissolved into *Confusion* and *Enthusiasme*.[1]

The "misfortune," however, heightened Traherne's "love" for the "beautiful order and *Primitive* Devotions of this

our excellent Church" (1:xxxii), which he served as rec-
tor of Credenhill, near Hereford, from 1661 to 1669, having
replaced the Puritan minister, the aptly-named Quarrell, at
the Restoration.

Too sweepingly, Traherne's editor, H. M. Margoliouth, in
the two pages he devotes to "Traherne the Writer," claims that

> there is nothing conventional, second-hand, or merely "ortho-
> dox" about Traherne's Christianity. (1:xl)

In fact, there is a good deal that falls into these categories
in the scholar-parson's writing. What is distinctive is the
particular emphases that Traherne gives to the principal
themes of Christian orthodoxy and — as importantly and
memorably — the individuality of expression that breathes
new life into these familiar convictions in his poetry and
meditative prose.

The eccentricities of Traherne's revelation of his Christian-
ity derive from the assertiveness of its Anglo-Catholic char-
acter: he speaks, for instance, of "King Charles the Martyr,"
whose "tutor" was the crucified Lord, in the familiar linkage
of Anglo-Catholicism and royalism (1:31). His partisanship
had its source in his reaction both to the iconoclasts and regi-
cides of the Presbyterian Commonwealth and the spiritual
tepidity of Restoration Anglicanism. This had similarly pro-
voked Izaak Walton, in his *Lives*, to provide models of the
parish priest for the clergy of a less saintly Charles in his ide-
alized biographies of such as George Herbert (1670). Indeed,
the influence of Herbert on Traherne is explicit in "The
Church's Year-Book," with its liturgical cadences and in the
anatomy of Christianity that the titles of Traherne's poems
propose, with their catalog of moral experience and of the
ordinances of the Church. Like the similarly learned Herbert,
he enjoys occasional recourse to rustic, proverbial lore:

> A Christian is an Oak flourishing in Winter (1:220);
> A little Grit in the Ey destroyeth the Sight of the very Heavens (1:178)

and the parabolic:

> If you com into an Orchard with a person you lov, and there be but one ripe cherry you prefer [give] it to the other. (1:197)

But in Traherne's ecstatic celebration of felicity — the focus of his spirituality — nothing less attuned to Herbert's temperate restraint in his poetry of the *via media* could be imagined, while his kindred focus on the Creation and the Incarnation contrasts markedly with the elder poet's emphasis on the Atonement and Redemption:

> What Could I O my Lord Desire more then such a World! . . . so Magnificent a Theatre, so Bright a Dwelling Place; so Great a Temple, so Stately a Hous replenished with all kind of Treasure . . . O Adorable *Trinity*! What hast Thou don! (1:33–34, 37)

In Traherne's principal sequence of poems, the Fall and the Resurrection make late and unengaging appearances. There is a lyric "On Christmas-Day" but nothing entitled "Good Friday" or "Easter." Drawing extensively on the psalms in his poetry, it is the celebratory rather than the penitential ones that Traherne favours in his quest (as he exclaims in his "Thanksgivings for the Body") to be "as *David*, the sweet Singer of *Israel*!" (2:223). For Traherne, as for his contemporary Crashaw, whom he resembles in so many ways, "sweet" is a favourite adjective.

To the extent that Traherne expresses fervently his individual experiences of a felicitous faith, in spite of his alleged abhorrence of *"Enthusiasme,"* his is a Protestant poetics — in Barbara Lewalski's sometimes misleadingly Procrustean phrase.[2] But it is a body of individual revelation discovered within a theology, ecclesiology and spirituality that are demonstrably and, indeed, demonstratively Catholic in character. This paradox is reminiscent of Vaughan's fidelity to the Church and its doctrine (heightened by the death of his younger brother William in the Civil War, which affected Henry's conversion) in company with his intensely private spiritual intimations, poeticized in *Silex Scintillans*. When Vaughan writes, "I walked the other day (to spend my hour)," it is both his personal hour (as the pronouns emphasize), with its unusual location in "a field" and poignant references to William, and the codified hour of meditation of classical Christian divinity, with its New Testament origins.

The Revolution (in spite of itself) had produced an *aggiornamento* of Anglican spirituality that consisted of a sharpened appreciation of orthodox doctrine in combination with an intensified personal faith that, in its impassioned idiosyncrasy, recalls that of the sectaries. Traherne, author of a poem entitled "The Rapture," tells us what his writing plainly reveals: that he is "Ravished in Spirit" (1: 28). His combination of a zeal for the central doctrines of Catholic Christianity — especially, the Incarnation — and the nurturing of an apostolic individuality in his spiritual life anticipate nineteenth century Tractarianism which similarly had its unexpected genesis and departure-point (in the case of John Henry Newman, for example) in the Protestantism of the Wesleys and the Evangelical revival.

It has often been noted that Traherne and Vaughan look forward to the early Romantics, in their appreciation of the natural world and in their neo-Platonic philosophizing. What has not been noticed is that Traherne is also a precursor of the nineteenth century Anglo-Catholics (Romantics, too, in their recovery of the medieval "ages of faith" in gothic architecture, vesture and ceremonial) who, in turn, drew inspiration from the seventeenth century Church. *The Library of Anglo-Catholic Theology* (published from 1841), a series of reprints of the writings of the Caroline divines, such as

Lancelot Andrewes, introduced "anglo-catholic" into the English language.

By setting Traherne and his literary achievement in the context of his Anglo-Catholicism, I would argue that it is the necessary milieu for the informed appreciation of his art, such an approach, more generally, proposing a "rejoinder," in Michael Edwards's phrase, "to the often ill-informed dismissal of Christianity in current literary theory."[3]

II

As an Anglican in the Catholic tradition, Traherne, in his life and his writings, demonstrates several of the characteristics of that ambiguous confession. Of first importance to Anglo-Catholics, as much in the seventeenth as in the nineteenth century, was the promotion of Anglicanism as a purer expression of the primitive Catholicism that (they alleged) had been subsequently corrupted by the Church of Rome. In a vivid anecdote included in the preface to his *Roman Forgeries*, Traherne recalls emerging from the Bodleian Library in Oxford and encountering, in its quadrangle, "a man that had spent many thousand pounds in promoting Popery." Agreeing to walk in the University Parks to discuss their differences, Traherne is subjected to a recital of the achievements of Romanism, its "Eleven Millions of *Martyrs*, Seventeen *Oecumenical Councils*" and so forth. Traherne responds that the martyrs of the early Christian centuries were "Martyrs of the *Catholick*, but not of the *Roman* Church":

> they only being Martyrs of the *Roman Church*, that die for *Transubstantiation*, the *Popes Supremacy*, the Doctrine of *Merits*, *Purgatory*, and the like. (1:xxix)

Further, Traherne points out forgeries of canons in the apostles' names and the invention of Councils "that never were" to the "utter disguizing and defacing of Antiquity." Such allegations, his interlocutor retorts, are nothing but lyes whereby the Protestants endeavour to disgrace the Papists. (1:xxix–xxx)

In response, Traherne offers to take him through the Bodleian the next day to prove his case, forgery by forgery. To which, the Roman Catholic says "he would not come; but made this strange reply: *What if they be forgeries? what hurt is that to the Church of* Rome?" This is too much for the meticulous scholar:

> *I have done with you!* whereupon I turned from him as an obdurate person. (1:xxx)

In spite of this, Traherne has regular recourse in his writings to Roman Catholic authorities. In this way, he is more precisely an Anglo-Catholic *in embryo* than a proto-Tractarian. He quotes Thomas à Kempis, the medieval ascetical friar and author of *The Imitation of Christ*, as an authority (1:5), and enrolls (approvingly) "the Pope from Rome" in a catalogue of exotic devotees, including the Queen of Sheba and the Wise Men, who make obeisance at the throne of God:

> With Rev'rence would approach unto that Ground,
> At that sole Altar be adoring found.
> ("Churches," 2:117)

He is an enthusiast for the contemplative life — "what is more Easy and Sweet than Meditation," he asks, rhetorically (1:5). This signals Traherne's debt, like many before him, such as Donne (with his Roman Catholic childhood in "a family of martyrs," Jesuits amongst them), to the continental tradition of disciplined contemplation with its sources in the manuals of St. Ignatius (founder of the Society of Jesus) and St. François de Sales. And in Traherne's meditation on the Cross, for example, his ecstatic emotion — only matched by his febrile evocations of Christ as his lover — exhales the mystical spirit of the Counter-Reformation in its rapturous combination of sensuous immediacy and intimate piety:

Is this He that was transfigured upon Mount Tabor! Pale, Withered! Extended! Tortured! Soyld with Blood and Sweat and Dust! Dried! Parched! O Sad! O Dismal Spectacle! All His Joynts are dissolved . . . O JESUS the more vile I here behold Thee, the more I Admire Thee . . . I here Adore thee! I prize and Desire always to see these Stripes and these Deformities. It is sweeter to be with Thee in thy Sufferings, then with Princes on their Thrones . . . I Tremble also to see thy Condescentions . . . my only Lover is Dead upon the Cross . . . (1:48)

Of his "Lover," in "Love," Traherne's baroque effusion is more Crashavian than Crashaw:

O Nectar! O Delicious Stream!
O ravishing and only Pleasure! Where
Shall such another Theme
Inspire my Tongue with Joys, or pleas mine Ear!
Abridgement of Delights
And Queen of Sights!
O Mine of rarities! O Kingdom Wide!
O more! O Caus of All! O Glorious Bride!
O God! O Bride of God! O King!
O Soul and Crown of evry Thing . . . (2:167)

the poem culminating in an allegory of delighted submission to pederastic abduction by Zeus:

His Ganimede! His Life! His Joy!
Or he comes down to me, or takes me up
That I might be his Boy. (2:168)

Liturgically, both in his private devotions and public ministrations, Traherne's Anglo-Catholicism is clear. He used daily the offices of Morning and Evening Prayer,[4] derived from the monastic hours, as prescribed for the clergy in *The Book of Common Prayer* (but seldom rigorously observed). The recovery of the discipline of the Daily Office was one of the liturgical achievements of the Tractarians, extended and further catholicized by the later Anglo-Catholics in their religious orders. A prototype for this Catholic monastic detail in an

Anglican setting could be found at Nicholas Ferrar's seventeenth century community at Little Gidding — the subject of the last poem of the *Quartets* of T. S. Eliot, "anglo-catholic in religion."[5] And like Eliot in *Ash-Wednesday*, Traherne, in "The Dialogue," adapts the style of the versicles and responses of the Office to his poetry.

The settings of liturgy, desecrated by the Cromwellians, are compensatingly appreciated in Traherne's celebration of the church building as the consecrated House of God. Beyond Herbert's restrained architectural anatomy, this appreciation, again, anticipates the nineteenth century Anglo-Catholic (and Romantic) fervour for rich ecclesiastical adornment:

> The Arches built (like Hev'n) wide and high
> Shew his Magnificence and Majesty
> Whose House it is: With so much Art and Cost
> The Pile is fram'd, the curious Knobs embost,
> Set off with Gold, that me it doth more pleas
> Than Princes Courts or Royal Palaces . . .
> Where Towers, Pillars, Pinnacles, and Spires
> Do all concur to match my great Desires,
> Whose Joy it is to see such Structures rais'd
> To th' end my God and Father should be prais'd. (2:116)

The variegated ornamentation of this diptych-poem, "Churches," represents the exterior and interior decoration the poet praises. In contradiction of Protestant teachings about the availability of the presence of God to the believer, anywhere in the world, Traherne argues that he is specially present in buildings consecrated to his worship:

> For Churches are a place
> That nearer stand
> Than any part of all the Land
> To Hev'n; from whence som little Sense I might
> To help my Mind receiv, and find som Light.
>   ("Solitude," 2:99–100)

As the poet of felicity and light, praising the created world as "the Beautifull Frontispiece of Eternitie, the Temple of God, the Palace of his children" (1:10), and (in "Nature") noting that "The Worlds fair Beauty set my Soul on fire" (2:60), Traherne, nonetheless, reserves a special place for his numinous communion with heaven in the church building and in the order of worship. Several poems in praise of bells and music counteract the Puritan disdain for such things and anticipate the Tractarian innovation of robed choirs and the subsequent Anglo-Catholic recovery of a full and solemn liturgy of which music was an essential component. Milton regarded priestly vestments as

> deformed, and fantastick dresses in Palls, and Miters, gold, and guegaws fetcht from Arons old wardrope, or the Flamins vestry.[6]

Traherne takes the opposite, Catholic view and would set a "fair Miter" on the heads of those with "Order, Ministry and Service" in the churches:

> Cloath them with Garments; and let thine Angels stand by.
> ("A Thanksgiving and prayer for the NATION," 2:329)

With the angels were the saints. Not surprisingly, Traherne isolates Mary, as the Mother of God, for particular praise — another mark of his Anglo-Catholicism. The Tractarians were restrained about her, nervous of the cult which the Anglo-Catholics were to develop. She was a "Mother out of sight," for John Keble, who could only suggest, through coy negatives, the devotion she might be accorded:

> Therefore, as kneeling day by day
> We to our Father duteous pray,
> So unforbidden may we speak
> An Ave to Christ's Mother meek:
> (As children with "good morrow" come
> To elders in some happy home).

He detains her in the company of the saints:

> Inviting so the saintly host above
> With our unworthiness to pray in love.[7]

Traherne, however, emphasizes the singularity — and, of course, felicity — of the co-redemptrix:

> . . . the Blessed Virgin (and no other)
> Obtain'd the Grace to be the Happy Mother
> Of God's own Son; for, of her pious Care
> To treasure up those Truths which she did hear
> Concerning Christ.
>
> ("The Inference," 2:142)

Yet nowhere, it must be said, is there evidence of his belief in the intercession of the Virgin and the saints — one of the articles of Anglo-Catholicism curiously absent from his writing but which even Keble tentatively envisages.

III

It is in the presentation of the sacramental life and the holy communion itself that the focus of Traherne's Anglo-Catholicism is most explicit, for it is in the doctrine of the sacrament of the altar that the discriminations of churchmanship are clarified. Traherne's celebration of the Real Presence indicates his unreservedly Catholic interpretation of the eucharistic sacrifice:

> O holy JESUS who didst for us die,
> And on the Altar bleeding lie.
>
> (Poems from *Christian Ethicks*, VI; 2:190)

The immediacy of this portrayal of the sacred victim — in the conflation of the altar of the Cross and the altar of the re-presentation of that sacrifice in the eucharist, where the wine becomes Christ's blood — is (again) redolent of Counter-Reformation piety. So much depends here, not only doctrinally but temperamentally, on the present participle. Traherne repeatedly uses the Catholic term "Altar" (the place of sacrifice, usually capitalized) for the Protestant "God's board" — as in Herbert's "The Collar" — which is the holy table of the commemorative Lord's Supper, the elements of bread and wine being unchanged upon it, but symbolizing the body and blood.[8] Traherne, we have seen, spurned transubstantiation (or, at least, martyrs for it), yet he indisputably held a high doctrine of the presence in the sacrament, contradicting Protestant memorialism and receptionism.

Inevitably linked to Traherne's Anglo-Catholic references to the altar is his sacerdotal conception of the Church's priests (such as himself) offering the eucharist at it. He affirms the threefold apostolic ministry, denied by Protestantism, although preserved (in a protestantized form, according to Roman Catholics) by the Church of England:

> Priests and Bishops serve at thine Altar, guiding our Bodies to eternal Glory.
>
> ("Thanksgivings for the Body," 2:223)

This is a triple provocation, with priests, altars, and the *sacerdos* in his role as the dispenser of the sacraments and, thereby, the conduit to God, in the wake of the Puritan Commonwealth and its ministers of the Word, its priesthood of all believers. Moreover, liturgically, Traherne includes in his poetry (in English) the petition of the priest in the *Missale Romanum* (in Latin) before he goes to the altar to offer that sacrifice:

> Enable me to wash my hands in Innocency.
> That I may compass thine altar about,
> And lift up my Hands
> To thy Holy Oracle.
>
> ("Thanksgivings for the Body," 2:227)

The manual actions — in the *lavabo* and the extending of the hands ("*extensis manibus prosequitur*," also in the missal) — are those of the Roman rite, not prescribed in *The Book of Common Prayer* and offensive to the Cromwellians ("the

Priest set to con his motions, and his Postures his Liturgies . . . "[9]) but appropriated by Anglo-Catholicism.

Obviously, in spite of his close study of Roman forgeries, Traherne gleaned much that he regarded as authentic from the old Church and, thereby, not only worthy of preservation but demanding it, as of Catholic provenance. This is the characteristic Anglo-Catholic position he repeatedly affirms — as in his praise of

> Festivals and Sabbaths,
> Sacraments and solemn Assemblies,
> Bishops, Priests and Deacons.
> ("Thanksgivings for the Glory of God's Works," 2:252)

IV

Essential to Traherne's traditionally Catholic emphasis on the sacraments, in his prose and poetry, is his celebration of the doctrine of the Incarnation (of which it is said that the sacraments are extensions). This is a doctrinal disposition which, in his writings, is also the source of his individuality of vision and utterance, his intense perception of the material world, where the "Word was made flesh, and dwelt among us" (John 1.14), and the felicity he derives from it. Traherne sharply rebuked those who denied the doctrine of the Incarnation. The Socinians (Unitarians) are "the Enemies of our Saviors Diety in this World" (1:75). Similarly, the sour Puritans are lambasted for theorizing an otherworldly felicity but failing to experience it now, in creation: "is no deceit more Odious, then that of Spending many Days in Studying, and none in Enjoying, Happiness" (1:175).

Traherne's joyous response to the created order began, he tells us in prose-poetry of breathtaking beauty, in his childhood:

> I remember the Time, when the Dust of the Streets were as precious as Gold to my Infant Eys . . . (1:13–14)

> O what Venerable and Reverend Creatures did the Aged seem!
> Immortal Cherubims. And yong Men Glittering and Sparkling
> Angels and Maids strange Seraphick Pieces of Life and beauty!
> Boys and Girles Tumbling in the Street and Playing, were
> moving jewels. (1:111)

Such *joie de vivre* is encountered in the poetry, too — as in
"Innocence," anticipating Blake both in its song-like style and
simple but striking vision:

> The very Night to me was Bright
> Twas Summer in December. (2:16)

The human body is not envisaged by Traherne as the prison-
house of the soul, as was usual in earlier seventeenth century
religious poetry (such as the emblems of Quarles, where a
characteristic text was the Pauline plea — "O wretched Man
that I am: who shall deliver me from the body of this Death?").
Rather, he praises it both as evidence of the Creator's abun-
dance and (correctly subordinating the physical to the meta-
physical) as "a Lantern . . . to the Candle of Lov that shineth
in thy soul" (1:83). In "Ease," he declares

> that evry Man
> Is like a God Incarnat on the Throne,
> Even like the first for whom the World began. (2:66)

His theological disposition is to return to the paradise of
prelapsarian Eden. In terms of a Christian Platonism, he yearns,
Wordsworth-like, for a recovery of childhood innocence with
its proximity to preexistent purity. "An Infant Ey" is a sus-
tained celebration of this theme:

> O that my Sight had ever Simple been! . . .
> Then might I evry Object still have seen . . .
> In such an hev'nly Light, as to descry
> In it, or by it, my Felicity. (2:86)

His bodily creation is the subject of Traherne's detailed appre-
ciation in the anatomy of "The Salutation":

These little Limmes
These Eys and Hands which here I find,
These rosie Cheeks wherwith my Life begins . . .

Long time before
I in my Mothers Womb was born,
A GOD preparing did this Glorious Store,
The World for me adorne.
Into this Eden so Divine and fair,
So Wide and Bright, I com his Son and Heir. (2:4,6)

"The Salutation" appropriately introduces Traherne's princi-
pal sequence of poems, but it also recalls the angelic salu-
tation to the Virgin announcing that she would bear the Christ
child. Traherne conflates his incarnation with the Incarna-
tion itself — here, and in the next poem, "Wonder," which
also recalls the Adamic creation:

How like an Angel came I down!
How bright are all Things here!
When first among his Works I did appear
O how their GLORY me did Crown? (2:6)

In the *apologia pro vita sua* that unfolds, in the sequence of
poems at large, while the emphasis is on Traherne's felicity,
there are also records of rebellion — as in "The Approach,"
which contains this self-reproach:

Thy Gracious Motions oft in vain
Assaulted me: My Heart did Hard remain
Long time: I sent my God away,
Grievd much that he could not impart his Joy. (2:38)

But prevalent is Traherne's exultation in his very existence,
as in this audacious anatomy in the aptly named poem, "The
Person":

The Naked Things
Are most Sublime, and Brightest shew . . .
They best are Blazond when we see
The Anatomie,

> Survey the Skin, cut up the Flesh, the Veins
> Unfold: The Glory there remains.
> The Muscles, Fibres, Arteries and Bones
> Are better far then Crowns and precious Stones. (2:76)

A physiological blazon of himself, penetrating beneath the skin, this celebration of carnality in all its detail as the expression of the Creator's bounty is, so far as I can find, unique in the explicitly religious poetry of the period, although Traherne's contemporaries, Abraham Cowley (in his "Ode: Upon Dr. Harvey") and Jane Barker in her long philosophical digression on anatomy explore the same fleshly territory. Barker, for example, writes of

> How th'walls consist of carneous parts within,
> The outsid pinguid overlayd with skin,
> The fretwork muscles arteries and veins
> With their implexures . . .[10]

These do not belong, however, to the specific theological and devotional contexts of Traherne's poem:

> Shall I not then
> Delight in these most Sacred Treasures
> Which my Great Father gave,
> Far more then other Men
> Delight in Gold? (2:76)

V

In those poems where Traherne is most himself, not sounding remotely like anyone else, "Shadows in the Water" and "On Leaping over the Moon," it is the doctrine of the Incarnation which is at the source of his inspiration and of his felicity.

The dominant conceit of "Shadows in the Water," of revelations of "Another World" perceived "as by som Puddle I did play," describes the juxtaposition of our physical domain and its spiritual transformation, as articulated in Traherne's vision of a "new *Antipodes*,"

> throu a little watry Chink.

In this world, creation is turned upside down,

> Peeple's feet against Ours go.

The double wit of the conceit is, first, that the puddle is also a mirror — he is seeing himself (his "brother," as he describes him in "On Leaping over the Moon") — and, second, that Traherne construes the antipodean domain as an "inferior World," which it was, geographically (down under), while, metaphorically, it is superior, disclosing "our second Selvs." Very importantly, theologically, while the domain in which this self-discovery occurs has dimensions redolent of eternity:

> Great Tracts of Land there may be found
> Enricht with Fields and fertil Ground (2:129)

it is, nonetheless, the creation and ourselves seen *sub specie aeternitatis*. It is this doctrinal restraint that makes the poem specifically incarnational. It is not transcendental. Rather, Traherne's orthodoxy is akin to Hopkins's in "Hurrahing in Harvest," where another poet of Anglo-Catholic provenance corrects himself in recognition of, at once, the joy which an incarnational interpretation of the world produces, but its ultimate incompleteness:

> And hurls for him, O half hurls earth for him off under his feet.[11]

It is a poetic way of saying that the Incarnation has to be completed in the Resurrection.

This is the teaching, too, of "On Leaping over the Moon" where Traherne extends his vision of the "new Peeple," seen through the chink, and, discovering his "brother" — his *alter ego* — there, portrays him as one who would hurl himself beyond this world:

Up in the Skies
His Body flies . . . (2:130)

in pursuit of the Sun (with the usual pun on "Son" in the seventeenth century): "As he went tripping o'r the King's highway."

Yet this wise aspirant knew not to "trust *Icarian* Wings," such overreaching pride leading to a dismal fall to

the deep Abyss where Satan crawls
Where horrid Death and Despair lies (2:131).

His better course is but to leap over the lesser planet, and felicitously:

How *happy he* o'r-leapt the Moon . . . (2:131)

in recognition both that the joys of Heaven can be known — are incarnated, indeed — on earth and that, in this meantime, "this middle Center," this is a sufficient revelation:

Thus did he yield me in the shady Night
A wondrous and instructiv Light,
Which taught me that under our Feet there is
As o'r our Heads, a Place of Bliss. (2:132)

This felicitous recognition depends, in Traherne's poetry, as indeed in his Christianity, on his acknowledgment of the truth of the doctrine of the Incarnation — whereby Christ visited the earth, blest it and crowned the year with his goodness — which is the conviction binding together the range of beliefs Traherne so enthusiastically espoused, and that determined the Catholic persuasion of his Anglicanism and his poetics.

14 • Revisiting Joseph Beaumont

P. G. Stanwood

The writings of Joseph Beaumont (1616–99), both poetry and prose, in English and Latin, are abundant. Most of his work remains in manuscript, such as the 25 large folio volumes of theological studies, carefully preserved in the library of Peterhouse, Cambridge. Yet easily available and amply sufficient is his epic poem *Psyche* (1648, 1651); published in a second and expanded edition posthumously in 1702, with over 40,000 lines, it dwarfs *The Faerie Queene*. His shorter lyric poems, a collection of which was first printed in 1749, number about 200. Such a large outpouring of verse ought at least to have secured Beaumont a firm place in English literature of the late Renaissance, and there is some evidence that his major poem was once commonly read. Pope, for example, included *Psyche* in his reading, allegedly saying that "there are in it a great many flowers well worth gathering, and a man who has the art of stealing wisely will find his account in reading it," and he adapted a few lines from it. So also does Keats echo Beaumont in his "Ode on Melancholy."[1]

Beaumont's modest fame rests almost entirely on *Psyche*, while his religious lyrics, certainly undervalued, have largely escaped notice. Although *Psyche* does contain lyric moments, even detachable passages that may be read independently, my wish now is to discuss Beaumont's "minor" poems principally for their own considerable merit, not as wayward effusions or fragments cast off from the capacious epic; and so I hope to extend my earlier and incomplete reflections about the lyric Beaumont and move toward a fuller analysis of this "metaphysical" poet.[2] My plan is to comment on certain especially characteristic poems and also to reveal Beaumont as the composer of a "poetic book," a work that is no accidental collection, but a thoughtfully organized whole, in a fashion that may recall George Herbert's *The Temple*. This point will be illustrated through special attention to the concluding "cycle" of poems that begins in May 1652 with "The Journè" [sic].

Proper awareness of Beaumont's lyric verse was not possible until Eloise Robinson's 1914 edition of the autograph manuscript, now in the Houghton Library, Harvard University, of 177 poems, only 30 of which had appeared in John Gee's 1749 edition, but with various omissions. Gee printed as well 11 more poems that appeared in a second manuscript, now lost, which was entitled *Cathemerina*, after Prudentius's fourth century *Cathemerinon*. The first and longer collection contains poems written between early 1644 and the end of June 1652; the second appears to continue until September of the same year, after which Gee says that Beaumont ceased writing poetry — the point may be disputed, yet Gee knew Beaumont's son and executor Charles, and Gee is therefore likely to have had correct knowledge of the facts. Gee included also some 17 Latin poems in his edition, likewise from the lost *Cathemerina*; and Gee's edition of Beaumont's verse, both English and Latin, appears in the second volume of Grosart's reprint of the 1702 edition of *Psyche* (1880). But the Robinson edition is the concern of this study, being based upon a completed manuscript in the author's own hand (All subsequent references are to her edition, and page numbers are in parentheses).

Joseph Beaumont, like his more famous contemporary Richard Crashaw, flourished in that remarkable collegiate society of Peterhouse, Cambridge, in the early part of the seventeenth century. Peterhouse, the oldest and the smallest foundation in the university, was now enjoying the most notable period in its long history. This time was anticipated by Andrew Perne, master from 1554 to 1589. He had been a chaplain to Edward VI, later complied with the Marian reforms, and yet easily accommodated himself to Elizabeth, preaching before her on her state visit to Cambridge in 1564. He was in regular contact with Elizabeth's great secretary Cecil, Lord Burghley, and was a friend of John Whitgift, archbishop of Canterbury (1583–1604), who was a fellow of Peterhouse from 1555 to 1567. Perne was always close to the court; he cultivated his powerful connections there, allowing — often uncomfortably — Peterhouse to become a familiar and favorite extension of royal prerogative and influence. Moreover, Perne was at the same time a deeply learned and widely read scholar who had a passion for books, which he indulged by collecting most of the new, humanist editions of the classics and the patristic fathers, as well as the most recent scriptural commentary and theological work of the Reformation — and also current works of geography, mathematics, and literature. Perne left his splendid collection to Peterhouse, which formed the core of the library that Beaumont — and Crashaw — must have known and used.[3]

The royalist outlook of the Peterhouse where Beaumont matriculated in 1631, and where Crashaw took up his fellowship in 1635, was a natural consequence of its Tudor past which flowered in Stuart times. Matthew Wren was now master (1626–34); he had attracted the attention of King James through his skill at disputation on a royal visit to Cambridge, and he was subsequently selected to accompany Prince Charles to Spain (in 1623, also with Leonard Mawe, then master of Peterhouse) to help with the ill-fated marriage negotiations to the Infanta. Wren's favor with court and church led to numerous promotions, and he became one of the most steadfast of Archbishop William Laud's bishops, ending finally as bishop of Ely (1638–67). In succession to Wren's mastership, Laud made certain that Peterhouse remained firmly royalist and high church by helping to secure John Cosin's election as master in 1634. Cosin was already well known for his strongly partisan high church views, particularly because of his famous book of *Devotions* that he had prepared for the court at King Charles's request, and because of his encouragement of suitably Laudian ritualism at Durham Cathedral, where he had held a prebendal office.[4]

Joseph Beaumont was thus an undergraduate member, and in time a fellow, of a college clearly identified with the monarchy and with the ruling ecclesiastical authorities. He undoubtedly accepted these dominant values and made them his own, for they found expression in his theological and political outlook. So too did Beaumont respond warmly to the influence of humanistic learning cultivated at Peterhouse, and also to the kind of religious devotion encouraged by Wren and Cosin, and other proponents of the Laudian revival. In poetry this was likely to mean orderliness, sacramentalism, sensuousness, adoration of the unseen and unknowable, devotion to the saints, and a struggle to uncover and correct false longings of the conscience and heart. Beaumont would soon have the leisure to cultivate his poetic muse, for when the Long Parliament began its examination of the universities in the early 1640s, Peterhouse was at once singled out for its alleged Laudian excesses and its determinedly royalist leanings. A committee of Parliament set about to "regulate" the universities, and it expelled almost all of the fellowship of Peterhouse in March 1644. But most of them had fled in the preceding months. Crashaw went to the continent, and he was followed by Cosin, who acted as chaplain to the royalist exiles of Charles's court in Paris during the long years of the

Interregnum; Wren was confined to the Tower; Beaumont re-
tired to his family home in Hadleigh, Suffolk, where he wrote
most of his poetry.[5]

Beaumont's lyrics as printed by Robinson, and indeed his
epic *Psyche*, echo in many places the verbal characteristics of
his more familiar contemporaries, especially Crashaw and
Herbert. Such common rhymes as light-bright-night, hearts-
darts, streams-beams, things-wings, eyes-rise, breast-nest, and
more, occur regularly in Beaumont, of course reminding us of
Crashaw. Beaumont's variety of stanza structures is reminis-
cent of Herbert, with their frequent alternation of short and
long lines, occasional shaped verses, and clever interlocking
or interweaving of rhymes, though generally not, as in Herbert,
with the same attention to the subtle modulation of mean-
ing. Robinson (xxxi–xl) provides many examples of Beaumont's
indebtedness to his predecessors, and in doing so seems to
diminish his own uniqueness and value — similarly, some read-
ers of Henry Vaughan have emphasized that poet's debt to
Herbert without also adequately demonstrating Vaughan's inde-
pendence. Perhaps Robinson's decision to place Beaumont
in "the school of Donne" obscures the differences of the mem-
bers of this supposed "fellowship." But she is right to portray
Donne, Herbert, Crashaw, Vaughan, and Traherne by "the re-
ligious temper" of much of their poetry; and because of his
similar devotional interests, she allows Beaumont entrance
into their excellent "school" and some grudging association
with it (Robinson xxviii–xxxi).[6]

Beaumont's shorter devotional verse touches a number of
familiar themes, which occur with regular frequency, espe-
cially poems on apostolic saints; on various scriptural events —
mainly of the New Testament; of principal feast days; on the
sacraments; on his birthday, and on the anniversary of his
baptism. The first poem in Robinson's edition to bear a date is
March 13, 1644; this is Beaumont's birthday poem of that year;
the last poem, which begins a concluding section, is May 17,

1652. There are a number of pleasing lyric poems that celebrate or respond to particular moods or circumstances, sometimes marked to be sung or instrumentally accompanied, often "To a Base and 2 Trebles." "A Morning Hymn," obviously paired with "An Evening Hymn" that follows at once, lacks such a direction, yet its song-like qualities inspired the recent setting by Nicholas Maw.[7] The short, seven syllable lines, with their regularly falling stresses on the first, third, fifth, and seventh syllables, the clarity of diction and syntax, the occasionally off-rhymed pairs, the quiet and objective poise of the whole poem, with its resolution in a final octosyllabic line, are characteristic of Beaumont's best effects:

> What's this Morns bright Eye to Me,
> Yf I see not thine, & Thee,
> Fairer JESU; in whose Face
> All my Heavn is spred! Alas
> Still I grovel in dead Night,
> Whilst I want thy living Light;
> Still I sleep, although I wake,
> And in this vain Sleep I Talk,
> Dreaming with wide open eyes,
> Fond fantastik Vanities.
>
> Shine, my onely Daystarr, shine:
> So mine Eyes shall wake by Thine;
> So the Dreams I grope in now
> To clear Visions shall grow;
> So my Day shall measured be
> By thy Graces Claritie;
> So shall I discern the Path
> Thy sweet Law prescribed hath;
> For thy Wayes cannot be shown
> By any Light, but by *thine own.* (325)

This felicitous poem is reminiscent perhaps of Herbert, or of Vaughan. Beaumont plays on the multiple senses of morning light, and the radiant face of Jesus that shines over the poet and his world, illuminating the darkness of his sleep. The poet's path becomes clear, firmly governed through the clarity of

God's grace whose light discovers light. The final couplet contains the mystery of this gleaming dawn and the sense of the whole poem, with the last line and its significant medial pause helping rightly to direct the traveler's way.

"Loves Mysterie" occurs near the beginning of the *Minor Poems*, and it is indeed marked "For a Base & 2 Trebles," and its theme hovers about the definition of love — in no way like Marvell's limpid division into two parallel lines that never meet. Beaumont struggles feelingly to find love in a fiery and mysterious paradox, much in the style of Crashaw's "Flaming Heart":

> The bright inamour'd *Yeouth* above
> I askd, What kind of thing is *Love*?
> I askd yᵉ Saints; They could not tell,
> Though in their bosomes it doeth dwell.
> I asked yᵉ lower Angels; They
> Liv'd in its Flames, but could not say.
> I asked yᵉ Seraphs: These at last confes'd
> We cannot tell how *God* should be expres'd.
>
> Can you not tell, whose amorous Eyes
> Flame in *Love's* Sweetest Ecstacies?
> Can you not tell whose pure thoughts move
> On Wings all feathered with *Love*?
> Can you not tell who breathe & live
> No life but what Great *Love* doth give?
> Grant *Love* a *God*: Sweet *Seraphs* who should know
> The nature of this Dietie, but you?
>
> And who, bold Mortall, more than Wee
> Should know, that *Love's* a *Mysterie*?
> Hid under his owne flaming Wing
> Lies *Love* a secret open thing.
> And there lie Wee, all hid in Light,
> Which gives Us, & denies Us Sight.
> We see what dazells & inflames our Eyes,
> And makes them Mighty *Love's* Burnt-Sacrifice. (11)

Here Beaumont defines the mystery of love primarily by declaring its indefinability, but in the highly affective terms of erotic sweetness, fire, and sacrifice. These may be familiar expressions, but the paradoxes embraced by them are aptly managed. The questioning "I" at the opening becomes the "bold Mortall" at the end, who informs all of us that the sight of love — secular and divine (for the two are inextricably mixed in this poetry) — is obvious but impossible; for love is known through its consuming flame.

Yet another poem that illustrates well Beaumont's devotional temper is "Jesus inter Ubera Maria[e]," (Jesus at Mary's breasts), on "Cantcl. 6," that is, the Canticles or the Song of Solomon 6: "My beloved is gone down into his garden, to the beds of spices, to feed in the gardens, and to gather lilies. I am my beloved's, and my beloved is mine: he feedeth among the lilies." These verses (2–3) provide Beaumont the devotional environment for his elaboration on the Nativity, a poem of five stanzas with a chorus, "To a Base and 2 Trebles," brief enough to quote in full:

> In yᵉ coolnesse of yᵉ day
> The old Worlds Even, *God* all undrest went downe
> Without His Roab, without His Crowne,
> Into His private garden, there to lay
> On spicey Bed
> His sweeter Head.
>
> There He found two Beds of Spice,
> A double Mount of Lillies, in whose Top
> Two milkie Fountaines bubled up.
> He soon resolv'd: & well I like, He cries,
> My table spread
> Upon my Bed.
>
> Scarcely had He 'gun to feed,
> When troops of *Cherubs* hover'd round about;
> And on their golden Wings they brought
> All *Edens* flowers. But We cry'd out; No need
> Of flowers heere;
> Sweet Spirits, forbeare.
>
> True, He needs no Sweets, say They,
> But Sweets have need of Him, to keep them so.

> Now *Paradise* springs new with you,
> Old *Edens* Beautie's all inclin'd this way;
>   And We are come
>   To bring them home.

> *Paradise* springs new with you,
> Where 'twixt those Beds of Lillies you may see
>   Of Life ye Everlasting Tree.
> Sweet is your reason, then said Wee, come strow
>   Your pious showres
>   Of Easterne Flowres.

CHORUS

> Winds awake, & with soft Gale
> Awake ye Odours of our Garden too;
>   By wch your selv's perfumed goe
> Through every Quarter of your World, that All
>   Your sound may heare,
>   And breathe your Aire. (16–17)

The regularity of the metrical and rhyme pattern reinforces the delicacy and elegance of this majestic yet intimate scene. As in "The Morning Hymn," Beaumont devises a form that places emphasis upon an initial word, here on the beginning of each stanza, in a short, seven syllable line that is rhymed with the fourth, ten syllable line, which makes a curious quatrain of abba, with 7, 10, 8, 10 syllables in iambic stress, with a deficient foot in the first line of each stanza. Each of these four quatrains (and the "chorus") is enjambed with the four syllable, two stress iambic couplets that close each stanza. The overall effect is to induce in the reader a sense of motion and unexpectedness that is yet held in a momentary and unmoving balance. The action produces calmness, poise, and continuity, which are precisely the qualities of the Nativity, of the once and ever occurring Incarnation.

The similarity of Beaumont's poem to Crashaw's "Hymne of the Nativity" (1646, 1648) is obvious. Crashaw's poem is much longer and more elaborately and skillfully conceited;

but the tone is the same, and so is the essential idea of the infant king who is both son and father of the maid and mother, the paradoxes at the heart of these poems. Crashaw provides for a chorus, too, in parts, which at the end join in full voice to celebrate the marvels of the Incarnation:

> Wellcome, all WONDERS in one sight!
>   Æternity shutt in a span.
> Sommer in Winter. Day in Night.
>   Heauen in earth, & GOD in MAN.
> Great little one! whose all-embracing birth
> Lifts earth to heauen, stoopes heau'n to earth.
>
> WELLCOME. Though nor to gold nor silk.
>   To more then Cæsar's birthright is;
> Two sister-seas of Virgin-Milk,
>   With many a rarely-temper'd kisse
> That breathes at once both MAID & MOTHER,
> Warmes in the one, cooles in the other.
>
> (Martin 250, lines 79–90)

Since Crashaw and Beaumont were writing these poems at about the same time, one cannot quite be sure which is earlier — or later; for Beaumont might have influenced Crashaw to expand the Nativity theme in his more abundant verse, or else Beaumont felt moved to comment with a smaller poem. Yet Beaumont was to write, probably influenced or inspired by Crashaw, at much greater length on the Incarnation in his *Psyche*, where he splendidly describes "The Great Little One" — the title and the subject of the whole of canto 7 — in language highly reminiscent of these earlier poems:[8] "The Day which made *Immensity* become/A *Little one*. . . . the Day/ Which shrunk *Eternity* into a *Span/Of Time, Heav'n* into *Earth, God* into *Man*" (7.156).

Beaumont's *Minor Poems* might appear at first to be a miscellaneous collection gathered haphazardly together. But they do have a systematic and meaningful arrangement that is also chronological — that is, Beaumont composed the poems in the order in which they appear while deliberately planning their sequence. The several poems on his birthday, along with the poems on his baptism, occur at yearly intervals and these poems mark divisions in the book. The first of these poems, "Natalitium," followed at once by "Anniversarium Baptismi," is dated March 13, 1643/44 — the first date, as I have noted, in the book.[9] The poem on his birthday is full of personal reference, being a review of the year just past — and recalling perhaps the themes of the preceding 34 poems, including the two just discussed (the "Morning Hymn" belongs to a later section of the book). Beaumont laments the passing of "eight & twenty long & tedious *yeares*," remembers his childhood, his school days, his time at Cambridge, and now he prays for the wisdom to carry on in the midst of his own and the world's darkness (82). He seems to allude to the raging of the Civil War and the troubled English church at the conclusion of his meditation, but he sees external events as a metaphor for the perpetual distress he feels over his own "civil war" of the heart. If only, he beseeches God, "I can understand but how to be/A genuine Member of thy Church & Thee"; finally, he resigns himself to be content: "though furious Warre/On every Minute heaps a thousand feares,/And does all Comfort, & all Hopes debarre,"

> If Thy propitious Eye will be my Starre
> No Tempest shall deterre me, for no Sea
> Can swell so high, as is thy Heavn, & Thee. (85)

Beaumont writes no poem for his birthday in 1645; but the next year "Natalitium" begins with a lament, a reference to his *Psyche*:

> Tire'd with my PSYCHE, (for y[e] Song
> Though wondrous hudled, yet was long,
> And near
> A year
> Consumed in such singing, well may force
> A stronger Voice then mine, & make it hoarse.)

"I took some time to breathe," he continues (280).

Following the next poem, the customary meditation on his spiritual birth through sacramental baptism, Beaumont writes "A Friend," not specifically directed toward any person, but to the lofty and idealized concept of friendship, grandly celebrated in the final two stanzas (15–16):

> Parentall Kindeness cold may grow
> And Filial Dutie cease to glow;
> Ev'n Matrimoniall Fervour may
> Be chill & faint & die away;
>   But Friendship's resolute Heat
> In Loyaltie's eternall Pulse doth beat.
>
> Tell all things else by thy slight Eye
> Thou scornst their glozing Treacherie;
> But, next to thy Devotions, spend
> Thy holyest Powers upon thy Friend:
>   None but thy God, & He
> Inseparably linked are to Thee. (291)

Perhaps Beaumont may be thinking of Richard Crashaw, a friendship that Beaumont notably commemorated in *Psyche*, which he was composing at about the same time. In a splendid section on the muses and their primary effect on numerous writers, both ancient and modern, including (in Beaumont's ordering) Cicero, Pindar, Herbert ("by the spheres/He tunes his Lute, and plays to heav'nly ears"), Homer, Tasso, and Spenser, Beaumont turns to Crashaw and calls on "this heart-attracting Pattern *Thou/My only worthy self*, thy Songs didst frame":

> Witness those polish'd *Temple Steps*, which now
> Stand as the Ladder to thy mounting fame;
>   And, spight of all thy Travels, make't appear
>   Th'art more in *England* than when Thou wert here.
>
> More unto others, but not so to me
> Privy of old to all thy secret Worth:
>   What half-lost I endure for want of *Thee*,
>   The World will read in this mishapen *Birth*.

Fair had my *Psyche* been, had she at first
By thy judicious hand been drest and nurst.

(canto 4, 107–08)

Again, Beaumont misses a year (1647), then writes in 1648, further in 1649, now with the title "Γενεθλιακόν" (that is, *Genethliakon*, Birthday feast), the year of Charles's execution to which Beaumont alludes, yet typically understanding the commotion of the state to stand for his own supposed spiritual emptiness. But "Γενεθλιακόν" of 1650 is most explicit:

Though I have seen our wretched Britain made
The Isle of Monsters; though the onely Trade
   Our England drives be Frensy, and
   Rebellious Desperation; Yet
   I finde a more enormous Band
   Of Rebells in my Bosome mett:
Rebells, whose furious stomach dares disdain
Not *Britains Monarch*, but *Heavns Soverain.* (378–79)

The next birthday poems, for 1651 and 1652, follow at once, the latter being of special interest for its domestic references. Beaumont was married in May 1650, to Elizabeth Brownrigg, the step-daughter of Matthew Wren; in this poem, he writes of the first child of this marriage, the young Elizabeth who died within the year of her birth.

"Γενεθλιακόν Marti 13. 1651 [52]" is remarkable also for beginning a final section of the *Minor Poems*, all of them dated. The several poems on his birthday, usually followed by a poem commemorating his baptism, mark out the progress of the book, often with intervening poems on saints' days and high points of the liturgical year, along with poems in which Beaumont peers into his own life and spiritual condition.[10] After "Annivers: Baptismi Mart. 21 [1652]," Beaumont begins a concluding cycle. He has shown before in his nativity and baptism poems the obvious movement of his life along a spectrum. Although he knows that he is living temporally, he must in an orderly way take note of the passing years, with its feasts and fasts, and he must also record the conflicts and troubles that beset him, as if writing a spiritual diary. The poem for May 17, which is followed by a daily poem until June 13, the last of the book, is called "The Journè," not "Journey" — the title of an earlier poem — for Beaumont evidently wishes to emphasize the sense not only of pilgrimage, but also of struggle or opposition, a meaning that the French word *"la Journée"* may convey better than the English "journey." Beaumont does not wish to signify a traveler who means to go from one place to another, as a pilgrim might do, but rather one who moves to meet a spiritual crisis and battle to overcome it. This is the kind of journeying that goes nowhere literally — not from Cambridge to Hadleigh or abroad — but looks for an opening, a resolution to distress, the seeking of a calm harbor for the soul's exile. Beaumont expresses the idea well (and uses the unusual form *"journè"* three times, once in each of the three stanzas of this poem), apostrophizing God as that "Great King of Bliss! in that sweet soveraintie/Of thine, O may poor I a Subject be." He ends:

> So shall I gain brave strength to stretch
> Through that laborious journè, which
> I going am; (& needs must go)
> Ev'n whilst I stay at home; for to
> The unknown Land of Death am I
> Hurried by Sinn & Destiny.
> Vain hopes of Rest, adieu: my birth I scorn
> To cross, since I a Traveller am born. (398)

Like Herbert before him, Beaumont offers in much of his poetry "a picture of the many spiritual Conflicts that have past betwixt God and my Soul, before I could subject mine to the will of Jesus my Master, in whose service I have now found perfect freedom."[11] Surely, like Herbert, Beaumont is troubled by the oppositions encountered in pilgrimage, though unlike Herbert he seldom reaches the same kind of quietness and rest.

The poems that follow "The Journè" (399–452) are typically descriptive of Beaumont's spiritual conflicts, for in them he defines his daily moods, observing also the general and personal significance of the special liturgical events that fall during this time — Ascension, Pentecost, St. Barnabas, (and tacitly) Trinity, in the final poem of the book. Beaumont now greets "The Winter-Spring" on May 18, writing of a spring that is suddenly overtaken by a late winter blast: "Mark well, my Heart, too plainly painted heer/An embleme of thy self in this sad Year" (399). Then comes "The Gentle Check" (May 19), a complaint for his "tardy" verse that the poet recollects on hearing the early morning birds. "The Sentinel" (May 20) follows, addressed "To my Friend" a figure (literal and metaphorical) that strikes his conscience and heart into higher and more sensitive awareness. "The Farm" (May 21), "News" (May 22), "The Duell" (May 23), "The World" (May 24), "The Servant" (May 25), and "Game" (May 26) all play upon the theme of the stubborn will, on the broken and tormented journey toward right action.

"Ascension" (May 27) considers the strangeness of Jesus's earthly departure, for "this happy day must be / The holy Feast of Sympathie." We must wait, fasting "by sad authority," for the coming of Pentecost, ten days hence. But "Heavns Kingdome now is open sett:/And yf we will not frustrate it,/ Our Heads is our Ascension too" (418–19). In continuing his meditation the next day, Beaumont declares that "Friends" is singular; for "who is thy souls Spouse but He?" (421) "The Bankrupt" (May 29) and "Detraction" (May 30, the Sunday after Ascension) analyze harmful tendencies; "Virtue" (May 31) should offer a corrective, but paradoxically "She's viley troublesome," for virtue is no quick conqueror: "deer Virtue, he/By blaming praiseth thee./Wise eyes would strait suspect thy rays/Should Fools thy Lustre praise" (427). "Thrift" (June 1) and "Avarice" (June 2) follow as a pair, commenting on each other, with "Honor" (June 3) forming an ironic reflection on them both. "Physik" (June 4) is necessary for treating pride, and its accompanying "Spittle of Diseases," but only if one recognizes that the mind, not the body, is diseased:

> The Aigue of cold Fear
> Doth nip thee up; or Lusts dogdays
> A burning Fever in the rayse.
> The Boulimie of Avarice doth tear
> Thy restless ever-hungry heart,
> Or thou in Prodagalities Consumption art. (434)

"Selflove" (June 5) forms the subject of the subsequent meditation, on the eve of "Pentecost" (June 6), or Whitsunday. This "Seasonable Feast" comes to heal heavy and sorrowful hearts — and Beaumont prays that the Comforter will tame the country's chaos:

> Thou, mighty Spirit, who
> Confusion from
> The Worlds first wombe
> Didst sweetly chase: Our Waves of Woe
> Now crave thy ayd; oh gently move on them,
> And Britains Chaos into order tame! (439)

The poems for Whitsuntide begin with "Witt" (June 7), a poem that playfully asks for a definition. Like Abraham Cowley's famous "Ode of Wit" ("Tell me, O tell, what kind of thing is wit"), Beaumont begins also with a request: "But who has Witt enough to tell/Me what it is?" (440). Beaumont is now in a cheerful mood, reflected in "Entertainment" (June 8) and "Riches" (June 9), but he catches himself in "The Alarm" (June 10), which appears to respond to a sudden sickness that makes the poet think of his mortality. The next day is June 11, the feast of St. Barnabas, an apostolic saint whose approval of and later dispute with St. Paul (Acts 15.39) encourages Beaumont: "Pluck courage then/From hence: since Saints themselves are Men,/Men may be Saints, & humane Passions be/Cohabitants with Sanctity" (449).

The final poems of this cycle are "The Gardin," on the eve of Trinity Sunday (June 12) and the curious "Palmestrie" (June 13). Beaumont is once more wracked by absence, loss, and inadequacy. There is no garden wherein he may walk, for he has been turned out of Paradise into this wide and desolate world. "O Miserable Me," writes Beaumont. Yet he ends the poem with hopefulness:

> That Tree, made Fertile by his own dear blood;
> And by his Death with quickning virtue fraught.
>   I now dread not the thought
> Of barracado'd Eden, since as good
>   A Paradise I planted see
>   On open Calvarie. (451)

Perhaps "Palmestrie," the last of the *Minor Poems*, is a suitable climax to the collection and to this daily series which began with "The Journè" on May 17, 1652. Now it is Trinity, but journeying must and always will continue. With a glancing reference to the Trinity, the poem contains three stanzas, each one with six lines in an interlocking rhyme scheme and a pattern that emphasizes the combination of two threes:

> Art sure th'ast given so much to the Poor?
>   Was't not thy meaning to bestow
> Part on thine own Vain-glory? Never score
>   Up that on Gods account, which thou
> Spendst on the Devil; nor make Charitie
> Hell purveyor, who should Heavns steward be.

Beaumont is once more turning inward to test his motives and worry over his darkest thoughts. But he continues in the next stanza:

> I'l not inquire thorough what trumpets throat
>   Thou spak'st the prologue to thy Gift;
> Nor in what carefull pomp thou gav'st thy groat;
>   Nor what a hard & piteous shift
> Thou mad'st to let Spectators know that thou
> Didst three weeks since another groat bestow.

Charity may be told through prophecy and the ready reckoning of the metonymic hand — the right or the left? But one should see what ought to be obvious and openly known, and so Beaumont concludes:

> Indeed no such intelligence; for I
>   By Palmestrie can read it plain:
> Thy right hand to thy left did it descry,
>   And now thy left tells tales again.
> What canst thou answer, who dost guilty stand
> By the cleer evidence of thine own hand?

"The cleer evidence" is the paradoxical close of the journey that has already begun but refuses to end.

15 • Ravishing Embraces and Sober Minds

The Poetry of Joseph Beaumont

Paul A. Parrish

The poetry of Joseph Beaumont (1616–99) has, with only a few notable exceptions, been largely ignored during the 350 years of its existence.[1] Indeed, if one sets aside commentary on Beaumont's best-known work, his long and various epic, *Psyche: or Loves Mysterie* (1648), recognition of Beaumont as a poet is thin to the point of virtual nonexistence.[2] My aim here is to identify, describe, and contextualize Beaumont's accomplishment as a lyric poet, both to argue that it is worthy of some continuing interest and, in the process, to reconsider some of the reasons for its having been — to say the least — slighted.

The time for this reconsideration seems especially apt, as the lines between canonical and noncanonical, the literary and the nonliterary, the professional writer and the amateur dilettante, the "authoritative" print publication and the "dubious" manuscript version are ever more blurred. Robinson notes Gee's observation that "poetical excursions were not Mr. Beaumont's studies, but his amusements; not the serious busines of his life, but reliefs from the ennui and irksomeness of being, which in that long divorce from Books [resulting from his expulsion from Cambridge], could not but oppress his active and vigorous mind," and she adds that Beaumont's "real occupation," even during the time of his Hadleigh "retirement," was writing his extensive commentaries on Ecclesiastes and the Pentateuch (xxiii). The implied distinction and differential evaluation between theological writings taken seriously and poetry written casually or even frivolously is not so much wrong as misleading; the sheer volume of Beaumont's verse, particularly when *Psyche* and the shorter poems are considered in the aggregate, demands at least a more even-handed approach to his poetic achievement.[3]

I

Since Beaumont's life, like his art, is not well known, it is useful to situate it historically before proceeding.[4] Beaumont's life divides conveniently into four segments: 1616–31, from his birth to his admission into Peterhouse; 1631–44, his years as a student and Fellow of Peterhouse;[5] 1644–60, his retirement years at Hadleigh and Tatingston Place; and 1660–99, his post-Restoration years as Doctor of Divinity and Regius Professor of Divinity at Cambridge. Unlike his friend Crashaw — for whom there was a marked pilgrimage from a childhood dominated by a father with apparently Puritan sympathies, to an absorption into the Laudian perspective of Pembroke College and Peterhouse, to eventual conversion to Rome — Beaumont's views appear to have steadily maintained their Laudian cast. Born into a family supportive of the High Church position, Beaumont was admitted into a college that was, to the increasingly aggressive Puritan forces, suspected of a kind of dangerous, if unacknowledged, complicity with

Rome.[6] Beaumont, we can be sure, found the religious and political environment of Peterhouse encouraging and nourishing, not dangerous or complicitous. Stanwood captures the spirit of Peterhouse — a spirit that must have been equally appealing to Crashaw and other Fellows — as well as the particular tasks Beaumont assumed for himself:

> An agreeable life, these years at Peterhouse. Heartened by its ceremony and tradition; surrounded by friends of like spirit, among them Richard Crashaw, from 1635 a Fellow at Peterhouse; guided by the order, watchful and strict, of Cosin, Beaumont flourished. He must have enjoyed his work and his contemplation, peacefully pursued. . . . Beaumont's wide reading in traditional writers is not so unusual as his study of contemporary authors: he read not merely Hebrew, Latin, and Greek, but Italian, Spanish, and French as well . . . ("Portrait" 30–31)

For Beaumont, however, the satisfactions of Peterhouse were not to last; like Crashaw and other Royalists, he was, on his ejection, forced to abandon friends, studies, students, and the nurturing environment of Peterhouse to take up a very different life at Hadleigh.

II

Beaumont himself downplays the value and originating forces of the poetry written during his years at Hadleigh and Tatingston Place, where he settled with his wife, observing in a letter that he wrote poetry during his exile from Peterhouse "that I might not live in mere Idleness," further dissociating his poetic endeavors from his scholarly ones by adding that he wrote "when I was stormed from my books and had not so much as one Book with me, but Marino, and only his Adoring [Beaumont presumably means *L'Adone*]" (quoted in Stanwood, "Portrait" 33). But Beaumont's productivity remains nonetheless extensive; if the whole of his writings reveals someone more attentive to theological matters than literary ones, the poetry testifies as well to his thorough and varied response to topics of importance to him and his contemporaries.[7]

The 179 poems in Robinson's *Minor Poems* can be identified, described, and grouped in various ways; I offer the following not to be overly prescriptive but to suggest a guide to understanding related and relatable topics:[8] (1) fourteen poems are written as pairs, one half of each pair commemorating Beaumont's birthday (March 16), the other commemorating the anniversary of his baptism (March 21). At least one poem in each pair is dated, and we can thus identify the years of composition as 1643, 1645, 1647, 1648, 1649, 1650, and 1651; (2) twenty-six poems celebrate New Testament figures and saints (or, in one instance ["Ad S. Angelum Custodem"], a guardian angel), including in the hagiolatry Andrew, Thomas, Stephen, Mark, Barnabas, John the Baptist, Peter, Luke, the Virgin Mary, and Mary Magdalen, as well as less familiar subjects such as Simeon Stylites and Gregory of Nazianzus;[9] (3) thirty-two poems are grounded in church ritual and sacraments (e.g., "The Waters of H. Baptisme," "Fasting," "H. Sacrament") or holy days (e.g., "SS. Innocents Day," "Christmasse Day," "Purification of the B. Virgin" [two poems], "Annunciatio B. V.," "Whitsunday" [five poems] , "Good Fryday" [two poems], "Easter," "Trinitie Sunday" [two poems], and others); (4) ten poems have a titular and topical association with identified scripture ("Jesus inter Ubera Maria" ["Cantcl. 6"], "Davids Elegie upon Jonathan" ["2 Sam. i. Chap. 26 x"], "Cantic. Chap. 2. XX^{ss} 10–11–12–13" ["Rise up, my Love, my Fairest One"] , "Thou shalt call His Name Jesus" ["S. Luc. i. 31"], "Love" ["Exod. 3"], "The True Love-Knott" ["I am my Beloveds, & my Beloved is mine. Cant. 6, 3. Turne away thine eyes, etc., v. 5"], "The Little Ones Greatnes" ["Suffer little Children to come unto Mee, & forbid them not, for of such is the Kingdome of God"], "The Admirable Conversion of S. Paul" ["Acts 9"], "The two Fires" ["Depart from Me yee Cursed into everlasting Fire, *prepared for ye* Deveill & his Angells. S. Mat. 25.41"], and "Charity seeketh not her own" ["I Cor. 13.5"]);[10] (5) thirteen poems are brief parables or stories from which moral or religious lessons are drawn (e.g., "The Gnat," "The Sluggard," "Bedtime," "The Voyage," "House & Home," "The Candle," "The Losse," "The Houreglasse," "The Sheepherd," "The Pilgrim"); (6) thirteen poems focus on love and particularly the "Lord of Love" (e.g., "Suspirium," "Loves Mysterie," "Love" [two poems of this title, in addition to the poem on Exod. 3 above], "Loves Monarchie," "Loves Adventure," "A Love bargaine," "Once & Ever," and three poems that are among those that testify to the influence of Crashaw: "The Complaint," "The Wound," and "The Combat"); (7) six poems are, for want of a better definition, "occasional," arising from particular moments in Beaumont's life other than the anniversaries noted above ("Hymnus ad Christum, proxime cooptandi in S. Presbyteratus Ordinem," "Paulo post Ordinationem," "Upon my Fathers Sudden & Dangerous Sickness" [Oct. 11, 1649], "Novemb. 5, 1644" (the anniversary of the Gunpowder Plot) or from subjects that have a particular topical interest ("Tobacco," "The Fashion"); (8) the largest grouping consists of some 38 poems that treat of virtues or attributes or personified values and events in the Christian life and that are usually meditations on and contemplations of the meaning and importance of such subjects to the speaker's life (e.g., "Reasonable Melancholy," "Death," "Civill Warr," "Dull Devotion," "Affliction," "Melancholie," "Patience," "Life," "Conscience," "The Heart," "Will," "Faith," "Censure," "Temporall Success," "Humane Revenge," "Hope," "Idleness," "Submission," "The Relapse," "Jealousy," "The Surrender"); (9) and, finally, Beaumont gives us a sequence of 28 poems commencing with "The Journè," dated May 17, 1652, and ending with "Palmestrie," dated June 13, 1652, and including 26 other poems, each dated between May 17 and June 13. The poems in this sequence are expositions and expostulations reminiscent of the poems in (8) above, with headings such as "The Duell," "The World," "The Servant," "Detraction," "Virtue," "Thrift," "Honor," and "Witt."[11]

Even this brief survey of topics and titles suggests some variety of interests and perspectives, a diversity that is more evident upon closer reading. I begin a more detailed study, however, by looking at poems that are more accurately noted for their personal quality, a constancy of tone and a similarity of perspective — the poems celebrating his birthday and baptism day.

III

Beaumont's poems on his birthday and the day of his baptism are largely all of a piece, poems conceived as companion poems that, in each instance, revisit and reconsider the implications of the day remembered. Inevitably Beaumont looks at his birthday as a time for contemplation and regret, an occasion to recognize the passing of years and with them to accept that his "Paths were but the ways of Sinn" (17) (Birthday 1648 [364]):[12]

> I'v liv'd thus long said I? Let me unspeak
> That Word, more hasty & more rash by far
> Then all those posting *yeares*: If I must make
> A true confession what my Fortunes are,
> I must leave Life to such as Live, and take
> With dull unworthy Things my proper Share.
>   A Thing within tells me theres no denying;
>   I have these eight & twenty yeares been Dying.
>   (9–16)
>   (Birthday 1643 [82])

> Whilst I behinde Me cast my annual Ey,
>   What do I but my *Sodome* spy!
> . . .
> Alas! that I must these twelve Moneths discount,
>   In which my Life did not amount
>   To more than Death.
>   (1–2, 11–13)
>   (Birthday 1648 [364])

How true that Day paints out to me
This Years sweet-soure repugnancie!
A Year in which my Joyes grew up
Into the blade of cheerly Hope:
But blasted then, did onely yeild
A Crop of Greif from Comforts Feild:
 A Year which taught me how
  To grow
Into a sad beleif that heer
Delight's bright Perl's but a mistaken Tear.
            (21–30)
         (Birthday 1651 [393])

The most interesting of the birthday poems is the first (1643 [82]), as Beaumont rehearses the stages of his life to that point, both the disappointments he has experienced and the knowledge he has gained. The "lingring Death" (17) that defines his life is in this poem only momentarily brightened by anticipation of the subject of its companion piece on his baptism, the hope that will come from a drenching "in a heavnly Fount, whence I/Rose faire as new borne Light from Easterne Skie" (23–24). That hope is, however, reserved for the second poem, as here thc poet stresses the various means by which he has become "o're grown with sinfull Rust" (28), from his childhood, through his apprenticeship "to the Bookish Trade/At full fifteene ith' Universitie" (59–60), to his Faustian ambition for greater knowledge:

My itching mind proudly desir'd to prie
Into whatever Learnings Title wore.
With unfledgd Wings I often towred high,
And snatch'd at things above my pitch, before
I had sure hold of what beneath did lie.
Yet on I ventur'd still, & caught at more;
 I caught the Wind of Words, which by a Blast
 Of following Notions soon away were past.
            (65–72)

"At length," Beaumont says, he learns a different kind of knowledge, as worldly learning yields to *"ETERNALL WISDOME,"* a willingness to "rest content/With shallow knowledge of such Objects, as/Can never blesse their Knower," to be seen as foolish among men in order "not to be a foole/ In that, which Saints and Angells draws to Schoole" (73–75, 79–80).

But this understanding he cannot sustain on his own, and in this poem, as in all of the birthday poems, he turns to God:

> O guide Me thou, Deare *Lord*, who in my Heart
> Dost read a simple & unfain'd Desire
> To follow Truth & Thee.
>
> (105–07)

The poems celebrating the anniversary of Beaumont's baptism are, not surprisingly, more exuberant in tone:

> Welcome sweet & happy Day:
>> O let me pay
> In thy blest Light the debt I owe
> The Fount, from which my better life doth flow.
>
> (1–4)
> (Baptism 1643 [86])

> Still, still deer LOVE, must I
>> In spight of HERESY,
> My thanks on this Days Altar heap;
> Thy Goodnes still I must adore,
>> Which washd a poor
> And sin-besmeard Thing, in that deep
> And spotless Fount of Purity
>> Which thy
> Compassion broachd to clense that fatal Stain
> Which from old Adam, o'r all Soules did reign.
>
> (1–10)
> (Baptism 1647 [334])

> How much worse than in vain
>>   Had I been *Born*
>>   That *other Morn*,
>   Had I not now been *Born again*!
>   For that was but my Death's, but this
> Alone of my true *Life* the *Birthday* is.

(1–6)
(Baptism 1648 [369])

These poems, too, however, point to evidences of sin and separation from the hope that "Lifes blessed Fountain" (24) (Baptism 1647 [335]) offers. Indeed, the 1645 poem uncharacteristically stresses that "woe" from its opening word:

> Woe is me, but even now
>>   Proud & fond I studied how
> To erect some gallant Vow
> On this pretious Mornings Brow,
> Whoe to Heavn allready ow
> Whatsoe'r I can bestow.

(1–6 [285])

More usually, the baptism poems remind the poet and the reader of the life-giving significance of the occasion, celebrate the event with hope and appreciation, confront the reality of a "deadly Prodigality" (26) (Baptism 1650 [390]) that threatens to undo what the baptism accomplished, and end by urging God or his soul to hold him and his faith fast:

> O no, sweet Lord, I would
>>   Be Thine, & none
>   But Thine alone:
> And though fond I my Bliss have sold
> To Vanity; I will not sell
> My Hope, since Thou art my Redeemer still.

(49–54)
(Baptism 1648 [371])

IV

While Beaumont's meditations on the anniversaries of his birth and his baptism are prompted by days of personal significance, his poems on biblical figures and saints take as their typical focus important and familiar events from their lives or attributes traditionally associated with them (e.g., Paul's conversion, Thomas's doubting, Peter's crucifixion head downwards, Luke's practice as physician, the stoning of Stephen, the faith and loyalty of Joseph, the love of John). Among these traditional associations and relatively conventional tributes, there are interesting variations. The poems differ considerably in style, tone, length and effect. At one extreme is "S. Johan. ad Port. Latin," which in 11 lines succinctly responds to the death by burning of St. John by mocking the foolishness and futility of those who would seek to stifle his life and spirit by feeding the flames with oil. It is, in fact and paradoxically, a song of celebration, set, as a headnote indicates, "To a Base & 2 Trebles":[13]

> Foolish Tryant, spare thy cost,
>   All thine Oile & Labour's lost:
> This is a *Seraph* all on fire;
> Oile will but feed his Flames up higher.
> If Thou would'st kill Him, let Him live:
> Death his best Life to Him will give.
>
>   Foolish Tyrant
> Who anoint'st thine Enemie
> Too strong before for Hell and Thee;
> And dost for streams of Torments, shed
> Soft Oile of Gladnes on His Head.

"S. John Baptist," in marked contrast, is a 600–line poem that amounts to a retelling of the whole of John's life, from Gabriel's surprise announcement of his coming birth to his parents "Grown old in spotlesse Pietie" (25), to his decision to seek "Deserts freedome" so that "He can goe/Living alone with

God" (238–39), to his development into the "Noble Preacher" (289), to his baptism of Jesus, and ultimately to his death at the hands of Herod.

More interesting still are poems on lesser known figures such as Simeon Stylites ("Lemniscus ad Columnam S. Simeonis Stylitae appensus") and Gregory of Nazianzus ("S. Gregorie Nazianzen").[14] The former praises the steadfastness of the saint who is best remembered for pole-sitting. That "reverend Pillar," says Beaumont, still stands,

> And all religious eyes commands.
> Still it stands erected high
> On fairest Mount of Memorie:
> High as the top of highest Glorie,
> Which writes from hence its noblest Storie.
> Higher then the PRINCE of FLIES
> With his swarthy Wings can rise:
> High as the flight of soules: as high
> As LOVE'S illustrious Wing could flie.
>
> (1–10)

Later in the poem Simeon is praised with words that might have been taken from Crashaw or St. Teresa, or both:

> Sure Simeon feels no blow
> Nor wound, but those, which LOVE'S sweet Darts
> Bestow on Saints Delicious Hearts.
>   Twas LOVE, which on the Pillar set
> Him as his fairest Mark, whereat
> To aime, & trie his Heavnly skill,
> Which with Darts of Life doth kill,
> And in ten thousand Deaths doth give
> A sweet Necessitie to Live:
> To Live a LIFE of WOUNDS, but those
> So healing, that the Soule would choose
> Rather Ease's pangs, then not
> By those Arrows to be shot.
>   LOVE shot full oft, & every Dart
> Flew directly to the Heart
> Of this fair Mark; At last He cries,

Mine alone, Mine is the Prize:
The Tempters Arrows are in vain,
Mine alone the Man have slain:
Mine He is, & Mine shall be;
No Title to Himselfe hath He:
Him I challange by the Law
Of greatest Arms, & mean to draw
Him home in Triumph after Me
In token of my Victorie.

(198–222)

"S. Gregorie Nazianzen" is reminiscent of Crashaw as well, but more in its images and perspective than in particular words or phrases. Gregory's mother is depicted and praised in words that might be deemed more fitting for the Virgin Mary:

And now not as the Mother, but the Maid
And nurse to Heavns great Pledge, she is afraid
    To use the Infant but as One,
    Whom God had made her foster-son:
        With tender Care
        She doth prepare
        All things that may
        Another Day
Proclaime as much: His tender Heart
    Shee seasons with religious Art,
And brings Him up as if Shee Tutoresse were
To educate some tender Angell heere.

(85–96)

The most remarkable moments in this 492–line poem are those that describe and celebrate the friendship of St. Gregory and St. Basil, a union of souls that is cast in terms that are strikingly physical, sensuous, and erotic:

But that which Athens did to Thee indeare
Was that thy Soule met with another there
    Right fit for thy sweet Company,
    A Soule, which did with thine agree
        In every part
        Of thy best Art,

A Soule whose Pulse
Beat nothing else
But love & Heavn, a Soule so nigh
Resembling thine, that Amitie
At length mistook, counting thy Heart to be
In Basils Breast, & his to pant in Thee.

Never did Chance of Nature tie a knott
Into so strait a Union, as that
Which Virtues knitt, & Graces tie
In a Band of Pietie.
Now Basil loves,
And lives, & moves
In Gregorie;
And mutuall He
Loves Basil back againe, & lives
By that Life away He gives.
Thus when two Floods imbrace, they loose each other
In the pellucid Bosome of his Brother.
. . .
Thus wert Thou marryed to thy Masculine Spouse:
When the Soule weds, no uselesse Sex she knows;
And heere thy Soule, & that alone
Enters NUPTIALL UNION.
No Female shall
Think to prevaile
By blandishment
On thy consent:
Though thy breast be large, yet Thou
Hast but one Heart to bestow,
And that is BASILS, who esteems it so
That for the World He will not let it goe.

(229–52, 265–76)

Although we have no way of knowing, it seems hardly a stretch to imagine that, in writing these lines about Gregory and Basil, Beaumont had in mind his relationship to Crashaw, his own "worthy friend" and his "onely worthy self" (*Psyche* IV.94), a poet and friend whom he likened to Gregory and about whom he claimed a special knowledge of "thy secret worth" (*Psyche* IV.95).

The poems on saints exhibit a Beaumont exuberant about love and devotion and celebrating faith and the faithful in enthusiastic and often sensuous terms: Mary Magdalene's "Zealous Fire" (5) of love is a "Noble Passion" that, in its "Immoderation," imitates Jesus's "excessive" love for her (58–60) ("S. Mary Magdalen's Ointment"); John is, both in the shorter poem cited above and in "S. John The Disciple, whom Jesus loved," on fire with the flame of love and desire for his "Friend" ("Thou, who dost live by Fire,/And in whose Breast such amorous streams doe boile,/Canst feele no other Flames. O, no: some higher/Fervor of Love must melt thine owne, & send/Thee to the flaming Bosome of thy Friend" (68–72). Elsewhere we read of Mary, "the *Virgin Spouse of Chastitie*" (64) ("Virginitie"), of Philip who speaks "The Heavnly heat of *JESU'S* LOVE" (51) ("S. Philip"), and of Andrew on whose tongue "Heavn & JESUS" sit "sweet" (30) ("S. Andrew").

V

This quality of exuberant or sensuous celebration derives in part from who Beaumont was and what he believed, in part from the subjects about which he was writing. We should not be surprised to find Beaumont giving full rein to the senses in some of the poems I have identified above, or in other examples, including many of the poems whose subject is love, or the Virgin Mary, or holy days such as Easter, the Annunciation or the Purification of the Blessed Virgin, or poems drawn from scripture that is itself sensuous and erotic. The choices of subjects may be suggestive of style or temperament, particularly if, as Beaumont and some of his readers claim, he was writing under no particular strictures except his own choices and preferences. But the subject may also, to an extent, determine tone and style, masking individual characteristics and nuances. The Beaumont thus far revealed is, in the main, one we might most readily associate with the Baroque in general and Crashaw in particular, but much as it is

inadequate and unrepresentative to speak *only* of a Baroque
Crashaw, so is it unfair to characterize Beaumont in terms
that suggest that he is little more than an emulator of Crashaw,
and a decidedly inferior one at that.[15] To be sure, the influence
of Crashaw, in some instances, or, in others, their mutual
response to similar aesthetic, theological, and political forces
is important and substantial. One cannot read key lines from
poems such as "The Complaint," "The True Love-Knott,"
"Loves Monarchie," "S. Matthew," "Cantic. Chap. 2.XX[ss] 10–
11–12–13," or "Purification of the B. Virgin" without acknowl-
edging the similar sensibilities of the two poets:

> Mighty *Love*, oh how dost Thou
>   By not fighting, overthrow;
>
> . . .
>
>   Dy I must, yf thus I live;
> Life to Me no Life can give;
> Wounds & Death bought Life for Me,
> Wounds & Death my life must be:
> Wounds of present Love; not such
> As pierce deep, but never touch
> Death which liveth in *Loves* Darts,
> Into Life to murder Harts;
> Wounds, & Death, which never from
> *Absence's* cold spring did come.
>   ("The Complaint" 1–2, 17–26)

>   These two,
> Which in an endlesse Combate throw
> Their fiery Darts from eithers Eyes,
> At once both win & loose the prize.
>
>   Both yeild,
> And boast that they have lost the feild;
> For by that losse they doe obteine
> Themselves, & that double againe.
>   ("The True Love-Knott" 17–24)

O MIGHTY *LOVE*
Thou Universall Life & Soule
Whose Powers doe move
And reigne alone from Pole to Pole,
Give Me thy Worthlesse Subject leave to sing
My due Allegiance to the Worlds Sweet King.
. . .

And heere does Thou
Display thine absolute Monarchie,
And not allow
The conquer'd Heart its owne to bee.
'Tis not its owne: And yet by being Thine
'Tis more its owne, then if it still were mine.

("Loves Monarchie" 1–6, 103–08)

O LOVE Thou art Almighty! This
Sole Day can prove Thee so, which is
Not onely Matthews, but from thence
The Feast of thy Omnipotence.

("S. Matthew" 1–4)

Rise up, my Love, my Fairest One
            Make no delay;
Now *Winters* utmost Blast hath blown
            Himselfe away.
. . .
All Sweets invite Us to lay downe
            Our dull delay
Rise up, my Love, my Fairest One
            And come away.

1–4, 21–24
("Cantic. Chap. 2.XX^ss 10–11–12–13")

How shall Chrystall purer grow?
            What shall purge, & whiten Snow?
In this Sacred Virgin-Mother
Snow & Chrystall joyne together.
What shall Days faire gate adorne,
What shall gild the face of Morne?

Ne'r did East so pure as Shee
Beare a Sun of Majestie.
    Yet must Chrystall, yet must Snow,
    Yet must th'East to clensing goe:
    By no Law, but onely the
    Sweet Law of Humilitie.
                ("Purification of the B. Virgin" [160] 1–12)

But Beaumont is capable of more than one voice, and in other poems there is evidence of a purposeful and deliberative consideration of topics, of occasions, of Christian virtues and daily expectations. Some of these poems are more reminiscent of Herbert than of Crashaw, and in many instances Beaumont is best seen as emulating neither.[16] They show Beaumont identifying his subjects, both grand and small, and working toward a kind of meditative application and understanding appropriate for his own life and circumstances. Such an effort can be seen in so slight a poem as "The Gnat," as well as in a more formidable poem such as "Life." "The Gnat" describes the speaker's nighttime combat with a pesky gnat, a "little flie" that pesters him and then abruptly flies away, leaving him to contemplate the pitiful state of humankind that is subject to being disturbed by so idle a creature:

    How true
A worme is Man, whom flies their sport can make!
Poor worme; true Rest in no Bed can he take,
    But one of Earth,
    Whence He came forth
    And grew.
                  (35–40)

"The Gnat" does not stretch the speaker's understanding, a quality in keeping with its light subject. In contrast, "Life" moves the speaker and reader through a range of responses to the serious illness of a 12-year old girl. The speaker first attacks "Life" for being hypocritical, for ravaging the soul and body of the sick girl while refusing her "the Courtesie of

Death" (132). If what he witnesses in the condition of the girl is to be called "life," the speaker asserts, he must reject it:

> O *Life*, some other Title I
> Must print upon thy Treacherie.
> Life is a Name pure as the Day
> > And sweet as Light,
> > But Thou like Night
> To blackest horrors dost poore Man betray.

> (133–38)

Rejecting this life, the speaker affirms another life,

> A Life, which with Eternitie
> Doth in its Noble date agree:
> A Life, whose foot tramples the Head
> > Of all that wee
> > Still changing see,
> A Life, that lives when every Death is dead.

> (163–68)

Moving from the deliberative to the emotional and personal, the speaker addresses "DEARE JESU" (181), expressing his hope "to end this living Death, & die!" (186) or, at least, to be "Dead to those Sins, which murdered/Thee on thy Crosse, & which would doe/The like to Me" (188–90).

More deliberative still are the poems that function much as parables or stories, a compelling example of which is "The Net." The controlling metaphor of the poem is the effort of a birdcatcher (a "Fowler") to capture elusive birds in his net. So long as the birds remain high in the trees they are invulnerable to the snares of the fowler; but if the sounds of his decoys are successful, the birds yield to the temptation to swoop down and are caught in the fowler's net, an illustration that functions as a lesson for human conduct. "Take warning then my Heart," the speaker urges:

> this Earth below
> All thick with snares doth grow.

This Net hath caught Me, & convinc'd me so
              That there's no saying No.
If Hearts but hover neere the Dust, straitway
The Serpent, that dwells there, makes them his prey.

(19–24)

Like the birds, however, the speaker can avoid that fate by using "those active Wings of thine,/Whose flight should be divine":

The Region of thy busines is above,
              In the cleare Orbe of Love,
Where Thou with Birds of Paradise mayst sing
And on the Tree of Life mayst rest thy Wing.

(25–30)

What I am calling Beaumont's deliberative mode is evident throughout most of the occasional verse and in many of those poems that remind us at times of the meditations and contemplations of Herbert. All of the poems in the May 17–June 13, 1652 sequence are of this sort, suggesting that, if Gee is correct in saying that the whole of the now-lost second manuscript was a series of poetical exercises or daily meditations, we might have a different and more balanced view of the kind of poet he tried to be. Poems in that sequence are aligned topically into three groups: (1) several are prompted by specific events or observations that give rise to the speaker's meditation on and inquiry into the meaning and application of what he has witnessed to his own life; (2) three ("Ascension," "Pentecost," and "S. Barnabie") are written on or about holy days or feast days; and (3) the majority appear not to be prompted by either specific events or religious occasions but are more general considerations of, for example, "Friends," "Detraction," "Virtue," "Thrift," "Honor," and "Witt."

A poem representative of the first sort is "The Gentle Check" (May 19). The speaker is caught between sleeping and waking "One half of me was up & drest,/The other still in lazy rest" (1–2) not yet having said his morning prayers, only to have his laziness be brought up short when he hears the "Mattens" of a "dainty-tongued Bird" (4–5). The song of a mere bird produces in him guilt and regret for the "Tardy guilty Tone" (16) that his "lazie Rhyme" (19) produces. Tomorrow, the speaker vows, he will be up and early at his prayers, to "strive/Before the Lark to be at heavn" (23–24). Other poems follow this simple, accessible, and effective structure: "The Winter-Spring" (May 18) is prompted by a late frost, reminding the speaker of his own need to avoid late and unexpected "Indevotions cold" (19); "The Duell" (May 23) opens over the bodies of a "Shandoys" and a "Compton," one wounded, one dead, from a "gallant" duel, and leads to a recognition of the more encompassing duel between Flesh and Spirit that all must confront; "The Alarm" is addressed to "Mortalitie" and is a response to an episode (an illness? a sudden fear of death?) during the previous night that has made the speaker better prepared for his eventual death. Of the additional poems that are identified with a person, place, or occasion, two are atypical in that neither attempts a moral or spiritual lesson. "Entertainment" (June 8) is reminiscent of Jonson's poems celebrating the simple joys of good food, good drink, and good companions, but with a twist. It is less the food and drink that pleases the speaker than the virtues of his host; his "*Good cheer*" (2) his "wellcome look" (8), his "Mess of Smiles gentiley garnishd out/With spruce Discourse" (13–14) are the important "entertainment" the speaker experiences: "In thine own Sweetnes I the banquet place" (23). "Game" (May 26) is a poem on hunting, a sport in which the speaker chooses not to participate and which he gently mocks as mere "Play" (54). He prefers, he says, "to hunt, as high/As Nimrod in the feilds of History" (59–60).

Of the poems of the more general sort, I will point only to two. "Honor" (June 3) is a skilled and effective poem that in its repetitive and rhythmical style offers a persistent warning to an "Ambitious Sir" who is threatened with dishonor by a

"deceitfull," "treacherous," "uncertain," and "banefull She."
The opening stanza addresses the apparently unwary acquain-
tance and sounds the initial warning, while the last offers the
final and "wholesome Lesson":

> Ambitious Sir, take heed;
>   For thou on Glass dost tread.
> No Glass more beautiful & cleer
> Than all the paths of Honor are;
> No Glass more slippery can be
> Or brittle, than deceitfull She.
>
> . . .
>
> Ambitious Sir take heed,
>   And in brave Haman read
> A wholesome Lesson: who but He
> Honor's own Darling was! Yet see
> his ruines monstrous mockery,
> Who fell full fifty cubits high.

(1–6, 25–30)

In light of the usual estimation of Beaumont as an undistin-
guished and pedestrian versifier, his poem "Witt" (June 7) is
amusingly suggestive and self-effacing. "But who has Witt
enough to tell/Me what it is?," the speaker asks about wit
in the opening lines, and he maintains this skeptical pose
throughout the poem. Perhaps responding to praises of wit in
others or to suggestions that he embody more wit in his own
writings, he professes (or admits) to being unsettled by the
sheer variousness of the definitions of wit:

> Now old, now young again; now low,
>   And now as high;
>   Now corsive, now
> Gratious with tickling Lenity;
> Proud Spanish now, now smug & sleek
> French, portly Roman now, now most delicious Greek.
>
> Sometimes her looser garb is Prose,
>   Sometimes in verse
>   Straitlac'd she goes;

> Now she as low as hell doth curse,
> Now swear as high as heavn: her paint
> Shews her sometimes a Devil, & few times a Saint.
>
> (7–18)

Wit, the speaker concludes, is not for him: "Let the World call/Me as they list: whats that to me?/Tis best, and I had rather Wise than Witty be" (28–30).

I conclude with two examples, "Tobacco" and "The Fashion," that, in spite of the self-effacing modesty of "Witt," give evidence of Beaumont's capacity to be effective, witty, and engaging. They are not, surely, "typical" of Beaumont, but they stand as useful reminders that if his verse more frequently places him in the company of Crashaw and Herbert, he can sound his own interesting and original notes as well. "Tobacco" is witty and humorous and is, to a contemporary ear, at times surprisingly prescient in its perspective and tone. In his opening words the speaker attacks the "Incroaching Weed" for leaving India "To taint another world" (1, 4). Tobacco is seen to be seductive and alluring, thought first to be "But tame & honest poyson, which good Art/Might mix into a wholsomenes" (8–9), but then discovered to be a product that effectively destroys the soul. There is a lesson in tobacco, but it is a lesson in vanity and prodigality:

> And art Thou not a vapour full as vain
> As Man himselfe? O costly smoke, could We
> But estimate thy Nothing, we might gain
> A Virtue for our Prodigalitie,
> > And spend in Incense Altars to perfume,
> > What in thy empty stink We now consume.
>
> (25–30)

But the lesson from tobacco also leads the speaker to recant: it is not tobacco that is to blame for ruining humankind, but humankind for encroaching on, terrorizing, and capturing tobacco for its own uses. Ultimately, in fact, the problem is not so much tobacco itself, which is even said to be of value, but fashion:

> I know thou cheer'st the Spirits, help'st the Braine,
> Repell'st bad Aires, to Students art a Freind,
> If us'd with sober Reason: but our vaine
> Humor prevails; Our Selves & Time We spend
>   We know not why; Such is our Affectation,
>   Our nose must smoak onely to be in fashion. (55–60)

Fashion comes in for an even greater measure of abuse in "The Fashion." Fashion might be worthy of approval, the speaker suggests, if it only made sense:

> I likewise might inamour'd be
> Of it, the Fashion, could I see
>   But what it is, & how
>   It comes to grow,
> But (like the Phantomes of a troubled Head)
> Before tis finished, tis quite vanished.
>
> (1–6)

The problems of fashion are its vanity, its lack of substance, its attempted regulation of beauty and ugliness, its constant and meaningless change. "Bodies of a comely Look/A META-MORPHOSIS can brook/From SHEERS & NEEDLE, and / Be at command/Of every gew gaw fancie, that they meet/ 'Mongst other Butter-flies about the Street" (13–18). There is no substance in fashion, "for the Fashion/Is Nothing else but Variation./And therefore Nothing" (19–21). That which would otherwise be considered "Deformitie" (26) is, if fashionable, considered beautiful: "It is enough if they/Can plead & say,/ Wee are the newest Cut: the ugliest dresse/Trimm'd with the Name of Fashion, beauteous is" (27–30).

"Tobacco" and "The Fashion" are among a number of poems by Beaumont that stand effectively on their own and that are most fairly considered and appreciated apart from a forced association with the poetry of Donne, Herbert, or Crashaw. These poems also serve as a reminder of the value of reading anew poets whom conventional judgment has rendered unimportant or unworthy. Reading Beaumont will not supplant our fuller attention to more established writers, nor should it. But as with many poets forever stuck with the label of being "minor," there is an equal danger of unexamined or unfair generalizations or simple neglect. Good and interesting poetry can be found in Beaumont, and if it is seen amidst more ordinary versifying it nonetheless merits attention and consideration on its own terms. As we move beyond a "great poets" approach to literary history to a more inclusive understanding of what it meant to read and write poetry in the seventeenth century, we are obligated, I believe, to look at the wide range of poets, women and men — Beaumont among them — who are not found in our anthologies, textbooks, or critical studies. Only then can we claim a deeper appreciation of the role poetry truly played in seventeenth century English society and culture.

16• John Roberts, Bibliographer

Claude Summers

John Roberts is, according to Joseph Summers, "our best criti-
cal bibliographer of English seventeenth century studies."[1]
Roberts is, of course, not only a bliographer. He has contrib-
uted a number of critical and scholarly studies of his own and
has edited an anthology of English Recusant devotional prose
and important collections of essays on Donne, Herbert,
Crashaw, and the seventeenth century religious lyric, and has
coedited the commentary in the elegies volume of *The
Variorum Edition of the Poetry of John Donne*. But it is surely
as a bibliographer that Roberts has made his most significant
contribution to the study of seventeenth century literature.
Roberts's bibliographies are distinguished by thoroughness,
scrupulous accuracy, intelligent and sympathetic annotations,
reader-friendly formats and useful indexes. They are indispens-
able research tools for students of seventeenth century litera-
ture. But they are more than that, and John Roberts is not
only a bibliographer both in the sense that he has done other
kinds of work and also in the sense that his bibliographies
transcend the narrow category of secondary bibliography as it
is popularly conceived and as all too frequently executed.

Roberts's first bibliography was *John Donne: An Annotated Bibliography of Modern Criticism, 1912–1967*, published in 1973 by the University of Missouri Press. He then issued *George Herbert: An Annotated Bibliography of Modern Criticism, 1905–1974* in 1978, also from the University of Missouri Press. These two seminal works have since been augmented by two additional volumes from the same publisher. In 1982, Roberts extended the Donne bibliography a decade in *John Donne: An Annotated Bibliography of Modern Criticism, 1968–1978*; and in 1988, he issued a revised and expanded edition of the Herbert bibliography as *George Herbert: An Annotated Bibliography of Modern Criticism, Revised Edition, 1905–1984*. In addition to the Donne and Herbert bibliographies, Roberts has also published the standard bibliography of criticism on Crashaw in *Richard Crashaw: An Annotated Bibliography of Criticism, 1632–1980*, issued by Missouri in 1985. He also included an important selective (and unannotated) bibliography of criticism of the seventeenth century religious lyric from 1952 to 1990 in his collection of essays entitled *New Perspectives on the Seventeenth-Century English Religious Lyric*, published by Missouri in 1994. These works, coupled with such bibliographical essays as "John Donne's Poetry: An Assessment of Modern Criticism" (published originally in the inaugural number of the *John Donne Journal* [1982] and reprinted in the second edition of Arthur L. Clements's Norton Critical Edition of *John Donne's Poetry* [1992]) and "Crashavian Criticism: A Brief Interpretive History" (included in Roberts's collection of essays entitled *New Perspectives on the Life and Art of Richard Crashaw* [1990]), as well as Roberts's service as principal bibliographer of *The Variorum Edition of the Poetry of John Donne*, constitute a major contribution to seventeenth century studies.

The Roberts bibliographies are arranged chronologically by year of publication, and within each year the ordering is alphabetical according to author. At first blush, this may seem an awkward or inefficient arrangement, particularly when one is using a secondary bibliography in its narrowest scope as a research tool — when, for example, one simply wants to find quickly the most extensive discussions of, say, Herbert's "The British Church" or Donne's "A Valediction: of my name, in the window." But arrangement by individual poem or even groups of poems is not practical since most criticism of Donne and Herbert fails to restrict itself neatly to clearly defined categories. Moreover, whatever difficulties may be created by the chronological arrangement are alleviated by the presence of indexes keyed to authors, subjects, and individual works referred to in the annotations. With the use of the indexes, it is easy to discover the fullest discussions of particular works. Hence, the bibliographies actually function quite well as reference tools. More significantly, however, the chronological arrangement facilitates other uses of the bibliographies. It permits them to go beyond Roberts's rather modest claim, as stated in the second Donne bibliography, that the primary purpose of his work "is to provide students, scholars, and critics of John Donne with a useful aid to research" (1).

In fact, Roberts's bibliographies of Donne, Herbert, and Crashaw are as much contributions to literary history as to secondary bibliography, narrowly conceived. The chronological arrangement, coupled with the fullness and fairness of the annotations, means that the bibliographies reliably chart the various directions and developments of scholarship and criticism during the years they encompass. In the case of Crashaw, Roberts's bibliography constitutes a history of the poet's reception across three and one-half centuries. While the scope of the other bibliographies is more restricted, limited to the period 1905–1984 in the case of Herbert and 1912–1978 in the case of Donne, they also subsume an enormous amount of scholarly and critical activity during periods in which the reputations of their subjects fluctuated and the assumptions and methods of literary criticism altered. Indeed, the critical attention paid to Herbert and Donne in the twentieth century has in crucial ways been paradigmatic of the modern institutionalization of scholarship and criticism. From this perspective, it is worth noting that the critical reputations of both poets were significantly revised as their work became the subject of academic study and the beneficiary of scholarly effort. Only in the twentieth century did Donne and Herbert regain, after centuries of relative neglect, the status of major poet that each enjoyed in his own age, at least among select coteries. It is not coincidental, then, that the beginning dates of the bibliographies of Herbert and Donne are the dates of significant editions, works that newly subjected the poetry to a systematic scholarly examination using the most advanced editorial theories and techniques of their day. Roberts begins the Herbert bibliography in 1905, the date of the publication of George Herbert Palmer's three-volume edition of *The English Poems of George Herbert*; he begins the Donne bibliography in 1912, the date of Herbert J. C. Grierson's *The Poems of John Donne*. Both editions, monumental in scope and ambition, had the effect of codifying the poetry for academic study and making it available for scholarly revaluation.

There is no better way to grasp the shifting currents of modern academic criticism than to read Roberts's bibliographies of Herbert and Donne straight through. There are not many secondary bibliographies that repay such an approach, but the thoroughness and openness of Roberts's annotations make his bibliographies repositories and epitomes of arguments that, seen in the aggregate, come to embody an oblique narrative of historical and critical development, as attitudes toward religious and erotic poetry change from era to era and as critical approaches come in and out of fashion. The history of Herbert criticism during the years 1905–1984 as redacted in Roberts's bibliographies is especially interesting, not merely as an account of Herbert's steadily emerging reputation as a major poet but also as a fascinating chronicle of changing

critical and cultural preoccupations. In the course of this co-
herent yet somewhat jerky chronicle that proceeds in fits and
starts, as the annual number of entries grows from a trickle to
a flood, attempts to define Herbert's religious positions are
largely (but never entirely) displaced by a New Critical em-
phasis on textual and rhetorical strategies, which in turn yields
finally (but by no means completely) to a New Historicist
examination of Herbert's work as a site of religious and social
controversy. The Herbert bibliographies function as a record
of the critical approaches to which the poetry has proven sus-
ceptible, as it is examined from a large number of (sometimes
antithetical) perspectives and subjected to a variety of meth-
odologies. The growth of Herbert's reputation in the twen-
tieth century, his recognition as an artist in his own right, is
in large measure a direct result of the poetry's responsiveness
to a number of quite different kinds of critical interventions.

The key to the bibliographies' success as contributions to
literary history is the quality and discrimination of the anno-
tations. Believing, as he states in the 1978 Herbert bibliogra-
phy, that "what is important and/or useful to one scholar or
critic is not equally significant to another" (x), Roberts pro-
vides annotations that are essentially descriptive rather than
evaluative. That is, he summarizes the entries with apparent
neutrality and almost never adds evaluative modifiers such
as "important" or "insignificant." Nor does he attempt to ref-
eree scholarly controversies, though he does cross-reference
disagreements. In other words, Roberts aims at a high stand-
ard of objectivity and stands aloof from critical disputation.
At the same time, however, the thoroughness of the annota-
tions tends to expose works of little or no value and he does
note errors of fact and make crucial decisions as to the amount
of space he allocates each entry. That is to say, the even-hand-
edness of the annotations is not an evasion of responsibility
but a calculated strategy of restraint. Rather than using his

bibliographies as a means of promoting a particular critical agenda or approach, Roberts effaces himself in the interest of his commitment to objectivity. While he makes responsible choices that signal the relative significance of the entries, he does not intrude to editorialize in his own voice about the worth of the items. Moreover, his awareness that contributions that may appear insignificant or insubstantial to one scholar might nevertheless prove valuable to another bespeaks his understanding of the winding ways of scholarship and the mysteriousness of the creative process.

Roberts's concise summaries frequently include direct quotations from the works being summarized, and this has the effect of capturing somewhat more than merely the thesis of an entry. The quotations convey something of the style, sophistication, and accessibility of the work being annotated, and items that are trivial or tendentious or jargon-ridden generally betray themselves in their own words. Moreover, the annotations are roughly proportional in size to the length and significance of the entries themselves. Book-length studies are sometimes allotted in excess of two printed pages of annotation, and an important essay might receive three-quarters of a page, while a note or peripheral material might be annotated in a single sentence. Hence, the annotations are by no means mechanical summaries of entries presented as of equal value. Most important of all, the annotations are remarkably sensitive to nuance and suggestiveness. Surely, the temptation in annotating lengthy books and articles is to summarize grossly and approximately, but Roberts consistently notes qualifications and contingencies and achieves a remarkable level of precision. The annotations are thus quite useful in the bibliography's function as a research tool: they provide sufficient information to let one know whether any particular item is likely to be pertinent and useful for the researcher's purposes. But, again, they are detailed and nuanced enough to serve the interests of the literary historian as well. Roberts's ability to communicate in a brief compass the subtleties of a sophisticated and elaborate scholarly argument is extraordinary.

The Roberts bibliographies are a valuable resource for the study of Donne, Herbert, and Crashaw, and of seventeenth century literature generally. All serious students of these poets and of the period owe a large debt to these volumes. Although it is always the fate of bibliographies to be outdated when they achieve print, because these particular bibliographies transcend their immediate usefulness as research tools, they remain valuable even as they grow increasingly dated. Happily, the Donne bibliography is due to be augmented soon by a volume to be issued by Duquesne University Press in 2003 under the title *John Donne: An Annotated Bibliography of Modern Criticism, 1979–1998*. Referred to by Roberts as "Donne III," this volume will contain some 1600 items and will follow the same principles and format as the earlier volumes. Cumulatively, Roberts's Donne bibliographies will constitute a thorough and detailed history of Donne's reputation in the twentieth century, one likely to be matched only by the massive Donne Variorum project currently underway.

While the news of the plans for the publication of "Donne III" is an occasion for celebration, it seems to me that the most appropriate mode of publication for secondary bibliographies is not print but electronic publication. What I would like to see is the inclusion of the Roberts bibliographies in an on-line journal or web site, where they could be systematically and regularly updated. Such on-line publication of the bibliographies would dramatically increase their usefulness as research tools since they could easily be augmented. With such periodic additions, they would not suffer from the built-in obsolescence of secondary bibliographies in print. I hope that an on-line journal or archive will undertake the project of maintaining and augmenting these important works, which are essential to all of us who work in seventeenth century studies. But, of course, the success of such an undertaking is crucially dependent on Roberts himself. That is, the bibliographies could not easily be continued by someone else or by a group of bibliographers, for despite their compiler's strategy of self-effacement they are, perhaps most surprisingly, a highly individual expression.

In objectively reporting the research of others, Roberts has himself not only compiled secondary bibliographies that facilitate the research of still others, but he has also made his own original contribution to scholarship by amassing and subtly shaping the materials of literary history. His bibliographies are far more than mechanical listings; in their careful organization and authoritative annotations they exhibit seasoned judgment and wide learning. For all their objectivity and self-restraint, they are, finally, quite personal documents, the oblique manifestation of a particular sensibility. If criticism is a form of autobiography, as Oscar Wilde maintained, then it really should not be so surprising that Roberts's bibliographies also function to illuminate their compiler as well as their subjects. These significant works reflect the scholarly commitment and expertise of John Roberts, Bibliographer, who is so much more than a bibliographer.

Notes

Notes to Chapter 1/McBride

1. Thanks to John C. Ulreich and Herbert N. Schneidau for reading early versions of this study and making thoughtful suggestions. This paper (in a much abbreviated form) was originally delivered at the Southwest Regional Renaissance Conference at the Huntington Library, San Marino, 10 May 1996, supported by a travel grant from the Renaissance Conference of Southern California. A later version was given at the Conference on Medieval Studies in Kalamazoo in May 1999.

2. Louis Martz, *The Poetry of Meditation: A Study in English Religious Literature of the Seventeenth Century* (New Haven: New Haven Univ. Press, 1954). On Southwell, see, for instance, Ronald J. Corthell's "'The secrecy of man': Recusant Discourse and the Elizabethan Subject," *English Literary Renaissance* 19 (1989): 272–90, and F. W. Brownlow's *Robert Southwell* (New York: Twayne, 1996).

3. Marshall Grossman, "The Gendering of Genre: Literary History and the Canon." *Aemilia Lanyer: Gender, Genre, and the Canon*, ed. Marshall Grossman (Lexington: Univ. Press of Kentucky, 1998), 128, 140.

4. Michelle Cliff, "Object Into Subject: Some Thoughts On the Work of Black Women Artists," *Making Face, Making Soul/Haciendo Caras: Creative and Critical Perspectives by Feminists of Color*, ed. Gloria Anzaldúa (San Francisco: Aunt Lute Books, 1990), 271, 272, 274.

5. See Martin Hengel, *Crucifixion in the Ancient World and the Folly of the Message of the Cross* (Philadelphia: Fortress Press, 1977).

6. The Jewish historian Josephus recounts that "Pilate . . . hearing him accused by men of the highest standing amongst us . . . condemned him to be crucified" (qtd. in Crossan, 147). I am indebted to John Dominic Crossan's *Who Killed Jesus?: Exposing the Roots of Antisemitism in the Gospel Story of the Death of Jesus* (San Francisco: Harper, 1991) for much of my understanding of these ancient materials.

7. Crossan, *Who Killed Jesus?*, 152.

8. One could argue that the creation of identity by a kind of Saussurean negative relationship (knowing oneself by what one is not) has precedent in Judaism: Jews are Jews because they are not Canaanites, they do not eat pork, they do not practice sacred prostitution or infanticide, they do not worship idols.

9. Note, for instance, the obsession of the early second century Pastoral Letters (1 and 2 Timothy and Titus) with obedience (by women, youth, and slaves to men, elders, and master) and with hierarchy in contrast to the earlier Pauline statement that in Christ "there is no longer Jew or Greek, . . . slave or free, . . . male and female" (Gal. 3.28).

10. Many Christians today and throughout the centuries have thought of Jesus, his followers, and his family as non-Jews. For instance, Elisabeth Schüssler Fiorenza relates a story of a woman who taught a parish adult education class on "Jesus, the Jew." At the end of the class, a participant said, "If you are so insistent that Jesus was Jewish, then you are probably right. But the Blessed Mother for sure is not." *In Memory of Her: A Feminist Theological Reconstruction of Christian Origins* (New York: Crossroad, 1985), 105–06.

11. Perhaps present in the singling out Eve as the one "deceived" in 2 Cor. 11.3; certainly a given in 1 Tim. 2.13 where Eve, and not Adam, is the one who was "deceived" and who "transgressed."

12. See *The Book of Common Prayer, 1559: The Elizabethan Prayer Book*, ed. John E. Booty (Charlottesville: Univ. Press of Virginia for the Folger Shakespeare Library, 1976). The text comes from 1 Cor. 11.23. Two factors might mitigate the impact of these eucharistic reminders of the Passion: the utter or relative incomprehensibility of the Latin Mass for most Christians and their rare and/or limited participation in the eucharistic liturgy. These factors must be weighed, however, against the portrayals of the Passion in graphic and plastic arts "readable" by all people, the popularity of Bible stories that had their own oral tradition throughout the premodern Christian world, and the existence of vernacular missals. Even so, literate laity and clergy would have an influence beyond their numbers on the creation of antisemitic rhetoric and policies.

13. The dramatic reenactment of Palm Sunday originated in fourth century Jerusalem and was practiced by the Roman church as early as the sixth century. The custom of reading the Passion narrative during Holy Week (from the four gospels, in canonical order) "goes back to very ancient times," and, by the Middle Ages, the Passion was being performed as a dramatic oratorio with cantors taking the various individual parts and the choir playing the Jews (a custom that was instrumental, of course, in reviving drama in the medieval world as the biblical enactments moved onto the church porch and then into the streets as

Mystery plays). See Massey Hamilton Shepherd, Jr., *The Oxford American Prayer Book Commentary* (New York: Oxford Univ. Press, 1950), 134–37.

14. Louis Martz cites the studies of Helen C. White and Maria Hagedorn in *The Poetry of Meditation*, 5–6. See Helen C. White, *English Devotional Literature*, Wisconsin Studies in Language and Literature, no. 29 (Madison: [Univ. of Wisconsin], 1931), and Maria Hagedorn, *Reformation und spanische Andachtsliteratur: Luis de Granada in England* (Bonn: J. Duckwitz, 1934).

15. The 1290 expulsion of the Jews from England is traditionally attributed to Edward I. However, the 1290 date is largely symbolic, a final expulsion that followed on decades of persecution. For a discussion of the history of fixation on Edward I's 1290 expulsion, see James Shapiro, *Shakespeare and the Jews* (New York: Columbia Univ. Press, 1996), 46–55.

16. Shapiro, *Shakespeare and the Jews*, 15.

17. The manuscript context of the poem provides little help in identifying the author — in addition to her poem, it includes a Calvinist prose tract, "A Soveraign Antidote agayst [sic] Despayre fitt to be taken of all those who are afflicted eyther outwardlye in Boddy or Inwardly in Mynde, or both," and an incomplete version of William Austin's "Ecce Homo" in addition to Middleton's poem, which quotes extensively from Robert Southwell's "Saint Peter's Complaint." In *Kissing the Rod: An Anthology of Seventeenth-Century Women's Verse* (London: Virago, 1988), Germaine Greer et al. speculate that the presence of both Calvinist and Roman Catholic writings in the manuscript suggests that Middleton was related to a family of devout Anglicans with Puritan allies and English Catholic contacts. Unfortunately, Elizabeth was a popular given name in the three generations of Middletons who lived during the time when the poem could have been written (94–96).

18. Reference to Middleton's poem is by stanza number from Bod. Don. E.17. Actually, to be fair, Lanyer's rendering is pretty pedestrian:

> Although the Spirit was willing to obay,
> Yet what great weakeness in the Flesh was found!

But the lines that follow redeem it:

> They slept in Ease, whilst thou in Paine didst pray;
> Loe, they in Sleepe, and thou in Sorrow drown'd" (425–28).

All quotations from Lanyer are by line number from *The Poems of Aemilia Lanyer: Salve Deus Rex Judaeorum*, ed. Susanne Woods (New York: Oxford Univ. Press, 1993).

19. Thanks to John Ulreich for his reading of this passage.

20. See *The Poems of Robert Southwell, S. J.*, ed. James H. McDonald

and Nancy Pollard Brown (Oxford: Clarendon Press, 1967), lxxxvi–xcii, for a discussion of the internal and historical arguments for dating the poem to the early 1590s.

21. See Mario Praz, "Robert Southwell's 'Saint Peter's Complaint' and its Italian Source," *Modern Language Review* 19 (1924): 273–90, and Louis Martz's discussion in *The Poetry of Meditation*, 194–95.

22. All quotations are from the McDonald and Brown edition of the *Poems*, cited by line number.

23. *Between Men: English Literature and Male Homosocial Desire* (New York: Columbia Univ. Press, 1985).

24. In Mark, a single servant girl accuses him twice, after which he is accused by "bystanders" (14.66–72). In Matthew, Peter is accused of being one of Jesus's followers by two different servant girls, and then by "bystanders" (26.69–75). In Luke, he is accused by a servant girl, then by "someone else," and then by "another" (22.54–62). In John, he is accused by "the woman who guarded the gate," by unidentified "they," and by "one of the slaves of the high priest" (18.15–27).

25. Significantly for my argument, Southwell borrows heavily from Tanzillo's the misogynistic tenor of Peter's "complaint," though the homoerotic elements I delineate in Southwell's poem seem to be original with him. I would argue, however, that, whatever the immediate source of particular images or descriptions, the self-fashioning achieved through the poem is no less Southwell's, just as Middleton's antisemitism must be attributed to her, whatever its larger context. Poets make choices from a variety of poetic and religious possibilities, and we can learn as much from their borrowings as from their seemingly original compositions.

26. Some biographers, including Alexander B. Grosart, who edited Southwell's works in the nineteenth century, have argued that Southwell had a wide and significant influence on Shakespeare. See Grosart's "Memorial-Introduction," in *The Complete Poems of Robert Southwell* (1872; reprint, Westport, CN: Greenwood Press, 1970) and Christopher Devlin's *Life of Robert Southwell, Poet and Martyr* (New York: Farrar, Straus and Cudahy, [1956]).

27. Lorna Hutson provides a contrast between the kind of male authority constructed in Shakespeare's sonnet — and, by implication, Southwell's poem — and the alternative authority Lanyer is attempting in the "Salve Deus":

> "All *Hews* in his controwling" thus indicates the reader's specifically masculine relation to the text. . . . The relation between masculine author and masculine patron/reader emerges as inherently "virtuous" (in the Renaissance sense of conducive to good action, rather than to theoretical speculation on the nature of good) by implicit

comparison with the relation between masculine author and feminine pretext/reader, since the usual pretext of Petrarchan discourse — love for a woman — can only generate a "face" or textual surface of rhetorical colours to be exploited by men. . . . So, since only a man can effectively reproduce from a discourse which celebrates beauty, this power of discursive reproduction becomes his intrinsic beauty, and only a man can therefore be "truly" beautiful.

"Why the Lady's Eyes Are Nothing Like the Sun," in *Women, Texts and Histories 1575–1760*, ed. Clare Brant and Diane Purkiss (London: Routledge, 1992), 18.

28. Of course, this image of adulterous human and faithful God has precedents in the Hebrew prophets, who picture the syncretist Israelites as whoring after false gods.

29. Lanyer's Jewish background has been well established. See Leeds Barroll, "Looking for Patrons," in *Gender, Genre, and the Canon*, ed. Marshall Grossman (Lexington: Univ. Press of Kentucky), 29–48, and the sources he cites, especially David Lasocki with Roger Prior, *The Bassanos: Venetian Musicians and Instrument Makers in England, 1531–1665* (Aldershot: Scolar Press, 1995). However, see Susanne Woods, *Lanyer: A Renaissance Woman Poet* (Oxford Univ. Press, 1999), 5–7, where Woods argues that "[m]ore likely than Jewish origins is the possibility that Baptista [Bassano] and Margaret [Johnson, Lanyer's parents] were radical Protestant partisans" (7).

30. Leeds Barroll questions the likelihood of Lanyer's having known Bertie (32–34). However, Barroll is "looking for patrons" in Lanyer's life; her relationship with Bertie might not have been one of patronage in the literary sense at all (not even in some kind of nascent form). She might merely have been, as Barroll suggests, taken by her mother as a young child to Bertie's household where Lanyer's mother may have been serving Bertie. It would not be at all surprising for Lanyer to make more of this relationship than the circumstances warranted.

31. A. L. Rowse, *The Poems of Shakespeare's Dark Lady: Salve Deus Rex Judaeorum by Emilia Lanier* (London: Jonathan Cape, 1976), 14, 35–36.

32. See Catherine Keohane's discussion of Lanyer's Jewishness and its relationship to her portrayal of Jews in "'That Blindest Weakenesse Be Not Over-Bold': Aemilia Lanyer's Radical Unfolding of the Passion," in *English Literary History* 64 (1997), 359–89. Keohane quotes Janel Mueller's argument that "Lanyer's Jewish background may have enabled her to conceive the agency at issue in the Crucifixion in gendered terms rather than the ethnic ones that were commonplace throughout Christian Europe," but notes that "Lanyer does not fully exonerate the Jews," adding that "Lanyer's rewriting of the Passion story is not one that specifically seeks to absolve the Jews (only Jewish women perhaps)" (365).

33. *Christ's Victorie and Triumph in Heaven, and Earth, over and after Death* consists of four poems. The section "Christ's Triumph Over Death" is the Passion narrative. "Christ's Victorie in Heaven" portrays personified Mercy pleading with God for Adam's pardon; "Christ's Victorie on Earth" recounts the temptation in the desert; and "Christ's Triumph after Death" describes the resurrection, ascension, and the "beatificall vision of God . . . And of Christ" (The Argument), where Christ is figured as a type of Orpheus.

34. Though (as Mueller notes) Fletcher's stanzas conclude with an alexandrine, a form that produces a very different — Spenserian — effect. "The Feminist Poetics of 'Salve Deus Rex Judaeorum," *Aemilia Lanyer: Gender, Genre, and the Canon*, ed. Marshall Grossman (Lexington: Univ. Press of Kentucky).

35. Mueller, "Feminist Poetics," 107–08.

36. Quoted in Grosart, "Memorial-Introduction," *The Complete Poems of Giles Fletcher, B. D.* (London: Chatto and Windus, 1876), 15, from *The Poems of Phineas Fletcher . . . .*, ed. Alexander Grosart, Fuller Worthies' Library (Blackburn: C. Tiplady, 1869).

37. Grosart, "Memorial-Introduction," 46–47.

38. For instance, note the epic echoes of the opening stanzas:

> The birth of Him that no beginning knewe,
> Yet giues beginning to all that are borne;
>
>   *　　*　　*
>
> How God and Man did both embrace each other,
> Met in one person, Heau'n and Earth did kiss;
> And how a Virgin did become a Mother,
> And bare that Sonne, Who the world's Father is,
>
>   *　　*　　*
>
> Is the first flame, wherewith my whiter Muse
> Doth burne in heauenly loue, such loue to tell.
>
>   *　　*　　*
>
> Ye Sacred Writings, in whose antique leaues
> The memories of Heau'n entreasur'd lie,
> Say, what might be the cause that Mercie heaues
> The dust and sinne aboue th'industrious skie,
> And lets it not to dust and ashes flie? (1,2,3,4)

Reference to Fletcher's poems is from Alexander B. Grosart's edition of *The Complete Poems of Giles Fletcher*, by stanza number.

39. In Matt. 27.57–60, Mark 15.43–46, Luke 23.50–53, and John 19.38. He is variously portrayed as "a disciple of Jesus" (Matt.); "a respected

member of the council, who was also himself waiting expectantly for the kingdom of God" (Mark); "a good and righteous man . . . who, though a member of the council, had not agreed to their plan and action" (Luke); and "a disciple of Jesus, though a secret one because of his fear of the Jews" (John).

40. See Susan Haskins's *Mary Magdalene: Myth and Metaphor* (New York: Harcourt Brace, 1993) on Mary Magdalene's life as a hermit (105–13) and the importance of weeping in her iconography (187–90).

Notes to Chapter 2/Pilarz

1. This presumption is reflected in the Second Vatican Council's Decree on the Renewal of Religious Life which states, "the up-to-date renewal of religious life comprises . . . a constant return to the primitive inspiration of the institutes. . . . Therefore, the spirit and aims of each founder should be faithfully accepted and retained, as indeed should each institute's sound traditions, for all of these constitute the patrimony of an institute" (*Perfectae Caritatis* #2).

2. Southwell entered the Society on October 17, 1578. In the second year of his noviceship he was transferred to the Roman College, soon to become the Pontifical Gregorian University, to begin the study of philosophy. He pronounced his first vows on October 18, 1580, and completed his "Public Defense" in philosophy a year later. From the Roman College he moved to the English College where he would serve as a prefect and tutor to his fellow countrymen while completing his own training in theology. The exact date of his ordination is difficult to determine, but Parsons refers to him as "Father Southwell" in a letter of 1585 (Devlin 66).

3. Included among these documents are the *Formula of the Institute*, which is to the Jesuits what the Rule is to other religious orders; the *Constitutions*, which, according to John O'Malley, "articulated the broad principles according to which the Society was to achieve its goals and reduced the vague generalities of the *Formula* to concrete structures and procedures" (7); Ignatius's *Autobiography*, a narrated story of his life up to 1538, which best models the Jesuits' "way of proceeding"; and, lastly, Loyola's voluminous correspondence which "contains theory and ideals . . . interpreted against the background of everyday reality" (9).

4. According to O'Malley, this expression, *noster modus procedendi; nuestro modo de proceder,* was the Jesuits' "most inclusive and pregnant expression for their style of life and ministry," and "while it of course indicated official documentation, it transcended it by suggesting more spontaneous and actualized ideals and attitudes that distinguished Jesuit life and ministry from that of others" (8).

5. Mercurian's reluctance was at least twofold. As Basset reports, "part of the General's hesitancy about the proposed mission to England was due to his knowledge that Jesuits were over committed in other parts of the world ... [since] in 1579 Jesuits had been dispatched to India, Japan, the West Indies, Poland, and Syria" (30). The General was also concerned about committing his men to so dangerous an operation. He was so wary of things English that the Pope had to command him to have Jesuits assume control of the English College in Rome, which had been founded for the express purpose of training missionary priests who would return and reconvert their homeland. Once control of the College was forced upon Mercurian, the inevitability of missioning Jesuits to accompany their students became clear. "It was pointed out to the General," Basset explains, "that the Fathers could hardly train the English seminarians for so dangerous a mission if they were unwilling to share the risks" (33).

6. Claudio Aquaviva, Mercurian's successor, continued the policy of avoiding conflict. To this end he ordered Southwell and Garnet to steer clear of politics. As Philip Caraman reports, "They were not to meddle in the affairs of state; in their reports to Rome, they were to avoid political news and gossip; in company they were to shun talk about the Queen and were not to countenance it in others" (2).

7. Contrary to what earlier biographers surmised about Southwell's career, McDonald and Brown use the poet's letters to his superiors in Rome to show how he enjoyed "a most active pastoral and administrative career" (xvii). Southwell did not spend all his time hiding in the homes of Catholic aristocrats. He frequently visited prisons, provided shelter for priests who were newly arrived in London, and set up his secret printing press. Finally, in the year before his arrest his local superior, Henry Garnet, sent him on a tour of England during which he met with large numbers of recusants. He wrote his English prose and poetry while carrying on these activities, and "his achievement as a writer was already making his influence widespread among Catholic families of great distinction" (xxix).

8. Referring to his formation in *A Humble Supplication*, Southwell notes how "we must limit our myndes to the restrained and severe course of the Society of Jesus, . . . where the place is exile, the Rules strict, the government austere, our wills broken, our least faults chastised, and a most absolute vertue exacted" (7). The "end of all our warlike preparations," Southwell argues, are "the wrastling with our wills, the mortifying of our bodies, and a continual warfare with nature, to get victory over ourselves" (13).

9. John O'Malley's *The First Jesuits* is especially important in this regard. His work is a result of efforts launched in response to the Second Vatican Council's *Perfectae Caritatis*, a Decree on the Renewal of

Religious Life. This document mandated that religious orders return to "the primitive inspiration" of their institutes by means of careful study and contemplation [2].

10. The dress of Jesuits in England was a source of criticism. For example, John Gee writes, "If, about Bloomesbury or Holborne, thou meet a smug young fellow in a gold-laced suit, a cloak lined thorow with velvet, one that hath gold rings on his fingers, a watch in his pocket, which he will value above 20 pounds, a very broad-laced band, a stiletto by his side, a man at his heeles, . . . then take heed of a Jesuit" (*Foote out of the Snare* 127). Southwell responds to such criticism in *A Humble Supplication*, insisting that "much more weighty is the salvation of our souls, than the external decency of our apparel; which though it be necessary in time and place; yet is it not so essential a point, as for the Care thereof to neglect the Charge of gods flock and the safety of our lives" (9).

11. Nadal's argument is treated at length by O'Malley in "To Travel to Any Part of the World: Jeronimo Nadal and the Jesuit Vocation," *Studies in the Spirituality of Jesuits* 16/2 (1984):7. This translation is taken from O'Malley's article.

12. Because so many have understood the Jesuits in terms of the Reformation for so long, there is warrant for belaboring this point. Ignatius himself reiterated it, often instructing his men to avoid "controversies" and "doubtful matters" in their preaching. He urged Jesuits in Prague, for example, "not to enter into polemics with the Protestants in the pulpit" (O'Malley 96). Promoting sound spirituality was, he insisted, "the bulwark against the errors of the times" (221). The attitudes of the first Jesuits to enter Germany is instructive in this regard. After careful observation they came to the conclusion that among the first and principal causes of "the calamity that afflicted Germany . . . were the depraved morals and vices of ecclesiastics." The solution was obvious enough: "If the bad lives of Christians were the cause of the Reformation, good lives must be the cure" (277).

13. For an insight into anxieties generated by the elevation of the host, see Richard McCoy's "The Wonderful Spectacle: The Civic Progress of Elizabeth I and the Troublesome Coronation." McCoy notes that "to confirmed Protestants, the elevation of the host was the essence of popish idolatry." Rather than witness the elevation at her Coronation Mass, and thereby alienate her Protestant subjects, the new queen is reported to have "retorned to her closet hearing the Consecration of the Mass" (220).

14. Dyer's "My Mind to Me a Kingdom is" can be found in McDonald and Brown, 150–51.

15. Southwell's remarks on Parsons may be wishful thinking. Not all Jesuits were as peaceable as Southwell, and Parsons is reputed to be among the most truculent. When Parsons seemed on the verge of

advocating the assassination of Queen Elizabeth, the Jesuit general intervened. He warned Parsons, "it will behoove the Society to keep out of it, since it little becomes our Institute." Nevertheless, after James and Elizabeth ratified the Anglo-Scottish League on 5 July 1586, Parsons began instigating a Spanish invasion of England (Hicks 108–9).

16. In a survey of recusant consolatory writing, Josephine Evetts-Secker concurs that More's emphasis differs from Southwell's. More's *Dialogue*, written in the Tower in 1534, urges "euery man & euery woman both, [to] appoynt with goddes helpe in their owne mynd beforehand what thyng they intend to do yf the very worst fall." Southwell, writing his *Epistle* "in a medieval mode," dramatizes Christ as the "faithfull paramour of our soule," who languishes for our love (124; 128).

17. Evetts-Secker points out how Southwell admits that his apprecia tion of epistolary discourse is based on early Christian as well as Jesuit precedent (125). In his opening he writes, "It hath bene always a laudable custome in Gods Church, for such were afflicted in time of persecution not onlye by continuall prayer, and good works, but also by letters and bookes to comforte one another" (*Epistle* 3).

18 Jesuits traditionally make the full 30-day version of the *Spiritual Exercises* shortly after entering the order and then again several years after they have been ordained to the priesthood. An abbreviated 8-day version of the retreat is made anually.

19. Southwell contemplated joining a Carthusian monastery before entering the Society. He discusses the process of discernment in a letter written in 1580: "I was in two minds about my vocation — tossed on a tide of suggestions, now making for the good ship 'Bruno,' now for the ship 'Ignatius,' and reaching neither; in fact I was drowning in a torrent of temptations, until at last I steered a sensible course and went to my Confessor. But he would say nothing except the same thing over and over again in different words: 'Stick to the Society, stick to your first vocation'" (Devlin 30–31).

20. Trussle writes to members of the Sackville family, who were the sons and daughters of Philip Howard's half sister, Lady Margaret Howard. Philip was the child of Lady Mary Fitzalan, the first wife of Thomas Howard, third Duke of Norfolk. Margaret was the daughter of his second wife, Margaret Audley. Margaret Howard married Robert Sackville. She died in 1521 at the age of 29, and it was to assuage her brother's grief that Southwell wrote *Triumphs Over Death*.

Notes to Chapter 4/Rienstra

1. All quotations from Lanyer in this essay are taken from *The Poems of Aemilia Lanyer*. Numbers in parentheses following quotations from Lanyer indicate line numbers. Important introductions of Lanyer since

Rowse include Beilin, "The Feminization of Praise: Aemilia Lanyer," in *Redeeming Eve*; Lewalski, "Of God and Good Women"; Lewalski, "Re-writing Patriarchy and Patronage"; and McGrath, "'Let us have our libertie againe': Aemilia Lanier's 17th-Century Feminist Voice." Lanyer scholarship has shifted emphasis in the last ten years from what the introduction to this volume has termed the "re-covery mode" to the "dis-covery mode," as is exemplified in a recent volume of criticism on Lanyer, edited by Marshall Grossman, exhibiting a variety of critical approaches. An additional recent article describing Lanyer's possible sources and also exploring the issue of exegesis in the "Eves Apologie" section is Richey, "'To Undoe the Booke': Cornelius Agrippa, Aemilia Lanyer and the Subversion of Pauline Authority." References to other scholarship treating specific issues will appear below, throughout.

2. The phrase is from Ann Baynes Coiro ("Writing in Service: Sexual Politics and Class Position in the Poetry of Aemilia Lanyer and Ben Jonson"), who explores Lanyer's construction of her own authorship within a complex determined by class as much as or more than gender. Coiro compares Lanyer to Jonson as well as to Spenser and Milton.

3. Janel Mueller ("The Feminist Poetics of Aemilia Lanyer's 'Salve Deus Rex Judaeorum'") confirms Lanyer's ambition to be a truth-teller. Her account of Lanyer's salutations is especially helpful.

4. All quotations from the *Psalmes* and from Pembroke's dedicatory poem are from the recent edition, *The Collected Works of Mary Sidney Herbert, Countess of Pembroke*. I am grateful to the editors for the use of page proofs of the edition while preparing this article, and particu-larly to Noel Kinnamon for verifying quotations against the final version.

5. The introductory material in *Collected Works* provides extensive accounts of Sidney's and Pembroke's roles in composing the *Psalmes*, their differing methods of composition, the nature of the extant manu-scripts, and the known history of its circulation. The edition also con-veniently gathers references to previously available scholarship on the psalter. For Mary Sidney's role in promoting her brother's reputation and the contemporary association of her with the psalter, see Hannay, *Philip's Phoenix*.

6. For the most recent account of contemporary reception of the *Psalmes*, see Hannay, "'Bearing the livery of your name.'"

7. For an account of Pembroke's revision process, see Rienstra and Kinnamon, "Revisioning the Sacred Text." Further examples of her method of composition, including many places in which Pembroke de-viated from Calvinist doctrine or commentaries in her poems, appear in *Collected Works*. An extensive consideration of Sidney's and Pembroke's style and method, particularly in comparison to the metrical psalm tra-dition, appears in Rienstra, "Aspiring to Praise."

8. John Donne, "Upon the translation of the Psalms by Sir Philip Sidney, and the Countess of Pembroke his sister."

9. Roland Greene, in "Sir Philip Sidney's Psalms, the Sixteenth-Century Psalter, and the Nature of Lyric," articulates the merged modes of ritual and lyric in the Psalms. Greene's intriguing remarks about Sidney's psalms lack, unfortunately, any reference to Pembroke's psalms. He regards Sidney's poems merely as an incomplete psalter. The idea of a ritual mode is not as relevant to this essay as the tension between lyric and prophetic modes, and thus will not be discussed.

10. A useful summary of contemporary Psalm commentary appears in Lewalski, *Protestant Poetics*.

11. Lisa Schnell, in "Breaking 'the rule of *Cortezia*': Aemilia Lanyer's Dedications to *Salve Deus Rex Judaeorum*," proposes that Lanyer may not have even known her chief addressee, Margaret Clifford, Countess of Cumberland, despite the intimacy the poem everywhere implies. Certainly, the so-called "community of good women" Lanyer constructs is no secure assemblage. The dedicatory poems contain numerous indications of Lanyer's anxiety about these women's virtue and benevolence toward her. Lanyer is well aware that the audience she writes into existence is as fragile and ephemeral as the edenic Cookeham of her "To Cooke-ham."

12. Not all the extant copies of *Salve Deus* contain the full set. See the "Textual Introduction" in the Woods edition. Also, Leeds Barroll has noted that Lanyer placed the poem dedicated to Pembroke ahead of the one to Lucy, Countess of Bedford, whose poem, by rank, should come first. Barroll terms this a "major mistake (as regards any hope of penetrating the queen's circle)" for Lanyer. However, it may reflect Lanyer's more intimate and hopeful imagined relationship to Pembroke. See Barroll, "Looking for Patrons," 40.

13. These associations are suggested in Beilin, *Redeeming Eve*, 189.

14. As Elaine Beilin has observed: "To men and perhaps to some women, a woman's desire for knowledge was a frightening prospect, recalling images of Eve's hand reaching for the apple. But by claiming that learning would increase a woman's virtue (her chastity, obedience, humility), the humanists and their successors reassured society that a woman's knowledge was under control and directed only to enhancing her womanliness" (Beilin xxi–xxii).

For discussions of learned women in the period, see Hannay, *Silent But for the Word*, 1–14. Also in that volume, see Mary Ellen Lamb, "The Cooke Sisters."

15. In the section following the *"vates"* passage, Sidney takes pains to establish that the poet is much more than a stenographer. The poet's singular nobility is that he is a maker: "Only the Poet, disdaining to be tied to any such subjection, lifted up with the vigor of his own

invention, doth grow in effect into another nature, in making things either better than Nature bringeth forth, or, quite anew, forms such as never were in Nature, . . . so as he goeth hand in hand with Nature, not enclosed within the narrow warrant of her gifts, but freely ranging only within the zodiac of his own wit" (100).

Looking back to the section on David, one sees that Sidney lists the specific virtues of the Psalms under the heading of David's "handling" of the prophetic material received through divine inspiration. David's initiative in the process is acknowledged.

16. Lanyer's depictions of her own work as compared to Pembroke's reflect the Nature-Art complex she has been exploring thus far. Pembroke's poetry is natural, but refined, a harmony of nature and art, like sugar. Lanyer's is purely natural (as she claimed in her poem to the queen), like honey, but wholesome even so, as it springs from virtue. While McGrath assesses Lanyer's "feminine poetics" as associated with nature and not with art, Lanyer's account of Pembroke's superior harmonizing of the two undercuts any such straightforward account of what Lanyer values in poetry. See Lynette McGrath, "'Let us have our libertie againe': Aemilia Lanier's 17th–Century Feminist Voice," 340.

17. Schnell also remarks at this point that "Lanyer appears to be bestowing on herself a privilege that is very nearly prophetic," an idea I obviously affirm and wish to account for and define in greater detail. See also Susanne Woods's interesting analysis of the ambiguous pronouns in this passage ("Aemilia Lanyer and Ben Jonson" 23).

18. McBride ("Remembering Orpheus in the Poems of Aemilia Lanyer") writes: "Rather than fictionalizing a female mentor poet on the body of a dead woman in the manner of Milton's Lycidas/Edward King, Lanyer intimates Mary Sidney's symbolic death, silencing the live Mary Sidney by placing her in a mythic heavenly landscape — the realm of the happy dead, but dead nonetheless — and by fusing her poetic person to that of her dead brother" (94).

19. The previous pages in the Woods edition give a brief summary of women's religious writing before 1611 and refer to other works already mentioned here.

20. I refer to Catherine Keohane's essay, "'That blindest weaknesse be not overbold': Aemilia Lanyer's Radical Unfolding of the Passion," which treats the radical nature of Lanyer's exegesis in the long, central poem of her volume in the kind of thorough detail not possible here. Achsah Guibbory's article, "The Gospel according to Aemilia: Women and the Sacred," also considers the details of Lanyer's treatment of the gospel narratives. While these studies explore the results of Lanyer's radical exegesis, I have attempted to account instead for the way in which she engineered the hermeneutical stance that made these results possible.

21. This raises the possibility that Lanyer never read the Sidney-Pembroke Psalter. However, this seems unlikely considering her praise of Pembroke's heart-ravishing hymns and the powerful influence over her imagination that Pembroke *as a writer* seems to have had. It may be simply that while Lanyer did have access to a manuscript long enough to become familiar with it, she did not have a copy available to which to refer during her own writing process. Living as she did at this period on the edges of noble families and court life, she may have had less access to manuscript copies of the psalter than her social superiors or even her male counterparts such as Donne, Daniel, or Jonson.

22. See Appendix for a list of Psalm references for this passage. Lewalski (*Writing Women* 228) has identified Lanyer's Psalm references as being "chiefly Psalms 18, 84, 89, and 104." While Psalms 18 and 104 are surely important, I have found only one distant reference to 84 and none at all to 89.

23. The narratives mentioned occur in Exodus 3, Isaiah 6, and Acts 10. Jeremiah 1, Acts 9, and, of course, the Book of Revelation are other biblical examples of prophetic initation through visions or dreams. The connection of poetry with prophecy is an ancient one, and is reflected in modern criticism with examinations of the "poetic/prophetic" in poets as diverse as Blake, Whitman, and D. H. Lawrence. A helpful essay connecting the hebraic tradition of dreaming and prophecy to Milton is William B. Hunter, "Prophetic Dreams and Visions." The essay is reprinted in *The Descent of Urania: Studies in Milton*. For a broader treatment of Milton's understanding of his own prophetic vocation, see John Spencer Hill, *John Milton: Poet, Priest and Prophet*.

24. Guillaume de Salluste du Bartas's poem "La Muse Chrétienne" was published in France in 1574. King James VI published an English translation in Edinburgh in 1584 and Josuah Sylvester published his translation in London in 1605. For a classic account of Du Bartas's influence on English poets' self-perception, see Lily B. Campbell's "The Christian Muse."

25. Rienstra, "Aspiring to Praise."

Notes to Chapter 5/Cook

1. For historical accounts of the country-house poem, see Hibbard, "The Country-house poem of the Seventeenth Century"; Molesworth, "Property and Virtue: The Genre of the Country-House Poem in the Seventeenth Century"; Fowler, "Country-House Poems: The Politics of a Genre"; McClung, *The Country House in English Renaissance Literature*; and Dubrow, "The Country-House Poem: A Study in Generic Development." At its most basic generic level, Lanyer is yoking the celebration of the country house to the "farewell to a place" poem, the

classical *syntaktikon* (on which, see Cairns, *Generic Composition in Greek and Roman Poetry*, 1972, 38–51). Studies that touch upon Lanyer's feminist version of the country-house poem include Coiro, "Writing in Service: Sexual Politics and Class Position in the Poetry of Aemelia Lanyer and Ben Jonson"; Lewalski, "The Lady of the Country-house poem" and "Rewriting Patriarchy and Patronage: Margaret Clifford, Anne Clifford, and Aemilia Lanyer"; Mueller, "The Feminist Poetics of Aemelia Lanyer's 'Salve Deus Rex Judaeorum'"; Schnell, "'So Great a Difference is There in Degree': Aemilia Lanyer and the Aims of Feminist Criticism"; and Woods, "Aemilia Lanyer and Ben Jonson: Patronage, Authority, and Gender." The best argument for Lanyer's radical feminism is McGrath, "'Let Us Have Our Libertie Againe': Aemilia Lanyer's 17th Century Feminist Voice."

2. Most discussions of country-house poems note the pervasiveness of the *sponte sua* convention. The fullest survey of the subject is in McClung, *The Country-house poem in English Renaissance Literature*, 12–13, 16–17, and 118–22.

3. All quotations of Lanyer's poems are taken from *The Poems of Aemilia Lanyer: Salve Deus Rex Judaeorum*, ed. Susanne Woods, Oxford UP, 1995.

4. On the Protestant return to the Augustinian preoccupation with conversion through grace, as opposed to the Catholic emphasis on salvation through works, see Halewood, *The Poetry of Grace: Reformation Themes and Structures in English Seventeenth Century Poetry*.

5. Arthur Clements's analysis of "the poetry of contemplation" relies heavily on the traditional mystic itinerary of purgation, illumination, and union. For traditional definitions of the terms, see his chapter 1, "Contemplative Tradition," *Poetry and Contemplation*, 1990.

6. The sight of 13 shires has not been explained. My analysis suggests to me that seeing what is physically impossible represents a meditative vision, and the number 13 may reflect the presence of Christ and his 12 apostles, but I cannot offer an adequate explanation. For an argument that the Song of Roland uses the number 13 to associate Charlemagne and his 12 peers with Christ and his apostles, see Bulatkin, *Structural Arithmetic in the Oxford "Roland."* Hieatt, "Numerical Structures in Verse: Second Generation Studies Needed (Exemplified in Sir Gawain and the Chanson de Roland)," evaluates Bulatkin's argument.

7. Margaret Hannay, "Mary Sidney and the Admonitory Dedication," considers Queen Elizabeth's identification with David and her interest in the Psalms. Beth Fisken, "Mary Sidney's Psalmes: Education and Wisdom," discusses Mary Sidney's psalm translations, noting especially the attractiveness of mother-child imagery to a woman writer.

8. For the importance of David as the dominant model for the seventeenth century devotional lyricist and of the Psalms in the period's

conception of lyric poetry, see Lewalski, *Protestant Poetics and the Seventeenth-Century Religious Lyric* (1979), 39–53 and 300–04.

9. All quotations from *On Christian Doctrine* are taken from *The Works of John Milton, 1931–38*, vol. 15. Numbers refer to book and line.

10. For an extended account of the paradox of exaltation through humility in both classical and Christian epic poetry, see my *Milton, Spenser and the Epic Tradition*.

11. *The Complete Poetry of Ben Jonson* (1963), cited by line number.

12. Gerard Genette develops this distinction in his chapter entitled "Voice," *Narrative Discourse: An Essay in Method* (1980), 212–62.

13. The oak introduces associations of the sacred drawn from both classical and biblical traditions. The temple of Jupiter at Dodona was surrounded by a grove of oaks. Abraham planted a grove of oaks in honor of the Lord at Beer-Sheba (Genesis 21.33) and built a shrine to God surrounded by oaks at Mamre (Genesis 13.18). For a lucid discussion of Protestant reliance on emblems in meditation, see Lewalski, *Protestant Poetics and the Seventeenth-Century Religious Lyric*, chapter 6.

14. In his footnote to *Paradise Lost* 4.139 Milton's editor Fowler cites this passage from Psalm 92 and DuBartas's *Divine Weeks*, line 189, where the poet asks that the adulteress "Blush (at the least) at Palm-Trees loyalty,/Which never bears, unless her Male be by."

15. I follow Woods's retention of the spelling "steame" in line 94, though editors commonly, and sensibly, amend this to "streame." I am hesitant to perceive here a commentary on the hot blood of Anne's betrothed, the Count of Dorset, though he was a notorious philanderer.

16. On the union of souls through a kiss, see Perella's comprehensive treatment *in The Kiss Sacred and Profane*. In addition to outlining the concept's history through the Church Fathers, *fin amors*, and Renaissance Neoplatonism, Perella briefly discusses seventeenth century examples by Donne, Cartwright, Cowley, Herrick, and others.

17. Catherine Keohane observes that "'paschal' refers to both the Passover and Easter" since Lanyer has chosen to narrate "a moment in which Judaism and Christianity overlap," "'That Blindes Weakenesse Be Not Over-Bold: Aemelia Lanyer's Radical Unfolding of the Passion" (1997), 364. I would add that in such passages Lanyer locates her poem's discursive moment in that same time, collapsing the centuries in between. While such collapse does not constitute a shift in diegetic positions in the manner of "Cooke-ham," the merging of temporalities suggests how profoundly meditative techniques shape the narratological program of *Salve Deus Rex Judaeorum* as a whole.

18. As Eleanor McNees observes in an excellent account of Donne's treatment of the Eucharist, "[T]he virtualists sought to defer Real presence, relegating it to a renewal of virtue within the communicant after he or she had partaken of the eucharistic elements"; "John Donne and

the Anglican Doctrine of the Eucharist" (1987), 96. This ambiguity of a virtue both bestowed and renewed closely resembles Lanyer's studied ambiguity.

Notes to Chapter 6/Evans

1. Nearly every writer on Drummond discusses the imitative nature of his verse. Kastner's edition of *The Poetical Works of William Drummond of Hawthornden* (1913) famously traces many of his debts; Wallerstein ("The Style of Drummond of Hawthornden in Its Relation to His Translations," 1933) offers an intelligent assessment of the general ways in which Drummond found his own voice even when working with others' models; see also Morgan (*Crossing the Border: Essays on Scottish Literature*, 67–74). However, the best student of the whole subject is Jack, especially in his book *The Italian Influence on Scottish Literature* (113–44). Meanwhile, Jack's article in *MLR* ("Petrarch in English and Scottish Renaissance Literature") shows how innovative Drummond's Petrarchism was in its original Scottish context. Jonson himself could hardly have objected to the fact that Drummond imitated other writers; it was simply that, for Jonson and England, the Petrarchan fashion had already come and gone.

2. Stull's articles ("Sacred Sonnets in Three Styles", 1982; "'Why Are Not *Sonnets* Made of Thee?'", 1982) help place Drummond's religious verse, especially his sonnets, in a larger context. See also Atkinson's studies ("The Religious Voices of Drummond of Hawthornden," 1986, and "William Drummond as a Baroque Poet," 1991).

3. Although I have consulted all the cited printings of Drummond's poems, I quote from the versions printed in Robert MacDonald's edition (1976). DiPasquale ("William Drummond of Hawthornden," 1992) offers a good primary bibliography. The titles of the poems do not appear in all printings; the numbering of the poems is borrowed from MacDonald.

4. My purpose here is not to discuss the poems in broad terms (as, for instance, Severance [1981] does in her study of their structural interrelations) but examine them closely as individual works of art.

5. Drummond himself was obviously aware of the complexities of translation and of how each translation produces, in effect, a different poem. The best evidence involves two Italian sonnets, each of which he translated in three different ways: "In the same sort of rime"; "In frier sort of rime"; and "Paraphrasticalie translated." See Kastner's edition (2:231–34).

Notes to Chapter 7/Narveson

1. The number of studies of the early Stuart church have multiplied in recent years. There is a useful review in Durston and Eales, *The Culture of English Puritanism, 1560–1700*. Peter Lake gives his view of the revisionist controversy in "Calvinism and the English Church 1570–1635." Recent major studies include Julian Davies, *The Caroline Captivity of the Church: Charles I and Remoulding of Anglicanism 1625–1641* and Anthony Milton, *Catholic and Reformed*: The *Roman and Protestant Churches in English Protestant Thought 1600–1640*.

2. Within the past few years, Richard Strier has placed Donne as a proto-Laudian, part of what Peter Lake calls "avant-garde" conformity; see "Donne and the Politics of Devotion" (93–114). Mary Papazian, on the other hand, sees telling parallels between Donne and Bunyan in their soteriology; see "Literary 'Things Indifferent': the Shared Augustinianism of Donne's *Devotions* and Bunyan's *Grace Abounding*" (324–49). In the same volume, Daniel Doerksen takes a position closer to my own; he sees Donne as typical of Jacobeans comfortable with the established church's balance of prayer and preaching, and friendly with conformable Puritans; see "Saint Paul's 'Puritan': John Donne's 'Puritan' Imagination in the Sermons," (350–65).

3. While recent Renaissance criticism has read such moments as creating a radical destabilization or skepticism, Katharine Eisaman Maus points out that for Walter Ralegh and George Hakewill, consideration of a similar problem, that of access to other minds, "eventuates . . . not in epistemological despair but in an attempt to articulate a remedy, even though the remedy itself seems unavoidably inadequate." These writers, Maus argues, are not seeking a philosophically coherent position but practical answers (*Inwardness and the Theater in the English Renaissance* [Chicago: University of Chicago Press, 1995], p. 8).

4. It is worth noting that Donne had written a poem on "The Annunciation [Lady-Day] and Passion" when the two fell on the same date in 1608. Austin's funeral sermon, if written soon before Austin's death in January 1633/4, comes shortly after "Death's Duell."

5. In his Christmas meditation, Austin writes "As You have heretofore exhorted Me . . . so my turne fals now, to exhort you," and a marginal note explains: "Sir Edward Spencer sup. Heb. 10.34. . . . Consanguineorum" (36). There is a further reference in the meditation for St. Bartholomew's Day to his audience as "You, of the Consanguinity" (231).

6. It is reasonable to assume that Donne's preaching may have had a direct influence on Austin's views. Besides their mutual connection with Alleyn, they overlapped at Lincoln's Inn. Austin was called to the bar in 1611 and was appointed Steward of the Reader's dinner for Lent 1620,

indicating that he was active at Lincoln's Inn during Donne's tenure as Reader in Divinity (*Black Book* 214). Given his active piety and substantial means, it seems more than likely that he would have been involved in the building of the new Lincoln's Inn chapel, also a concern of Donne's, who preached both to raise funds and at the dedication, an event Austin would almost certainly have attended. The latter sermon was one of the few published in Donne's lifetime, as *Encoenia The Feast of Dedication* (London, 1623); see also Potter and Simpson 4:362–79. The perspective I present runs counter to the characterization of Austin by Wilfrid Prest, who calls his theology "distinctly non-Calvinist" (215).

7. Featley, *Ancilla Pietatis, or, the Handmaid to Private Devotion* (London, 1626), 142–3; Hodgkins, *Authority, Church, and Society in George Herbert: Return to the Middle Way* (Columbia: University of Missouri Press, 1993), 64–86.

8. Austin quotes from the *Faerie Queene* both in his "Essay of Tutelar Angels" (255) and in *Haec Homo.*

9. In an undated sermon preached at Lincoln's Inn, Donne similarly distinguishes between delight and joy, "for delight is in sensual things, and in beasts, as well as in men, but joy is grounded in reason, and in reason rectified" (Potter and Simpson 3:342).

10. The apparent indecorum of Austin's holy scourging or Donne's rape was perhaps less shocking or more conventional to their piety than has often been argued. James Howell writes to thank Austin for the poem Austin sent on the Passion of Christ, and declares that "all the while I was perusing it, it committed holy rapes upon my Soul . . . there were such flexanimous strong ravishing strains thro'out it" (211).

Notes to Chapter 8/McDowell

1. John Horden offers the most convincing case for Cary as a minor emblem book writer. His essay on the Brotherton manuscript ("A New Emblem Manuscript by Patrick Cary (1623/4–1657)," 1988) reproduces pictures from Cary's emblems and contextualizes Cary's emblematic practices against those of the poet's contemporaries.

2. Delany discusses the question of dating in the third section (lxix–lxxxi) of her "General Introduction" to Cary's life and work (*The Poems of Patrick Cary*, 1978). My quotations of Cary's work come from this edition.

3. I take the details of Cary's life story from Delany's introduction (the fullest account), Douglas Bush's review of Delany's edition (Lord Falklands Brother, 1978), Pamela Willett's work on Cary's Italian poems ("Patrick Cary and His Italian Poems," 1976, and "Patrick Cary: A Sequel," 1978), and the entry on Cary in the *Dictionary of National Biography* (3:1160–61).

4. Some evidence exists that Cary possibly met Milton and certainly met Crashaw at the English College in Rome, in 1638 and 1646, respectively. Crashaw especially shares Cary's attitudes about the senses, the mind, and the affections. Milton also espouses similar views about the passions (see, for instance, his depiction of the way psychological turmoil mars Satan's disguise as a cherubim in book 3.114–30 of *Paradise Lost*). On balance, however, Milton is more suspicious of the senses, especially sight (e.g. in the portrayal of Eve). Not surprisingly, Catholic writers generally view the senses as potentially productive, but firm distinctions between Catholic and Protestant views of the senses are misleading, especially in regard to Anglicans. Both Herbert and Vaughan, for example, approach the senses in the same way Cary does, which is why Cary's clearly defined educational paradigm helps explain references to the senses in their work.

5. Brathwaite was himself a poet of minor note, who wrote mainly secular works but also a few religious ones, including translations of some of the Psalms. For more on his life, see the *Dictionary of National Biography* (2:1141–42).

6. Coeffeteau's psychological theory comes from *A Table of Humane Passions With their Causes and Effects*, first published in France in 1615 and translated by Edward Grimeston into English in 1621. H. James Jensen thinks this work "in general agrees with all other theories" (*Muses' Concord* 6). See *Muses' Concord*, ch. one, for a more in depth explication of Coeffeteau's psychological theory and its relevance to the arts. Reynolds's ideas appear in *A Treatise of the Passions and Faculties of the Soul of Man* (1640, rep. 1678). Reynolds is an interesting figure because his moderate views and willingness to compromise enabled him to secure prominent religious employment before, during, and after the English Civil War. The main difference between Reynolds and Coeffeteau in their psychological maps is that Reynolds does not call the vegetative and sensitive parts "soules" the way Coeffeteau does; however, he does consider them parts of the soul. They are simply the ones firmly attached to the body.

7. The most thorough treatment of the passions and their connections with rhetoric, literature, music, and the visual arts in the seventeenth century is Jensen's *The Muses' Concord: Literature, Music, and the Visual Arts in the Baroque Age* (1976). This book is especially valuable on the ways in which artistic works were intended to affect readers, viewers, and audience members. Jensen's recent book, *Signs and Meaning in Eighteenth-Century Art: Epistemology, Rhetoric, Painting, Poesy, Music, Dramatic Performance, and G. F. Handel* (1997), expands on these issues by reconstructing the ways in which artistic signs were interpreted in eighteenth century aesthetics generally and in Handel's dramatic oratorios. Both books are of interest in reference to my discussion of the mind, the passions, and the senses.

8. Thomas Wright (1561–1624), the Catholic controversialist, voices the opinion of many in avowing the value of the passions: "Moreouer, the Scriptures exhort vs to these passions, *Irascimini, & nolite peccare,* Be angry, and sinne not. *Cum metu & tremere salutem operamini,* with feare and trembling worke your saluation: And therefore it were blaspemous [sic] to say, that absolutely all passions were ill, for so the Scriptures should exhort vs to ill" (15–16). As Thomas O. Sloan notes in his introduction to the facsimile edition of *The Passions of the Minde in Generall,* Wright's treatise is one of the most rhetorical of the works on faculty psychology, in that Wright consistently is interested in the means by which one can stir the passions of others. J. F. Senault, in *The Use of Passions* (trans. 1649), agrees with Wright: "Briefly, there is no Passion which is not serviceable to vertue, when they are governed by reason, and those who have so cryed them down [the Stoiks], make us see they never knew their use, nor worth" (qtd. in Wright xxxii).

9. Louis L. Martz's *The Poetry of Meditation* continues to be the best source on the first two forms of meditation. As is well-known, Barbara Lewalski offers Protestant forms of meditative practices in the work of Protestant poets as alternatives to the Ignatian and Salesian methods. The education of the senses in this poem seems to derive from neither expressly Catholic nor Protestant sources directly but from a more generalized understanding of faculty psychology.

10. For a sweeping account of the paradoxes, biblical precedents, and some significant outbreaks of iconoclasm in Christian history, see David Freedberg's *The Power of Images,* ch. 14 (378–428). The violence done to images throughout history stems from a lack of confidence in the ability of the general populace to regulate the effects of the visual on human thoughts, feelings, and behavior. In England, the same anxiety informed the Parliamentary act of 28 August 1643, which sanctioned the destruction of religious images at Cambridge and elsewhere.

11. In a recent essay, John R. and Lorraine M. Roberts provide a concise, helpful description of Southwell's life and aesthetic premises. In comparison to Southwell's desire for martyrdom as the highest form of imitation of Christ, Cary's religious dedication seems almost half-hearted. But both poets shared assumptions about the homeopathic potential of poetic description and both attempt to move the passions of readers through emphatic presentations of the Crucifixion, meant to place the reader imaginatively at the scene.

Notes to Chapter 9/Demers

1. Graham Parry includes plates of the three other portraits completed between 1633 and 1638: "Charles I Riding through the Triumphal Arch," "Le Roi à la chasse," and "Charles I in Armor on Horseback." See "Van Dyck and the Caroline Court Poets" (248–50).

2. Margaret Spufford draws a critical distinction between ages seven and eight: "children who had the opportunity to go to school until they were seven were likely to be able to read. Those who remained at school until eight were likely to be able to write." See "first steps in literacy" (412).

3. Jonathan Keates reviews a recent performance very favourably on account of the choreographer's deliberate use of the medium "to create the closest possible engagement between his spectators and the aural pictures devised by Handel and Milton"; see "The soul's embrace: George Frederic Handel and John Milton *L'Allegro, Il Penseroso, Ed Il Moderato*" (22).

4. In her prize-winning *Visionary Women; Ecstatic Prophecy in Seventeenth-Century England*, Phyllis Mack examines women's "wide-ranging and utopian . . . prophecy during the Civil War period" (412). Patricia Crawford's *Women and Religion in England 1500–1720* looks at major religious movements of the early modern period to trace "the significance of the male/female distinction in religious belief" (2). A special issue of *Bunyan Studies* (Number 7, 1997), edited by Vera J. Camden, is devoted to "Dissenting Women in John Bunyan's World and Work." While each study is instructive and suggestive, none attends specifically or exclusively to the subjects of female melancholy and meditative withdrawal. In *The Gendering of Melancholia: Feminism, Psychoanalysis, and the Symbolics of Loss in Renaissance Literature*, Juliana Schiesari weaves contemporary theory and the poetry of the Italian Renaissance as a way of exploring the differences between male and female melancholia; Schiesari does not set up a simple polarity, but argues the "existence of male melancholia as precluding the possibility of female melancholics" (15). She shows how the discourse of melancholia "legitimates that neurosis as culturally acceptable for particular men, . . . while the viability of such appropriation seems systematically to elude women" (15).

5. Klibansky *et al.* devote a whole chapter, with material stretching from the seventeenth to the nineteenth centuries, to the idea of "Melancholy as Heightened Self-Awareness" (228–40).

6. Burton is citing Erasmus, *Epist. ad Dorphium.*

7. All references to "Eliza," Collins and Major will be based on the single seventeenth century editions of their work listed in Works Cited; since these editions are unlineated, parenthetical citations will refer to page numbers.

8. Although the text was in Latin with English titles, the 1560 edition of *Hore Beatissime Virginis ad legtimum Sarisburiensis Ecclesie ritum* includes a prayer "for womne in travelynge of childe"; three prayers about childbirth were added to William Seres's *A primer or Book of private prayers* (1553), the official Elizabethan primer. The 16th edition of Samuel Hieron's *A helpe unto devotion* (1635) "included a prayer to be

said by a woman in labour and a prayer of thanksgiving for a safe delivery," while John Norden's *A pensive man's practice* (1627) had "five prayers covering pregnancy, childbirth, thanksgiving, and midwives." See Judith Hurtig, "Death in Childbirth" (614).

9. With her disquisition on the Trinity, "Three in One conjoyn'd . . . yet each Person differing" ("To My Sister, S. S." 27), and on the bread and wine of the Eucharist as "the pleadges of thy grace" ("On going to the Sacrament" 58), there is little compelling evidence of her strong "Calvinist sentiments."

10. The three citations come from Thomas More's *Dialoge of Comforte Against Tribulation* (1534), Thomas Raynalde's translation of Roesslin's *Byrth of Mankynde otherwyse called the Womans Boke* (1545), and Helkiah Crooke's *A Description of the Body of Man, Microcosmographia* (1615).

11. Joseph Caryl, who supplies the text's Imprimatur, was a nonconformist leader, minister of St. Magnus Church, and contributor to Cromwell's London "commission of 'triers' to approve public ministers"; see *DNB*, 3. 1162–63 and Skerpan, *The Rhetoric of Politics* (160).

Notes to Chapter 10/Rex

1. This title is inspired by the PBS series *Eyes on the Prize: The Civil Rights Struggle in America*.

2. *Eliza's Babes: or the Virgins-Offering* (Laurence Blaiklock: London, 1652) Title page.

3. A quick review of the items published by Laurence Blaiklock establishes an interesting context for *Eliza's Babes*. The titles in the Short Title Catalogue fall into two time periods: early 1640s and 1648–1653. Between 1642 and 1644, Blaiklock published ten Parliamentary tracts dealing mainly with the rights of Englishmen to disobey the king. These tracts include works against paying custom duties to the king, the right of Parliament to pass laws without the king's consent, and the right of Parliament to control both shipping and the navy. He also published several newspapers in the 1640s, including the *Perfect Journal of Some Passages in Parliament* and the Scotch Mercury. Blaiklock apparently quit publishing sometime after 1653 when he published W. Young's *A Vade Mecum*, making *Eliza's Babes* one of his last publications.

In addition to these Parliamentary tracts, Blaiklock also published several collections of poetry, including most notably two volumes of poetry which he termed the collected poems of Francis Beaumont. The others, in addition to *Eliza's Babes*, included William Fenwick's *True Ancient Forms of Worship*, and H. Mill's *Poems*. But, according to William Ringler, Blaiklock was far from an honest and reliable publisher. Specifically, he manipulated both the appearance and amount of poetry attributed to Beaumont in both editions (1640 & 1653). Beyond this information about her publisher, little is known about the personal circumstances of the author of *Eliza's Babes.*

4. Margaret J. M. Ezell, *The Patriarch's Wife: Literary Evidence and the History of the Family* (Chapel Hill: U of North Carolina P, 1987) 84–85. Also, Wall 283–86.

5. There are two "Of Submission" poems in *Eliza's Babes.* The first, quoted here, "Of Submission" (I) is on page 4. "Of Submission" (II) is on page 14.

Notes to Chapter 11/Hurley

1. I wish to thank Lisa Navarro, Skidmore College 1996, for her enthusiastic essay on An Collins, which first brought to my attention the possibilities for critical analysis of Collins's verse.

2. Single poems by Collins once appeared in anthologies: see S. Austin Allibone, *Critical Dictionary of English Literature* (1898); Sir Egerton Brydges, *Restituta* (1815); A. F. Griffith, ed., *Bibliotheca Anglo-Poetica* (1815); and Frederick Rowton, *The Female Poets of Great Britain* (1853). Current anthologies including Collins are those edited by Elizabeth Graham et al., *Her Own Life: Autobiographical Writings by Seventeenth-Century Englishwomen*; Germaine Greer et al., *Kissing the Rod: An Anthology of Seventeenth-Century Women's Verse*; and Ann Stanford, *The Women Poets in English.* An abridged facsimile of the *Divine Songs and Meditacions., ed.* Stanley N. Stewart (Augustan Society Reprint, 1961) is still in print and a xeroxed copy of the original is available through University Microfilms. An entry on Collins, by Eugene Cunnar, appears in the *Dictionary of Literary Biography, vol. 131, Seventeenth-Century Non-Dramatic Poets*, third series. Most recently, Sidney Gottlieb has edited a complete edition of the poems, *An Collins, Divine Songs and Meditacions* (1996). All citations here are from that edition.

3. Barbara Kiefer Lewalski, *Protestant Poetics and the Seventeenth-Century Religious Lyric*, 234.

4. Thomas Healy, *New Latitudes. Theory and English Renaissance Literature*, 49–52.

5. Notably, those who have tried to infer Collins's theology from one or two phrases extracted from the verse have dramatically contradicted each other, labeling her as "not in sympathy with the left-wing of the Puritan movement" (Stewart iv), and "if not a Catholic, she was devoutly anti-Calvinist" (Greer et al. 148). After reading her complete work, I agree with Cunnar's carefully generalized conclusion that Collins "develops a Protestant theology influenced by Calvinism" (49). We can say, for example, that she articulates a theology that is Protestant in its emphasis on scripture and on the application of the Word of God to the

self; she is Calvinist in passages which carry echoes of the doctrines of the elect and of total depravity (see passages cited from "The Discourse"; also lines like "Touching my selfe and others, I conceive,/That all men are by nature dead in sin" (Gottlieb 16); and in her stress on justification by faith (passages cited from "The Discourse"). Nevertheless, she backs away from too rigid an application of the harsher Calvinist doctrines by giving her greatest emphasis to grace and to the process of faith.

6. See, among others, Louis Martz, *The Poetry of Meditation* for the first; Arnold Stein, *George Herbert's Lyrics* and Stanley Fish, *Self-Consuming Artifacts* for the second. A strongly persuasive dissenting voice has been Barbara Kiefer Lewalski's. She argues, in her *Protestant Poetics and the Seventeenth-Century Religious Lyric*, that "the primary poetic influences upon the major devotional poets of the century — Donne, Herbert, Vaughan, Traherne, Taylor — are contemporary, English and Protestant" and supports her argument through extensive discussion of the English backgrounds in "biblical genre theory, biblical topics, Protestant ways with emblem, metaphor, typology and Protestant theory regarding the uses of art in religious subjects" (283).

7. The poets listed are those for whom there exist Norton critical editions, for example, specifically the edition of Donne's poems edited by A. L. Clements and the edition of *George Herbert and the Seventeenth-Century Religious Poets* (i.e., Crashaw, Marvell, Vaughan and Traherne) edited by Mario Di Cesare.

8. Lewalski, for example, observes "At first glance, the Sidney-Pembroke psalms seem not to be part of the development I am tracing because they are true paraphrases, close to their originals and without a clearly-delineated persona" (241). And Lily B. Campbell, whose pioneering study, *Divine Poetry and Drama in Sixteenth-Century England* laid the groundwork for much of Lewalski's restoration of Protestant poetics by retrieving the vast number of sixteenth century verse translations and poetic versions of the poetic parts of the Bible, apologizes in her "Preface" for writing "the secondary story" of the art of making the Bible part of English literature.

9. For a complete discussion of Mary Sidney's manuscripts see Gary F. Waller, *Mary Sidney, Countess of Pembroke: A Critical Study of Her Writings and Literary Milieu* (Salzburg, 1979). Recent work by the scholar Margaret Hannay has been essential in establishing Mary Sidney's literary reputation.

Notes to Chapter 12/Long

I gratefully acknowledge Karen Cunningham for her invaluable suggestions on this essay.

1. I follow Ann Rosalind Jones's definition of the term "negotiation," as the "range of interpretive positions through which subordinated groups respond to the assumptions encoded into dominant cultural forms and systems of representation" (2). That these "forms and systems" have some variation, for example based on differences in class, nationality, or religious belief, allows for the appropriation of those elements which women wish to "emphasize . . . [in] pursuing their own interests" (3).

2. The 1998 Shakespeare Association seminar "Early Modern Women Writers and Genre," chaired by Elaine Beilin, produced evidence that women participated in a wide range of genres in the period. For a useful bibliography, see *English Literary Renaissance* 23.3 (Fall 1993).

3. See also Jacqueline Pearson, "Women reading, reading women" (93–4). For a broader critique of this practice, see Debora K. Shuger, *Habits of Thought* (5–6).

4. In *Obstetrics and Gynaecology in Tudor and Stuart England*, a fascinating study of early modern obstetrical and gynecological literature, Audrey Eccles notes, for example, that Francoise Mauriceau thought the remedy of taking shredded crimson silk in egg yolk to avoid miscarriage after a fall "superstitious and ridiculous, but 'one may give it to those that desire it to content them, because these Remedies, though useless, can yet do no hurt'" (73).

5. See John Roberts's selective but extensive bibliography of modern critical studies of the seventeenth century English religious lyric, 1952–1990, in *New Perspectives on the Seventeenth-Century English Religious Lyric* edited by John Roberts (1994). See also *Religion, Literature, and Politics in Post-Reformation England*, Donna Hamilton, et al., Editors (1986); *"Glow-Worm Light": Writings of 17th Century English Recusant Women from Original Manuscripts*, Dorothy Latz, Editor (1989); *Religion and Culture in Renaissance England*, Claire McEachern and Debora Shuger, Editors (1997); and *Representing Women in Renaissance England*, Claude J. Summers and Ted-Larry Pebworth, Editors (1997).

6. For specific sources, see Wilcox, "Curious Frame" (22–3).

7. Fisken suggests Mary Sidney's psalms were "grounded in the Protestant tradition" and "adhered . . . faithfully" to scriptural meaning, "because to do otherwise would be to set [her] own work above that of God" ("Mary Sidney's Psalmes: Education and Wisdom," 168).

8. For a description of these "methods," see Martz (2). On women's access to religious treatises, see Betty S. Travitsky, "The Possibilities of Prose." For evidence of women's familiarity with contemporary religious lyric poetry, see Wilcox, "Entering *The Temple*: women, reading, and devotion in seventeenth-century England."

9. Anthony Low makes a distinction between "two basic kinds of metrical psalms . . . in the period": those in "Common Meter," which fit "the Reformers' conviction that music should not interfere with

scriptural meaning," and "the literary or court psalm," a more sophisticated form employed, for example, by the Sidneys (*Love's Architecture: Devotional Modes in Seventeenth-Century English Poetry*, 28–29). Low argues, "the Sidneys probably chose to write their psalter in a variety of stanza forms not for poetic reasons only, . . . but in order to fit them to the new styles of music" (29).

10. See Hannay, "'Wisdome the Wordes': Psalm Translation and Elizabethan Women's Spirituality" (65).

11. Crawford argues it is not surprising that "assumptions about the two sexes remained virtually unchallenged" even during the period 1640–1660 since religious "reform . . . intensified emphasis upon the Bible rather than diminished it" (9). But Crawford finds evidence that "women could both accept beliefs about their inferiority and transcend them" (1).

12. See also Dennis Kay, *Melodious Tears: The English Funeral Elegy from Spenser to Milton*; Peter Sacks, *The English Elegy: Studies in the Genre from Spenser to Yeats*; Eric Smith, *By Mourning Tongues: Studies in English Elegy*.

13. Similar expressions are found in men's diaries. See Beier, "The Good Death in Seventeenth-Century England."

14. For a discussion of gender differences in mourning and melancholia, see Juliana Schiesari, *The Gendering of Melancholia*; and Sharon T. Strocchia, "Funerals and the Politics of Gender in Early Renaissance Florence."

15. I am indebted to Marcy North for bringing this absence in *Monument* to my attention. I use the compound noun to indicate that the experience of childloss in the period was nearly as ubiquitous as childbirth.

16. A review of the MLA Bibliography for the period 1981 to May 1998 reveals fewer than ten publications focusing solely on early-modern, women-authored elegy, and the majority of these are concerned with Anne Bradstreet.

17. An analogy may be made to early scholarship on women's autobiography which, when read through a canonical lens, was often deemed a failure of the genre. Women's elegy, like women's autobiography, invites us to recognize and celebrate the distinctiveness of women's writing.

18. See Valerie Fildes, "Maternal feelings re-assessed: child abandonment and neglect in London and Westminster, 1550–1800"; and Allyson May, "'She at first denied it': Infanticide Trials at the Old Bailey."

19. For example, Betty Travitsky argues that Elizabeth Egerton's grief over the loss of her daughter Katherine "provide[s] yet another set of refutations to one of Lawrence Stone's most controversial contentions — the idea that 'low affect', or a low level of emotional attachment,

characterized parent-child relationships in early modern England" ("'His Wife's Prayers and Meditations': MS Egerton 607," 251). The vehement resistance to Stone's argument suggests the intensity with which our culture holds the maternal bond inviolate, and any suggestion that maternal feeling is (partially) learned and not instinctive, that it is present to varying degrees in individual women, and that the early modern period, generally speaking, may have felt less affection toward children than we supposedly do now make our culture uncomfortable. To cite a telling example from my own classroom, in Svava Jakobsdottir's "A Story for Children," the mother's exaggerated level of sacrifice — allowing her children to remove her brain among other physical brutalities — is initially read by the majority of my students as familiar and appropriate maternal behavior.

20. A woman's relationship with her child was mediated not only by her relationship to God but by her relationship with her husband as well: his needs took precedence over a child's needs; Galenic medical theories credited him with the greater part in reproduction; and the law sided with him — or required he take responsibility for a child — in disputes over paternity.

21. This relationship with God is in contrast to, for example, Donne's *Holy Sonnets*, which, Young suggests, "emphasize that God must take [Donne's] part and 'fight for' or 'defend' the sinner, who is helpless without such assistance" (28). Both Carey and Donne require God's intervention, but Carey demands it, sure she is deserving of it, while Donne begs for it, unsure whether he is worth saving.

22. In her *Meditations*, Carey constructs a prose "Dialogue Betwixt the Soul and the Body," which further suggests her concern over the relationship 'betwixt' the two states of being (13).

23. Boulger notes of Calvin's view that "God is good but He is also arbitrary . . . usually [drove] a pious mind to the belief that God is arbitrarily good" (201).

24. In his essay, "Donne's Holy Sonnets and the Theology of Grace," Young cites John Stachniewski's representation of Calvinism as "a theology which brutalized self-esteem" (30), and it is the case that early modern reformists usually don't expect God to reward good works but believe He is "a jealous and a punitive creator" (Tyacke, *Anti-Calvinists: The Rise of English Arminianism*, 1).

25. Wilcox notes a similar moment in Lady Jane Cheyne's elegy for her sister, the Countess of Bridgewater, when her "questioning of the rightness of God's actions is expressed in the phrase 'unto sinfull eye', suggesting that the speaker is well aware that her perspective on the event is so doubting as to be 'sinfull'" ("Soule" 16). This may be construed as a Calvinistic "sin-consciousness," as a rhetorical device, typically gendered feminine, or indicative of the Reformation's

emphasis on God and Christ as masculine figures and the relatively femi-
nized supplicant of either sex.

26. Germaine Greer notes, "Verbal correspondences show that Carey
used the Geneva Bible" (161). All citations here are from facsimile edi-
tions of the Geneva Old and New Testaments unless otherwise noted.

27. As Boulger's *The Calvinist Temper in English Poetry* shows, these
parallel to some degree Calvin's "religious system and theology" (58).

28. Carey provides a foil for scholars who argue, as Collinson does in
his analyses of letters between noblewomen and English Protestant di-
vines, that gentlewomen "seem to have found perplexing" new doctrines
like election (275).

29. Boulger notes this doctrine "remained vague and therefore sub-
ject to vast difference of interpretation within Protestantism and to ridi-
cule from without" (20). He also notes it "may sometimes be the source
or undercurrent of confidence in a writer, but where it appears directly
as defining principle, we are moving from Calvinist-Puritanism to the
'left' spiritual tradition" (20). How far "left" we may situate Carey will
require further study of her whole diary.

30. Crawford notes that "Protestant reformers were deeply troubled
by Catholic veneration of the Virgin, particularly given the widespread
popular belief in her power over Christ" (36), but they "had a fine line to
tread, for they sought to give Mary due honour without encouraging
exalted views of her power" (37). This moment in the poem also recalls
Young's caution against the recent tendency among scholars to label all
early modern poems "Protestant," to the exclusion of other influences,
including Catholicism and the finer distinctions to be made within Prot-
estantism.

Notes to Chapter 13/Spurr

1. Unsigned preface, "To The Reader," to *A Serious and Pathetical
Contemplation* (1699), containing Traherne's *Thanksgivings*, in *Centu-
ries, Poems, and Thanksgivings*, ed. H. M. Margoliouth, 2 vols. (Oxford:
Clarendon Press, 1958), I: xxxii. All references to Traherne's prose and
poetry are to this edition, with volume and page numbers given paren-
thetically within the text.

2. In arguing that Traherne's "most striking departure from the Prot-
estant consensus is his ecstatic celebration of infant innocence" (*Prot-
estant Poetics and the Seventeenth-Century Religious Lyric*, 352), Lewalski
emphasizes what the poet avoids in Protestantism (especially, the
emphasis on Original Sin), but overlooks what he affirms in Catholic
teaching (especially, the doctrine of the Incarnation). In referring to
Traherne's focus on himself and his body, she argues that this fits the

"location of and exploration of the paradigm of salvation . . . a primary characteristic of Protestant poetics" (357). But it also — and more obviously — fits the theology of the Incarnation, more strongly stressed in the Catholic tradition.

3. Review of David Lyle Jeffrey, *People of the Book* (1996), blurb.

4. "He never failed any one day either publickly or in his private Closet, to make use of her publick Offices," Preface, *A Serious and Pathetical Contemplation*, "Introduction," *Centuries, Poems, and Thanksgivings*, I: xxxii.

5. "Preface," *For Lancelot Andrewes* (1928), p. 7.

6. "Of Reformation" (May, 1641), *The Prose of John Milton*, 42.

7. *The Christian Year* (1827), 218. This poem comes from Keble's collection, *Lyra Innocentium*.

8. Herbert's emblem poem, "The Altar," which introduces his sequence in *The Church*, is representative at once of a classical stone altar and the speaker's broken and contrite heart. It is not the Catholic altar of the eucharistic sacrifice. Until the Anglo-Catholic movement of the nineteenth century, altars in Anglican churches were usually wooden in order to stress the difference between a table of communion — a board both in substance and as the setting for a supper — and the "pagan" altar of sacrifice.

9. Milton, "Of Reformation" (May, 1641), *The Prose of John Milton*, 42.

10. In Cowley, *Selected Poetry and Prose*, ed. J. Taaffe, 78. See Barker in *Kissing the Rod*, eds. Greer et al., 363. I am grateful to my colleague, Dr. Bruce Gardiner, for these references.

11. *The Poems*, 70.

Notes to Chapter 14/Stanwood

1. The quotation from Pope is reported in John Gee's introduction to his edition of Beaumont's *Original Poems in English and Latin* (Cambridge, 1749), xxii. See Mark Notzon, "A New Source for Pope's *Dunciad*, Book IV, 21–24," *Notes and Queries* 26 (1979): 543, and also James A. Means, "Keats's 'Ode on Melancholy' and Beaumont's *Psyche* (1648)," *Notes and Queries* 32 (1985): 341.

2. See my "St. Teresa and Joseph Beaumont's *Psyche: or Loves Mysterie*," *Journal of English and Germanic Philology* 62 (1963): 533–50, rpt. in Stanwood, *The Sempiternal Season: Studies in Seventeenth-Century Devotional Writing* (New York: Peter Lang, 1992), in which see esp. 139–42. This book of collected essays includes also "A Portrait of Stuart Orthodoxy," a biographical summary and study of Beaumont, 125–36, which originally appeared in the *Church Quarterly Review* 165 (1964): 27–39.

Beaumont's verse has attracted sporadic attention, mostly on his epic poem. The pioneering study is that by Austin Warren in *Richard Crashaw: A Study in Baroque Sensibility* (Baton Rouge: Louisiana State University Press, 1939), esp. 41–46, 111–32, the inspiration of my doctoral dissertation (University of Michigan, 1961), a critical edition of "The Dereliction" canto of *Psyche*. Philip I. Herzbrun wrote on "*Psyche* and Seventeenth Century Poetic Traditions" (Ph.D. diss., The Johns Hopkins University, 1956); Natalie Maynor, "Joseph Beaumont's *Psyche* in the Seventeenth-Century Context" (Ph.D. diss., University of Tennessee, 1978); and Claire Warwick devotes a long and fascinating chapter to Beaumont in her "'Love is Eloquence': Richard Crashaw and the Development of a Discourse of Divine Love" (Ph.D. diss., University of Cambridge, 1994). A. O. Reesink writes on Beaumont's Latin oration of 1638 in *LIAS* 24/2 (1997): 197–211, first noticed by Austin Warren (118) and edited with a translation in my dissertation. The oration is notable for its reference to St. Teresa (see Warren 44).

3. On Perne, see the article in the *Dictionary of National Biography*, and also H. C. Porter, *Reformation and Reaction in Tudor Cambridge* (Cambridge: Cambridge University Press, 1958), 56–57 and *passim*. Much important information about Andrew Perne (1519?–1589) is unpublished, being contained in the British Library Harleian MS 7045, in the Cambridge University Library Baker MSS 27 and 34, and in the Peterhouse Treasury, which possesses the catalogue of books given to the Library by Perne. But see T. A. Walker's still useful but very sketchy history, *Peterhouse* (Cambridge: W. Heffer, 1935), esp. chapters 4 and 5. The best general survey of Peterhouse in Tudor and Stuart times remains that by the late Professor Sir Herbert Butterfield in volume 1 of the *Victoria History of the County of Cambridge and the Isle of Ely*, ed. L. F. Salzman (London, 1938). Perne's most important seventeenth-century successors to the mastership of Peterhouse included Leonard Mawe (1617–26); Matthew Wren (1626–34); John Cosin (1634–44, 1660); Joseph Beaumont (1663–99) — all royalists and high churchmen.

4. See "Portrait of Stuart Orthodoxy," and also the introduction to my edition of Cosin's *A Collection of Private Devotions* (Oxford: Clarendon Press, 1967). A great liturgist whose influence on the Book of Common Prayer is the most substantial after Cranmer himself, Cosin was chaplain during the Interregnum to the exiled Royalist court in Paris. At the Restoration, he became bishop of Durham.

While not usually remembered as a poet, Cosin's achievement as a translator and writer of hymns and devotional verse deserves to be better known. J. R. Watson gives an excellent description of Cosin's hymns, especially his translation of the "Veni Creator," in *The English Hymn: A Critical and Historical Study* (Oxford: Clarendon Press, 1997), 82–86.

5. In addition to works already cited about Beaumont's life, one should

see also the excellent summary by Lorraine M. Roberts in the *Dictionary of Literary Biography*, vol. 126: *Seventeenth-Century British Nondramatic Writers*, second series, ed. M. Thomas Hester (Detroit: Gale Research, 1991), 3–9.

6. Robinson concludes her estimation of Beaumont with these characteristic comments, full both of praise and deprecation: "There are not many who will care for pleasure's sake to read all the poems of Beaumont. Yet in our hurried times, these verses, wrought through long hours of leisure by a workman who loved his task, hold the charm of a beautiful epoch and an irrecoverable one. Furthermore, there is value in coming to know one whom even a small meed of fame has kept for us past the years, especially if he be, as Beaumont is, a faithful reflection of the influences and environment which made men like Herbert and Vaughan and Traherne, and the greatest, Milton" (xliii).

7. Nicholas Maw (b. 1935) composed *Three Hymns for SATB and organ* (London: Faber Music, 1990) that includes two other contemporary works. Beaumont's "Morning Hymn" is followed by a "Pastoral Hymn" from John Hall's *Second Booke of Divine Poems* (Cambridge, 1647), and finally by "Evening Hymn," from Sir Thomas Browne's *Religio Medici*, II.12 (1642, 1643). Maw's *Three Hymns* was commissioned by the Lichfield Festival for the Choir of Lichfield Cathedral, and the work was first performed in 1989.

8. Beaumont writes elaborately of the Nativity in this canto, deriving much of his language, as his marginal notes clearly indicate, from the Canticles (stanzas 158 ff.).

9. Beaumont, for the most part, is arranging his poems in chronological order, and his dating follows the old style calendar. Yet Robinson assumes that this poem on "Natalitium," which Beaumont dates "Martij 12, 1643," belongs to 1643, not 1644. Yet the next dated poem that soon follows (after only 15 poems) is called "Novemb. 5, 1644," obviously commemorating the Gunpowder Plot. Then the next poem clearly dated is "Jan. 1, 1643," which I would take to mean "1644" new style. There is some disruption or confusion of the sequence here, or displacement of the poems in the manuscript; for Beaumont has placed "Epiphanie Oblation" before "Christmasse Day," after which appears a series of poems on Holy Week followed by "Newyear Day" and its companion "Jan. 1, 1643." The earlier date of 1643 is important to Robinson, for she wishes to date Beaumont's departure from Peterhouse, Cambridge well before the official ejection order of June 11, 1644 (xxi–xxii). Establishing the date of Beaumont's departure from Peterhouse by reference to the *Minor Poems* is, however, risky; surely he may have left long before the ejection order, and he would have been able to start writing his poetry — both "minor" and epic — at any time before or after his removal to his home in Hadleigh. The best and most recent discussion of these issues

of residence, and also of Beaumont's friendship with Crashaw, is by Hilton Kelliher, "Crashaw at Cambridge" in *New Perspectives on the Life and Art of Richard Crashaw*, ed. John R. Roberts (Columbia: University of Missouri Press, 1990), 180–214; see also, in the same volume, Elsie Elizabeth Duncan-Jones, "Who was the Recipient of Crashaw's Leyden Letter?" (174–79).

10. A. B. Chambers calls attention to the last 13 poems of the book, noting that Beaumont's baptism poems could not have been given in sequential order, yet they are linked through their titles and general subject matter. There are seven of these baptismal poems, too, and Chambers argues that this "perfect" number necessarily completes the whole work (21–32), a judgment that seems to me difficult to prove.

11. I quote from Herbert's dying message to Nicholas Ferrar about the manuscript of *The Temple*, reprinted in *The Works of George Herbert*, ed. F. E. Hutchinson (Oxford: Clarendon Press, 1941), xxxvii.

Notes to Chapter 15/Parrish

1. The title of this essay attempts to identify two important qualities of Beaumont's poetry while also alluding to terms that Beaumont himself used. In "The two Fires" he speaks exuberantly of the "Flames of eternall Love" and the "blisse/Of ravishing Imbraces" (15–16) that consume a life devoted to God. In a very different mood, he argues in a simple and unadorned fashion in "House & Home" for the value of looking inward to find genuine freedom: "turne thine eye/Inward, & observe thy Breast;/There alone dwells solid Rest," for "In a cleanly sober Mind/ Heavn it selfe full Room doth find" (24–26, 33–34).

2. Beaumont's poetry was written largely between 1643–44 and 1652, when, following his ejection from his Fellowship at Peterhouse, Cambridge, because of his royalist and Laudian views, he retired (initially) to Hadleigh, his birthplace. While in this forced "retirement," Beaumont remained busy, though with activities that had not occupied him when he was Fellow, scholar, and tutor at Peterhouse. In 1650 he married Elizabeth Brownrigg, stepdaughter of Matthew Wren, Bishop of Ely and Master of Peterhouse from 1625/26 to 1634, with whom he had four children. During this period he also wrote *Psyche*, two manuscript volumes of shorter poems, and a large quantity of biblical commentary.

Psyche was first published in London in 1648; although Beaumont apparently had some hesitancy about having it appear in print, at least in part because of its anti-Puritan perspective, he was encouraged to do so by friends (Stanwood, "Portrait," 32–33). Of the two manuscripts of shorter poems, one is the basis for Eloise Robinson's edition of *The Minor Poems of Dr. Joseph Beaumont, D. D.* (1914). The second has been lost though a few poems from it have been printed. In 1749, John Gee,

Master of Peterhouse, edited a volume of 41 poems in English and 17 in Latin. Robinson says that Gee's edition includes 30 poems from the surviving manuscript she consulted, but she mistakenly includes "David's Elegie upon Jonathan," which is not, in fact, in Gee. She also says that Gee includes 11 poems from the now lost manuscript, but there are 12 English poems in Gee (and, following Gee, in Grosart) that are not in Robinson (xv). In 1880, A. B. Grosart edited *The Complete Poems of Dr. Joseph Beaumont* as part of the Chertsey Worthies' Library, though, in fact, the edition was far from complete. Grosart printed *Psyche* and the English and Latin poems that appeared in Gee's 1749 edition. Of the more than 200 poems identifiable as Beaumont's, most were not printed until 1914, when Robinson, working with the autograph manuscript then owned by Professor George Herbert Palmer of Harvard University, edited *The Minor Poems*.

Beaumont's life and *Psyche* have received occasional attention, much of it in connection with other figures (especially Crashaw) or other writings (see, for example, the items by Duncan-Jones, Healy, Maynor, Means, Notzon, Pritchard, and, especially, Stanwood, in Works Cited). Comments on his poetry apart from *Psyche* are largely confined to passing remarks made in the context of fuller considerations of *Psyche* (e.g., Stanwood) or of writers such as Crashaw (e.g., Healy).

3. Stanwood turns the assumptions about Beaumont's casual approach to poetry into a positive, observing that the years at Peterhouse

> were his most attractive, and they bore their best fruit in the short period of intensive poetic activity after his ejection. His most natural communication was the sermon, the lecture, the tract; but his poetry, the most memorable of all his work, was perhaps a happy accident: in his poetry, he was at leisure, less self-consciously disputative, and most informal ("Portrait" 37).

4. The most valuable overview of Beaumont's life is found in P. G. Stanwood's "A Portrait of Stuart Orthodoxy." There are also biographical memoirs in Gee and Grosart and a biographical sketch in Robinson's introduction to her edition of *The Minor Poems*.

5. Some have dated Beaumont's ejection from his Fellowship in 1644, others in 1643. The former claim derives from an April 1644 written order executed by the Earl of Manchester responding to a January 1644 ordinance from Parliament pertaining to the reforming and regulating of the universities. Beaumont, Crashaw and others were formally ejected for not being in residence, indicating that they had left the university some time before, likely before William Dowsing's destructive purge of December 1643. Hence they may well have experienced the results of ejection in 1643. See, e.g., Gee *Memoirs* 2; Robinson, xxi–xxiii; Stanwood, "Portrait," 32; and Parrish 25–30. We cannot identify Beaumont's exact

movement during this turbulent time (the uncertainty of location is even more true with respect to Crashaw), but by 1644 he is at his family home in Hadleigh.

6. By no means would this view have been accepted by most residents of Peterhouse, but that such an association was made by Puritan forces is evident in the record of several Puritan writers who commented on "Popery" at Cambridge and of those who destroyed offensive elements of the University during its sacking in the 1640s. In an anonymous manuscript dated from early 1641 ("Innovations in Religion & Abuses in Government in [the] University of Cambridge," BM MS. Harley 7019, fol. 73) , the author or authors single out Peterhouse as a College particularly guilty of exhibiting the luxurious trappings and dangerous doctrines of the "Papists." The "schollers" of the College, we are told,

> are exceedingly Imployed to learne pricksong to the great losse of theire time & prejudice of theire studdyes, and the preferments of the Colledge are cast vpon them according to theire skill & proficiency therein. After the second yeare, the third part of Aquinas *Summes* is appointed to be read by them, that betimes they may suck in the doctrine of the Papists. It is credibly reported that there are divers private oratories & Altars in the Colledge with Crucifixes & several other popish pictures. (Quoted in Pritchard 578)

Pritchard further notes that among the offenders, Beaumont and Crashaw are accused by name (see also Stanwood, "Portrait," 29–30).

7. Because my interests in this essay are focuscd on the shorter poems, I do not intend to discuss *Psyche*. Stanwood offers the most succinct and insightful commentary on that long poem, saying that it

> is a more useful guide to Beaumont's thought by far than his formal Scriptural exegesis [such as his commentaries on Ecclesiastes and the Pentateuch]; for the many enthusiasms of his life find expression in his capacious epic: probably there is no poem in English longer than this one, nor one more subject to digressions of all sorts. . . . Everything finds its place in *Psyche*, and the very range of subjects, so randomly chosen, gives bizarre charm and variety to Beaumont's poem ("Portrait" 33).

8. Largely for convenience, I am focusing my remarks on the texts in Robinson's edition. The additional 12 lyric poems in English printed by Gee and Grosart (see n. 2) do not challenge the observations I make in what follows. These poems, much like those in Robinson, reveal Beaumont writing on love, responding to scriptural texts and incidents, and meditating on attributes and qualities he judges characteristic of humankind.

9. For titles and texts of the poems I am citing Robinson's edition. I have silently modernized such words as "y^e" (the), "y^t" (that), "wth" (with), and "w^{ch}" (which), both in the poetry and in other seventeenth century documents. Although Robinson does not number lines of poetry, I have for convenience inserted line numbers of quoted poems within parentheses following each passage.

10. Many other poems, of course, are related to biblical events or scriptural commentary. The poems I identify here, however, develop more specifically from and respond to words, phrases and images in passages that are identified (and are typically printed as a kind of subtitle). These poems should, of course, be read in other important contexts as well. The poem on St. Paul's conversion is explicitly dependent for its development on the opening verses of Acts 9, but is also one of a number of lives of saints to which Beaumont pays tribute; "Jesus inter Ubera Maria" and "Rise up, my Love, my Fairest One" derive from and include paraphrases of the Canticles but are, more importantly, among those poems in which Beaumont celebrates the sensuous love of God.

11. As mentioned in n. 2 above, in his 1749 selected edition, Gee included 29 poems from the surviving manuscript of Beaumont's verse (those that form the basis of Robinson's edition) and 12 from the manuscript now lost. Gee says that the latter was entitled *Cathemerina* and was intended to be a collection of poetical exercises written between May 17 and September 3, 1652, each poem a meditative preparation for the day. The 28 poems in Robinson's edition would then be conceptually part of the stratagem that encompassed 4–5 months of Beaumont's life in 1652.

12. These 14 poems are variously titled, including several headings in Greek. I am for convenience identifying the poems by subject and year, inserting the page number from Robinson's edition in brackets. I have elsewhere also identified page numbers in brackets if more than one poem carries the same title.

13. This is one of a number of poems headed to indicate that it is to be played or sung. Several, though not this one, have the initials "R. C.," suggesting the probability that Crashaw worked on the musical composition. See, for example, "Ascension" [190–91] ("The Hymn Sett to 5 Parts for voices & violls. by R. C.").

14. Interesting, too, is the fact that both of these poems have clear associations with Crashaw. The first, as I suggest later, echoes the language and tone of Crashaw's Teresa poems; the second is on a saint whose verse Beaumont himself compares to Crashaw's. In *Psyche*, Beaumont praises Crashaw in two stanzas that follow his recognition of other poets, including Gregory. Having acknowledged the achievements of such as Homer, Tasso, and Spenser ("Colin"), Beaumont gives greater praise to Gregory and then to Crashaw, whom he calls his *"onely worthy self"* and who, he says, emulated Gregory's "Pattern":

> And by this soul-attracting Pattern, *Thou,*
> *My onely worthy self*, thy Songs didst frame:
> Witnesse those polish'd *Temple-Steps*, which now
> Whether thou wilt or no, this Truth proclaim,
> And, spight of all thy Travels, make't appear
> Th'art more in *England*, than when thou wert here. (Canto IV.94)

15. In her discussion of Beaumont's poetry, Robinson gives much of her attention to a comparison between Beaumont and other writers, including Donne (to whose "school," she says, he surely belongs [xxx]), Herbert, Traherne, Milton, Vaughan, and, especially, Crashaw (xxviii–xliii). Insisting on Beaumont's literary ancestry, she also acknowledges his lesser stature. She finds his poetry characteristically too long and rambling to be compared satisfactorily to Herbert's, and while finding his poetic affinities with Crashaw notable and important, she nonetheless concludes that "he had none of Crashaw's power" (xli). Writing much later in this century, Thomas Healy is even more dismissive. In the context of a book-length study of Crashaw, he notes that Beaumont "is the only figure whose poetry readily reveals an extensive Crashaw influence," but he adds that there "is little to be gained elaborating the parallels Robinson draws attention to. Beaumont is not a distinguished poet, and one is too often aware, with both his *Psyche* and minor poems, of reading second-rate imitations of the Fletchers, Crashaw, and Herbert" (156–57).

16. One poem that in a very visible way recalls Herbert is "Suspirium ad Amorem," one of Beaumont's few pattern poems, each stanza of which appears as does the first:

> O LOVE
>   Come prove
>   Thy Dart
>   On Me;
>   And deigne
>   To gaine
>   My Hart
> To Thee!

Notes to Chapter 16/Summers

1. Review of *George Herbert: An Annotated Bibliography of Modern Criticism, 1905–1974* by John R. Roberts, *Renaissance Quarterly* 32 (1979): 441.

Works Cited

Alabaster, William. *The Sonnets*. Eds. G. M. Story and Helen Gardner. London: Oxford Univ. Press, 1959.

Alighieri, Dante. *The Divine Comedy. The Carlyle-Okey-Wicksteed Translation*. New York: Random House, 1932.

Anderson, Judith H. *Words that Matter: Linguistic Perception in Renaissance English*. Stanford: Stanford Univ. Press, 1996.

Archaeologia. Or Miscellaneous Tracts relating to Antiquity. The Society of Antiquaries of London. Vol. 32. London: J. Nichols and Son, 1847.

Atkinson, David W. "The Religious Voices of Drummond of Hawthornden." *Studies in Scottish Literature* 21 (1986): 197–209.

Augustine, John. "'Cleared by Faith': The Use of Scriptural Precedent in English Protestant Defenses of Poetry." *The Geneva Bible* (The Annotated New Testament, 1602 Facsimile). Ed. Gerald T. Sheppard. New York: Pilgrim, 1989.

Austin, William. *Cato Major. Or, The Book of Old Age*. London, 1648.

———. *Devotionis Augustinianae Flamma or Certayne Devout, Godly, & Learned Meditations*. London, 1635.

———. *Haec Homo*. London, 1637.

———. "William Drummond as a Baroque Poet." *Studies in Scottish Literature* 26 (1991): 394–408.

Barroll, Leeds. "Looking for Patrons." *Aemilia Lanyer: Gender, Genre, and the Canon*. Ed. Marshall Grossman. Lexington: Univ. of Kentucky Press, 1998.

Bassett, Bernard. *The English Jesuits: From Campion to Martindale*. New York: Herder and Herder, 1968.

Beaumont, Joseph. *The Complete Poems of Dr. Joseph Beaumont*. Ed. Alexander Grosart. Chertsey Worthies' Library. Edinburgh: Printed for Private Circulation, 1880. Rpt. 2 vols. Edinburgh: T. & A. Constable, 1880.

————. *The Minor Poems of Joseph Beaumont, D.D. 1616–1699.* Ed. Eloise Robinson. London: Constable, 1914.

————. *Original Poems in English and Latin.* Ed. John Gee. Cambridge, 1749.

————. *Psyche: or Loves Mysterie in XX Cantos: Displaying the Intercourse Betwixt Christ, and the Soule.* London: Printed by John Dawson for George Boddington, 1648.

————. *Psyche, or Loves Mystery, In XXIV Cantos: Displaying the Intercourse Betwixt Christ, and the Soul.* [Ed. Charles Beaumont.] Second ed. Cambridge: Cambridge Univ. Press, 1702.

Beier, Lucinda McCray. "The Good Death in Seventeenth-Century England." *Death, Ritual, and Bereavement.* Ed. Ralph Houlbrooke. New York: Routledge, 1989.

Beilin, Elaine V. *Redeeming Eve: Women Writers of the English Renaissance.* Princeton: Princeton Univ. Press, 1987.

Bell, Ilona. "'Setting Foot into Divinity': George Herbert and the English Reformation." *Modern Language Quarterly* 38 (1977): 219–41.

Berley, Marc. "Milton's Earthly Grossness: Music and the Condition of the Poet in L'Allegro and Il Penseroso." *Milton Studies* 30 (1993): 149–61.

Blain, Virginia, Patricia Clements, and Isobel Grundy, eds. *Feminist Companion to Literature in English: Women Writers from the Middle Ages to the Present.* London: B. T. Batsford Ltd., 1990.

The Booke of Common Prayer, and Administration of the Sacraments, And other Rites and Ceremonies of the Church of England. London: [Robert Barker], 1615.

————. Cambridge: Cambridge Univ. Press [n.d.].

Booty, John E., ed. *The Book of Common Prayer, 1559: The Elizabethan Prayer Book.* Charlottesville: Univ. of Virginia Press for the Folger Shakespeare Library, 1976.

Boulger, James D. *The Calvinist Temper in English Poetry.* New York: Mouton, 1980.

Braithwaite, Richard. *ESSAIES VPON THE FIVE SENSES. With a pithie one vpon DETRACTION. LONDON.* Printed by E: G: for Richard Whittaker, and are to be sold at his shop at the Kings Head in Paules Church-yard. 1620.

Brown, Christopher. *Van Dyck.* Oxford: Phaidon, 1982.

Brownlow, F. W. *Robert Southwell.* New York: Twayne, 1996.

Bulatkin, Eleanor. *Structured Arithmetic in the Oxford "Roland."* Columbus: Ohio State Univ. Press, 1972.

Burton, Robert. *The Anatomy of Melancholy.* 3 vols. Intro. Holbrook Jackson. London: J. M. Dent, 1932.

———. *The Anatomy of Melancholy.* Eds. F. Dell and P. Jordan Smith. New York: Tudor Publishing Co., 1948.

Bush, Douglas. "Lord Falkland's Brother." *TLS* (November 10, 1978): 1309.

Cairns, Francis. *Generic Composition in Greek and Roman Poetry.* Edinburgh: Edinburgh Univ. Press, 1972.

Camden, Vera J., ed. *Bunyan Studies: Dissenting Women in John Bunyan's World and Work* 7 (1997).

Campbell, Lily B. "The Christian Muse." *Huntington Library Bulletin* 8 (1935): 29–70.

———. *Divine Poetry and Drama in Sixteenth-Century England.* Cambridge and Berkeley: Cambridge Univ. Press and Univ. of California Press, 1959.

Caraman, Philip. *Robert Southwell and Henry Garnet: A Study of Friendship.* St. Louis: The Institute of Jesuit Sources, 1995.

Carey, Mary. *Meditations from Her Note Book of 1649–1657.* Printed & sold by Francis Meynell, 67 Romney Street, Westminster, 1918.

Cary, Patrick. *The Poems of Patrick Cary.* Ed. Sister Veronica Delany. Oxford: Clarendon Press, 1978.

Chambers, A. B. *Transfigured Rites in Seventeenth-Century English Poetry.* Columbia: Univ. of Missouri Press, 1992.

Clancy, Thomas. "The First Generation of Jesuits." *Archivum Historicum Societatis Jesu* 57 (1998): 137–62.

Clements, Arthur L. *Poetry and Contemplation: John Donne, George Herbert, Henry Vaughan, and the Modern Period.* Albany: State Univ. Press of New York, 1990.

Cliff, Michelle. "Object into Subject: Some Thoughts on the Work of Black Women Artists." *Making Face, Making Soul/Haciendo Caras: Creative and Critical Perspectives by Feminists of Color.* Ed. Gloria Anzaldúa. San Francisco: Aunt Lute Books, 1990.

Coeffeteau, F. N. *Table of the Humane Passions with Their Causes and Effects.* Trans. Edward Grimeston. *LONDON. Printed by Nicholas Okes.* 1621.

Coiro, Ann Baynes. "Writing in Service: Sexual Politics and Class Position in the Poetry of Aemilia Lanyer and Ben Jonson." *Criticism* 35 (1993): 357–76.

Collins, An. *Divine Songs and Meditacions.* London: Printed by R. Bishop, 1653.

———. *Divine Songs and Meditacions.* Ed. Sidney Gottlieb. Tempe, AZ: Medieval & Renaissance Texts and Studies, 1996.

———. *Divine Songs and Meditacions.* Ed. Stanley N. Stewart. Abridged facsimile. Los Angeles: William Andrews Clark Memorial Library, Univ. of California, 1961.

Collinson, Patrick. *Godly People: Essays on English Protestantism and Puritanism.* London: Hambleton Press, 1983.

Cook, Patrick J. *Milton, Spenser and the Epic Tradition.* Aldershot: Scolar Press, 1996.

Corns, Thomas N. *Uncloistered Virtue: English Political Literature, 1640–1660.* Oxford: Clarendon Press, 1992.

Corthell, Ronald J. "'The secrecy of man': Recusant Discourse and the Elizabethan Subject." *English Literary Renaissance* 19 (1989): 272–90.

Cosin, John. *A Collection of Private Devotions.* Ed. P. G. Stanwood. Oxford: Clarendon Press, 1967.

Cowley, Abraham. *Selected Poetry and Prose.* Ed. J. Taaffe. New York: Twayne, 1972.

Crashaw, Richard. *The Poems English, Latin, and Greek of Richard Crashaw.* Ed. L. C. Martin. Oxford: Clarendon Press, 1957.

Crawford, Patricia. *Women and Religion in England 1500–1720.* London: Routledge, 1993.

Cressy, David. "Literacy in pre-industrial England." *Societas: A Review of Social History* 4 (1974): 229–40.

Crossan, John Dominic. *Who Killed Jesus?: Exposing the Roots of Anti-Semitism in the Gospel Story of the Death of Jesus.* San Francisco: Harper, 1991.

Cunnar, Eugene. "An Collins." *Dictionary of Literary Biography: Seventeenth-Century Nondramatic Poets.* Vol. 131. Third Series. Ed. M. Thomas Hester. Detroit: Bruccoli Clark Layman, 1993.

———. "*Ut Pictura Poesis*: Thomas Cole's Painterly Interpretations of *L'Allegro* and *Il Penseroso*." *Milton Quarterly* 24.3 (1990): 85–98.

Cust, Richard and Ann Hughes. *Conflict in Early Stuart England: Studies in Religion and Politics 1603–1642.* London: Longmans, 1989.

Davies, H. Neville. "Milton's Nativity Ode and Drummond's 'An Hymne of the Ascension.'" *Scottish Literary Journal* 12 (1985): 5–23.

Davies, Horton. *Worship and Theology in England.* Vol. I. Princeton: Princeton Univ. Press, 1970.

Davies, Julian. *The Caroline Captivity of the Church: Charles I and the Remoulding of Anglicanism 1625–1641.* Oxford: Clarendon Press, 1992.

Davies, Stevie. *Unbridled Spirits: Women of the English Revolution: 1640–1660.* London: The Women's Press, 1998.

Dawson, Edward. "The Practical Methode of Meditation." Preface to *An Abridgment of Meditations of the Life, Passion, Death, and Resurrection of our Lord and Saviour Iesus Christ.* Vincentius Bruno. St. Omer: 1614. Rpt. Louis Martz, *The Meditative Poem.* New York: New York Univ. Press, 1963.

D'Evelyn, Charlotte. *Meditations on the Life and Passion of Christ.* London: Oxford Univ. Press, 1929. Rpt. New York: Krause Reprint Co., 1971.

De Sales, St. Francis. *Introduction to the Devout Life* (1608). Ed. Allan Ross. Westminster, MD: The Newman Press, 1948.

Devlin, Christopher. *The Life of Robert Southwell, Poet and Martyr.* New York: Farrar, Straus, and Cudahy [1956].

Dictionary of National Biography. Vols. 2 and 3. Eds. Leslie Stephen and Sidney Lee. London: Oxford Univ. Press, 1917.

DiPasquale, Theresa M. "William Drummond of Hawthornden." *Dictionary of Literary Biography.* Vol. 121. Detroit: Gale Research Co., 1992.

Doerksen, Daniel W. "'Saint Pauls Puritan': John Donne's 'Puritan' Imagination in the *Sermons.*" *John Donne's Religious Imagination.* Eds. Raymond-Jean Frontain and Frances M. Malpezzi. Conway: Univ. of Central Arkansas Press, 1995.

Donne, John. *The Complete Poetry of John Donne.* Ed. John T. Shawcross. Garden City: Doubleday, 1967.

———. "On the Translation of the Psalms by Sir Philip Sidney, and the Countess of Pembroke his sister." *John Donne: The Complete English Poems.* Ed. A. J. Smith. London: Penguin, 1971.

———. *The Sermons of John Donne.* Ed. George R. Potter and Evelyn L. Simpson. 10 vols. Berkeley: Univ. of California Press, 1953–62.

Drummond, William. *Flowres of Sion. By William Drummond of Hawthornedenne. To Which is Adjoyned His* Cypresse Grove. 1623. New York: Da Capo Press, 1973.

———. *Poems and Prose.* Ed. Robert H. MacDonald. Edinburgh and London: Scottish Academic Press, 1976.

———. *The Poems of William Drummond of Hawthornden.* Ed. Wm. C. Ward. 2 vols. New York: Scribner's, 1894.

———. *The Poetical Works of William Drummond of Hawthornden.* Ed. L. E. Kastner. 2 vols. Manchester: Manchester Univ. Press, 1913.

DuBartas, Guillaume de Saluste. *The Divine Weeks and Works.* Trans. Joshua Sylvester. Ed. Susan Snyder. Oxford: Oxford Univ. Press, 1979.

Dubrow, Heather. "The Country-House Poem: A Study in Generic Development." *Genre* 12 (1979): 153–79.

Duncan-Jones, Elsie E. "Who Was the Recipient of Crashaw's Leyden Letter?" *New Perspectives on the Life and Art of Richard Crashaw.* Ed. John R. Roberts. Columbia: Univ. of Missouri Press, 1990.

Durston, Christopher and Jacqueline Eales. *The Culture of English Puritanism, 1560–1700.* New York: St. Martin's Press, 1996.

Eccles, Audrey. *Obstetrics and Gynaecology in Tudor and Stuart England.* Kent, OH: Kent State Univ. Press, 1982.

Eliot, T. S. *For Lancelot Andrewes.* London: Faber & Faber, 1970.

Eliza's Babes: or The Virgins-Offering. Being Divine Poems and Meditations. London: Laurence Blaiklock, 1652.

Elrod, Eileen Razzari. "'Mouth Put in the Dust': Personal Authority and Biblical Resonance in Anne Bradstreet's Grief Poems." *Studies in Puritan American Spirituality* 5 (1995): 35–62.

Engel, William E. *Mapping Mortality: The Persistence of Memory and Melancholy in Early Modern England.* Amherst: Univ. of Massachusetts Press, 1995.

Enterline, Lynn. *The Tears of Narcissus: Melancholia and Masculinity in Early Modern Writing.* Stanford: Stanford Univ. Press, 1995.

Evelyn, John. *Numismata, A Discourse of Medals, Ancient and Modern. Together with some Account of Heads and Effigies of Illustrious and Famous Persons, in Sculps and Taille-Douce, of whom we have no Medals extant. To which is added A Digression concerning Physiognomy.* London, 1697.

Evetts-Secker, Josephine. "Consolatory Literature of the English Recusants." *Renaissance and Reformation* 6.2 (1982): 122–41.

Ezell, Margaret J. M. *The Patriarch's Wife: Literary Evidence and the History of the Family.* Chapel Hill: Univ. of North Carolina Press, 1987.

———. *Writing Women's Literary History.* Baltimore: Johns Hopkins Univ. Press, 1993.

Featley, Daniel. *Ancilla Pietatis, or, the Handmaid to Private Devotion.* London, 1626.

Ferguson, Harvie. *Melancholy and the Critique of Modernity: Søren Kierkegaard's Religious Psychology.* London: Routledge, 1995.

Fildes, Valerie. "Maternal feelings re-assessed: child abandonment and neglect in London and Westminster, 1550–1800." *Women as Mothers in Pre-Industrial England.* Ed. Valerie Fildes. London: Routledge, 1990.

Finzi, Silvia Vegetti. *Mothering: Toward a New Psychoanalytic Construction.* Trans. Kathrine Jason. New York: The Guilford Press, 1996.

Fiorenza, Elisabeth Schüssler. *In Memory of Her: A Feminist Theological Reconstruction of Christian Origins.* New York: Crossroad, 1985.

Fish, Stanley. *Self-Consuming Artifacts.* Berkeley: Univ. of California Press, 1992.

Fisken, Beth Wynne. "Mary Sidney's Psalmes: Education and Wisdom." *Silent But for the Word.* Ed. Margaret P. Hannay. Kent, OH: Kent State Univ. Press, 1985.

Flannery, Austin, ed. *Vatican Counsel II: The Conciliar and Post Consiliar Documents.* Northport, NY: Costello Publishing, 1988.

Fletcher, Anthony and John Stevenson. "Introduction." *Order and Disorder in Early Modern England.* Eds. Anthony Fletcher and John Stevenson. Cambridge: Cambridge Univ. Press, 1985.

Fletcher, Giles. *The Complete Poems of Giles Fletcher, B. D.* Ed. Alexander B. Grosart. London: Chatto and Windus, 1876.

Fogle, French Rowe. *A Critical Study of William Drummond of Hawthornden.* New York: King's Crown, 1952.

Fowler, Alastair. "Country-House Poems: The Politics of a Genre." *Seventeenth-Century* 1 (1986): 1–14.

Freedberg, David. *The Power of Images: Studies in the History and Theory of Response.* Chicago: Univ. of Chicago Press, 1989.

Friedman, Donald. "Christ's Image and Likeness in Donne." *John Donne Journal* 15 (1996): 75–94.

Frontain, Raymond-Jean and Frances M. Malpezzi, eds. *John Donne's Religious Imagination.* Conway: Univ. of Central Arkansas Press, 1995.

Gee, John. *Foot Out of the Snare.* Ed. T. H. B. Harmsen. Nijmegen: Cicero Press, 1992.

———. *Memoirs of Joseph Beaumont....* Annotated by Thomas Alfred Walker. Cambridge: Cambridge Univ. Press, 1934.

———, ed. *Original Poems in English and Latin ... by Joseph Beaumont, D.D.* Cambridge: J. Bentham, 1749.

Genette, Gerard. *Narrative Discourse: An Essay in Method.* Trans. Jane E. Lewin. Ithaca: Cornell Univ. Press, 1980.

The Geneva Bible. (1560 Facsimile). Madison: Univ. of Wisconsin Press, 1969.

———. (The Annotated New Testament, 1602 Facsimile). Ed. Gerald T. Sheppard. New York: Pilgrim, 1989.

Graham, Elspeth, Hilary Hinds, Elaine Hobby, and Helen Wilcox, eds. *Her Own Life: Autobiographical Writings by Seventeenth-Century Englishwomen.* London and New York: Routledge, 1989.

Greene, Guy Shepard. "Drummond's Borrowing from Donne." *Philological Quarterly* 11 (1932): 26–38.

Greene, Roland. "Sir Philip Sidney's Psalms, the Sixteenth-Century Psalter, and the Nature of Lyric." *SEL* 30 (1990): 19–40.

Greer, Germaine, et al., eds. *Kissing the Rod: An Anthology of Seventeenth-Century Women's Verse.* London: Virago, 1988.

Griffith, A. F., ed. *Bibliotheca Anglo-Poetica.* London, 1815.

Grosart, Alexander B. "Memorial-Introduction." *The Complete Poems of Giles Fletcher, B. D.* London: Chatto and Windus, 1876.

Grossman, Marshall, ed. *Aemilia Lanyer: Gender, Genre, and the Canon.* Lexington: Univ. of Kentucky Press, 1998.

―――. "The Gendering of Genre: Literary History and the Canon." *Aemilia Lanyer: Gender, Genre, and the Canon.* Ed. Marshall Grossman. Lexington: Univ. of Kentucky Press, 1998.

Guibbory, Achsah. "Enlarging the Limits of the 'Religious Lyric': The Case of Herrick's *Hesperides.*" *New Perspectives on the Seventeenth-Century English Religious Lyric.* Ed. John R. Roberts. Columbia: Univ. of Missouri Press, 1994.

―――. "The Gospel According to Aemilia: Women and the Sacred." *Aemilia Lanyer: Gender, Genre, and the Canon.* Ed. Marshall Grossman. Lexington: Univ. of Kentucky Press, 1998.

Guiney, Louise. *Recusant Poets.* New York: Sheed and Ward, 1939.

Hageman, Elizabeth. "Women's poetry in early modern Britain." *Women and Literature in Britain 1500–1700.* Ed. Helen Wilcox. Cambridge: Cambridge Univ. Press, 1996.

Halewood, William H. *The Poetry of Grace: Reformation Themes and Structures in English Seventeenth-Century Poetry.* New Haven: Yale Univ. Press, 1970.

Hall, Joseph. *Heaven vpon Earth and Characters of Vertves and Vices.* Ed. Rudolf Kirk. New Brunswick, NJ: Rutgers Univ. Press, 1948.

Hamilton, Donna B. and Richard Strier, eds. *Religion, Literature, and Politics in Post-Reformation England 1540–1633.* Cambridge: Cambridge Univ. Press, 1995.

Hannay, Margaret P. "'Bearing the livery of your name': the Countess of Pembroke's Agency in Print and Scribal Publication." *Sidney Journal* (forthcoming).

―――. "Mary Sidney and the Admonitory Dedication." *Silent But for the Word.* Ed. Margaret P. Hannay. Kent, OH: Kent State Univ. Press, 1985.

―――. *Philip's Phoenix: Mary Sidney, Countess of Pembroke.* New York: Oxford Univ. Press, 1990.

―――, ed. *Silent But for the Word: Tudor Women as Patrons, Translators, and Writers of Religious Works.* Kent, OH: Kent State Univ. Press, 1985.

―――. "'Wisdome the Wordes': Psalm Translation and Elizabethan Women's Spirituality." *Religion & Literature* 23.3 (1991): 65–82.

―――, Noel J. Kinnamon, and Michael G. Brennan, eds. *The Collected Works of Mary Sidney Herbert, Countess of Pembroke.* 2 vols. Oxford; Clarendon Press, 1998.

Haskins, Susan. *Mary Magdalene: Myth and Metaphor.* New York: Harcourt Brace, 1993.

Healy, Thomas. *New Latitudes: Theory and English Renaissance Literature.* London, Melbourne, Auckland: Hodder & Stoughton, 1992.

———. *Richard Crashaw.* Medieval and Renaissance Authors, vol. 8. Leiden: E. J. Brill, 1986.

Hengel, Martin. *Crucifixion in the Ancient World and the Folly of the Message of the Cross.* Philadelphia: Fortress Press, 1977.

Herbert, George. *The Works of George Herbert.* Ed. F. E. Hutchinson. Oxford: Clarendon Press, 1941.

Herz, Judith Scherer. "Reading [out] Biography in 'A Valediction forbidding Mourning.'" *John Donne Journal* 13 (1994): 137–42.

Hibbard, G. R. "The Country House Poem of the Seventeenth Century." *Journal of the Warburg and Courtauld Institutes* 19 (1956): 159–74.

Hicks, Leo, ed. *Letters and Memorials of Fr. Robert Parsons, S. J.* London: Catholic Record Society, 1942.

Hieatt, A. Kent. "Numerical Structures in Verse: Second-Generation Studies Needed (Exemplified in *Sir Gawain* and the *Chanson de Roland*)." *Essays in the Numerical Criticism of Medieval Literature.* Lewisburg, PA: Bucknell Univ. Press, 1980.

Hill, John Spencer. *John Milton: Poet, Priest and Prophet.* Totowa, NJ: Rowman and Littlefield, 1979.

Hobby, Elaine. *Virtue of Necessity: English Women's Writing 1649–88.* Ann Arbor: Univ. of Michigan Press, 1989.

Hodgkins, Christopher. *Authority, Church, and Society in George Herbert: Return to the Middle Way.* Columbia: Univ. of Missouri Press, 1993.

Hopkins, Gerard Manley. *The Poems.* Eds. W. H. Gardner and N. H. MacKenzie. London: Oxford Univ. Press, 1970.

Horden, John. "A New Emblem Manuscript by Patrick Cary (1623/24–1657)." *Word and Visual Imagination: Studies in the Interaction of English Literature and the Visual Arts.* Eds. Karl Josef Höltgen, Peter M. Daly, and Wolfgang Lottes. Erlangen: Univ.-Bibliothek Erlangen-Nürnberg, 1988.

Houlbrooke, Ralph. "Introduction." *Death, Ritual, and Bereavement.* Ed. Ralph Houlbrooke. New York: Routledge, 1989.

Howell, James. *Epistolae Ho-Elianae: familiar letters Domestic and foreign, divided into four books: partly historical, political, philosophical. Upon emergent occasions.* London: R. Ware, 1754.

Hughes, Ann. *The Causes of the English Civil War.* New York: St. Martin's Press, 1991.

Hunter, William B. *The Descent of Urania: Studies in Milton, 1946–1988.* Lewisburg, PA: Bucknell Univ. Press, 1989.

———. "Prophetic Dreams and Visions in *Paradise Lost.*" *Modern Language Quarterly* 9 (1948): 277–85.

Hurtig, Judith W. "Death in Childbirth: Seventeenth-Century English Tombs and Their Place in Contemporary Thought." *Art Bulletin* 65 (1983): 603–15.

Hutson, Lorna. "Why the Lady's Eyes are Nothing Like the Sun." *Women, Texts and Histories 1575–1760.* Eds. Clare Brant and Diane Purkiss. London: Routledge, 1992.

Jack, Ronald D. S. "Drummond of Hawthornden: The Major Scottish Sources." *Studies in Scottish Literature* 6 (1969): 36–46.

———. *The History of Scottish Literature.* Vol. 1. Origins to 1660. Aberdeen: Aberdeen Univ. Press, 1987.

———. *The Italian Influence on Scottish Literature.* Edinburgh: Edinburgh Univ. Press, 1972.

———. "Petrarch in English and Scottish Renaissance Literature." *Modern Language Review* 71 (1976): 801–11.

Jeffrey, David Lyle. *People of the Book.* Cambridge: William B. Eerdmans, 1996.

Jensen, H. James. *The Muses' Concord: Literature, Music, and the Visual Arts in the Baroque Age.* Bloomington: Indiana Univ. Press, 1976.

———. *Signs and Meaning in Eighteenth-Century Art: Epistemology, Rhetoric, Painting, Poesy, Music, Dramatic Performance, and G. F. Handel.* New York: Peter Lang, 1997.

Johnson, Jeffrey. "Wrestling with God: John Donne at Prayer." *John Donne's Religious Imagination.* Eds. Raymond-Jean Frontain and Frances M. Malpezzi. Conway: Univ. of Central Arkansas Press, 1995.

Jones, Ann Rosalind. *Currency of Eros: Women's Love Lyric in Europe 1540–1620.* Bloomington: Indiana Univ. Press, 1990.

Jonson, Ben. *The Complete Poetry of Ben Jonson.* Ed. William B. Hunter, Jr. New York: Norton, 1963.

———. *Ben Jonson.* Eds. C. H. Herford and Percy and Evelyn Simpson. 11 vols. Oxford: Clarendon Press, 1925–52.

———. *Ben Jonson's Timber, or Discoveries.* Ed. R. S. Walker. Syracuse: Syracuse Univ. Press, 1953.

Kay, Dennis. *Melodious Tears: The English Funeral Elegy from Spenser to Milton.* Oxford: Clarendon Press, 1990.

Keates, Jonathan. "The Soul's Embrace: George Frederic Handel and John Milton: *L'Allegro, Il Penseroso, Ed Il Moderato.*" *TLS* (June 13, 1997): 22.

Keble, John. *The Christian Year.* London: Church Literature Association, 1877.

Keohane, Catherine. "'That Blindest Weakenesse be not Over-Bold': Aemilia Lanyer's Radical Unfolding of the Passion." *ELH* 64 (1997): 359–90.

Kierkegaard, Søren. *For Self-Examination/Judge for Yourself!* Trans. and eds. Howard V. Hong and Edna H. Hong. Bloomington: Indiana Univ. Press, 1990.

King, John N. "Recent Studies in Southwell." *English Literary Renaissance* 13 (1983): 221–27.

Kinsley, James, ed. *Scottish Poetry: A Critical Survey.* London: Cassell, 1973.

Klawitter, George. "Craft and Purpose in Alabaster's Incarnation Sonnets." *University of Hartford Studies in Literature* 15.3/16.1 (1984): 60–66.

Klibansky, Raymond, Erwin Panofsky, and Fritz Saxl, eds. *Saturn and Melancholy: Studies in the History of Natural Philosophy, Religion and Art.* London: Nelson, 1964.

Kouffman, Avra. "'Why feignest thou thyselfe to be another woman?': Constraints on the Construction of Subjectivity in Mary Rich's Diary." *Women's Life Writing: Finding Voice/Building Community.* Ed. Linda S. Coleman. Bowling Green, OH: Bowling Green State Univ. Popular Press, 1997.

Kristeva, Julia. *Black Sun: Depression and Melancholia.* Trans. Leon S. Roudiez. New York: Columbia Univ. Press, 1989.

———. *Powers of Horror: An Essay on Abjection.* Trans. Leon S. Roudiez. New York: Columbia Univ. Press, 1982.

Lake, Peter. "Calvinism and the English Church 1570–1635." *Past and Present* 114 (1987): 32–76.

Lamb, Mary Ellen. "The Cooke Sisters: Attitudes toward Learned Women in the Renaissance." *Silent But for the Word.* Ed. Margaret P. Hannay. Kent, OH: Kent State Univ. Press, 1985.

Lanyer, Aemilia. *The Poems of Aemilia Lanyer: Salve Deus Rex Judaeorum.* Ed. Susanne Woods. New York: Oxford Univ. Press, 1993.

Lasocki, David and Roger Prior, eds. *The Bassanos: Venetian Musicians and Instrument Makers in England, 1531–1665.* Aldershot: Scolar Press, 1995.

Latz, Dorothy. *"Glow-Worm Light": Writings of 17th Century English Recusant Women from Original Manuscripts.* Salzburg: Elizabethan and Renaissance Studies 92:21, 1989.

Laurence, Anne. "Godly Grief: Individual Responses to Death in Seventeenth-Century Britain." *Death, Ritual, and Bereavement.* Ed. Ralph Houlbrooke. New York: Routledge, 1989.

Leishman, J. B. *The Monarch of Wit.* London: Hutchinson and Co., 1965.

Lewalski, Barbara. "The Lady of the Country House Poem." *The Fashioning and Functioning of the British Country House.* Ed. Gervase Jackson-Stops et al. Hanover: National Gallery of Art, 1989.

———. "Of God and Good Women: The Poems of Aemilia Lanyer." *Silent But for the Word.* Ed. Margaret P. Hannay. Kent, OH: Kent State Univ. Press, 1985.

———. *Protestant Poetics and the Seventeenth-Century Lyric.* Princeton: Princeton Univ. Press, 1979.

———. "Re-writing Patriarchy and Patronage: Margaret Clifford, Anne Clifford, and Aemilia Lanyer." *The Yearbook of English Studies* 21 (1991): 87–106.

———. *Writing Women in Jacobean England.* Cambridge: Harvard Univ. Press, 1993.

Lilley, Kate. "True State Within: Women's Elegy 1640–1700." *Women, Writing, History 1640–1740.* Eds. Isobel Grundy and Susan Wiseman. Athens: Univ. of Georgia Press, 1992.

Linday, Maurice. *History of Scottish Literature.* Second ed. London: Robert Hale, 1992.

Low, Anthony. *Love's Architecture: Devotional Modes in Seventeenth-Century English Poetry.* New York: New York Univ. Press, 1978.

Loyola, Ignatius. *The Constitutions of the Society of Jesus.* Trans. George Ganns. St. Louis: The Institute of Jesuit Sources, 1970.

———. *The Spiritual Exercises.* Trans. David Fleming. St. Louis: The Institute of Jesuit Sources, 1978.

Mack, Phyllis. *Visionary Women: Ecstatic Prophecy in Seventeenth-Century England.* Berkeley: Univ. of California Press, 1992.

Major, Elizabeth. *Honey on the Rod; or a comfortable Contemplation for one in Affliction; with sundry Poems on several Subjects.* London: Printed for Thomas Maxey, 1656.

Malpezzi, Frances. "Thy Cross, My Bower: The Greening of the Heart." *"Too Rich to Clothe the Sunne": Essays on George Herbert.* Eds. Claude J. Summers and Ted-Larry Pebworth. Pittsburgh: Univ. of Pittsburgh Press, 1980.

Marcus, Leah. *The Politics of Mirth: Jonson, Herrick, Milton, Marvell, and the Defense of Old Holiday Pastimes.* Chicago: Univ. of Chicago Press, 1986.

Marshall, Peter. *The Catholic Priesthood and the English Reformation.* Oxford: Clarendon Press, 1994.

Martz, Louis L. *The Meditative Poem.* New York: New York Univ. Press, 1963.

————. *The Poetry of Meditation: A Study in English Religious Literature of the Seventeenth Century.* New Haven: Yale Univ. Press, 1954.

Masson, David. *Drummond of Hawthornden: The Story of His Life and Writings.* 1873. New York: Haskell House, 1969.

Maus, Katharine Eisaman. *Inwardness and the Theater in the English Renaissance.* Chicago: Univ. of Chicago Press, 1995.

May, Allyson N. "'She at first denied it': Infanticide Trials at the Old Bailey." *Women & History: Voices of Early Modern England.* Ed. Valerie Frith. Toronto: Coach House Press, 1995.

Maynor, Natalie. "Joseph Beaumont's *Psyche* in the Seventeenth-Century Context." Diss. Univ. of Tennessee, 1979.

McBride, Kari Boyd. "Remembering Orpheus in the Poems of Aemilia Lanyer." *SEL* 38 (1998): 87–108.

McClung, William Alexander. *The Country House in English Renaissance Literature.* Berkeley: Univ. of California Press, 1977.

McCoy, Richard. "The Wonderful Spectacle: The Civic Progress of Elizabeth I and the Troublesome Coronation." *Urban Life in the Renaissance.* Eds. Susan Zimmerman and Ronald F. E. Weissman. Newark: Univ. of Delaware Press, 1989.

MacDonald, Michael. *Mystical Bedlam: Madness, Anxiety, and Healing in Seventeenth-Century England.* Cambridge: Cambridge Univ. Press, 1981.

MacDonald, Robert H. *The Library of Drummond of Hawthornden.* Edinburgh: Edinburgh Univ. Press, 1971.

McEachern, Claire and Debora Shuger, eds. *Religion and Culture in Renaissance England.* Cambridge: Cambridge Univ. Press, 1997.

McGrath, Lynette. "'Let us have our libertie againe': Aemilia Lanier's 17th-Century Feminist Voice." *Women's Studies* 20 (1992): 331–48.

————. "Metaphoric Subversions: Feasts and Mirrors in Aemilia Lanier's *Salve Deus Rex Judaeorum.*" *LIT* 3 (1991): 101–13.

McNees, Eleanor. "John Donne and the Anglican Doctrine of the Eucharist." *Texas Studies in Language and Literature* 29 (1987): 91–114.

MacQueen, John. *The Enlightenment and Scottish Literature. Volume I: Progress and Poetry.* Edinburgh: Scottish Academic Press, 1982.

Means, James A. "Keat's 'Ode on Melancholy' and Beaumont's *Psyche* (1648)." *N&Q* 32 (1985): 341.

Middleton, Elizabeth. "The Death and Passion of our Lord Jesus Christ; As it was Acted by the Bloodye Jewes, And Registred by The Blessed Evangelists." Bod. Don. E.17.

Millar, Oliver. *The Age of Charles I: Painting in England 1620–1649.* London: The Tate Gallery, 1972.

———. *Van Dyck in England.* London: National Portrait Gallery, 1982.

Milton, Anthony. *Catholic and Reformed: The Roman and Protestant Churches in English Protestant Thought 1600–1640.* Cambridge: Cambridge Univ. Press, 1995.

Milton, John. *Complete Poems and Major Prose.* Ed. Merritt Y. Hughes. New York: Macmillan, 1957.

———. *On Christian Doctrine. The Works of John Milton.* Vol. 15. Gen. ed. Frank Allen Patterson. New York: Columbia Univ. Press, 1931–38.

———. *Paradise Lost.* Ed. Alastair Fowler. London: Longman, 1971.

———. *The Prose of John Milton.* Ed. J. Max Patrick. New York: Anchor, 1967.

Moffitt, John F. "Who is The Old Man in a Golden Helmet?" *Art Bulletin* 66 (1984): 417–27.

Molesworth, Charles. "Property and Virtue: The Genre of the Country-House Poem in the Seventeenth Century." *Genre* 1 (1968): 141–77.

Mordaunt, Elizabeth, Countess of. *The Private Diarie of Elizabeth, Countess of Mordaunt.* Duncairn, 1856.

Morgan, Edwin. *Crossing the Border: Essays on Scottish Literature.* Manchester: Carcanet, 1990.

Mueller, Janel. "The Feminist Poetics of '*Salve Deus Rex Judaeorum.*'" *Feminist Measures: Soundings in Poetry and Theory.* Eds. Lynn Keller and Christianne Miller. Ann Arbor: Univ. of Michigan Press, 1994. Rpt. *Aemilia Lanyer: Gender, Genre, and the Canon.* Ed. Marshall Grossman. Lexington: Univ. of Kentucky Press, 1998.

Mullins, Maire. "Introduction." *Religion & Literature, Special Issue on Women, Spirituality, and Writing* 23.2 (1991): 1–7.

Notzon, Mark. "A New Source for Pope's *Dunciad*, Book IV, 21–24." *N&Q* 26 (1979): 543.

O'Malley, John. *The First Jesuits.* Cambridge: Harvard Univ. Press, 1993.

———. "'To Travel to Any Part of the World': Jeronimo Nadal and the Jesuit Vocation." *Studies in the Spirituality of Jesuits* 16.2 (1984): 1–28.

Ostriker, Alicia. "A Word Made Flesh: The Bible and Revisionist Women's Poetry." *Religion & Literature* 23.3 (1991): 9–26.

Ottenhoff, John. "The Shadow and the Real: Typology and the Religious Sonnet." *University of Hartford Studies in Literature* 15.3/16.1 (1984): 43–59.

Parrish, Paul A. *Richard Crashaw.* Twayne's English Authors Series, 299. Boston: G. K. Hall, 1980.

Pascal, Blaise. *Pensées and Other Writings.* Trans. Honor Levi. New York: Oxford Univ. Press, 1995.

Pearson, Jacqueline. "Women reading, reading women." *Women and Literature in Britain 1500–1700.* Ed. Helen Wilcox. Cambridge: Cambridge Univ. Press, 1996.

Perella, Nicolas James. *The Kiss Sacred and Profane: An Interpretative History of Kiss Symbolism and Related Religio-Erotic Themes.* Berkeley: Univ. of California Press, 1969.

Pigman, G. W. *Grief and English Renaissance Elegy.* Cambridge: Cambridge Univ. Press, 1985.

Plomer, Henry. *A Dictionary of the Booksellers and Printers Who Were Working in England, Scotland, and Ireland from 1641 to 1667.* London: Bibliographical Society, 1907.

Plutarch. *Plutarch's Moralia.* Vol. 1. Trans. Frank Cole Babbit. London: Heinemann, 1927.

Praz Mario. "Robert Southwell's 'Saint Peter's Complaint' and its Italian Source." *Modern Language Review* 19 (1924): 273–90.

Prest, Wilfrid R. *The Inns of Court under Elizabeth and the Early Stuarts, 1590–1640.* London: Longman, 1972.

Pritchard, Allan. "Puritan Charges Against Crashaw and Beaumont." *TLS* (July 2, 1964): 578.

Rabelais, François. *The Histories of Gargantua and Pantagruel.* Trans. J. M. Cohen. Harmondsworth: Penguin, 1955.

Rae, Thomas Ian. "The Political Attitudes of William Drummond of Hawthornden." *The Scottish Tradition: Essays in Honor of Ronald Gordon Cant.* Eds. Geoffrey Wallis Steuart Barrow and Dugald MacArthur. Edinburgh: Scottish Academic Press, 1974.

Raspa, Anthony. *The Emotive Image: Jesuit Poetics in the English Renaissance.* Fort Worth: Texas Christian Univ. Press, 1983.

Rathmell, J. C. A. *The Psalms of Sir Philip Sidney and the Countess of Pembroke.* New York: New York Univ. Press, 1963.

Records of the Honourable Society of Lincoln's Inn. Admissions. Vol. 1. London: Lincoln's Inn, 1896.

———. *Black Book.* Vol. 2. London: Lincoln's Inn, 1898.

Reynolds, Edward. *A Treatise of the Passions and Faculties of the Soul of Man.* LONDON: Printed by *Tho. Newcomb,* for *Robert Boulter* at the *Turks Head* in *Cornhil.* 1678.

Richey, Esther Gilman. "'To Undoe the Booke': Cornelius Agrippa, Aemilia Lanyer and the Subversion of Pauline Authority." *English Literary Renaissance* 27.1 (1997): 106–28.

Rienstra, Debra K. "Aspiring to Praise: The Sidney-Pembroke Psalter and the English Religious Lyric." Diss. Rutgers Univ., 1995.

——— and Noel J. Kinnamon. "Revisioning the Sacred Text." *Sidney Journal* 17.1 (1999): 51–74.

Ringler, William. "The 1640 and 1653 Poems by Francis Beaumont Gent." *Studies in Bibliography* 40 (1987): 120–39.

Roberts, John R. "John Donne's Poetry: An Assessment of Modern Criticism." *John Donne Journal* 1 (1982): 55–67.

———, ed. *New Perspectives on the Life and Art of Richard Crashaw.* Columbia: Univ. of Missouri Press, 1990.

———, ed. *New Perspectives on the Seventeenth-Century English Religious Lyric.* Columbia: Univ. of Missouri Press, 1994.

——— and Lorraine M. Roberts. "'To weave a new webbe in their owne loome': Robert Southwell and Counter-Reformation Poetics." *Sacred and Profane: Secular and Devotional Interplay in Early Modern British Literature.* Eds. Helen Wilcox, Richard Todd, and Alasdair MacDonald. Amsterdam: VU Univ. Press, 1996.

Roberts, Lorraine M. "Joseph Beaumont." *Dictionary of Literary Biography.* Vol. 126. Detroit: Gale Research Co., 1991.

Rowse, A. L. *The Poems of Shakespeare's Dark Lady: Salve Deus Rex Judaeorum by Emilia Lanyer.* London: Jonathan Cape, 1978.

Russell, Conrad. *The Causes of the English Civil War.* Oxford: Oxford Univ. Press, 1990.

Sacks, Peter. *The English Elegy: Studies in the Genre from Spenser to Yeats.* Baltimore: Johns Hopkins Univ. Press, 1985.

Schenck, Celeste M. "Feminism and Deconstruction: Re-Constructing the Elegy." *Tulsa Studies in Women's Literature* 5 (1986): 13–28.

Schiesari, Juliana. *The Gendering of Melancholia: Feminism, Psycho-analysis, and the Symbolics of Loss in Renaissance Literature.* Ithaca: Cornell Univ. Press, 1992.

Schnell, Lisa. "Breaking 'the rule of *Cortezia*': Aemilia Lanyer's Dedications to *Salve Deus Rex Judaeorum.*" *Journal of Medieval and Early Modern Studies* 27.1 (1997): 77–101.

———. "'So Great a Difference is There in Degree': Amelia Lanyer and the Aims of Feminist Criticism." *Modern Language Quarterly* 57 (1996): 23 35.

Schoenfeldt, Michael C. "The gender of religious devotion: Amelia Lanyer and John Donne." *Religion and Culture in Renaissance England.* Eds. Claire McEachern and Debora Shuger. Cambridge: Cambridge Univ. Press, 1997.

———. *Prayer and Power.* Chicago: Univ. of Chicago Press, 1991.

Schwoerer, Lois G. "Women's public political voice in England: 1640–1740." *Women Writers and the Early Modern British Political Tradition.* Ed. Hilda L. Smith. Cambridge: Cambridge Univ. Press, 1998.

Sedgwick, Eve Kosofsky. *Between Men: English Literature and Male Homosocial Desire.* New York: Columbia Univ. Press, 1985.

Severance, Sibyl Lutz. "'Some Other Figure': The Vision of Change in *Flowres of Sion,* 1623." *Spenser Studies* 2 (1981): 217–25.

Shakespeare, William. *The Complete Works.* Ed. Alfred Harbage. New York: Viking, 1969.

Shapiro, James. *Shakespeare and the Jews.* New York: Columbia Univ. Press, 1996.

Sharpe, Kevin. *Criticism and Compliment: The Politics of Literature in England of Charles I.* Cambridge: Cambridge Univ. Press, 1987.

Shawcross, John T. "Poetry, Personal and Impersonal: The Case of Donne." *The Eagle and the Dove: Reassessing John Donne.* Eds. Claude J. Summers and Ted-Larry Pebworth. Columbia: Univ. of Missouri Press, 1986.

Sheperd, Massey Hamilton, Jr. *The Oxford American Prayer Book Commentary.* New York: Oxford Univ. Press, 1950.

Sherwood, Terry G. *Fulfilling the Circle: A Study of John Donne's Thought.* Toronto: Univ. of Toronto Press, 1984.

Shuger, Debora K. *Habits of Thought in the English Renaissance: Religion, Politics and the Dominant Culture.* Berkeley: Univ. of California Press, 1990.

———. *The Renaissance Bible: Scholarship, Sacrifice, and Subjectivity.* Berkeley: Univ. of California Press, 1994.

Sidney, Sir Philip. *An Apology for Poetry.* Ed. Geoffrey Shepherd. London: Nelson, 1965.

Skerpan, Elizabeth. *The Rhetoric of Politics in the English Revolution 1642–1660.* Columbia and London: Univ. of Missouri Press, 1992.

Smith, Eric. *By Mourning Tongues: Studies in English Elegy.* Totowa, NJ: Rowan and Littlefield, 1977.

Smith, Lacey Baldwin. *This Realm of England.* Lexington, MA: Heath, 1988.

Southwell, Robert. *An Epistle of Comfort.* Ed. Margaret Waugh. Chicago: Loyola Univ. Press, 1966.

———. *An Humble Supplication to her Majesty.* Ed. R. C. Bald. Cambridge: Cambridge Univ. Press, 1953.

———. *The Poems of Robert Southwell, S. J.* Eds. James Harold McDonald and Nancy Pollard Brown. Oxford: Clarendon Press, 1967.

———. *Spiritual Exercises and Devotions.* Ed. J. M. Buck. London: Sheed and Ward, 1931.

———. *Triumphs Over Death*. Ed. J. W. Trotman. London: Manresa Press, 1914.

Spufford, Margaret. "First steps in literacy: the reading and writing experiences of the humblest seventeenth-century spiritual autobiographers." *Social History* 4.3 (1979): 407–35.

Stace, W. T. *Mysticism and Philosophy*. New York: Lippincott, 1960.

Stanford, Ann, ed. *The Women Poets in English*. New York, St. Louis, San Francisco: McGraw-Hill, 1972.

Stanwood, P. G. "A Portrait of Stuart Orthodoxy." *Church Quarterly Review* 165 (1964): 27–39.

———. "St. Teresa and Joseph Beaumont's *Psyche*." *JEGP* 62 (1963): 533–50.

———. *The Sempiternal Season: Studies in Seventeenth-Century Devotional Writing*. New York: Peter Lang, 1992.

Starkey, David. "The Real Image of Regal Power." *TLS* (March 12, 1999): 18–19.

Steen, Sara Jayne, ed. "Recent Studies in Women Writers of the Seventeenth Century, 1604–1674 (1990 to mid-1993)." *English Literary Renaissance* 24.1 (Winter 1994): 243–74.

Stevens, Mark. "Master of the Grand Manner." *ART News* 90.2 (1991): 108–13.

Stone, Lawrence. *The Family, Sex and Marriage in England 1500–1800*. Abridged ed. New York: Harper & Row, 1979.

Strier, Richard. "Changing the Object: Herbert and Excess." *George Herbert Journal* 2 (1978): 24–37.

———. *Love Known*. Chicago: Univ. of Chicago Press, 1983.

Strocchia, Sharon T. "Funerals and the Politics of Gender in Early Renaissance Florence." *Refiguring Woman: Perspectives on Gender and the Italian Renaissance*. Eds. Marilyn Migiel and Juliana Schiesari. Ithaca, NY: Cornell Univ. Press, 1991.

Strong, Roy. *Van Dyck: Charles I on Horseback*. London: Allen Lane, Penguin, 1972.

Stull, William L. "Sacred Sonnets in Three Styles." *Studies in Philology* 79 (1982): 78–99.

———. "'Why Are Not *Sonnets* Made of Thee?': A New Context for the 'Holy Sonnets' of Donne, Herbert, and Milton." *Modern Philology* 80 (1982): 129–35.

Summers, Claude J. and Ted-Larry Pebworth, eds. *Representing Women in Renaissance England*. Columbia: Univ. of Missouri Press, 1997.

Summers, Joseph H. Review of *George Herbert: An Annotated Bibliography of Modern Criticism, 1905–1974* by John R. Roberts. *Renaissance Quarterly* 32 (1979): 440–42.

Taylor, William. *The Annals of St. Mary Overy: an Historical and Descriptive Account of St. Saviour's Church and Parish.* London: Nichols and Son, 1833.

Traherne, Thomas. *Centuries, Poems, and Thanksgivings.* 2 vols. Ed. H. M. Margoliouth. Oxford: Clarendon Press, 1958.

Travitsky, Betty. "'His Wife's Prayers and Meditations': MS Egerton 607." *The Renaissance Englishwoman in Print: Counterbalancing the Canon.* Eds. Anne M. Haselkorn and Betty Travitsky. Amherst: Univ. of Massachusetts Press, 1990.

———. "The Possibilities of Prose." *Women and Literature in Britain 1500–1700.* Ed. Helen Wilcox. Cambridge: Cambridge Univ. Press, 1996.

Tuve, Rosemond. *A Reading of George Herbert.* Chicago: Univ. of Chicago Press, 1952.

———. "Sacred 'Parody' of Love Poetry and Herbert." *Studies in the Renaissance* 8 (1961): 249–90.

Tyacke, Nicholas. *Anti-Calvinists: The Rise of English Arminianism 1590–1640.* Oxford: Clarendon Press, 1987.

Walker, Thomas Alfred. *Memoirs of Joseph Beaumont.* Cambridge: Cambridge Univ. Press, 1934.

———. *Peterhouse.* Cambridge: W. Heffer, 1935.

———. *A Peterhouse Bibliography.* Cambridge: Cambridge Univ. Press, 1924.

Wall, Wendy. *The Imprint of Gender: Authorship and Publication in the English Renaissance.* Ithaca, NY: Cornell Univ. Press, 1993.

Wallerstein, Ruth C. "The Style of Drummond of Hawthornden in Its Relation to His Translations." *PMLA* 48 (1933): 1090–1107.

Warren, Austin. *Richard Crashaw: A Study in Baroque Sensibility.* Baton Rouge: Louisiana State Univ. Press, 1939.

Watson, Roderick. *The Literature of Scotland.* New York: Schocken, 1985.

Wayne, Don E. *Penshurst: The Semiotics of Place and the Poetics of History.* Madison: Univ. of Wisconsin Press, 1984.

Webber, Joan. *Contrary Music: The Prose Style of John Donne.* Madison: Univ. of Wisconsin Press, 1963.

Wheelock, Arthur K., Jr. *et al. Van Dyck Paintings.* Washington DC: National Gallery of Art, in association with Thames and Hudson, 1991.

Wilcox, Helen. "'Curious Frame': The Seventeenth-Century Religious Lyric as Genre." *New Perspectives on the Seventeenth-Century English Religious Lyric.* Ed. John R. Roberts. Columbia: Univ. of Missouri Press, 1994.

———. "Entering *The Temple*: women, reading, and devotion in seventeenth-century England." *Religion, Literature, and Politics in Post-Reformation*

England, 1540–1688. Eds. Donna B. Hamilton and Richard Strier. Cambridge: Cambridge Univ. Press, 1996.

————. "Exploring the Language of Devotion in the English Revolution." *Literature and the English Civil War.* Eds. Thomas Healy and Jonathan Sawday. Cambridge: Cambridge Univ. Press, 1990.

————. "'My Soule in Silence?': Devotional Representations of Renaissance Englishwomen." *Representing Women in Renaissance England.* Eds. Claude J. Summers and Ted-Larry Pebworth. Columbia: Univ. of Missouri Press, 1997.

————, ed. *Women and Literature in Britain 1500–1700.* Cambridge: Cambridge Univ. Press, 1996.

Willett, Pamela. "Patrick Cary and His Italian Poems." *The British Library Journal* 2.2 (1976): 109–19.

————. "Patrick Cary: A Sequel." *The British Library Journal* 4.2 (1978): 148–60.

Woods, Susanne. "Aemilia Lanyer and Ben Jonson: Patronage, Authority, and Gender." *Ben Jonson Journal* 1 (1994): 15–30.

Wright, Thomas. *The Passions of the Minde in Generall, a reprint based on the 1604 edition.* Ed. Thomas O. Sloan. Urbana: Univ. of Illinois Press, 1971.

Young, R. V. "Donne's Holy Sonnets and the Theology of Grace." *"Bright Shootes of Everlastingnesse": The Seventeenth-Century Religious Lyric.* Eds. Claude J. Summers and Ted-Larry Pebworth. Columbia: Univ. of Missouri Press, 1987.

Young, William. *The History of Dulwich College . . . with a Life of the Founder, Edward Alleyn.* 2 vols. Edinburgh: Morrison and Gibb, 1889.

Zeiger, Melissa F. *Beyond Consolation: Death, Sexuality, and the Changing Shapes of Elegy.* Ithaca: Cornell Univ. Press, 1997.

Ziegler, Georgianna M., ed. "Recent Studies in Women Writers of Tudor England, 1485–1603 (1990 to mid-1993)." *English Literary Renaissance* 24.1 (Winter 1994): 229–42.

About the Contributors

PATRICK COOK is associate professor of English at George Washington University. He is the author of *Milton, Spenser and the Epic Tradition* (1996), as well as articles and reviews on Renaissance and medieval literature, film, and cyber-culture. He is currently working on a study of the drama of Thomas Middleton.

EUGENE R. CUNNAR (coeditor) teaches at New Mexico State University and has published widely on Crashaw, Donne, Milton, An Collins, Herbert and others, as well as on art history. He is currently a contributing editor to the *Variorum Edition of the Poetry of John Donne* and working on Aemelia Lanyer and Margaret Cavendish.

PATRICIA DEMERS, professor of English at the University of Alberta, researches in the areas of early modern literature, biblical literature, and children's literature. Her publications include two edited anthologies of children's literature, *From Instruction to Delight* (1982) and *A Garland from the Golden Age* (1983), *Louis Hémon's Maria Chapdelaine: A Seasonal Romance* (1993), *Women as Interpreters of the Bible* (1992), *Heaven Upon Earth: The Form of Moral and Religious Children's Literature to 1850* (1993) and *The World of Hannah More* (1996).

ROBERT C. EVANS is University Alumni Professor at Auburn University at Montgomery. He has published on Ben Jonson, Renaissance women writers, and short fiction, particularly the works of Flannery and Frank O'Connor. He is an editor of the *Ben Jonson Journal* and Renaissance editor for *Comparative Literature*.

ANN HURLEY teaches Renaissance literature at Wagner College in New York. She is coeditor of *So Rich a Tapestry: The Sister Arts and Visual Culture* (1995) and has just finished a second book, *John Donne and Renaissance Visual Culture*.

JEFFREY JOHNSON (coeditor) is professor of English at College Misericordia. In addition to his articles on Crashaw, Donne, Herbert, and Vaughan, he is the author of *The Theology of John Donne*. He is also a contributing editor for two volumes of the *Variorum Edition of the Poetry of John Donne*.

GEORGE KLAWITTER teaches courses in Renaissance literature at St. Edward's University, where he chairs the English Literature Department. He has edited the complete poems of Richard Barnfield (1990) and published a study of John Donne's love poetry, *The Enigmatic Narrator* (1993).

DONNA LONG is assistant professor of English at Fairmont State College in Fairmont, WV. She has a second essay on maternal elegy forthcoming in *Speaking Grief in English Literary Culture, Milton to Shakespeare* (eds. Kent and Swiss). She was recently awarded a grant from Fairmont State, in collaboration with Dr. Rhonda Lemke Sanford, to develop and teach a course on Early Modern Women.

KARI BOYD MCBRIDE teaches in the Women's Studies Department at the University of Arizona. Her most recent publications include "Sacred Celebration: The Patronage Poems" in *Aemilia Lanyer: Gender, Genre, and the Canon*, ed. Marshall Grossman, and "Answerable Styles: Aemilia Lanyer and John Milton Rewriting the Social Text," coauthored with John C. Ulreich (forthcoming in *JEGP*).

SEAN MCDOWELL is currently associate instructor at Indiana University, where he is finishing work on a dissertation investigating acts of consecration in early modern religious lyrics. His work most recently appeared in *Discoveries: South-Central Renaissance Conference News and Notes*.

KATE NARVESON has published on Donne, Herbert, Lucy Hutchinson, and has just completed a book manuscript on early Stuart devotional disciplines and the construction of identity. She is currently working on a study of the tensions and intersections between physiological and Calvinist views of the body and the self in Lady Grace Mildmay.

PAUL PARRISH is professor of English at Texas A & M University. He is the author of a number of essays on Donne, Milton, Crashaw and other seventeenth century subjects and of *Richard Crashaw* (1980). The volume commentary editor of *The Anniversaries and Epicedes and Obsequies*, vol. 6 of *The Variorum Edition of the Poetry of John Donne* (1995), he serves as Chief Editor of the Commentary for the Donne Variorum.

SCOTT PILARZ is assistant professor of English at Georgetown University, where he received the Edward Bunn Award for Faculty Excellence in 1999. He has published on medieval drama, liturgical history and practice, the religious poetry of John Donne, and Robert Southwell.

MICHAEL REX recently completed his Ph.D. at Wayne State University in seventeenth and eighteenth century British literature, particularly women authors. He is currently turning his dissertation, The Heroines' Revolt: English Women Writing Epic Poetry 1654–1789, into a book.

DEBRA RIENSTRA teaches literature and writing at Calvin College. She received her Ph.D. from Rutgers University, where she began her work in the area of early modern women and English religious poetry. She is also a published poet.

BARRY SPURR is senior lecturer in English at the University of Sydney, Australia. He is author of books on liturgical language, Lytton Strachey and, most recently, *Studying Poetry* (1997). Dr. Spurr has published extensively on Renaissance and modernist poetics and is currently completing a book on T. S. Eliot's Anglo-Catholicism.

PAUL G. STANWOOD is professor emeritus of English at the University of British Columbia. He has edited a number of works, including *John Cosin's "A Collection of Private Devotions,"* William Law's *Serious Call to a Devout and Holy Life* and *The Spirit of Love* (with Austin Warren); *John Donne and the Theology of Language* (with Heather Ross Asals); and *Of Poetry and Politics: New Essays on Milton and His World*. He is a contributing editor to the *John Donne Variorum*. He is also the author of *The Sempiternal Season: Studies in Seventeenth-Century Devotional Writing* and the recent *Izaak Walton* (1998).

CLAUDE SUMMERS is William E. Stinton Professor in the Humanities and professor of English at the University of Michigan-Dearborn. Co-editor of collections of essays on a wide variety of topics and author of book-length studies of Marlowe, Jonson, Isherwood, Forester, and twentieth century English and American gay fiction, he has recently published an edition of the *Selected Poems of Ben Jonson* and the Lambda Award-winning *The Gay and Lesbian Literary Heritage*. He is past president of the John Donne Society.

Index